Who's Afraid of C++?

Who's Afraid of C++?

Steve Heller

AP Professional

AP Professional is a Division of Academic Press, Inc.

Boston San Diego New York
London Sydney Tokyo Toronto

AP PROFESSIONAL

An Imprint of ACADEMIC PRESS, INC.
A Division of HARCOURT BRACE & COMPANY

ORDERS (USA and Canada): 1-800-3131-APP or APP@ACAD.COM
AP Professional Orders: 6277 Sea Harbor Dr., Orlando, FL 32821-9816

Europe/Middle East/Africa: 0-11-44 (0) 181-300-3322
Orders: AP Professional 24-28 Oval Rd., London NW1 7DX

Japan/Korea: 03-3234-3911-5
Orders: Harcourt Brace Japan, Inc., Ichibancho Central Building   22-1, Ichibancho   Chiyoda-Ku, Tokyo 102

Australia: 02-517-8999
Orders: Harcourt Brace & Co. Australia, Locked Bag 16, Marrickville, NSW 2204 Australia

Other International: (407) 345-3800
AP Professional Orders: 6277 Sea Harbor Dr., Orlando FL 32821-9816

Editorial: 1300 Boylston St., Chestnut Hill, MA 02167 (617)232-0500

Web: http://www.apnet.com/approfessional

United Kingdom Edition published by
ACADEMIC PRESS LIMITED
24–28 Oval Road, London NW1 7DX

Heller, Steve, 1949–
        Who's Afraid of C++ / Steve Heller.
                p. cm.
            Includes index.
            ISBN 0-12-339097-4 (alk. paper).
            1. C++ (computer program language)   I. Title
        QA76.73.C153H455   1996
        005.13'3—dc20   96-13293
                                                                                    CIP

Printed in the United States of America
 96 97 98 99   IP   9 8 7 6 5 4 3 2

Contents

Acknowledgements   xiii

Preface   xv

Letter from a Novice   xix

Foreword   xxiii

Chapter 1: Prologue   1
- Introduction to Programming 1
  - How to Write a Program 5
  - Baby Steps 6
  - On with the Show 8

Chapter 2: Hardware Fundamentals   9
- Getting Started 9
- Objectives of This Chapter 10
- Behind the Curtain 10
  - Disk 11
  - 1985, a Space Odyssey 13
  - RAM 14
  - Return to Sender, Address Unknown 15
  - The CPU 17
  - Caching In 22
  - Please Register Here 22
- Odometer Trouble 25
  - Back to the Future 28
  - Over-Hexed 31
- Exercises 36
- Registering Relief 37
  - Some Assembly Required 37
  - On a RAMpage 40

Registering Bewilderment 40
Slimming the Program 42
A Fetching Tale 47
Review 48
Conclusion 49
Answers to Exercises 50

Chapter 3: Basics of Programming   53
Creative Programming? 53
Definitions 53
Objectives of This Chapter 54
Speed Demon 54
Blaming It on the Computer 55
That Does Not Compute 55
Lost in Translation 56
What's Going on Underneath? 60
Who's on First? 63
Exercises, First Set 64
Underware? 64
Compiler's Eye View 65
Execution Is Everything 72
A Cast of Characters 75
A Byte by Any Other Name. 81
Some Strings Attached 82
Exercises, Second Set 83
In and Out 84
If Only You Knew 86
Exercises, Third Set 88
While We're on the Subject 88
Just up the Block 90
At the Fair 90
Novice Alert 97
Take It for a Spin 98
Exercises, Fourth Set 99
Review 99
Conclusion 102
Answers to Exercises 102

Chapter 4: More Basics   111
A Modest Proposal 111
Objectives of This Chapter 111
Algorithmic Thinking 112
A Prize Catch 115
What a Tangled Web We Weave. 119

You May Already Have Won 119
   Variables, by the Numbers 121
   A Sorted Tale 133
   Details, Details 141
   To Err Is Human. 143
To Really Foul Things up Requires a
Computer 149
   What, Me Worry? 150
   Garbage in, Garbage Out 151
Review 154
Exercises 156
Conclusion 158
Answers to Exercises 158

Chapter 5: Functional Literacy   165
Form Follows Function 165
Definitions 167
Objectives of This Chapter 168
Functioning Normally 168
   Above Average 173
   Return to Sender 174
   For the Sake of Argument 176
   General Delivery 180
Using a Function 180
   A Convincing Argument 186
The Man behind the Curtain 187
   The Object of My Affections 188
   Operating Systematically 190
   Using Your Library Card 191
Automatic Pilot 192
   Stacking the Deck 195
   Don't Call Me, I'll Call You 197
   How It All Stacks Up 199
Scoped Out 202
   Static Cling 203
Exercises, First Set 213
Think Globally? 219
   A BASIC Difficulty 220
   I Say "Live It, or Live with It" 221
Nesting Instinct 221
Review 223
Exercises, Second Set 226
Conclusion 226
Answers to Exercises 227

Chapter 6: Taking Inventory 235
A class Act 235
Definitions 236
Objectives of This Chapter 237
Pay Some Attention to the Man Behind the
Curtain 237
Taking Stock 242
More Definitions 245
Common Behavior 245
    The Native Problem 246
    A Concrete Plan 246
Go to the Head of the class 258
Shop till You Drop 262
Price Fixing 267
    Vectoring In 270
References Required 274
    Don't Fence Me In 279
    Can I Help You? 281
    The Customer Is Always Right 286
    Next Customer, Please? 289
    Nothing Ventured, Nothing Gained 294
    Testing, 1, 2, 3. 301
    Paging Rosie Scenario 305
Review 306
Exercises 312
Conclusion 313
Answers to Exercises 313

Chapter 7: Stringing Along 317
Objectives of This Chapter 317
Playing out the string 317
    Passing Along a Few Pointers 322
The Dynamic Duo, new and delete 324
Caution: Construction Area 330
Constructive Criticism? 339
Tricky Assignment 341
Assignment of Responsibility 344
References Required 347
Hello, operator? 350
    What Is the Meaning of this? 351
Equality Now! 352
    Please delete Me, Let Me Go 354
    The Next Assignment 357
    The Terminator 361

Review 364
Exercises 365
Conclusion 367
    Answers to Exercises 368

Chapter 8: Down the Garden Path   373
Objectives of This Chapter 373
    For Reference Only 373
    Unfair Copy 375
    Temporary Help Wanted 378
Copy Cat 381
Screen Test 383
    A Character Study 385
    Array of Hope? 387
    A Slippery Character 389
    Overwrought 390
    private Property: Keep Out! 392
    Maintenance Required 394
First Review 397
Stringing Along 399
    Less than Obvious 403
    Down for the Count 405
    For Better or Worse? 411
    A Greater Cause 414
    Simple Pleasures 414
    Equalization of Opportunity 417
    Displaying Expertise 418
    Down by the Old cout Stream 419
    Gently Down the Stream 420
    Friends of Global Progress 421
    Members and Friends Only 422
    Reader and Advisor 424
Initial Here 425
    Pointers and Setters 428
Second Review 431
Exercises 433
Conclusion 434
Answers to Exercises 434

Appendix A: Tying up Loose Ends   441
Where Am I, Anyway? 441
Tying up Loose Ends 442
    Operator Precedence 442
    Other Native Data Types 443

protected Species 443

Glossary   445

About the Author   473

Index   475

This book is dedicated to Susan Patricia Caffee Spino, the light of my life. Without her, this book would not be what it is; even more important, I would not be what I am: a happy man.

Acknowledgements

I'd like to thank Claudia and David Rattazzi for their support during the traumatic times of late 1995 and early 1996. True friends are more valuable than gold (although perhaps not pound for pound!)

I'd also like to thank my supplementary beta readers: Adrian Burke, Donald Gray, Orville Fudpucker III, Phil Haney, and Beth Zelasky, who have provided valuable feedback on the manuscript.

Matthew J. W. Ratcliff has gone above and beyond the call of duty for beta readers. His thorough review has made a significant contribution to the completeness and accuracy of this book.

Of course, I'm indebted to Ed Yourdon for his glorious Foreword. I hope that the book lives up to his praise.

Finally, my editors at AP Professional, Chuck Glaser and Jeff Pepper, have both been everything that a technical author could hope for (and most don't get).

Preface

Is this book for you? If you're a programmer in a language other than C++, and want to upgrade your skills, then the answer is yes. But what if you have no previous programming experience? In that case, here's a little quiz that may help you decide:

1. Do you want to know how the programs in your computer work inside, and how to write some of your own?
2. Are you willing to exert yourself mentally to learn a complex technical subject?
3. Do you have a sense of humor?

If you've answered yes to these questions and follow through with the effort required, then you will get a lot out of this book.

The common wisdom states that programming is a difficult subject that should be reserved for a small number of specialists. One of the main reasons that I have written this book is that I believe this attitude is wrong; it is possible, and even desirable, for you to learn how programs work and how to write them. Those who don't understand how computers perform their seemingly magical feats are at an increasing disadvantage in a society ever more dependent on these extraordinary machines.

Regardless of the topic, I can see no valid reason for a book to be stuffy and dry, and I've done everything possible to make this one approachable. However, don't let the casual tone fool you into thinking that the subject is easy; there is no "royal road" to programming, any more than there is to geometry. Especially if you have no prior experience in programming, this book will stretch your mind more than virtually any other subject you could study.

One of the reasons that this book is different from other books is the participation of Susan, my primary "test reader", whose account of her involvement in this project immediately follows this Preface. I recommend that you read that account before continuing with the technical material following it, as it explains how and why she contributed to making your task easier and more enjoyable.

Speaking of Susan, here is a bit of correspondence between us on the topic of how one should read this book, which occurred after her first reading of what is now Chapters 2 and 3:

> **Susan**: Let me say this: to feel like I would truly understand it, I would really need to *study* this about two more times. Now, I could do this, but I am not sure you would want me to do so. I think reading a chapter once is enough for most people.

> **Steve**: As a matter of fact, I would expect the reader of my book to read and study this chapter several times if necessary; for someone completely new to programming, I imagine that it **would** be necessary. Programming is one of the most complex human disciplines, although it doesn't take the mathematical skills of a subject such as nuclear physics, for example. I've tried to make my explanations as simple as possible, but there's no way to learn programming (or any other complex subject) without investing a significant amount of work and thought.

After she had gone through the text a number of times and had learned a lot from the process, we continued this discussion as follows:

> **Susan**: Well then, maybe this should be pointed out in a Preface or something. Of course, it would eventually be obvious to the reader as it was to me, but it took me awhile to come to that conclusion. The advantage of knowing this in advance is that maybe I would not be so discouraged that I was not brilliant after one read of a chapter.

> **Steve**: I will indeed mention in the Preface that the reader shouldn't be fooled by the casual tone into thinking that this is going to be a walk in the park. In any event, please don't be discouraged. It seems to me that you have absorbed a fair amount of very technical material with no previous background; that's something to be proud of!

We'll be hearing from Susan many more times in the course of the book. She will be checking in frequently in the form of extracts from the e-mail discussion we engaged in during the testing and revising process. I hope you will find her comments and my replies add a personal touch to your study of this technical material.

While we're on the topic of your studying, this would be a good time to tell you how to get updates and help with any errors you might find in the book or any other questions you might have. The best way is to visit my WWW page:

http://ourworld.compuserve.com/homepages/steve_heller.

If you don't have WWW access, you can write to me at the following address:

2220 Coit Road Suite, 480-125
Plano, Texas 75075

Now that those preliminaries are out of the way, let's proceed. The next voice you will hear is that of Susan, my test reader. I hope you get as much out of her participation in this book as I have.

Letter from a Novice

One day last March I found myself reading this little message on my computer monitor:

```
[#: 288196 S10/Have You Heard?]
[25-Mar-95 20:34:55]
[Sb: Readers for my new book]
[Fm: Steve Heller 71101,1702]
[To: all]
```

Hi!

I'm looking for some readers for a book I'm working on, which teaches people how to program, using C++ as the language. The ideal candidate is someone who wants to learn how to program, but has little or no knowledge or experience in programming. I can't pay anything, but participants will learn how to program, and will be acknowledged in the book, as well as getting an autographed copy. If you're interested, please reply by e-mail.

Steve

As I considered my response to this message I felt a little trepidation for what was to come. I have only known one profession: nursing. I had owned and used a computer for only a little over two years at the time and thought DOS was too difficult to understand. Not only had I no prior knowledge of programming, I had very little knowledge of computers in general. Yet, what knowledge I did have of the computer fed my curiosity for more, and as my love of the computer grew, it soon was apparent I had no choice. I replied by e-mail.

Evidently I was considered an ideal candidate as I did not wait long for acceptance as a test reader. I then embarked upon a project that I thought would last a few weeks to a few months. It was my expectation that I would read a chapter at a time, submit a few comments occasionally and nothing more. Never in my wildest dreams would I have ever expected that I would end up reading every page of this book with utmost attention to detail, leaving no word unturned, no concept overlooked, no hair on my head left unpulled for the next nine months of my life. But, if we were going to make this book as clear as possible for anyone who wanted to read it, there was no other way.

The process of writing this book was an enormous effort on both our parts. Neither Steve nor I could have ever imagined the type of dialogue that would ensue. It just happened; as I asked the questions, he answered the questions and I asked again. The exchange would continue until we were both satisfied that I "had it". When that happened, Steve knew the right wording for the book, and I could move on to the next concept. It was an experience like no other in my life. It was a time filled with confusion, frustration, anger, acceptance, understanding, and joy. The process often gave cause for others to question my motivation for doing it. Admittedly, at times my frustration was such that I wanted to give up. But it was my mountain, and I had to climb it. I would not accept defeat.

The material was not the only source of my frustration. There was the inherent difficulty that Steve and I had in keeping communication flowing and speaking the same language. We found we had very different writing styles which added another obstacle to our undertaking. He, the ultimate professional, and I, the incorrigible misfit, finally managed a happy medium. We corresponded on a daily basis almost exclusively in e-mail. Through that medium it was our challenge to get into each other's minds. He had to learn how I thought and I had to learn how he thought, not an easy task for an "expert" and a "novice" who were total strangers.

What you are about to read is the refinement of the writings of the mind of a genius filtered through the mind of a novice. Ideally, the result of this combination has produced the best possible information written in the most understandable form. The book as you see it is considerably different from the original version, as a result of this filtering process. For that same reason, it is also different from any other book of its kind. To our knowledge, this is the first time that someone with no previous background in programming has been enlisted in the creation of such a book. Of course, it took tutoring, but that tutoring is what led to the simplification of the text so that future novices could enjoy a relatively painfree reading experience.

During the first few months of this process, I had to take it on faith that somehow all of this material would eventually make sense. But late one quiet night while first reading about object-oriented programming, (the creation of "classes") I was abruptly shaken by the most incredible feeling. I was held spellbound for a few moments, I gasped and was gripped with the sudden realization and awe of the profound beauty of the code. I had finally caught a glimpse of what programming was *really* all about. This experience later led me to write the following quotation to my sister:

> Programming is SOOOO gorgeous. So fine, so delicate. It is so beautifully spun with silk threads, tiny and intricate. Yet like silk it can be strong and powerful, it all depends on how you use it.

At last, I had "gotten it". Within these pages the beauty lies dormant waiting for those who embark on the task of learning, to be viewed only when the work has been done and the mountain scaled. It is an exquisite panorama and a most worthy journey.

Foreword

Argh! Another "Programming for Dummies" book! I have to admit that when Steve Heller prevailed upon me to read his manuscript and prepare a foreword for this book, I had serious misgivings. Steve is a talented, articulate fellow, and I've enjoyed corresponding with him on the Internet for the past few years — ever since he gleefully pointed out in one of his earlier books (*Efficient C/C++ Programming*) that I had made the outrageously shortsighted comment in my 1975 textbook, *Techniques of Program Structure and Design*, that "unless you're very rich or very eccentric, you'll never have the luxury of owning your own computer."

Still, I dreaded the task of reading his entry-level programming book: almost every one I've read during my career has either been deadly boring, or childishly condescending, or both. Imagine my surprise, then, when I discovered that *Who's Afraid of C++* was not only a *good* book, but an exciting one. Because I'm writing these words in mid-February 1996, you won't be impressed when I tell you that it's the best computer book that I've read in 1996 — so let me put it more strongly: this is the best technical book I've read since *Zen and the Art of Motorcycle Maintenance* appeared in the mid-1970s.

Before I explain this rather bizarre analogy, let me address the central theme of *Who's Afraid of C++*: learning a new programming language. Anyone who has gone through this process knows that it isn't easy. True, there are languages like LOGO and Basic that can be taught to novices within short periods of time; one of my most enjoyable experiences in the computer field was teaching LOGO to a group of 6- and 7- year old children during a two-week summer class on Fire Island. But languages like C++ — the subject of this book — are far more difficult, not only for novices but for veterans of other programming languages. Ask any COBOL programmer whether he found it difficult to absorb the intricate syntax and arcane vocabulary of C++ and you're likely to get a groan.

But for many of us, C++ has become a prerequisite to continued employment in the software industry. Groan though they may, more and more COBOL programmers are making the transition — for the simple reason that mainframe applications are being replaced by PC and client-server apps, and a lot of them are written in C++. Even if the main part of an application is written in a simpler language like Visual Basic, it's likely that some portions (e.g., the VBX components) will have to be programmed in C or C++. I often joke that C++ is the assembly language of the 90s, but I sometimes forget to remind my friends that assembly language was the first language I learned, and I would have been very nervous trying to program in any higher-level language if I didn't have a good idea of what was going on at the level of hardware registers and memory addresses.

Does this mean that all of today's veteran programmers will be required to learn C++? Well, perhaps not: after all, vast numbers of programmers *have* managed to make a comfortable living by creating applications in high-level languages without really understanding what was going on "under the covers." Judging from the employment ads in the newspapers, you can get a job today if you speak Visual Basic, PowerBuilder, or Smalltalk; but your odds of getting (or keeping) a programming job are usually *much* better if you also know C++. And for the beleaguered COBOL programmer, that's a key point to remember: whether it's fair or not, languages like Visual Basic are often regarded as "toys", while C++ is considered a "serious" language for building today's industrial-strength applications.

I got an inkling of the nature of this sea-change in programming languages in late 1995, at a panel session discussing IBM's newly-released version of object-oriented COBOL. It's an exciting, powerful new language, and I think that one could make a strong argument that OO-COBOL is a more logical migration path for today's legacy COBOL programmers and vintage-1972 application programs than any other alternative. Nevertheless, when I asked the audience of some 100 people — all of whom were COBOL fans of one kind or another — whether they would advise their children to learn COBOL if their children intended to pursue a programming profession, less than 5 percent raised their hands. I didn't have the opportunity to see how many would have recommended C++, but it's virtually certain that the number of raised hands would have been far higher.

In mid-1995, another reason for learning C++ appeared on the horizon without any advance warning: the introduction of Sun Microsystems' "Java" language. Unless you've been living in a cave for the past few years, you know about the frenzy surrounding all aspects of the Internet and the World Wide Web; and you may have heard about Java as the language that promises to bring "live content" to Web pages. As I write this foreword, it's too early to tell whether Java really will revolutionize the Internet to the degree promised by its supporters, but there is one thing for sure: Java is mostly a subset of C++, and if you've learned C++, it will be a lot easier to learn Java.

On the other hand, that raises an interesting question: why not learn Java first, and just forget about C++? It's similar to the argument one often hears about the relationship between C and C++. Presumably, it's a lot easier for an experienced C programmer to learn the additional syntax of C++, though the object-oriented paradigm supported by C++ typically requires a great deal of "un-learning". Similarly, one can assume that an existing knowledge of C++ will make it easier to learn Java — but since one of the most important aspects of Java is what it *eliminates* from the C++ language (e.g., pointers), there is a certain amount of un-learning required here as well.

All of this is particularly relevant for the novice programmer, who typically has no prior programming experience, and who barely has the time and patience to learn *one* language, let alone two or three. If we knew that we were going to be developing all of our applications to operate on the World Wide Web, and if we knew for certain that Sun would be able to withstand the onslaught of Microsoft and its Internet-friendly version of Visual Basic, maybe we could recommend to the novice that she skip C and C++ and just focus on Java ... or, following the lead of Netscape, perhaps learn only the "Java-lite" language known as JavaScript.

But we need a reality check here. For the time being, it's safe to assume that there will be a lot of programs that do *not* run on the Web. As of late 1995, the number of personal computers was estimated to be in the range of 200-300 million worldwide, but the number of Internet users has been pegged at the far lower figure of 30 million. Each of the 300 million PCs is a candidate for C++ programming (not to mention all the mainframes and mid-size machines). As for the Internet: well, if you express the number of Internet users as a fraction of the human race, it still rounds to zero. In any case, if Java does become a dominant language in the next few years, I'm confident that Steve Heller will be able to produce a modified version of *Who's Afraid of C++* with the same dramatic success.[*]

None of this explains why an utter novice who does *not* intend to become a professional computer programmer should necessarily learn to program in C++, or why she should learn to program in *any* language. There has been a great deal of debate about this since PCs first invaded the mainstream of society a dozen years ago; colleges, high schools, and even some elementary schools have adopted — and then sometimes abandoned — a policy that students should learn computer programming for the same reason they learn biology or chemistry or geometry. Indeed, one could argue that the odds are far better that you'll need to write a small computer program (or at least have a decent understanding of the logic behind an existing program) in your day-to-day life than that you'll have to prove the Pythagorean Theorem or dissect a frog or recite the chemical composition of aspirin.

But I'm not going to pursue this argument; after 30+ years in the software industry, I'm biased, and I suspect that professional educators are equally biased. And it really doesn't matter; regardless of the opinion of advocates and opponents of compulsory programming courses, the practical reality for the adults or college students who are the likely readers of this book is that it's a personal choice. And this is a key point: quite aside from the technical intricacies of syntax and structure, learning a programming language is an intensely personal experience. It's often agonizing, it's sometimes tedious (especially if you don't have the proper tools!), and it's occasionally fun. On very rare occasions — perhaps only once a year, and sometimes only once or twice in one's career — it's more than fun: it's exhilarating, it's a rush, it's a shot of pure adrenaline. For some, it's almost a religious experience. And religious experiences, no matter how much we talk about them or write about them, are ultimately *personal* experiences. In the case of programming, that personal experience is also solitary in most cases, for it occurs at 3 in the morning when you're exhausted and frazzled and at your wit's end, and about to give up — and the program you've been sweating over finally gets up on its hind legs and *runs*.

It's the personal nature of the programming experience that makes this book such an unexpected and powerful masterpiece. As you'll see from the outset, it was *not* a solitary experience, but an ongoing dialogue between mentor and student — not a make-believe student, but a real one. Perhaps it's a bit unfair comparing *Who's Afraid of*

---

[*]   Author's note: By a tremendous coincidence, I indeed have a book called *Who's Afraid of Java* in the works; it should be out sometime in 1997.

C++ to Robert Pirsig's *Zen and the Art of Motorcycle Maintenance*, for Mr. Heller and his student appear not to have suffered the same degree of psychic trauma as the characters in Mr. Pirsig's book. But the personal drama is intense nonetheless, and it would be interesting to read even if you had no interest in the technical subject matter. Assuming that you *do* intend to learn C++, the dialogue between the teacher and his often-frustrated student will suck you into a deeper level of involvement and participation than would ever have been possible in a normal "programming for dummies" book.

For those devoid of any emotion or interest in personal relationships, it's possible to skip over this part of the book and focus entirely on the technical stuff. It's all there, and it's all accurate, and it's all well-written. But there are other computer books of that ilk (even though very few at the introductory level), and the problem is that your mind begins to wander, about halfway through each chapter; by the end of the chapter, you can't even remember what the topic was. Such a fate is not likely with this book.

One last note: everything I've written here identifies Steve Heller as the sole author of *Who's Afraid of C++*. But his student, Susan Spino, is definitely more than a student; by the end of the book, she has become a full-fledged collaborator and approaches the status of co-author. I congratulate Steve for having written a superb piece of technical work, but I have some personal words of admiration for Susan: I offer you my congratulations for having the energy, the intellect, the tenacity, and the passion to bring this collaboration to its fruition. You did a helluva job — and it promises to be a long collaboration indeed, stretching far beyond the final page of the book. As my friends in New York City often like to say about such developments; *Mazel tov!*

Ed Yourdon
New York City
February 1996

Chapter 1

Prologue

Introduction to Programming

"Begin at the beginning, and go on till you come to the end: then stop." This method of telling a story is as good today as it was when the King of Hearts prescribed it to the White Rabbit. In this book, we must begin with you, the reader, since my job is to explain a technical subject to you. It might appear that I'm at a severe disadvantage; after all, I've never met you.

Nevertheless, I can make some pretty good guesses about you. You almost certainly own a computer and know how to use its most common application, word processing. If you use the computer in business, you probably also have an acquaintance with spreadsheets and perhaps some database experience as well. Now you have decided to learn how to program the computer yourself rather than relying completely on programs written by others. On the other hand, you might be a student using this book as a text in an introductory course on programming. In that case, you'll be happy to know that this book isn't written in the dry, overly academic style employed by textbook writers. I hope that you will enjoy reading it, as my "test readers" have.

Whether you are using this book on your own or in school, there are many good reasons to learn how to program. You may have a problem that hasn't been solved by commercial software; you may want a better understanding of how commercial programs function so you can figure out how to get around their shortcomings and peculiarities; or perhaps you're just curious about how computers perform their seemingly magical feats. Whatever the initial reason, I hope you come to appreciate the great creative possibilities opened

up by this most ubiquitous of modern inventions.[1] However, before
we begin, we should agree on definitions for some fundamental
words in the computing field.

Why start with words? Because knowing the correct meaning of
the words you're reading is really important, even more so than you
might suspect. If you don't understand words as they are used in a
subject, you'll get lost very quickly and decide that the subject is
"hard" or "not for you", when all along the problem may be just the
words that you don't know. We'll start with some definitions of
technical words that you'll need to know; however, if at any time you
run across a word that you're not sure you understand, take the time
to find a definition, understand it, and use the word in sentences until
you're sure you have it.

Susan had some incisive observations about this topic of the power
of words, which prompted me to include the preceding caution. Here
is our exchange on that issue:

> **Susan**: I will read something usually at face value, but often there is
> much more to it; that is why I don't get it. Then, when I go back and
> really think about what those words mean, it will make more sense. This
> book almost needs to be written in ALL CAPS to get the novice to pay
> closer attention to each and every word.
>
> **Steve**: IMAGINE WRITING A BOOK IN ALL CAPS! THAT
> WOULD BE VERY DIFFICULT TO READ, DON'T YOU THINK?

Many of the technical words used in this book are in the Glossary
at the end of the book; it is also very helpful to have a good technical
dictionary of computer terms. You should also be aware that the
word giving you trouble is not not necessarily a technical word; it
can be a very simple word in plain English. In any case, you should
not pass by a word you don't understand; you'll just get confused
later. Make sure you understand what you're reading, and you'll have
an easier time learning.

Of course, you may not be able to remember all of these technical
definitions the first time through. If you can't recall the exact
meaning of one of these terms, just look up the word or phrase in the
index, and it will direct you to the page where the definition is stated.
You could also look in the Glossary, at the end of the book.

---

1. Of course, it's also possible that you already know how to program in another language and
are using this book to learn how to do so in C++. If so, you'll have a head start; I hope that
you'll learn enough to make it worth your while to wade through some material you already
know.

Definitions of key technical terms are listed there in alphabetical order.

Before we continue, let's check in again with Susan. The following is from her first letter to me about the contents of this book:

> **Susan**: I like the one-on-one feel of your text, like you are just talking to me. Now, you did make a few references to how simple some things were (which ?) I didn't catch on to, so it kinda made me feel I was not too bright for not seeing how apparently simple those things were. . . .
>
> I think maybe it would have been helpful if you could have stated from the onset of this book just what direction you were taking, at least chapter by chapter. I would have liked to have seen a goal stated or a least a summary of objectives from the beginning. I often would have the feeling I was just suddenly thrown into something as I was reading along. Also (maybe you should call this *C++ for Dummies*, or is that taken already?)[2], you might even *define* what programming is! What a concept! Because it did occur to me that since I have never seen it done, or a language or anything, I really don't know what programming *is*! I just knew it was something that nerds do.

Susan's wish is my command, so I have provided a list of objectives at the beginning of each chapter after this one. I've also fulfilled her request for a definition of some programming terms, starting as follows:

An **algorithm** is a set of precisely defined steps to calculate an answer to a problem or set of problems, which is guaranteed to arrive at such an answer eventually. As this implies, a set of steps that might never end is *not* an algorithm.

Programming is the art and science of solving problems by the following procedure:[3]

1. Find or invent a general solution to a class of problems.
2. Express this solution as an algorithm or set of algorithms.

---

2. As it happens, that title is indeed taken. However, I'm not sure it's been applied appropriately, since the book with that title assumes previous knowledge of C! What that says about C programmers is better left to the imagination.

3. This definition is possibly somewhat misleading since it implies that the progression of a program is straightforward and linear, with no revisions required. This is known as the "waterfall model" of programming, since water going over a waterfall follows a preordained course in one direction. However, real-life programming doesn't usually work this way; rather, most programs are written in an incremental process as assumptions are changed and errors are found and corrected.

3.   Translate the algorithm(s) into terms so simple that a stupid machine like a computer can follow them to calculate the specific answer for any specific problem in the class.

At this point, let's see what Susan had to say about the above definition and my response:

Susan: Very descriptive. How about this definition: "Programming is the process of being creative using the tools of science such as incremental problem solving to make a stupid computer do what you want it to"? That I understand!

Your definition is just fine. A definition has to be concise and descriptive and that you have done and covered all the bases. But you know what is lacking? An example of what it looks like. Maybe just a little statement that really looks bizarre to me and then say that by the end of the chapter you will actually know what this stuff really means! Sort of like a coming attraction type of thing.

Steve: I understand the idea of trying to draw the reader into the "game". However, I think that presenting a bunch of apparent gibberish with no warning could frighten readers as easily as it might intrigue them. I think it's better to delay showing examples until they have some background.

Now let's return to our list of definitions:

Hardware refers to the physical components of a computer, the ones you can touch. Examples include the keyboard, the monitor, the printer.

Software refers to the other, nonphysical components of a computer, the ones you cannot touch. If you can install it on your hard disk, it's software. Examples include a spreadsheet, a word processor, a database program.

Source code is a program in a form suitable for reading and writing by a human being.

An **executable program** (or just an *executable*, for short) is a program in a form suitable for running on a computer.

Object code is a program in a form suitable for incorporation into an executable program.

Compilation is the process of translating source code into object code. Almost all of the software on your computer was created by this process.

A **compiler** is a program that performs compilation as defined above.

How to Write a Program

Now you have a definition of programming. Unfortunately, however, this doesn't tell you how to write a program. The process of solving a problem by programming in C++ follows these steps:[4]

Problem:	After discussions between the user and the programmer, the programmer defines the problem precisely.
Algorithms:	The programmer finds or creates algorithms that will solve the problem.
C++:	The programmer implements these algorithms as source code in C++.
Executable:	The programmer runs the C++ compiler, which must already be present on the programmer's machine, to translate the source code into an executable program.
Hardware:	The user runs the resulting executable program on a computer.

These steps advance from the most abstract to the most concrete, which is perfectly appropriate for an experienced C++ programmer. But you're not an experienced C++ programmer, or you wouldn't be reading this book. Before you can follow this path to solving a problem, you're going to need a fairly thorough grounding in all of these steps. It's not really feasible to discuss each step exhaustively before going to the next one, so I've created a little "step indicator" that you'll see on each right hand page of the text, with the currently active step shown in bold.

```
Problem
Algorithms
C++
Executable
Hardware
```

For example, when we're discussing algorithms, the indicator on the right hand page will have the word **Algorithms** in bold. The five steps of this indicator correspond to the five steps in problem solving just defined. I hope this device will make it easier for you to follow the sometimes tortuous path to programming knowledge. Let's see what Susan thinks of it:

> **Susan**: With all the new concepts and all the new language and terms, it is so hard to know what one thing has to do with the other and where things are supposed to fit into the big picture. With the key, you can see how these things all fit as logical steps to an end. Now, I know it isn't going to be easy, but at least I know what my destination is before I

---

4. This description is actually a bit oversimplified. We'll examine another step in the process of making an executable program, called *linking*, in a later chapter.

board the plane. Anyway, you have to understand; for someone like me, this is an enormous amount of new material to be introduced to all at once. When you are bombarded with so many new terms and so many abstract concepts, it is a little hard to sort out what is what. Will you have guidelines for each of the steps? Since I know a little about this already, the more I look at the steps, I just know that what is coming is going to be a big deal. For example, take step 1: you have to give the ingredients for properly defining a problem. If something is left out, then everything that follows won't work.

Steve: I hope you won't find it that frustrating, because I explain all of the steps carefully as I do them. Of course, it's possible that I haven't been careful enough, but in that case you can let me know and I'll explain it further.

Unfortunately, it's not possible for me to provide a thorough guide to all of those steps, as that would be a series of books in itself. However, there's a wonderful small book called *How to Solve It* by G. Polya, that you should be able to get at your local library. It was written to help students solve geometry problems, but the techniques are applicable in areas other than geometry. I'm going to recommend that readers of my book read it if they have any trouble with general problem solving.

Problem
Algorithms
C++
Executable
Hardware

The steps for solving a problem via programming might sound reasonable in the abstract, but that doesn't mean that you can follow them easily without practice. Assuming that you already have a pretty good idea of what the problem is that you're trying to solve, the Algorithms step is likely to be the biggest stumbling block. Therefore, it might be very helpful to go into that step in a bit more detail.

Baby Steps

Since we already understand the problem, we want to start writing a program that will solve it. That means that we have to figure out a plan of attack, which we will then break down into small enough steps to be expressed in C++. This is called **stepwise refinement**, since we start out with a "coarse" solution and refine it until the steps are within the capability of the C++ language. For a complex problem, this may take several intermediate steps, but let's start out with a simple example. Say that we want to know how much older one person is than another. We might start with the following general outline:

1.　　Get ages from user.

2. Calculate difference of ages.
3. Print the result.

This can in turn be broken down further as follows:

1. Get ages from user.

   a. Ask user for first age.
   b. Ask user for second age.

2. Subtract second age from first age.
3. Print result.

This looks okay, except that if the first person is younger than the second one, then the result will be negative. That may be acceptable. If so, we're just about done, since these steps are simple enough for us to translate them into C++ fairly directly. Otherwise, we'll have to modify our program to do something different depending on which age is higher. For example,

1. Get ages from user.

   a. Ask user for first age.
   b. Ask user for second age.

2. Compute difference of ages.

   a. If first age is greater than second, subtract second age from first age.
   b. Otherwise, subtract first age from second age.

3. Print result.

Problem
Algorithms
C++
Executable
Hardware

You've probably noticed that this is a much more detailed description than would be needed to tell a human being what you want to do. That's because the computer is extremely stupid and literal: it does only what you tell it to do, not what you meant to tell it to do. Unfortunately, it's very easy to get one of the steps wrong, especially in a complex program. In that case, the computer will do something ridiculous, and you'll have to figure out what you did wrong. This "debugging", as it's called, is one of the hardest parts of programming. Actually, it shouldn't be too difficult to understand why that is the case. After all, you're looking for a mistake you've made yourself. If you knew exactly what you were doing, you wouldn't have made the mistake in the first place.

I hope that this brief discussion has made the process of programming a little less mysterious. In the final analysis, it's basically just logical thinking.[5]

On with the Show

Now that you have some idea how programming works, it's time to see exactly how the computer actually performs the steps in a program, which is the topic of Chapter 2.

Problem
Algorithms
C++
Executable
Hardware

---

5. Of course, the word *just* in this sentence is a bit misleading; taking logical thinking for granted is a sure recipe for trouble.

Chapter 2

Hardware Fundamentals

Getting Started

Like any complex tool, the computer can be understood on several levels. For example, it's entirely possible to learn to drive an automobile without having the slightest idea of how it works. The analogy with computers is that it's relatively easy to learn how to use a word processor without having any notion of how such programs work. On the other hand, programming is much more closely analogous to designing an automobile than it is to driving one; therefore, we're going to have to go into some detail about the internal workings of a computer, not at the level of electronic components, but at the lowest level accessible to a programmer.

This is a book on learning to program in C++, not on how a computer works.[1] Therefore, it might seem better to start there and eliminate this detour, and indeed many (perhaps most) books on C++ do exactly that. However, in working out in detail how I'm going to explain C++ to you, I've come to the conclusion that it would be virtually impossible to explain *why* certain features of the language exist and how they actually work, without your understanding *how* they relate to the underlying computer hardware.

I haven't come to this position by pure logical deduction, either. In fact, I've worked backward from the concepts that you will need to know to program in C++ to the specific underlying information that you will have to understand first. For example, one specific concept is supposed to be extremely difficult for a beginning programmer in

---

1. Some people believe that you should learn C before you learn C++. Obviously, I'm not one of those people; for that matter, neither is the inventor of C++, Bjarne Stroustrup. On page 169 of his book, *The Design and Evolution of C++*, he says "Learn C++ first. The C subset is easier to learn for C/C++ novices and easier to use than C itself."

C++ to grasp, but you shouldn't have much trouble understanding it by the time you get to it in Chapter 7; it's noted as such in the discussion there. I'd be interested to know how you find my explanation there, given the background that you'll have by that point; don't hesitate to e-mail me about this topic (or any other, for that matter).[2]

On the other hand, if you're an experienced programmer, a lot of this will be just review for you. Nonetheless, it can't hurt to go over the basics one more time before diving into the ideas and techniques that make C++ different from other languages.

Now let's begin with some definitions and objectives for this chapter.

A **binary** number system is one that uses only two digits, 0 and 1.

A **hexadecimal** number system is one that uses 16 digits, 0–9 and a–f.

Objectives of This Chapter

Problem
Algorithms
C++
Executable
Hardware

By the end of this chapter, you should

1. Understand the programmer's view of the most important pieces of hardware in your computer.
2. Understand the programmer's view of the most important pieces of software in your computer.
3. Be able to solve simple problems using both the binary and hexadecimal number systems.
4. Understand how whole numbers are stored in the computer.

Behind the Curtain

First we'll need to expand on the definition of *hardware*. As noted earlier, *hardware* means the physical components of a computer, the ones you can touch.[3] Examples are the monitor, which displays your document while you're working on it, the keyboard, the printer, and

---

2. The concept I'm referring to is the *pointer*, in case you want to make a note of it here.

3. Whenever I refer to a *computer*, I mean a modern microcomputer capable of running MS-DOS; these are commonly referred to as *PCs*. Most of the fundamental concepts are the same in other kinds of computers, but the details differ.

all of the interesting electronic and electromechanical components inside the case of your computer.[4]

Right now, we're concerned with the programmer's view of the hardware. The hardware components of a computer with which you'll be primarily concerned are the disk, RAM (short for Random Access Memory), and last but certainly not least, the CPU (short for Central Processing Unit).[5] We'll take up each of these topics in turn.

Disk

When you sit down at your computer in the morning, before you turn it on, where are the programs you're going to run? To make this more specific, suppose you're going to use a word processor to revise a letter you wrote yesterday before you turned the computer off. Where is the letter, and where is the word processing program?

You probably know the answer to this question; they are stored on a disk inside the case of your computer.[6] Disks use magnetic recording media, much like the material used to record speech and music on cassette tapes, to store information in a way that will not be lost when the power is turned off. How exactly is this information (which may be either executable programs or data such as word processing documents) stored?

We don't have to go into excruciating detail on the storage mechanism, but it is important to understand some of its characteristics. A disk consists of one or more circular *platters*, which are extremely flat and smooth pieces of metal or glass covered with a material that can be very rapidly and accurately magnetized in either of two directions, "north" and "south". To store large amounts of data, each platter is divided into many millions of small regions,

Problem
Algorithms
C++
Executable
Hardware

---

4. Although it's entirely possible to program without ever seeing the inside of a computer, you might want to look in there anyway, just to see what the CPU, RAM chips, disk drives, etc., look like. Some familiarization with the components would give you a head start if you ever want to expand the capacity of your machine.

5. Other hardware components can be important to programmers of specialized applications; for example, game programmers need extremely fine control on how information is displayed on the monitor. However, we have enough to keep us busy learning how to write general data-handling programs; you can always learn how to write games later, if you're interested in doing so.

6. Technically, this is a hard disk, to differentiate it from a floppy disk, the removable storage medium often used to distribute software or transfer files from one computer to another. Although at one time, many small computers used floppy disks for their main storage, the tremendous decrease in hard disk prices means that today even the most inexpensive computer stores programs and data on a hard disk.

each of which can be magnetized in either direction independent of the other regions. The magnetization is detected and modified by *recording heads*, similar in principle to those used in tape cassette decks. However, in contrast to the cassette heads, which make contact with the tape while they are recording or playing back music or speech, the disk heads "fly" a few millionths of an inch away from the platters, which rotate at very high velocity.[7]

The separately magnetizable regions used to store information are arranged in groups called *sectors*; they are arranged in concentric circles called *tracks*. All tracks on one side of a given platter (a *recording surface*) can be accessed by a recording head dedicated to that recording surface; each sector is used to store some number of *bytes* of the data, generally a few hundred to a few thousand. "Byte" is a coined word meaning a group of 8 *bi*nary dig*its*, or *bits* for short.[8] You may wonder why the data aren't stored in the more familiar decimal system, which of course uses the digits from 0 through 9. This is not an arbitrary decision; on the contrary, there are a couple of very good reasons that data on a disk are stored using the binary system, in which each digit has only two possible states, 0 and 1. One of these reasons is that it's a lot easier to determine reliably whether a particular area on a disk is magnetized "north" or "south" than it is to determine 1 of 10 possible levels of magnetization. Another reason is that the binary system is also the natural system for data storage using electronic circuitry, which is used to store data in the rest of the computer.

While magnetic storage devices have been around in one form or another since the very early days of computing, the advances in technology just in the last 10 years have been staggering. To comprehend just how large these advances have been, we need to define the term used to describe storage capacities: the Megabyte. The standard engineering meaning of *Mega* is "multiply by 1 million", which would make a Megabyte equal to 1 million (1,000,000) bytes. As we have just seen, however, the natural number system in the computer field is binary. Therefore, "one

Problem
Algorithms
C++
Executable
Hardware

---

7. The heads have to be as close as possible to the platters because the influence of a magnet (called the *magnetic field*) drops off very rapidly with distance. Thus, the closer the heads are, the more powerful the magnetic field is and the smaller the region that can be used to read and write data reliably. Of course, this leaves open the question of why the heads aren't in contact with the surface; that would certainly solve the problem of being too far away. Unfortunately, this seemingly simple solution would not work at all. There is a name for the contact of heads and disk surface while the disk is spinning, *head crash*. The friction caused by such an event destroys both the heads and disk surface almost instantly.

8. In some old machines, bytes sometimes contained more or less than 8 bits, but the 8-bit byte is virtually universal today.

Megabyte" is often used instead to specify the nearest "round" number in the binary system, which is 2^20 (2 to the 20th power), or 1,048,576 bytes.[9] This wasn't obvious to Susan, so I explained it some more, as you can see here:

> **Susan**: Just how important is it to really understand that the Megabyte is 2^20 (1,048,576) bytes? I know that a meg is not really a meg; that is, it's more than a million. But I don't understand 2^20, so is it enough to just take your word on this and not get bogged down as to why I didn't go any further than plane geometry in high school? You see, it makes me worry and upsets me that I don't understand how you "round" a binary number.

> **Steve**: The ^ symbol is a common way of saying "to the power of", so 2^20 would be 2 to the power of 20; that is, 20 2s multiplied together. This is a "round" number in binary just as 10 * 10 * 10 (1000) is a "round" number in decimal.

1985, a Space Odyssey

With that detail out of the way, we can see just how far we've come in a short period of time. In 1985, I purchased a 20 Megabyte disk for $900 ($45 per Megabyte); its **access time**, which measures how long it takes to retrieve data, was approximately 100 milliseconds (milli = 1/1000, so a millisecond is one thousandth of a second). In December 1995, a 1600 Megabyte disk cost as little as $350, or approximately 22 *cents* per megabyte; in addition to this 200-fold decrease in cost, its access time was 10 milliseconds, which is approximately 10 times as fast as the old disk.[10] Of course, this significantly understates the amount of progress in technology in both economic and technical terms. For one thing, a 1995 dollar is worth considerably less than a 1985 dollar. In addition, the new drive is superior in every other measure as well: it is much smaller than the old one, consumes much less power, and has many times the projected reliability of the old drive.

Problem
Algorithms
C++
Executable
Hardware

---

9. In case you're not familiar with the ^ notation, the number on its right indicates how many copies of the number to the left have to be multiplied together to produce the final result. For example, 2^5 = 2 * 2 * 2 * 2 * 2, whereas 4^3 = 4 * 4 * 4. Of course, I've just introduced another symbol you might not be familiar with: the * is used to indicate multiplication in programming.

10. By the way, the reason I've specified the month as well as the year for the 1600 MB disk's price is that its price had gone down by approximately 50% in the previous six months. At that rate of decline, by the time you read this, 1600 MB disks will probably be given away in Crackerjack™ boxes.

This tremendous increase in performance and price has prevented the long-predicted demise of disk drives in favor of new technology. However, the inherent speed limitations of disks still require us to restrict their role to the storage and retrieval of data for which we can afford to wait a relatively long time.

You see, while 10 milliseconds isn't very long by human standards, it is a long time indeed to a modern computer. This will become more evident as we examine the next essential component of the computer, the *RAM*.

RAM

Problem
Algorithms
C++
Executable
Hardware

The working storage of the computer, where data and programs are stored while we're using them is called **RAM**, which is an acronym for Random Access Memory.[11] For example, your word processor is stored in RAM while you're using it. The document you're working on is likely to be there as well unless it's too large to fit all at once, in which case parts of it will be retrieved from the disk as needed. Since we have already seen that both the word processor and the document are stored on the disk in the first place, why not leave them there and use them in place, rather than copying them into RAM?

The answer, in a word, is *speed*. RAM is physically composed of millions of microscopic switches on a small piece of silicon known as a *chip*: a 4 megabit RAM chip has approximately 4 million of them.[12] Each of these switches can be either on or off; we consider a switch that is "on" to be storing a 1, and a switch that is "off" to be storing a 0. Just as in storing information on a disk, where it was easier to magnetize a region in either of two directions, it's a lot easier to make a switch that can be turned on or off reliably and quickly than one that can be set to any value from 0 to 9 reliably and quickly. This is particularly important when you're manufacturing millions of them on a silicon chip the size of your fingernail.

A main difference between disk and RAM is what steps are needed to access different areas of storage. In the case of the disk, the head has to be moved to the right track (an operation known as a *seek*), and then we have to wait for the platter to spin so that the region we

---

11. *RAM* is sometimes called "internal storage", as opposed to "external storage", that is, the disk.

12. Each switch is made of several transistors. Unfortunately, an explanation of how a transistor works would take us too far afield. Consult any good encyclopedia, such as the Encyclopedia Britannica, for this explanation.

want to access is under the head (called *rotational delay*). On the other hand, with RAM, the entire process is electronic; we can read or write any byte immediately as long as we know which byte we want. To specify a given byte, we have to supply a unique number called its **memory address** or just **address** for short.

Return to Sender, Address Unknown

What is an address good for? Let's see how my discussion with Susan on this topic started:

> **Susan**: About memory addresses: are you saying that each little itty bitty tiny byte of RAM is a separate address? Well, this is a little hard to imagine.

> **Steve**: Actually, each byte of RAM *has* a separate address, which doesn't change, and a value, which does.

In case the notion of an address of a byte of memory on a piece of silicon is too abstract, it might help to think of an address as a set of directions as to how to find the byte being addressed, much like directions to someone's house. For example, "Go three streets down, then turn left. It's the second house on the right". With such directions, the house number wouldn't need to be written on the house. Similarly, the memory storage areas in RAM are addressed by position; you can think of the address as telling the hardware which street and house you want, by giving directions similar in concept to the preceding example. Therefore, it's not necessary to encode the addresses into the RAM explicitly.

Problem
Algorithms
C++
Executable
Hardware

Susan wanted a better picture of this somewhat abstract idea:

> **Susan**: Where are the bytes on the RAM, and what do they look like?

> **Steve**: Each byte corresponds to a microscopic region of the RAM chip. As to what they look like, have you ever seen a printed circuit board such as the ones inside your computer? Imagine the lines on that circuit board reduced thousands of times in size to microscopic dimensions, and you'll have an idea of what a RAM chip looks like inside.

Since it has no moving parts, storing and retrieving data in RAM is much faster than waiting for the mechanical motion of a disk platter turning.[13] As we've just seen, disk access times are measured in milliseconds, or thousandths of a second. However, RAM access times are measured in *nanoseconds* (abbreviated *ns*); *nano* means one billionth. In late 1995, a typical speed for RAM was 70 ns, which means that it is possible to read a given data item from RAM about 150,000 times as quickly as from a disk. In that case, why not use disks only for permanent storage, and read everything into RAM in the morning when we turn on the machine?

The reason is cost. In late 1995, the cost of 16 Megabytes of RAM was approximately $600. For that same amount of money, you could have bought almost 3000 Megabytes of disk! Therefore, we must reserve RAM for tasks where speed is all-important, such as running your word processing program and holding a letter while you're working on it. Also, since RAM is an electronic storage medium (rather than a magnetic one), it does not maintain its contents when the power is turned off. This means that if you had a power failure while working with data only in RAM, you would lose everything you had been doing.[14] This is not merely a theoretical problem, by the way; if you don't remember to save what you're doing in your word processor once in a while, you might lose a whole day's work from a power outage of a few seconds.[15]

Problem
Algorithms
C++
Executable
Hardware

Before we get to how a program actually works, we need to develop a better picture of how RAM is used. As I've mentioned before, you can think of RAM as consisting of a large number of bytes, each of which has a unique identifier called an *address*. This address can be used to specify which byte we mean, so the program might specify that it wants to read the value in byte 148257, or change the value in byte 66666.

Susan wanted to make sure she had the correct understanding of this topic:

---

13. There's also another kind of electronic storage, called **ROM**, for Read-Only Memory; as its name indicates, you can read from it, but you can't write to it. This is used for storing permanent information, such as the program that allows your computer to read a small program from your *boot disk*; that program, in turn, reads in the rest of the data and programs needed to start up the computer. This process, as you probably know, is called *booting* the computer. In case you're wondering where that term came from, it's an abbreviation for *bootstrapping*, which is intended to suggest the notion of pulling yourself up by your bootstraps.

    You may have noticed that the terms RAM and ROM aren't symmetrical; why isn't RAM called RWM, Read-Write Memory? Because that's too hard to pronounce.

14. The same disaster would happen if your system were to crash, which is not that unlikely if you're using certain popular PC graphically oriented operating environments whose names start with *W*.

15. Most modern word processors can automatically save your work once in a while, for this very reason. I heartily recommend using this facility; it's saved my bacon more than once.

> **Susan**: Are the values changed in RAM depending on what program is loaded in it?

> **Steve**: Yes, and they also change while the program is executing. RAM is used to store both the program itself and the values it manipulates.

This is all very well, but it doesn't answer the question of how the program actually uses or changes values in RAM, or performs arithmetic and other operations; that's the job of the CPU, which we will take up next.

The CPU

The **CPU** (Central Processing Unit) is the "active" component in the computer. Like RAM, it is physically composed of millions of microscopic transistors on a chip; however, the organization of these transistors in a CPU is much more complex than on a RAM chip, as the latter's functions are limited to the storage and retrieval of data. The CPU, on the other hand, is capable of performing dozens or hundreds of different fundamental operations called *machine instructions*, or just *instructions* for short. While each instruction performs a very simple function, the tremendous power of the computer lies in the fact that the CPU can perform (or *execute*) tens or hundreds of millions of these instructions per second.[16]

> Problem
> Algorithms
> C++
> Executable
> **Hardware**

These instructions fall into a number of categories: instructions that perform arithmetic operations such as adding, subtracting, multiplying, and dividing; instructions that move information from one place to another in RAM; instructions that compare two quantities to help make a determination as to which instructions need to be executed next and instructions that implement that decision; and other, more specialized types of instructions.

Of course, adding two numbers together (for example) requires that the numbers be available for use. Possibly the most straightforward way of making them available is to store them in and retrieve them from RAM whenever they are needed, and indeed this is done sometimes. However, as fast as RAM is compared to disk drives (not to mention human beings), it's still pretty slow compared

---

16. Each type of CPU has a different set of instructions, so that programs compiled for one CPU cannot in general be run on a different CPU. Some CPUs, such as the very popular 80x86 ones from Intel, fall into a "family" of CPUs in which each new CPU can execute all of the instructions of the previous family members. This allows upgrading to a new CPU without having to throw out all of your old programs, but correspondingly limits the ways in which the new CPU can be improved without affecting this "family compatibility".

to modern CPUs. For example, the computer I'm using to write this book has a 66 Megahertz (abbreviated MHz) CPU, which can execute up to 66 million instructions per second (abbreviated MIPS),[17] or one instruction approximately every 16 ns.[18]

To see why RAM is a bottleneck, let's calculate how long it would take to execute an instruction if all the data had to come from and go back to RAM. A typical instruction would have to read some data from RAM, and write its result back there; first, though, the instruction itself has to be loaded (or *fetched*) into the CPU before it can be executed. Let's suppose we have an instruction in RAM, reading one data item also in RAM, and writing the result back to RAM. Then the minimum timing to do such an instruction could be calculated as in Figure 2.1.

```
Time          Function

 70 ns        Read instruction from RAM
 70 ns        Read data from RAM
 16 ns        Execute instruction
 70 ns        Write result back to RAM
------
226 ns        Total instruction execution time
```

Figure 2.1: RAM vs. CPU speeds

Problem
Algorithms
C++
Executable
Hardware

To compute the effective MIPS of a CPU, we divide 1 second by the time it takes to execute one instruction. Given the assumptions in this example, the CPU could execute only about 4.5 million instructions per second, which is a far cry from the peak performance of 66 MIPS claimed by the manufacturer.[19] If the manufacturer's claims have any relation to reality, there must be a better way.

In fact, there is. As a result of a lot of research and development, both in academia and in the semiconductor industry, it is possible to approach the rated performance of fast CPUs.[20] Some of these

---

17. You shouldn't get the idea from the coincidence of the Megahertz and MIPS numbers that 1 MIPS means the same as 1 MHz. It so happens that, for the 486, the fastest instructions take one clock cycle. Therefore, if most of the instructions your program executes are one-cycle instructions, you can approach 66 MIPS on a 66 MHz 486. This relationship doesn't hold in general; for example, the Pentium™ machines can execute two instructions simultaneously in some cases, and therefore a 90 MHz Pentium can run at up to 180 MIPS in the ideal case.

18. In the case of MHz, *Mega* really means "million" (that is, 1,000,000), in contrast to its use in describing storage capacities. I'm sorry if this is confusing, but it can't be helped.

19. 1 second/226 ns per instruction = 4,424,788 instructions per second.

20. As will be illustrated in Figure 2.12.

techniques have been around as long as we've had computers; others have fairly recently "trickled down" from supercomputers to microcomputer CPUs. One of the most important of these techniques is the use of a number of different kinds of storage devices having different performance characteristics; the arrangement of these devices is called the **memory hierarchy**. Figure 2.2 illustrates the memory hierarchy on my home machine at the time I started writing this book.

Susan and I had a short discussion of the layout of this figure:

> **Susan**: OK, just one question on Figure 2.2. If you are going to include the disk in this hierarchy, I don't know why you have placed it over to the side of RAM and not above it, since it is slower and you appear to be presenting this figure in ascending order of speed from the top of the figure downward. Did you do this because it is external rather than internal memory and it doesn't "deserve" to be in the same lineage as the others?

> **Steve**: Yes; it's not the same as "real" memory, so I wanted to distinguish it.

Before we get to the diagram, I should explain that a **cache** is a small amount of fast memory where frequently used data are stored temporarily. According to this definition, RAM functions more or less as a cache for the disk; after all, we have to copy data from a slow disk into fast RAM before we can use it for anything. However, while this is a valid analogy, I should point out that the situations aren't quite parallel. Our programs usually read data from disk into RAM explicitly; that is, we're aware of whether it's on the disk or in RAM, and we have to issue commands to transfer it from one place to the other. On the other hand, caches are "automatic" in their functioning. We don't have to worry about them, and our programs work in exactly the same way with them as without them, except faster. In any event, the basic idea is the same: to use a faster type of memory to speed up repetitive access to data usually stored on a slower storage device.

Problem
Algorithms
C++
Executable
Hardware

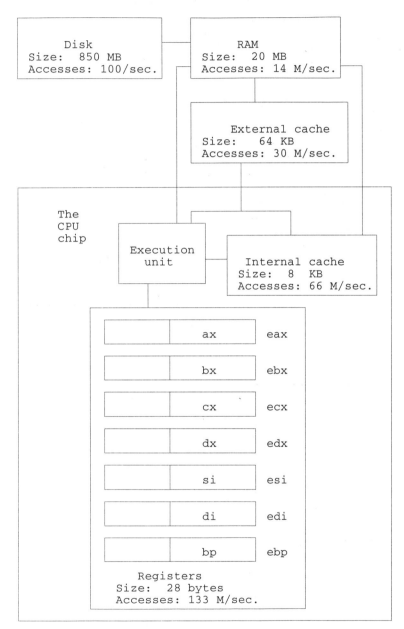

Figure 2.2: The memory hierarchy

We've already seen that the disk is necessary to store data and programs when the machine is turned off, while RAM is needed for its higher speed in accessing data and programs we're currently using.[21] But why do we need the *external cache*?

Actually, we've been around this track before, when we questioned why everything isn't loaded into RAM rather than being read from the disk as needed; we're trading speed for cost. To have a cost-effective computer with good performance requires the designer to choose the correct amount of each storage medium.

So just as with the disk vs. RAM trade-off before, the reason that we use the external cache is to improve performance. While RAM can be accessed about 14 million times per second, the external cache is made from a faster type of memory chips, which can be accessed about 30 million times per second. While not as extreme as the speed differential between disk and RAM, this difference is still significant. However, we can't afford to use external cache exclusively instead of RAM, because it would be too expensive to do so. In late 1995, the cost of 1 MB of external cache was in the neighborhood of $300. For that same amount of money, you could have bought 8 Megabytes of RAM. Therefore, we must reserve external cache for tasks where speed is all-important, such as supplying frequently used data or programs to the CPU.[22]

The same analysis applies to the trade-off between the external cache and the *internal cache*. The internal cache's characteristics are similar to those of the the external cache, but to a greater degree; it's even smaller and faster, allowing access at the rated speed of the CPU. Both characteristics have to do with its privileged position on the same chip as the CPU; this reduces the delays in communication between the internal cache and the CPU but means that chip area devoted to the cache has to compete with area for the CPU, as long as the total chip size is held constant.

Unfortunately, we can't just increase the size of the chip to accommodate more internal cache because of the expense of doing so. Larger chips are more difficult to make, which reduces their *yield*, or the percentage of good chips. In addition, fewer of them fit on one *wafer*, which is the unit of manufacturing. Both of these attributes make larger chips more expensive to make.

Problem
Algorithms
C++
Executable
Hardware

---

21. These complementary roles played by RAM and the disk explain why the speed of the disk is also illustrated in the memory hierarchy.

22. There are other reasons to limit the size of an external cache. For one thing, it uses a lot of power and thus produces a lot of heat; this isn't good for electronic components.

Caching In

To oversimplify a bit, here's how caching reduces the effects of slow RAM. Whenever a data item is requested by the CPU, there are three possibilities:

1. It is already in the internal cache. In this case, the value is sent to the CPU without referring to RAM at all.
2. It is in the external cache; in this case it will be "promoted" to the internal cache, and sent to the CPU at the same time.
3. It is not in either the internal or external cache. In this case, it has to be entered into a location in the cache. If there is nothing in that cache location, the new item is simply added to the cache. However, if there is a data item already in that cache location, then the old item is displaced to the external cache, and the new item is written in its place.[23] If the external cache location is empty, that ends the activity; if it is not empty, then the item previously in that location is overwritten by the one displaced from the internal cache.[24]

Problem
Algorithms
C++
Executable
Hardware

Please Register Here

Another way to improve performance that has been employed for many years is to create a small number of private storage areas, called **registers**, that are on the same chip as the CPU itself. Programs use these registers to hold data items that are actively in use; data in registers can be accessed within the time allocated to instruction execution (16 ns in our example), rather than the much longer times needed to access data in RAM.[25] This means that the

---

23. Here, I'm assuming that this is a *direct-mapped cache*, which means that each cache "location" can hold exactly one item. It's also possible to have a cache that stores more than one item in a "location", in which case one of the other items already there will be displaced to make room for the new one. The one selected is usually the one that hasn't been accessed for the longest time, on the theory that it's probably not going to be accessed again soon; this is called the *least recently used* (abbreviated LRU) replacement algorithm.

24. This is fairly close to the actual way caches are used to reduce the time it takes to get frequently used data from RAM (known as *caching reads*); reducing the time needed to write changed values back to RAM (*caching writes*) is more complicated.

25. In case you're wondering how a small number of registers can help the speed of a large program, I should point out that no matter how large a program is, the vast majority of instructions and data items in the program are inactive at any given moment. In fact, less than a dozen instructions are in various stages of execution at any given time even in the most advanced CPU available in 1995. The computer's apparent ability to run several

time needed to access data in registers is predictable, unlike data that may have been displaced from the internal cache by more recent arrivals and thus must be reloaded from the external cache or even from RAM. Most CPUs have some **dedicated register**s, which aren't available to application programmers (that's us), but are reserved for the operating system (e.g., DOS, Windows 95, Unix, OS/2) or have special functions dictated by the hardware design; however, we will be concerned primarily with the **general registers**, which are available for our use.[26]

The general registers are used to hold working copies of data items called **variables**, which otherwise reside in RAM during the execution of the program. These variables represent specific items of data that we wish to keep track of in our programs, such as weights and numbers of items.[27]

The notion of using registers to hold temporary copies of variables wasn't crystal clear to Susan. Here's our discussion on that topic:

> **Susan**: Here we go, getting lost. When you said "The general registers are used to hold working copies of data items called variables, which reside in RAM", are you saying RAM stores info when not in use?

> **Steve**: During execution of a program, when data aren't in the general registers, they are generally stored in RAM.

> **Susan**: See, this is confusing to me, because I didn't think RAM stores anything when turned off.

> **Steve**: You're correct; RAM doesn't retain information when the machine is turned off. However, it is used to keep the "real" copies of data that we want to process but won't fit in the registers.

Problem
Algorithms
C++
Executable
Hardware

You can put something in a variable, and it will stay there until you store something else there; you can also look at it to find out what's in it. As you might expect, several types of variables are used to hold

---

26. All of the registers are physically similar, being just a collection of circuits in the CPU used to hold a value. As indicated here, some registers are dedicated to certain uses by the design of the CPU, whereas others are generally usable. In the case of the general registers, which are all functionally similar or identical, a compiler often uses them in a conventional way; this stylized usage simplifies the compiler writer's job.

27. Since RAM doesn't maintain its contents when power is turned off, anything that a program needs to keep around for a long time, such as inventory data to be used later, should be saved on the disk. We'll see how that is accomplished in a future chapter.

different kinds of data; the first ones we will look at are variables representing whole numbers (the so-called **integer variables**), which are a subset of the category called **numeric variables**. As this suggests, there are also variables that represent numbers that can have fractional parts. We'll look at these so-called floating-point variables briefly in a later chapter.

Different types of variables require different amounts of RAM to store them, depending on the amount of data they contain; a very common type of numeric variable, known as a short, requires 16 bits (that is, 2 bytes) of RAM to hold any of 65536 different values, from −32768 to 32767, including 0. As we will see shortly, these odd-looking numbers are the result of using the binary system.

By no coincidence at all, the early Intel CPUs such as the 8086 had general registers that contained 16 bits each; these registers were named ax, bx, cx, dx, si, di, and bp. Why does it matter how many bits each register holds? Because the number (and size) of instructions it takes to process a variable is much less if the variable fits in a register; therefore, most programming languages, C++ included, relate the size of a variable to the size of the registers available to hold it. A short is exactly the right size to fit into a 16-bit register and therefore can be processed efficiently by the early Intel machines, whereas longer variables had to be handled in pieces, causing a great decline in efficiency of the program.

Progress marches on: more recent Intel CPUs, starting with the 80386, have 32-bit general registers; these registers are called eax, ebx, ecx, edx, esi, edi, and ebp. You may have noticed that these names are simply the names of the old 16-bit registers with an e tacked onto the front. The reason for the name change is that when Intel increased the size of the registers to 32 bits with the advent of the 80386, it didn't want to change the behavior of previously existing programs that (of course) used the old names for the 16-bit registers. So the old names now refer to the bottom halves of the "real" (that is, 32-bit) registers; instructions using these names behave exactly as though they were accessing the 16-bit registers on earlier machines. To refer to the 32-bit registers, you use the new names eax, ebx, and so on, for "extended" ax, "extended" bx, and so forth.

What does it mean to say that instructions using the 16-bit register names "behave exactly as though they were accessing the 16-bit registers on earlier machines"? Before I can explain this, you'll have to understand the binary number system, on which all modern computers are based. To make this number system more intelligible, I have written the following little fable.

Problem
Algorithms
C++
Executable
Hardware

Odometer Trouble

Once upon a time, the Acme company had a factory that made golf carts. One day, Bob, the president of Acme, decided to add an odometer to the carts, so that the purchaser of the cart could estimate when to recharge the battery. To save money, Bob decided to buy the little numbered wheels for the odometers and have his employees put the odometers together. The minimum order was a thousand odometer wheels, which was more than he needed for his initial run of 50 odometers. When he got the wheels, however, he noticed that they were defective: Instead of the numbers 0–9, each wheel had only two numbers, 0 and 1. Of course, he was quite irritated by this error, and attempted to contact the company from which he had purchased the wheels, but it had closed down for a month for summer vacation. What was he to do until it reopened?

While he was fretting about this problem, the employee who had been assigned to the task of putting the odometers together from the wheels came up with a possible solution. This employee, Jim, came into Bob's office and said, "Bob, I have an idea. Since we have lots of orders for these odometer-equipped carts, maybe we can make an odometer with these funny wheels and tell the customers how to read the numbers on the odometer."

Bob was taken aback by this idea. "What do you mean, Jim? How can anyone read those screwy odometers?"

Jim had given this some thought. "Let's take a look at what one of these odometers, say with five wheels, can display. Obviously, it would start out reading 00000, just like a normal odometer. Then when one mile has elapsed, the rightmost wheel turns to 1, so the whole display is 00001; again, this is no different from a normal odometer."

"Now we come to the tricky part. The rightmost wheel goes back to 0, not having any more numbers to display, and pushes the 'tens' wheel to 1; the whole number now reads 00010. Obviously, one more mile makes it 00011, which gives us the situation shown in the following diagram:

```
Normal odometer    Funny odometer
   00000              00000
   00001              00001
   00002              00010
   00003              00011
```

Figure 2.3: The first few numbers

Problem
Algorithms
C++
Executable
Hardware

Jim continued, "What's next? This time, the rightmost wheel turns over again to 0, triggering the second wheel to its next position. However, this time, the second wheel is already at its highest value, 1; therefore, it also turns over to 0 and increments the third wheel. It's not hard to follow this for a few more miles, as illustrated in Figure 2.4.

```
Normal odometer      Funny odometer
    00004                00100
    00005                00101
    00006                00110
    00007                00111
```

Figure 2.4: The next few numbers

Bob said, "I get it. It's almost as though we were counting normally, except that you skip all the numbers that have anything but 0s or 1s in them."

"That's right, Bob. So I suppose we could make up a list of the 'real' numbers and give it to the customers to use until we can replace these odometers with normal ones. Perhaps they'll be willing to work with us on this problem."

Problem
Algorithms
C++
Executable
Hardware

"Okay, Jim, if you think they'll buy it. Let's get a few of the customers we know the best and ask them if they'll try it; we won't charge them for the odometers until we have the real ones, but maybe they'll stick with us until then. Perhaps any odometer would be better than no odometer at all."

Jim went to work, making some odometers out of the defective wheels; however, he soon figured out that he had to use more than five wheels, because that allowed only numbers from 0 to 31. How did he know this?

Each wheel has two numbers, 0 and 1. So with one wheel, we have a total of two combinations. Two wheels can have either a 0 or a 1 for the first number, and the same for the second number, for a total of four combinations. With three wheels, the same analysis holds: 2 numbers for the first wheel * 2 for the second wheel * 2 for the third wheel = 8 possibilities in all; actually, they are the same 8 possibilities we saw in Figures 2.3 and 2.4.

A pattern is beginning to develop: for each added wheel, we get twice as many possible combinations. To see how this continues, take a look at Figure 2.5, which shows the count of combinations vs. number of wheels for all wheel counts up to 16 (i.e., 16-bit quantities).

Number of wheels	Number of combinations[28]
1	2
2	4
3	8
4	16
5	32
6	64
7	128
8	256
9	512
10	1024
11	2048
12	4096
13	8192
14	16384
15	32768
16	65536

Figure 2.5: How many combinations?

Jim decided that 14 wheels would do the job, since the lifespan of the golf cart probably wouldn't exceed 16,383 miles, and so he made up the odometers. The selected customers turned out to be agreeable and soon found that having even a weird odometer was better than none, especially since they didn't have to pay for it. However, one customer did have a complaint: The numbers on the wheels didn't seem to make sense when translated with the chart supplied by Acme. The customer estimated that he had driven the cart about 9 miles, but the odometer displayed the following number,

Problem
Algorithms
C++
Executable
Hardware

11111111110111

which, according to his translation chart, was 16375 miles. What could have gone wrong?

Jim decided to have the cart brought in for a checkup, and what he discovered was that the odometer cable had been hooked up backwards. That is, instead of turning the wheels forward, they were going backwards. That was part of the solution, but why was the value 16375?

Just like a car odometer, in which 99999 (or 999999, if you have a 6-wheel odometer) is followed by 0, going backwards from 0 reverses that progression. Similarly, the number 11111111111111 on the funny odometers would be followed by 00000000000000, since

---

28. If you think that last number looks familiar, you're right: it's the number of different values that I said could be stored in a type of numeric variable called a short. This is no coincidence; read on for the detailed explanation.

the "carry" off the leftmost digit is lost. Therefore, if you start out at 0 and go backward 1 mile, you'll get

11111111111111

The next mile will turn the last digit back to 0, producing

11111111111110

What happens next? The last wheel turns back to 1, and triggers the second wheel to switch as well:

11111111111101

The next few "backward" numbers look like this:

```
11111111111100
11111111111011
11111111111010
11111111111001
11111111111000
11111111110111
```

Problem
Algorithms
C++
Executable
Hardware

and so on. If you look at the right-hand end of these numbers, you'll see that the progression is just the opposite of the "forward" numbers.

As for the customer's actual mileage, the last one of these is the number the customer saw on his backward odometer. Apparently, he was right about the distance driven, since this is the ninth "backward" number. So Jim fixed the backward odometer cable and reset the value to the correct number, 00000000001001, or 9 miles.

Eventually, Acme got the right odometer wheels with 0–9 on them, replaced the peculiar ones, and everyone lived happily ever after.

THE END

Back to the Future

Of course, the wheels that made up the funny odometers contain only two digits, 0 and 1, so the odometers use the binary system for counting. Now it should be obvious why we will see numbers like 65536 and 32768 in our discussions of the number of possible different values that a variable can hold: variables are stored in RAM as collections of bytes, each of which contains 8 bits. As the list of combinations indicates, 8 bits (1 byte) provide 256 different combinations, while 16 bits (2 bytes) can represent 65536 different possible values.

But what about the "backward" numbers with a lot of 1s on the left? As the fable suggests, they correspond to "negative" numbers. That is, if moving 2 miles forward from 0 registers as 00000000000010, and moving 2 miles backward from 0 registers as 11111111111110, then the latter number is in some sense equivalent to –2 miles. This in fact is the way that negative integers are stored in the computer; integer variables that can store negative values are called signed *variables*. If we don't specify whether we want to be able to store negative values in a given variable, the C++ language assumes that we want that ability, and provides it for us by default.

However, adding the ability to represent negative numbers has a drawback: namely, that you can't represent as many positive numbers. This should be fairly obvious, since if we interpret some of the possible patterns as negative, they can't also be used for positive values. Sometimes, of course, we don't have to worry about negative numbers, such as counting how many employees our company has; in such cases, we can specify that we want to use unsigned *variables*, which will always be interpreted as positive (or 0) values. An example is an unsigned short variable, which uses 16 bits (that is, 2 bytes) to hold any number from 0 to 65535, which totals 65536 different values. This capacity can be calculated as follows: since each byte is 8 bits, 2 bytes contain a total of 16 bits, and 2^{16} is 65536.

It's important to understand that the difference between a short (that is, a signed short) and an unsigned short is exactly which 65536 values each can hold. An unsigned short can hold any whole number from 0 to 65535, whereas a short can hold any value from –32768 to +32767.

I hope this is clear to you, but in case it isn't, let's see how Susan and I worked over this point:

> **Susan**: I really don't think I understand what a short is besides being 2 bytes of RAM, and I don't really know what signed and unsigned mean.

> **Steve**: A short is indeed 2 bytes (that is, 16 bits) of RAM. This means that it can hold any of 2^{16} (65536) different values. This is a very nice range of values for holding the number of pounds that a pumpkin weighs (for example). You'll see some more uses for this type of variable later.

Problem
Algorithms
C++
Executable
Hardware

The difference between a (signed) short and an unsigned short is exactly which 65536 values each can hold. An unsigned short can hold any whole number from 0 to 65535, whereas a (signed) short can hold any value from −32768 to +32767. The difference between these is *solely* in the interpretation that we (and the compiler) give to the values. In other words, it's not possible to tell whether a given 2 bytes of RAM represent a short or an unsigned short by looking at the contents of those bytes; you have to know how the variable was defined in the program.

Susan: Ok, let's start over. A short is 2 bytes of RAM. A short is a variable. A short is a numeric variable. It can be signed (why is that a default?), meaning its value can be −32768 to +32767, or unsigned, meaning its value can be 0–65535. How's that?

Steve: That's fine. Since you've asked, the reason signed is the default is because that's the way it was in C, and changing it in C++ would "break" C programs that depended on this default. Bjarne Stroustrup, the inventor of C++, has a rule that C++ must be as close to C as possible but no closer. In this case, there's no real reason to change the default, so it wasn't changed.

Problem
Algorithms
C++
Executable
Hardware

Susan: Oh, why is it that every time you say something is fairly obvious, my mind just shuts down? When you say "if we interpret some of the possible patterns as negative, they can't also be used for positive values." Huh? Then if that is the case would not the reverse also be true? I can see how this explains the values of the signed and unsigned short, but really I don't think I have grasped this concept.

Steve: What I was trying to explain is that you have to choose one of the following two possibilities:[29]

1.   (signed) short range: −32768 to +32767
2.   unsigned short range: 0 to 65535

In other words, you have to decide whether you want a given variable to represent:

1.   Any of 32768 negative numbers, 0, or 32767 positive numbers, or
2.   Any of 65536 nonnegative numbers from 0 to 65535

If you want a variable with a range like that in selection 1, use a (signed) short; if you prefer the range in selection 2, use an unsigned short. For example, for the number of lines in a text file, you could use an

---

29. If neither of these does what you want, don't despair. Other types of numeric variables have different ranges; we'll go over them quickly in Appendix A.

unsigned short, since the maximum number of lines could be limited to less than 65,000 lines and couldn't ever be negative. On the other hand, to represent the number of copies of a book that have been sold in the last month, including the possibility of returns exceeding sales, a signed short would be better, since the value could be either positive or negative.

Susan: In other words, if you are going to be using variables that might have a negative value then use a signed short, and if you want strictly "positive" numbers then use an unsigned short. Right?

Steve: Exactly!

Susan: Well, then, how do you write a short to indicate that it is signed or unsigned?

Steve: When you define it, you have to specify that it is unsigned if you want it to be unsigned; the default is signed. In other words, if we define a variable x as short x;, it will be signed, whereas if we want a variable called x that is an unsigned short, we have to say unsigned short x;.

Susan: So does it make any difference if your variable is going to overlap the signed and unsigned short ranges? For example, if you are using numbers from 10,000 to 30,000, would it matter which short you used? It falls under the definition of both.

Steve: You can use whichever you wish in that case.

Problem
Algorithms
C++
Executable
Hardware

Over-Hexed

You may have noticed that it's tedious and error prone to represent numbers in binary; a long string of 0s and 1s is hard to remember or to copy. For this reason, the pure binary system is hardly ever used to specify numbers in computing. However, we have already seen that binary is much more "natural" for computers than the more familiar decimal system. Is there a number system that we humans can use a little more easily than binary, while retaining the advantages of binary for describing internal events in the computer?

As it happens, there is. It's called **hexadecimal**, which means "base 16". As a rule, the term *hexadecimal* is abbreviated to *hex*. Since there are 16 possible combinations of 4 bits (2*2*2*2), hexadecimal notation allows 4 bits of a binary number to be represented by one hex digit. Unfortunately, however, there are only

10 "normal" digits, 0–9.[30] To represent a number in any base, you need as many different digit values as the base, so that any number less than the base can be represented by one digit. For example, in base 2, you need only two digits, 0 and 1. In base 8 (*octal*), you need eight digits, 0–7.[31] So far, so good. But what about base 16? To use this base, we need 16 digits. Since only 10 numeric digits are available, hex notation needs a source for the other six digits. Because letters of the alphabet are available and familiar, the first six letters, a–f, were adopted for this service.[32]

Although the notion of a base-16 numbering system doesn't seem strange to people who are familiar with it, it can really throw someone who learned normal decimal arithmetic solely by rote, without understanding the concepts on which it is based. This topic of hexadecimal notation occupied Susan and me for quite awhile; here's some of the discussion we had about it:

> **Susan**: I don't get this at all! What is the deal with the letters in the hex system? I guess it would be okay if 16 wasn't represented by 10!
>
> **Steve**: Well, there are only 10 "normal" digits, 0–9. To represent a number in any base, you need as many "digits" as the base, so that any number less than the base can be represented by one "digit". This is no problem with a base less than ten, such as octal, but what about base 16? To use this base we need 16 digits, 0–9 and a–f. One way to remember this is to imagine that the "hex" in "hexadecimal" stands for the six letters a through f and the "decimal" stands for the 10 digits 0–9.
>
> **Susan**: OK, so a hex digit represents 16 bits? So then is hex is equal to 2 bytes? According to the preceding a hex digit is 4 bits.
>
> **Steve**: Yes, a hex digit represents 4 bits. Let's try a new approach. First, let me define a new term, a *hexit*. That's short for "hex digit", just like "bit" is short for "binary digit".
>
> 1. How many one-digit decimal numbers exist?
> 2. How many two-digit decimal numbers exist?
> 3. How many three-digit decimal numbers exist?

Problem
Algorithms
C++
Executable
Hardware

---

30. Paging Dr. Seuss. . .

31. In the early days of computing, base 8 was sometimes used instead of base 16, especially on machines that used 12-bit and 36-bit registers; however, it has fallen into disuse because almost all modern machines have 32-bit registers.

32. Either upper or lower case letters are acceptable to most programs (and programmers). I'll use lower case because such letters are easier to distinguish than upper case ones; besides, I find them less irritating to look at.

4.   How many four-digit decimal numbers exist?
5.   How many one-bit binary numbers exist?
6.   How many two-bit binary numbers exist?
7.   How many three-bit binary numbers exist?
8.   How many four-bit binary numbers exist?
9.   How many one-hexit hexadecimal numbers exist?
10.   How many two-hexit hexadecimal numbers exist?
11.   How many three-hexit hexadecimal numbers exist?
12.   How many four-hexit hexadecimal numbers exist?

The answers are:

1.   10
2.   100
3.   1000
4.   10000
5.   2
6.   4
7.   8
8.   16
9.   16
10.   256
11.   4096
12.   65536

Problem
Algorithms
C++
Executable
Hardware

What do all these answers have in common? Let's look at the answers a little differently, in powers of 10, 2, and 16, respectively:

1.   10 $= 10^1$
2.   100 $= 10^2$
3.   1000 $= 10^3$
4.   10000 $= 10^4$
5.   2 $= 2^1$
6.   4 $= 2^2$
7.   8 $= 2^3$
8.   16 $= 2^4$
9.   16 $= 16^1$
10.   256 $= 16^2$
11.   4096 $= 16^3$
12.   65536 $= 16^4$

That is, each digit multiplies the number of different values that can be represented by a number in any base by the size of the base. That's the way positional number systems such as decimal, binary, and hex work. If you need a bigger number, you just add more digits.

    Okay, so what does this have to do with hex? If you look at the above table, you'll see that 2^4 (16) is equal to 16^1. That means that 4 bits are exactly equivalent to one hexit in their ability to represent different numbers: exactly 16 possible numbers can be represented by four bits, and exactly 16 possible numbers can be represented by one hexit.

This means that you can write one hexit wherever you would otherwise have to use four bits, as illustrated in Figure 2.6.

```
4-bit value   1-hexit value

0000               0
0001               1
0010               2
0011               3
0100               4
0101               5
0110               6
0111               7
1000               8
1001               9
1010               a
1011               b
1100               c
1101               d
1110               e
1111               f
```

Problem
Algorithms
C++
Executable
Hardware

Figure 2.6: Binary to hex conversion table

So an 8-bit number, such as:
0101 1011
can be translated directly into a hex value, like this:
5   b

For this reason, binary is almost never used. Instead, we use hex as a shortcut to eliminate the necessity of reading, writing, and remembering long strings of bits.

Susan: A hex digit or hexit is like a four-wheel odometer in binary. Since each wheel is capable of only one of two values, being either (1) or (0), then the total number of possible values is 16. Thus your 2*2*2*2 = 16. I think I've got this down.

Steve: You certainly do!

Susan: If it has 4 bits and you have 2 of them then won't there be eight "wheels" and so forth? So 2 hex would hold XXXXXXXX places and 3 hex would hold XXXXXXXXXXXX places.

Steve: Correct. A one-hexit number is analogous to a one-digit decimal number. A one-hexit number contains 4 bits and therefore can represent any of 16 values. A two-hexit number contains 8 bits and therefore can represent any of 256 values.

Now that we've seen how each hex digit corresponds exactly to a group of four binary digits, here's an exercise you can use to improve your understanding of this topic: Invent a random string of four binary digits and see where it is in figure 2.6. I guarantee it'll be there somewhere! Then look at the "hex" column and see what "digit" it corresponds to. There's nothing really mysterious about hex; since we have run out of digits after 9, we have to use letters to represent the numbers 'ten', 'eleven', 'twelve', 'thirteen', 'fourteen', and 'fifteen'.

Now, here's a table showing the correspondence between some decimal, hex, and binary numbers, with the values of each digit position in each number base indicated, and the calculation of the total of all of the bit values in the binary representation, as shown in Figure 2.7.

Decimal Place Values 10 1	Hexadecimal Place Values 16 1	Binary Place Values 16 8 4 2 1		Sum of binary digit values
0	0 0	0 0 0 0 0	=	0 + 0 + 0 + 0 + 0
1	0 1	0 0 0 0 1	=	0 + 0 + 0 + 0 + 1
2	0 2	0 0 0 1 0	=	0 + 0 + 0 + 2 + 0
3	0 3	0 0 0 1 1	=	0 + 0 + 0 + 2 + 1
4	0 4	0 0 1 0 0	=	0 + 0 + 4 + 0 + 0
5	0 5	0 0 1 0 1	=	0 + 0 + 4 + 0 + 1
6	0 6	0 0 1 1 0	=	0 + 0 + 4 + 2 + 0
7	0 7	0 0 1 1 1	=	0 + 8 + 4 + 2 + 1
8	0 8	0 1 0 0 0	=	0 + 8 + 0 + 0 + 0
9	0 9	0 1 0 0 1	=	0 + 8 + 0 + 0 + 1
1 0	0 a	0 1 0 1 0	=	0 + 8 + 0 + 2 + 0
1 1	0 b	0 1 0 1 1	=	0 + 8 + 0 + 2 + 1
1 2	0 c	0 1 1 0 0	=	0 + 8 + 4 + 0 + 0
1 3	0 d	0 1 1 0 1	=	0 + 8 + 4 + 0 + 1
1 4	0 e	0 1 1 1 0	=	0 + 8 + 4 + 2 + 0
1 5	0 f	0 1 1 1 1	=	0 + 8 + 4 + 2 + 1
1 6	1 0	1 0 0 0 0	=	16 + 0 + 0 + 0 + 0
1 7	1 1	1 0 0 0 1	=	16 + 0 + 0 + 0 + 1
1 8	1 2	1 0 0 1 0	=	16 + 0 + 0 + 2 + 0
1 9	1 3	1 0 0 1 1	=	16 + 0 + 0 + 2 + 1

Figure 2.7: Different representations of the same numbers

Problem
Algorithms
C++
Executable
Hardware

Another reason to use hex rather than decimal is that byte values expressed as hex digits can be combined directly to produce larger values, which is not true with decimal digits. In case this isn't obvious, let's go over it in more detail. Since each hex digit (0–f) represents exactly 4 bits, two of them (00–ff) represent 8 bits, or one byte. Similarly, 4 hex digits (0000–ffff) represent 16 bits, or a short value; the first two digits represent the first byte of the 2-byte value, and the last two digits, the second byte. This can be extended to any number of bytes. On the other hand, representing 4 bits requires two decimal digits, as the values range from 00–15, whereas it takes three digits (000–255) to represent one byte. A 2-byte value requires five decimal digits, since the value can be from 00000 to 65535. As you can see, there's no simple relationship between the decimal digits representing each byte and the decimal representation of a 2-byte value.

Susan had some more thoughts on the hexadecimal number system. Let's listen in:

> **Susan**: I think you need to spend a little more time reviewing the hex system, like an entire chapter.<G> Well, I am getting the impression that we are going to be working with hex, so I am trying to concentrate my understanding on that instead of binary. I think this all moves a little too fast for me. I don't know what your other reviewers are saying but I just feel like I get a definition of a abstract concept, and the next thing I know I am supposed to be doing something with it, like make it work. Ha! I personally need to digest new concepts, I really need to think them over a bit, to take them in and absorb them. I just can't start working with it right away.

Problem
Algorithms
C++
Executable
Hardware

As usual, I've complied with her request; the results are immediately ahead.

Exercises

Here are some exercises that you can use to check your understanding of the binary and hexadecimal number systems. I've limited the examples to addition and subtraction, as that is all that you're ever likely to have to do in these number systems. These operations are exactly like their equivalents in the decimal system, except that as we have already seen, the hexadecimal system has six extra digits after 9: a, b, c, d, e, and f. We have to take these into account in our calculations: for example, adding 9 and 5, rather than producing 14, produces e.

1. Using the hexadecimal system, answer these problems:

   a.   1a + 2e = ?
   b.   12 + 18 = ?

c. $50 - 12 = ?$

2. In the binary system, answer these problems:

a. $101 + 110 = ?$
b. $111 + 1001 = ?$
c. $1010 - 11 = ?$

Consider the two types of numeric variables we've encountered so far, short and unsigned short. Let's suppose that x is a short, and y is an unsigned short, both of them currently holding the value 32767, or 7fff in hex.

3. What is the result of adding 1 to y, in both decimal and hex?
4. What is the result of adding 1 to x, in both decimal and hex?

Answers to exercises can be found at the end of the chapter.

Registering Relief

Before we took this detour into the binary and hexadecimal number systems, I promised to explain what it means to say that the instructions using the 16-bit register names "behave exactly as though they were accessing the 16-bit registers on earlier machines". After a bit more preparation, we'll be ready for that explanation. First, let's take a look at some characteristics of the human-readable version of machine instructions: assembly language instructions.

Problem
Algorithms
C++
Executable
Hardware

Some Assembly Required

The **assembly language** instructions we will look at have a fairly simple format.[33] The name of the operation is given first, followed by one or more spaces. The next element is the "destination", which is the register or RAM location that will be affected by the instruction's execution. The last element in an instruction is the "source", which represents another register, a RAM location, or a constant value to be used in the calculation. The source and destination are separated by a

---

33. I'm simplifying here. There are instructions that follow other formats, but we'll stick with the simple ones for the time being.

comma.[34] Here's an example of a simple assembly language instruction:

add   ax,1

In this instruction, add is the operation, ax is the destination, and the constant value 1 is the source. Thus, add ax,1 means to add 1 to the contents of ax, replacing the old contents of ax with the result.

Let's see what Susan has to say about the makeup of an assembly language instruction:

> **Susan**: So the destination can be a register, cache, or RAM?
>
> **Steve**: Yes, that's right. However, I should make it clear that the cache is transparent to the programmer. That is, you don't say "write to the cache" or "read from the cache"; you just use the RAM addresses and the hardware takes care of using the cache as appropriate to speed up access to frequently used locations. On the other hand, you do have to address registers explicitly when writing an assembly language program.

Problem
Algorithms
C++
Executable
Hardware

Now we're finally ready to see what the statement about using the 16-bit register names on a 32-bit machine means. Suppose we have the register contents shown in Figure 2.8 (indicated in hexadecimal).

32-bit register	32-bit contents	16-bit register	16-bit contents
eax	1235ffff	ax	ffff

Figure 2.8: 32 and 16 bit registers, before add ax,1

If we were to add 1 to register ax, by executing the instruction add ax,1, the result would be as shown in Figure 2.9.

---

34. Of course, the actual machine instructions being executed in the CPU don't have commas, register names, or any other human-readable form; they consist of fixed-format sequences of bits stored in RAM. The CPU actually executes machine language instructions rather than assembly language ones; a program called an **assembler** takes care of translating the assembly language instructions into machine instructions. However, we can usually ignore this step, because each assembly language instruction corresponds to one machine instruction. This correspondence is quite unlike the relationship between C++ statements and machine instructions, which is far more complex.

32-bit register	32-bit contents	16-bit register	16-bit contents
eax	12350000	ax	0000

Figure 2.9: 32 and 16 bit registers, after add ax,1

In case this makes no sense, consider what happens when you add 1 to 9999 on a four digit counter such as an odometer. It "turns over" to 0000, doesn't it? The same applies here: ffff is the largest number that can be represented as four hex digits, so if you add 1 to a register that has only four (hex) digits of storage available, the result is 0000.

As you might imagine, Susan was quite intrigued with the above detail; here is her reaction.

> **Susan**: I have a understanding retention half-life of about 30 nanoseconds, but while I was reading this I was understanding it except I am boggled as to how adding 1 to ffff makes 0000, see, I am still not clear on Hex. Question: When you show the contents of a 32-bit register as being 12350000, then is the 1235 the upper half and the 0000 the lower half? Is that what you are saying?

> **Steve**: That's right!

As this illustrates, instructions that refer to ax have no effect whatever on the upper part of eax; they behave exactly as though the upper part of eax did not exist. However, if we were to execute the instruction add eax,1 instead of add ax,1, the result would look like Figure 2.10.

32-bit register	32-bit contents	16-bit register	16-bit contents
eax	12360000	ax	0000

Figure 2.10: 32 and 16 bit registers, after add eax,1

In this case, eax is treated as a whole. Similar results apply to the other 32-bit registers and their 16-bit counterparts.

Problem
Algorithms
C++
Executable
Hardware

On a RAMpage

Unfortunately, it isn't possible to use only registers and avoid references to RAM entirely, if only because we'll run out of registers sooner or later. This is a good time to look back at the diagram of the "memory hierarchy" (figure 2.2) and examine the relative speed and size of each different kind of memory.

The "size" attribute of the disk and RAM are specified in Megabytes, whereas the size of an external cache is generally in the range from 64 Kilobytes to 1 Megabyte. As I mentioned before, the internal cache is considerably smaller, usually in the 8 to 16 Kilobyte range. The registers, however, provide a total of 28 *bytes* of storage; this should make clear that they are the scarcest memory resource. To try to clarify why the registers are so important to the performance of programs, I've listed the "speed" attribute in number of accesses per second, rather than in milliseconds, nanoseconds, and so forth. In the case of the disk, this is about 100 accesses per second. RAM can be accessed about 14 million times per second. The clear winners, though, are the internal cache and the registers, which can be accessed 66 million times per second and 133 million times per second, respectively.

Problem
Algorithms
C++
Executable
Hardware

Registering Bewilderment

In a way, the latter figure (133 million accesses per second for registers) overstates the advantages of registers relative to the cache. You see, any given register can be accessed only 66 million times per second; however, many instructions refer to two registers and still execute in one CPU cycle. Therefore, the maximum number of references per second is more than the number of instructions per second.

However, this leads to another question: Why not have instructions that can refer to more than one memory address (known as *memory-to-memory* instructions) and still execute in one CPU cycle? In that case, we wouldn't have to worry about registers; since there's (relatively) a lot of cache and very few registers, it would seem to make more sense to eliminate the middleman and simply refer to data in the cache.[35] Of course, there is a good reason for the provision of

---

35. Perhaps I should remind you that the programmer doesn't explicitly refer to the cache; you can just use normal RAM addresses and let the hardware take care of making sure that the most frequently referenced data ends up in the cache.

both registers and cache. The main drawback of registers is that there are so few of them; on the other hand, one of their main advantages is also that there are so few of them. Why is this?

The main reason to use registers is that they make instructions shorter: since there are only a few registers, we don't have to use up a lot of bits specifying which register(s) to use. That is, with eight registers, we only need 3 bits to specify which register we need. In fact, there are standardized 3-bit codes that might be thought of as "register addresses", which are used to specify each register when it is used to hold a variable. Figure 2.11 is the table of these register codes.[36]

Register address	16-bit register	32-bit register
000	ax	eax
001	cx	ecx
010	dx	edx
011	bx	ebx
100	sp	esp
101	bp	ebp
110	si	esi
111	di	edi

Figure 2.11: 32 and 16 bit register codes

Problem
Algorithms
C++
Executable
Hardware

By contrast, with a "memory-to-memory" architecture, each instruction would need at least 2 bytes for the source address, and 2 bytes for the destination address.[37] Adding 1 byte to specify what the instruction is going to do, this would make the minimum instruction size 5 bytes, whereas some instructions that use only registers can be as short as 1 byte. This makes a big difference in performance because the caches are quite limited in size; big programs don't fit in the caches, and therefore require a large number of RAM accesses. As a result, they execute much more slowly than small programs.

---

36. Don't blame me for the seemingly scrambled order of the codes; that's the way Intel's CPU architects assigned them to registers when they designed the 8086 and it's much too late to change them now. Luckily, we almost never have to worry about their values, because the assembler takes care of the translation of register names to register addresses.

37. If we want to be able to access more than 64 Kilobytes worth of data, which is necessary in most modern programs, we'll need even more room to store addresses.

Slimming the Program

This explains why we want our programs to be smaller. However, it may not be obvious why using registers reduces the size of instructions, so here's an explanation.

Most of the data in use by a program are stored in RAM. When using a 32-bit CPU, it is theoretically possible to have over 4 billion bytes of memory (2^{32} is the exact number). Therefore, that many distinct addresses for a given byte of data are possible; to specify any of these requires 32 bits. Since there are only a few registers, specifying which one you want to use takes only a few bits; therefore, programs use register addresses instead of memory addresses wherever possible, to reduce the number of bits in each instruction required to specify addresses.

I hope this is clear, but it might not be. It certainly wasn't to Susan. Here's the conversation we had on this topic:

Problem
Algorithms
C++
Executable
Hardware

> **Susan**: I see that you are trying to make a point about why registers are more efficient in terms of making instructions shorter, but I just am not picturing exactly how they do this. How do you go from "make the instructions much shorter" to "we don't have to use up a lot of bits specifying which registers to use"?
>
> **Steve**: Let's suppose that we want to move data from one place to another in memory. In that case, we'll have to specify two addresses: the "from" address and the "to" address. One way to do this is to store the addresses in the machine language instruction. Since each address is at least 16 bits, an instruction that contains two addresses needs to occupy at least 32 bits just for the addresses, as well as some more bits to specify exactly what instruction we want to perform. Of course, if we're using 32-bit addresses, then a "two-address" instruction would require 64 bits just for the two addresses, in addition to whatever bits were needed to specify the type of instruction.
>
> **Susan**: OK. . . think I got this. . .
>
> **Steve**: On the other hand, if we use registers to hold the addresses of the data, we need only enough bits to specify each of two registers. Since there aren't that many registers, we don't need as many bits to specify which ones we're referring to. Even on a machine that has 32 general registers, we'd need only 10 bits to specify two registers; on the Intel machines, with their shortage of registers, even fewer bits are needed to specify which register we're referring to.

Susan: Are you talking about the bits that are needed to define the instruction?

Steve: Yes.

Susan: How would you know how many bits are needed to specify the two registers?

Steve: If you have 32 different possibilities to select from, you need 5 bits to specify one of them, because 32 is 2 to the fifth power. If we have 32 registers, and any of them can be selected, that takes 5 bits to select any one of them. If we have to select two registers on a CPU with 32 registers, we need 10 bits to specify both registers.

Susan: So what does that have to do with it? All we are talking about is the instruction that indicates "select register" right? So that instruction should be the same and contain the same number of bits whether you have 1 or 32 registers.

Steve: There is no "select register" instruction. Every instruction has to specify whatever register or registers it uses. It takes 5 bits to select 1 of 32 items and only 3 bits to select 1 of 8 items; therefore, a CPU design that has 32 registers needs longer instructions than one that has only 8 registers.

Susan: I don't see why the number of registers should have an effect on the number of bits one instruction should have.

Steve: If you have two possibilities, how many bits does it take to select one of them? 1 bit. If you have four possibilities, how many bits does it take to select one of them? 2 bits. Eight possibilities require 3 bits; 16 possibilities require 4 bits; and finally 32 possibilities require 5 bits.

Susan: Some machines have 32 registers?

Steve: Yes. The PowerPC, for example. Some machines have even more registers than that.

Susan: If the instructions to specify a register are the same, then why would they differ just because one machine has more than another?

Steve: They aren't the same from one machine to another. Although every CPU that I'm familiar with has registers, each type of machine has its own way of executing instructions, including how you specify the registers.

Problem
Algorithms
C++
Executable
Hardware

Susan: OK, and in doing so it is selecting a register, right? An instruction should contain the same number of bits no matter how many registers it has to call on.

Steve: Let's take the example of an add instruction, which as its name implies, adds two numbers. The name of the instruction is the same length, no matter how many registers there are; that's true. However, the actual representation of the instruction in machine language has to have room for enough bits to specify which register(s) are being used in the instruction.

Susan: They are statements right? So why should they be bigger or smaller if there are more or fewer registers?

Steve: They are actually machine instructions, not C++ statements. The computer doesn't know how to execute C++ statements, so the C++ compiler is needed to convert C++ statements into machine instructions. Machine instructions need bits to specify which register(s) they are using; so, with more registers available, more bits in the instructions have to be used to specify the register(s) that the instructions are using.

Susan: Do all the statements change the values of bits they contain depending on the number of registers that are on the CPU?

Problem
Algorithms
C++
Executable
Hardware

Steve: Yes, they certainly do. To be more precise, the machine language instructions that execute a statement are larger or smaller depending on the number of registers in the machine, because they need more bits to specify one of a larger number of registers.

Susan: "It takes five bits to select one of 32 items. . ."
". . .and only three bits to select one of eight items." Why?

Steve: What is a bit? It is the amount of information needed to select one of two alternatives. For example, suppose you have to say whether a light is on or off. How many possibilities exist? Two. Since a single bit has two possible states, 0 or 1, we can represent "on" by 1 and "off" by 0 and thus represent the possible states of the light by one bit.

   Now suppose that we have a fan that has four settings: low, medium, high, and off. Is one bit enough to specify the current setting of the fan? No, because one bit has only two possible states, while the fan has four. However, if we use two bits, then it will work. We can represent the states by bits as follows:

```
bits    state
----    -----
 00     off
 01     low
 10     medium
 11     high
```

Note that this is an arbitrary mapping; there's no reason that it couldn't be like this instead:

```
bits    state
----    -----
 00     medium
 01     high
 10     off
 11     low
```

However, having the lowest "speed" (that is, off) represented by the lowest binary value (00) and the increasing speeds corresponding to increasing binary values makes more sense and therefore is easier to remember.

This same process can be extended to represent any number of possibilities. If we have eight registers, for example, we can represent each one by 3 bits, as noted previously in figure 2.11 on page 41. That is the actual representation in the Intel architecture; however, whatever representation might have been used, it would require 3 bits to select among eight possibilities. The same is true for a machine that has 32 registers, except that you need 5 bits instead of 3.

Problem
Algorithms
C++
Executable
Hardware

Susan: Okay, so then does that mean that more than one register can be in use at a time? Wait, where is the room that you are talking about?

Steve: Some instructions specify only one register (a "one-register" instruction), while others specify two (a "two-register" instruction); some don't specify any registers. For example, most "branch" instructions are in the last category; they specify which address to continue execution from. These are used to implement if statements, for loops, and other flow control statements.

Susan: So, when you create an instruction you have to open up enough "room" to talk to all the registers at once?

Steve: No, you have to have enough room to specify any one register, for a one-register instruction, or any two registers for a two-register instruction.

Susan: Well, this still has me confused. If you need to specify only one register at any given time, then why do you always need to have all the room available? Anyway, where is this room? Is it in RAM or is it in the registers themselves? Let's say you are going to specify an instruction that uses only 1 of 32 registers. Are you saying that even though you are going to use just one register you have to make room for all 32?

Steve: The "room" that I'm referring to is the bits in the instruction that specify which register the instruction is using. That is, if there are eight registers and you want to use one of them in an instruction, 3 bits need to be set aside in the instruction to indicate which register you're referring to.

Susan: So you need the bits to represent the address of a register?

Steve: Right. However, don't confuse the "address of a register" with a memory address. They have nothing to do with one another, except that they both specify one of a number of possible places to store information. That is, register ax doesn't correspond to memory address 0, and so on.

Susan: Yes, I understand the bit numbers in relation to the number of registers.

Problem
Algorithms
C++
Executable
Hardware

Steve: That's good.

Susan: So the "address of a register" is just where the CPU can locate the register in the CPU, not an address in RAM. Is that right?

Steve: Right. The address of a register merely specifies which of the registers you're referring to; all of them are in the CPU.

After that comedy routine, let's go back to Susan's reaction to something I said earlier about registers and variables:

Susan: The registers hold only variables. . . Okay, I know what is bothering me! What else is there besides variables? Besides nonvariables, please don't tell me that. (Actually that would be good, now that I think of it.) But this is where I am having problems. You are talking about data, and a variable is a type of data. I need to know what else is out there so I have something else to compare it with. When you say a register can hold a variable, that is meaningless to me, unless I know what the alternatives are and where they are held.

Steve: What else is there besides variables? Well, there are constants, like the number 5 in the statement x = 5;. Constants can also be stored in registers. For example, let's suppose that the variable x, which is a short, is stored in location 1237. In that case, the statement x = 5; might generate an instruction sequence that looks like this:

```
mov ax,5
mov [1237],ax
```

where the number in the [] is the address of the variable x. The first of these instructions loads 5 into register ax, and the second one stores the contents of ax (5, in this case) into the memory location 1237.

Sometimes, however, constants aren't loaded into registers as in this case but are stored in the instructions that use them. This is the case in the following instruction:

```
add ax,3
```

This means to add 3 to whatever was formerly in register ax. The 3 never gets into a register but is stored as part of the instruction.[38]

A Fetching Tale

Another way of reducing overhead is to read instructions from RAM in chunks, rather than one at a time, and feed them into the CPU as it needs them; this is called *prefetching*. This mechanism operates in parallel with instruction execution, loading instructions from RAM into special dedicated registers in the CPU before they're actually needed; these registers are known collectively as the *prefetch queue*. Since the prefetching is done by a separate unit in the CPU, the time to do the prefetching doesn't increase the time needed for instruction execution. When the CPU is ready to execute another instruction, it can get it from the prefetch queue almost instantly, rather than having to wait for the slow RAM to provide each instruction. Of course, it does take a small amount of time to retrieve the next instruction from the prefetch queue, but that amount of time is included in the normal instruction execution time.

Problem
Algorithms
C++
Executable
Hardware

> **Susan**: I don't understand prefetching. What are "chunks"? I mean I understand what you have written, but I can't visualize this. So, there is just no time used to read an instruction when something is prefetched?
>
> **Steve**: A separate piece of the CPU does the prefetching at the same time as instructions are being executed, so instructions that have already

---

38. We'll go into this whole notion of using registers to represent and manipulate variables in grotesque detail in Chapter 3.

been fetched are available without delay when the execution unit is ready to "do" them.

The effect of combining the use of registers and prefetching the instructions can be very significant. In our example, if we use an instruction that has already been loaded, which reads data from and writes data only to registers, the timing reduces to that shown in Figure 2.12.

```
Time          Function
0  ns         Read instruction from RAM[39]
0  ns         Read data from register[40]
16 ns         Execute instruction
0  ns         Write result back to register[41]
-----
16 ns         Total instruction execution time
```

Figure 2.12: RAM vs. CPU speeds, using registers and prefetching

As I indicated near the beginning of this chapter, the manufacturers aren't lying to us; if we design our programs to take advantage of these (and other similar) efficiency measures taken by the manufacturer, we can often approach the maximum theoretical performance figures.

You've just been subjected to a barrage of information on how a computer works. Let's go over it again before continuing.

Problem
Algorithms
C++
Executable
Hardware

Review

Three main components of the computer are of most significance to programmers: disk, RAM, and the CPU; the first two of these store programs and data that are used by the CPU.

Computers represent pieces of information (or data) as binary digits, universally referred to as *bits*. Each bit can have the value 0 or 1. The binary system is used instead of the more familiar decimal system because it is much easier to make devices that can store and retrieve 1 of 2 values than 1 of 10. Bits are grouped into sets of eight, called *bytes*.

---

39. Since the instruction is already in the prefetch queue, this step doesn't count against the execution time. Hence the 0 in the time column.

40. This time is included under "Execute instruction".

41. This time is included under "Execute instruction".

The disk uses magnetic recording heads to store and retrieve groups of a few hundred bytes on rapidly spinning platters in a few milliseconds. The contents of the disk are not lost when the power is turned off, so it is suitable for more or less permanent storage of programs and data.

RAM, which is an acronym for Random Access Memory, is used to hold programs and data while they're in use. It is made of millions of microscopic transistors on a piece of silicon called a *chip*. Each bit is stored using a few of these transistors. RAM does not retain its contents when power is removed, so it is not good for permanent storage. However, any byte in a RAM chip can be accessed in about 70 nanoseconds (billionths of a second), which is hundreds of thousands of times as fast as accessing a disk. Each byte in a RAM chip can be independently stored and retrieved without affecting other bytes, by providing the unique memory address belonging to the byte you want to access.

The CPU (also called the *processor*) is the active component in the computer. It is also made of millions of microscopic transistors on a chip. The CPU executes programs consisting of instructions stored in RAM, using data also stored in RAM. However, the CPU is so fast that even the typical RAM access time of 70 nanoseconds is a bottleneck; therefore, computer manufacturers have added both *external cache* and *internal cache*, which are faster types of memory used to reduce the amount of time that the CPU has to wait. The internal cache resides on the same chip as the CPU and can be accessed without delay. The external cache sits between the CPU and the regular RAM; it's faster than the latter, but not as fast as the internal cache. Finally, a very small part of the on-chip memory is organized as *registers*, which can be accessed within the normal cycle time of the CPU, thus allowing the fastest possible processing.

Problem
Algorithms
C++
Executable
Hardware

Conclusion

In this chapter, we've covered a lot of material on how a computer actually works. As you'll see, this background is essential if you're going to understand what really happens inside a program. In the next chapter, we'll get to the "real thing": how to write a program to make all this hardware do something useful.

Answers to Exercises

1. Hexadecimal arithmetic

    a. 48

        You probably won't be surprised to hear that Susan didn't care much for this answer originally. Here's the discussion on that topic:

        > **Susan**: Problem 1a. My answer is 38. Why? My own personal way of thinking: If a = 10 right? and if e = 14 and if 1 * 10= 10 and if 2 * 14 = 28 then if you add 10 + 28 you get 38. So please inform me how you arrived at 48? I didn't bother with the rest of the problems. If I couldn't get the first one right, then what was the point?
        > **Steve**: Here's how you do this problem:
        >   1(1 * 16) + a(10 * 1)
        >   2(2 * 16) + e(14 * 1)
        >   -------------------
        >   3(3 * 16) + 18(24 * 1 = 1 * 16 + 8 * 1)
        > Carry the 1 from the low digit to the high digit of the answer, to produce:
        >   4(4 * 16) + 8(8 * 1), or 48 hex, which is the answer.

Problem
Algorithms
C++
Executable
Hardware

    b. 2a
    c. 3e

2. Binary arithmetic

    a. 1011
    b. 10000
    c. 111

3. 32768 decimal, or 8000 in hex

4. −32768, or 8000 in hex

    Why is the same hex value rendered here as −32768, while it was 32768 in question 3? The only difference between short and unsigned short variables is how their values are interpreted. In particular, short variables having values from 8000h to ffffh are considered negative, while unsigned short values in that range are positive. That's why the range of short values is −32768 to +32767, whereas unsigned short variables can range from 0 to 65535.

Problem
Algorithms
C++
Executable
Hardware

Chapter 3

Basics of Programming

Creative Programming?

After that necessary detour into the workings of the hardware, we can now resume our regularly scheduled explanation of the creative possibilities of computers. It may sound odd to describe computers as providing grand scope for creative activities: Aren't they monotonous, dull, unintelligent, and extremely limited? Yes, they are. However, they have two redeeming virtues that make them ideal as the canvas of invention: They are extraordinarily fast and spectacularly reliable. These characteristics allow the creator of a program to weave intricate chains of thought and have a fantastic number of steps carried out without fail. We'll begin to explore how this is possible after we go over some definitions and objectives for this chapter.

Definitions

An **identifier** is a user defined name; variable names are identifiers. Identifiers must not conflict with keywords such as if and while; for example, you cannot create a function or a variable with the name while.

A **keyword** is a word defined in the C++ language, such as if and while. It is illegal to define an identifier such as a variable name that conflicts with a keyword; for example, you cannot create a function or a variable with the name while.

Objectives of This Chapter

By the end of this chapter, you should

1. Understand what a program is and have some idea how a program works.
2. Understand how to get information into and out of a program.
3. Understand how to use if and while to control the execution of a program.[1]
4. Understand how a portion of a program can be marked off so that it will be treated as one unit.
5. Be able to read and understand a simple program I've written in C++.

Speed Demon

```
Problem
Algorithms
C++
Executable
Hardware
```

The most impressive attribute of modern computers, of course, is their speed; as we have already seen, this is measured in MIPS (millions of instructions per second).

Of course, raw speed is not very valuable if we can't rely on the results we get. ENIAC, one of the first electronic computers, had a failure every few hours, on the average; since the problems it was used to solve took about that much time to run, the likelihood that the results were correct wasn't very high. Particularly critical calculations were often run several times, and if the users got the same answer twice, they figured it was probably correct. By contrast, modern computers are almost incomprehensibly reliable. With almost any other machine, a failure rate of one in every million operations would be considered phenomenally low, but a computer with such a failure rate would make dozens of errors per second.[2]

---

1. Please note that capitalization counts in C++, so IF and WHILE are not the same as if and while. You have to use the latter versions.

2. By comparison, the flap over the Pentium floating-point flaw, which ironically enough erupted while I was beginning to write this chapter, seems minor. The divide instruction in early versions of that processor lost precision in rare cases, estimated to happen once in 9 billion operations with values chosen at random. The error caused the accuracy of the results to be reduced from about 17 decimal places to about 5 in these cases. Most of the upset over this error could probably have been avoided by better customer communications from Intel.

Blaming It on the Computer

On the other hand, if computers are so reliable, why are they blamed for so much that goes wrong with modern life? Who among us has not been the victim of an erroneous credit report, or a bill sent to the wrong address, or been put on hold for a long time because "the computer is down"?[3] The answer is fairly simple: It's almost certainly not the computer. More precisely, it's very unlikely that the CPU was at fault; it may be the software, other equipment such as telephone lines, tape or disk drives, or any of the myriad "peripheral devices" that the computer uses to store and retrieve information and interact with the outside world. Usually, it's the software; when customer service representatives tell you that they can't do something obviously reasonable, you can count on its being the software. For example, I once belonged to a 401K plan whose administrators provided statements only every three months, about three months after the end of the quarter; in other words, in July I found out how much my account had been worth at the end of March. The only way to estimate how much I had in the meantime was to look up the share values in the newspaper and multiply by the number of shares. Of course, the mutual fund that issued the shares could tell its shareholders their account balances at any time of the day or night; however, the company that administered the 401K plan didn't bother to provide such a service, as it would have required doing some work.[4] Needless to say, whenever I hear that "the computer can't do that" as an excuse for such poor service, I reply "Then you need some different programmers."

Problem
Algorithms
C++
Executable
Hardware

That Does Not Compute

All of this emphasis on computation, however, should not blind us to the fact that computers are not solely arithmetic engines. The most common application for which PCs are used is word processing, which is hardly a hotbed of arithmetical calculation. While we have so far considered only numeric data, this is a good illustration of the

---

3. Monetary figures such as are used in business are probably the most common example of numeric data. However, they are not usually represented by integer types such as short variables, but use other representations such as the previously mentioned *floating-point variables*, which can represent numbers with fractional parts. We will go into these variables in a bit more detail in Appendix A.

4. This was apparently against the plan administrator's principles.

fact that computers also deal with another kind of information, which is commonly referred to by the imaginative term **nonnumeric variables**. Numeric variables are those suited for use in calculations, such as in totalling a set of weights. On the other hand, nonnumeric data are items that are not used in calculations like adding, multiplying, or subtracting: Examples are names, addresses, telephone numbers, Social Security numbers, bank account numbers, or drivers license numbers. Note that just because something is called a *number*, or even is composed entirely of the digits 0–9, does not make it numeric data by our standards. The question is how the item is used. No one adds, multiplies, or subtracts drivers license numbers, for example; they serve solely as identifiers and could just as easily have letters in them, as indeed some do.

For the present, though, let's stick with numeric variables. Now that we have defined a couple of types of these variables, short and unsigned short, what can we do with them? To do anything with them, we have to write a C++ program, which consists primarily of a list of operations to be performed by the computer, along with directions that influence how these operations are to be translated into machine instructions.

Problem
Algorithms
C++
Executable
Hardware

This raises an interesting point: Why does our C++ program have to be translated into machine instructions? Isn't the computer's job to execute (or *run*) our program?

Lost in Translation

Yes, but it can't run a C++ program. The only kind of program any computer can run is one made of machine instructions; this is called a **machine language** program, for obvious reasons. Therefore, to get our C++ program to run, we have to translate it into a machine language program. Don't worry, you won't have to do it yourself; that's why we have a program called a *compiler*.[5] The most basic tasks that the compiler performs are the following:

---

5. How is the compiler itself translated into machine language so it can be executed? The most common method is to write the compiler in the same language it compiles and use the previous version of the compiler to compile the newest version! Of course, this looks like an infinite regress; how did the first compiler get compiled? By manual translation into *assembly language*, which was then translated by an *assembler* into machine language. To answer the obvious question, at some point an assembler was coded directly in machine language.

1. Assigning memory addresses to variables. This allows us to use names for variables, rather than having to keep track of the address of each variable ourselves.
2. Translating arithmetic and other operations (such as +, −, etc.) into the equivalent machine instructions, including the addresses of variables assigned in the previous step.[6]

This is probably a bit too abstract to be easily grasped, so let's look at an example as soon as we have defined some terms. Each complete operation understood by the compiler is called a *statement*, and ends with a semicolon (;).[7] Figure 3.1 shows some sample statements that do arithmetic calculations.[8]

```
short i;
short j;
short k;
short m;

i = 5;
j = i * 3;        // j is now 15
k = j  i;         // k is now 10
m = (k + j) / 5;  // m is now 5
i = i + 1;        // i is now 6
```

Figure 3.1: A little numeric calculation

Problem
Algorithms
C++
Executable
Hardware

To enter such statements in the first place, you can use any text editor that generates "plain" text files, such as the EDIT program that comes with DOS or Windows' Notepad. Whichever text editor you use, make sure that it produces files that contain only what you type; stay away from programs like Windows Write™ or Word for Windows™, as they add some of their own information to indicate fonts, type sizes, and the like to your file, which will foul up the compiler.

---

6. The compiler also does a lot of other work for us, which we'll get into later.

7. By the way, blank lines are ignored by the compiler; in fact, because of the trailing semicolon on each statement, you can even run all the statements together on one line if you want to, without confusing the compiler. However, that will make it much harder for someone reading your code later to understand what you're trying to do. Programs aren't written just for the compiler's benefit but to be read by other people; therefore, it is important to write them so that they can be understood by those other people. One very good reason for this is that more often than you might think, those "other people" turn out to be *you*, six months later.

8. The // marks the beginning of a *comment*, which is a note to you or another programmer; it is ignored by the compiler. For those of you with BASIC experience, this is just like REM (the "remark" keyword in that language); anything after it on a line is ignored.

Once we have entered the statements for our program, we use the compiler, as indicated, to translate the programs we write into a form that the computer can perform; as defined in Chapter 1, the form we create is called *source code*, since it is the source of the program logic, while the form of our program that the computer can execute is called an *executable program*, or just an *executable* for short.

As I've mentioned before, there are several types of variables, the short being only one of these types. Therefore, the compiler needs some explanatory material so that it can tell what types of variables you're using; that's what the first four lines of our little sample program fragment are for. Each line tells the compiler that the type of the variable i, j, k, or m is short; that is, it can contain values from −32768 to +32767.[9]

After this introductory material, we move into the list of operations to be performed. This is called the *executable* portion of the program, as it actually causes the computer to do something when the program is executed; the operations to be performed, as mentioned above, are called **statements**. The first one, i = 5;, sets the variable i to the value 5. A value such as 5, which doesn't have a name, but represents itself in a literal manner, is called (appropriately enough) a **literal** value.

Problem
Algorithms
C++
Executable
Hardware

This is as good a time as any for me to mention something that experienced C programmers take for granted but has a tendency to confuse novices. This is the choice of the = sign to indicate the operation of setting a variable to a value, which is known technically as **assignment**. As far as I'm concerned, an assignment operation would be more properly indicated by some symbol suggesting movement of data, such as 5 => i;, meaning "store the value 5 into variable i". Unfortunately, it's too late to change the notation for the **assignment statement**, as such a statement is called, so you'll just have to get used to it. The = means "set the variable on the left to the value on the right".[10]

Now that I've warned you about that possible confusion, let's continue looking at the operations in the program. The next one, j = i * 3;, specifies that the variable j is to be set to the result of multiplying the current value of i by the literal value 3. The one after

---

9. Other kinds of variables can hold larger (and smaller) values; we'll go over them in some detail in future chapters.

10. At the risk of boring experienced C programmers, let me reiterate that = *does not mean* "is equal to"; it means "set the variable to the left of the = to the value of the expression to the right of the =. In fact, there is *no* equivalent in C++ to the mathematical notion of equality. We have only the assignment operator = and the comparison operator ==, which we will encounter in the next chapter. The latter is used in if statements to determine whether two expressions have the same value. All of the valid comparison operators are listed in Figure 4.4.

that, k = j − i;, tells the computer to set k to the amount by which j is greater than i; that is, j − i. The most complicated line in our little program fragment, m = (k + j) / 5;, calculates m as the sum of adding k and j and dividing the result by the literal value 5. Finally, the line i = i + 1; sets i to the value of i plus the literal value 1.

This last may be somewhat puzzling; how can i be equal to i + 1? The answer is that an assignment statement is *not* an algebraic equality, no matter how much it may resemble one. It is a command telling the computer to assign a value to a variable. Therefore, what i = i + 1; actually means is "Take the current value of i, add 1 to it, and store the result back into i." In other words, a C++ variable is a place to store a value; the variable i can take on any number of values, but only one at a time; any former value is lost when a new one is assigned.

This notion of assignment was the topic of quite a few messages with Susan. Let's go to the first round:

> **Susan**: I am confused with the statement i = i + 1; when you have stated previously that i = 5;. So, which one is it? How can there be two values for i?
>
> **Steve**: There can't; that is, not at one time. However, i, like any other variable, can take on any number of values, one after another. First, we set it to 5; then we set it to 1 more than it was before (i + 1), so it ends up as 6.
>
> **Susan**: Well, the example made it look as if the two values of i were available to be used by the computer at the same time. They were both lumped together as executable material.
>
> **Steve**: After the statement i = 5;, and before the statement i = i + 1;, the value of i is 5. After the statement i = i + 1;, the value of i is 6. The key here is that a variable such as i is just our name for some area of memory that can hold only one value at one time. Does that clear it up?
>
> **Susan**: So, it is not like algebra? Then i is equal to an address of memory and does not really equate with a numerical value? Well, I guess it does when you assign a numerical value to it. Is that it?
>
> **Steve**: Very close. A variable in C++ isn't really like an algebraic variable, which has a value that has to be figured out and doesn't change in a given problem. A programming language variable is just a name for a storage location that can contain a value.

Problem
Algorithms
C++
Executable
Hardware

With any luck, that point has been pounded into the ground, so you won't have the same trouble that Susan did. Now let's look at exactly what an assignment statement does. If the value of i before the statement i = i + 1; is 5 (for example), then that statement will cause the CPU to perform the following steps:[11]

1.   Take the current value of i (5).
2.   Add one to that value (6).
3.   Store the result back into i.

After the execution of this statement, i will have the value 6.

What's Going on Underneath?

Problem
Algorithms
C++
Executable
Hardware

In a moment we're going to dive a little deeper into how the the CPU accomplishes its task of manipulating data, such as we are doing here with our arithmetic program. First, though, it's time for a little pep talk for those of you who might be wondering exactly why this apparent digression is necessary. It's because if you don't understand what is going on under the surface, you won't be able to get past the "Sunday driver" stage of programming in C++. In some languages it's neither necessary or perhaps even possible to find out what the computer actually does to execute your program, but C++ isn't one of them. A good C++ programmer needs an intimate acquaintance with the internal workings of the language, for reasons which will become very apparent when we get to Chapter 7. For the moment, you'll just have to take my word that working through these intricacies is essential; the payoff for a thorough grounding in these fundamental concepts of computing will be worth the struggle.

Now let's get to the task of exploring how the CPU actually stores and manipulates data in memory. As we saw previously, each memory location in RAM has a unique *memory address*; *machine instructions* that refer to RAM use this address to specify which *byte* or bytes of memory they wish to retrieve or modify. This is fairly straightforward in the case of a 1-byte variable, where the instruction merely specifies the byte that corresponds to the variable. On the other hand, the situation isn't quite as simple in the case of a variable

---

11. If you have any programming experience whatever, you may think that I'm spending too much effort on this very simple point. I can report from personal experience that it's not necessarily easy for a complete novice to grasp. Furthermore, without a solid understanding of the difference between an algebraic equality and an assignment statement, that novice will be unable to understand how to write a program.

that occupies more than 1 byte. Of course, no law of nature says that an instruction couldn't contain a number of addresses, one for each byte of the variable. However, this solution is never adopted in practice, as it would make instructions much longer than they need to be. Instead, the address in such an instruction specifies the first byte of RAM occupied by the variable, and the other bytes are assumed to follow immediately after the first one. For example, in the case of a short variable, which as we have seen occupies 2 bytes of RAM, the instruction would specify the address of the first byte of the area of RAM in which the variable is stored.

However, there's one point that I haven't brought up yet: how the data for a given variable are actually arranged in memory. For example, suppose that the contents of a small section of RAM (specified as two hex digits per byte) look like Figure 3.2.

```
Address     Hex byte value

1000        41
1001        42
1002        43
1003        44
1004        00
```

Figure 3.2: A small section of RAM

Also suppose that a short variable i is stored starting at address 1000. To do much with a variable, we're going to have to load it into a *general register*, one of the small number of named data storage locations in the CPU intended for general use by the programmer; this proximity allows the CPU to operate on data in the registers at maximum speed. You may recall that there are seven general registers in the 386 CPU (and its successors); they're named eax, ebx, ecx, edx, esi, edi, and ebp.[12] Unfortunately, there's another complication here; these registers are designed to operate on 4-byte quantities, while our variable i, being of type short, is only two bytes long. Are we out of luck? No, but we do have to specify how long the variable is that we want to load. This problem is not unique to Intel CPUs, since any CPU has to have the ability to load different-sized variables into registers. Different CPUs use different methods of specifying this important piece of information; in the

Problem
Algorithms
C++
Executable
Hardware

---

12. Besides these general registers, a dedicated register called esp plays an important role in the execution of real programs. We'll see how it does this in Chapter 5.

Intel CPUs, one way to do this is to alter the register name.[13] As we saw in the discussion of the development of Intel machines, we can remove the leading e from the register name to specify that we're dealing with 2-byte values; the resulting name refers to the lower two bytes of the 4-byte register. Therefore, if we wanted to load the value of i into register ax (that is, the lower half of register eax), the instruction could be written as follows:[14]

mov ax,[1000][15]

As usual, our resident novice Susan had some questions on this topic. Here is our conversation:

Susan: If you put something into 1000 that is "too big" for it, then it spills over to the next address?

Steve: Sort of. When you "put something into 1000", you have to specify exactly what it is you're "putting in". That is, it must be either a short, a char, or some other type of variable that has a defined size.

Susan: Is that how it works? Why then is it not necessary to specify that it is going to have to go into 1000 and 1001? So what you put in is not really in 1000 anymore, it is in 1000 *and* 1001? How do you refer to its REAL address? What if there is no room in 1001? Would it go to 2003 if that is the next available space?

Problem
Algorithms
C++
Executable
Hardware

Steve: Because the rule is that you always specify the starting address of any item (variable or constant) that is too big to fit in 1 byte. The other bytes of the item are always stored immediately following the address you specify. No bytes will be skipped when storing (or loading) one item; if the item needs 4 bytes and is to be stored starting at 1000, it will be stored in 1000–1003.

Susan: I see. In other words, the compiler will always use the next bytes of RAM, however many need to be used to store the item?

Steve: Right.

---

13. This is not the only possible solution to this problem nor necessarily the best one; for example, in many Motorola CPUs, you specify the length of the variable directly in the instruction, so loading a *word* (i.e., 2-byte) variable might be specified by the instruction move.w, where the .w means "word". Similarly, a *longword* (i.e., 4-byte) load might be specified as move.l, where the .l means "long word".

14. It's also possible to load a 2-byte value into a 32-bit register such as eax and have the high part of that register set to 0 in one instruction, by using an instruction designed specifically for that purpose. This approach has the advantage that further processing can be done with the 32-bit registers.

15. The number inside the brackets [ ] represents a memory address.

Who's on First?

Now I have a question for you. After we execute the assembly language statement mov ax,[1000] to load the value of i into ax, what's in register ax? That may seem like a silly question; the answer is obviously the value of i. Yes, but what is that value exactly? The first byte of i, at location 1000, has the value 41 hexadecimal (abbreviated 41h), and the second byte, at location 1001, has the value 42h. But the value of i is 2 bytes long; is it 4142h or 4241h? These are clearly not the same!

That was a trick question; there's no way for you to deduce the answer with only the information I've given you so far. The answer happens to be 4241h, because that's the way Intel decided to do it; that is, the low part of the value is stored in the byte of RAM where the variable starts. Some other CPUs do it the opposite way, where the high part of the value is stored in the byte of RAM where the variable starts; this is called *big-endian*, since the big end of the value is first, while the Intel way is correspondingly called *little-endian*. And some machines, such as the Power PC, can use either of these methods according to how they are started up. This makes it easier for them to run software written for either of these memory orientations.

As you might have surmised, the same system applies to 4-byte values; therefore, if we wrote the instruction mov eax,[1000], since we're on a little-endian machine, it would load the eax register with the value 44434241h; that is, the four bytes 41, 42, 43, and 44 (hex) would be loaded into the eax register, with the byte having the lowest address loaded into the low end of the register.

Here's another example. A little-endian system would represent the number 1234 (hex) stored at address 5000 as in Figure 3.3.

```
Problem
Algorithm
C++
Executable
Hardware
```

```
Address    Value

5000       34
5001       12
```

Figure 3.3: One little endian

whereas a big-endian system would represent the same value 1234 (hex) as illustrated in Figure 3.4.

```
Address    Value

5000       12
5001       34
```

Figure 3.4: A big endian example

This really isn't much of a problem as long as we don't try to move data from one type of machine to another; however, when such data transportation is necessary, dealing with mixed endianness can be a real nuisance!

Before going on, let's practice a bit with this notion of how data are stored in memory.

Exercises, First Set

1. Assume that a short variable named z starts at location 1001 in a little-endian machine. Using Figure 3.5 for the contents of memory, what is the value of z, in hex?

```
Problem
Algorithms
                Address     Hex byte value
C++
                1000        3a
Executable      1001        43
Hardware        1002        3c
                1003        99
                1004        00
```

Figure 3.5: Exercise 1

Underware?

I can almost hear the wailing and tooth gnashing out there. Do I expect you to deal with all of these instructions and addresses by yourself? You'll undoubtedly be happy to learn that this isn't necessary, as the compiler takes care of these details. However, if you don't have some idea of how a compiler works, you'll be at a disadvantage when you're trying to figure out how to make it do what you want. Therefore, we're going to spend the next few pages "playing compiler"; that is, I'll examine each statement and indicate what action the compiler might take as a result. I'll simplify the statements a bit to make the explanation simpler; you should still get the idea (I hope). Figure 3.6 illustrates the set of statements that I'll compile:[16]

```
short i;
short j;

i = 5;
j = i + 3;
```

Figure 3.6: A really little numeric calculation

Compiler's Eye View

Here are the rules of this game:

1. All numbers in the C++ program are decimal; all addresses and numbers in the machine instructions are hexadecimal.[17]
2. All addresses are 2 bytes long.[18]
3. Variables are stored at addresses starting at 1000.
4. Machine instructions are stored at addresses starting at 2000.[19]
5. A number *not* enclosed in [] is a literal value, which represents itself. For example, the instruction mov ax,1000 means to move the value 1000 into the ax register.
6. A number enclosed in [] is an address, which specifies where data are to be stored or retrieved. For example, the instruction mov ax,[1000] means to move 2 bytes of data starting at location 1000, *not* the value 1000 itself, into the ax register.

Problem
Algorithm
C++
Executable
Hardware

Now, let's start compiling. The first statement, short i; tells me to allocate storage for a 2-byte variable called i that will be treated as signed (because that's the default). Since no value has been assigned

---

16. As I've mentioned previously, blank lines are ignored by the compiler; you can put them in freely to improve readability.

17. However, I've cheated here by using small enough numbers in the C++ program that they are the same in hex as in decimal.

18. The real compiler on the CD-ROM actually uses 4-byte addresses, but this doesn't change any of the concepts involved.

19. These addresses are arbitrary; a real compiler will assign addresses to variables and machine instructions by its own rules.

to this variable yet, the resulting "memory map" looks like Figure 3.7.

```
Address     Source code variable name

1000        i
```

Figure 3.7: Compiling, part 1

As you might have guessed, this exercise was the topic of a considerable amount of discussion with Susan. Here's how it started:

> **Susan**: So the first thing we do with a variable is to tell the address that its name is i, but no one is home, right? It has to get ready to accept a value. Could you put a value in it without naming it, just saying address 1000 has a value of 5? Why does it have to be called i first?

> **Steve**: The reason that we use names instead of addresses is because it's much easier for people to keep track of names than it is to keep track of addresses. Thus, one of the main functions of a compiler is to allow us to use names that are translated into addresses for the computer's use.

Problem
Algorithms
C++
Executable
Hardware

The second statement, short j; tells me to allocate storage for a 2-byte variable called j that will be treated as signed (because that's the default). Since no value has been assigned to this variable yet, the resulting "memory map" looks like Figure 3.8.

```
Address     Source code variable name

1000        i
1002        j
```

Figure 3.8: Compiling, part 2

Here's the exchange about this step:

> **Susan**: Why isn't the address for j 1001?

> **Steve**: Because a short is 2 bytes, not 1. Therefore, if i is at address 1000, j can't start before 1002; otherwise, the second byte of i would have the same address as the first byte of j, which would cause chaos in the program. Imagine changing i and having j change by itself.

> **Susan**: Okay. I just thought that each address represented 2 bytes for some reason. Then in reality each address always has just 1 byte?

Steve: Every byte of RAM has a distinct address, and there is one address for each byte of RAM. However, it is often necessary to read or write more than one byte at a time, as in the case of a short, which is 2 bytes in length. The machine instructions that read or write more than 1 byte specify only the address of the first byte of the item to be read or written; the other byte or bytes of that item follow the first byte immediately in memory.

Susan: Okay, this is why I was confused. I thought when you specified that the RAM address 1000 was a short (2 bytes), it just made room for 2 bytes. So when you specify address 1000 as a short, you know that 1001 will also be occupied with what you put in 1000.

Steve: Or to be more precise, location 1001 will contain the second byte of the short value that starts in byte 1000.

The next line is blank, so we skip it. This brings us to the statement i = 5; which is an executable statement, so we need to generate one or more machine instructions to execute it. We have already assigned address 1000 to i, so we have to generate instructions that will set the 2 bytes at address 1000 to the value that represents 5. One way to do this is to start by setting ax to 5, by the instruction mov ax,5, then storing the contents of ax (5, of course) into the location where the value of i is kept: namely 1000, via the instruction mov [1000],ax.

Figure 3.9 shows what our "memory map" looks like so far.

Problem
Algorithms
C++
Executable
Hardware

```
Address       Variable Name

1000          i
1002          j

Address       Machine Instruction         Assembly Language
                                          Equivalent

2000     | b8 05 00 |                      mov ax,5

2003     | a9 00 10 |                      mov [1000],ax
```

Figure 3.9: Compiling, part 3

Here's the next installment of my discussion with Susan on this topic:

Susan: When you use ax in an instruction, that is a register, not RAM?

Steve: Yes.

Susan: How do you know you want that register and not another one? What are the differences in the registers? Is ax the first register that data will go into?

Steve: For our current purposes, all of the 16-bit general registers (ax, bx, cx, dx, si, di, bp) are the same. Some of them have other uses, but all of them can be used for simple arithmetic such as we're doing here.

Susan: How do you know that you are not overwriting something more important than what you are presently writing?

Steve: In assembly language, the programmer has to keep track of that; in the case of a compiled language, the compiler takes care of it instead, which is another reason to use a compiler rather than writing assembly language programs yourself.

Susan: If it overwrites, you said important data will go somewhere else. How will you know where it went? How does it know whether what is being overwritten is important? Wait. If something is overwritten, it isn't gone, is it? It is just moved, right?

Problem
Algorithms
C++
Executable
Hardware

Steve: The automatic movement of data that you're referring to applies only to cached data being transferred to RAM. That is, if a slot in the cache is needed, the data that it previously held is written out to RAM without the programmer's intervention. However, the content of registers is explicitly controlled by the programmer (or the compiler, in the case of a compiled language). If you write something into a register, whatever was there before is gone. So don't do that if you need the previous contents!

Susan: How do you know that 5 will require 2 bytes?

Steve: In C++, because it's a short. In assembly language, because I'm loading it into ax, which is a 2-byte register.

Susan: Why do the the variable addresses start at 1000 and the machine addresses start at 2000?

Steve: It's arbitrary; I picked those numbers out of the air. In a real program, the compiler decides where to put things.

Susan: What do you mean by machine address? What is the machine? Where are the machine addresses?

Steve: A machine address is a RAM address. The machine is the CPU. Machine addresses are stored in the instructions so the CPU knows which RAM location we're referring to.

Susan: We talked about storing instructions before; is this what we are doing here? Are those instructions the "machine instructions"?

Steve: Yes.

Susan: Now, this may sound like a very dumb question, but please tell me where 5 comes from? I mean if you are going to move the value of 5 into the register ax, where is 5 hiding to take it from and to put it in ax? Is it stored somewhere in memory that has to be moved, or is it simply a function of the user just typing in that value?

Steve: It is stored in the instruction as a literal value. If you look at the assembly language illustration on page 67, you will see that the mov ax,5 instruction translates into the three bytes b8 05 00; the 05 00 is the 5 in "little-endian" notation.

Susan: Now, what is so magical about ax (or any register for that matter) that will transform the address 1000 to hold the value of 5?

Steve: The register doesn't do It; the execution of the instruction mov [1000],ax is what sets the memory starting at address 1000 to the value 5.

Susan: What are those numbers supposed to be in the machine instruction box? Those are bytes? Bytes of what? Why are they there? What do they do?

Steve: They represent the actual machine language program as it is executed by the CPU. This is where "the rubber meets the road". All of our C++ or even assembly language programs have to be translated into machine language before they can be executed by the CPU.

Susan: So this is where 5 comes from? I can't believe that there seems to be more code. What is b8 supposed to be? Is it some other type of machine language?

Steve: Machine language is exactly what it is. The first byte of each instruction is the "operation code", or "op code" for short. That tells the CPU what kind of instruction to execute; in this case, b8 specifies a "load register ax with a literal value" instruction. The literal value is the next 2 bytes, which represent the value 5 in "little-endian" notation; therefore, the full translation of the instruction is "load ax with the literal value 5".

Problem
Algorithms
C++
Executable
Hardware

Susan: So that is the "op code"? Okay, this makes sense. I don't like it, but it makes sense. Will the machine instructions always start with an op code?

Steve: Yes, there's always an op code first; that's what tells the CPU what the rest of the bytes in the instruction mean.

Susan: Then I noticed that the remaining bytes seem to hold either a literal value or a variable address. Are those the only possibilities?

Steve: Those are the ones that we will need to concern ourselves with.

Susan: I don't understand why machine addresses aren't in 2-byte increments like variable addresses.

Steve: Variable addresses aren't always in 2-byte increments either; it just happens that short variables take up 2 bytes. Other kinds of variables can and often do have other lengths.

Susan: So even though variable addresses are the same as instruction addresses they really aren't because they can't share the same actual address. That is why you distinguish the two by starting the instruction addresses at 2000 in the example and variable addresses at 1000, right?

Problem
Algorithms
C++
Executable
Hardware

Steve: Right. A particular memory location can hold only one data item at a time. As far as RAM is concerned, machine instructions are just another kind of data. Therefore, if a particular location is used to store one data item, you can't store anything else there at the same time, whether it's instructions or data.

The last statement, j = i + 3; is the most complicated statement in our program, and it's not that complicated. As with the previous statement, it's executable, which means we need to generate machine instructions to execute it. Since we haven't changed ax since we used it to initialize the variable i with the value 5, it still has that value. Therefore, to calculate the value of j, we can just add 3 to the value in ax by executing the instruction add ax,3. After the execution of this instruction, ax will contain i + 3. Now all we have to do is to store that value in j. As indicated in the translation of the statement short j; the address used to hold the value of j is 1002. Therefore, we can set j to the value in ax by executing the instruction mov [1002],ax.

Figure 3.10 shows what the "memory map" looks like now.

```
Address      Variable Name

1000            i
1002            j

Address      Machine Instruction          Assembly Language
                                          Equivalent
```

Address	Machine Instruction	Assembly Language Equivalent
2000	b8 05 00	mov ax,5
2003	a9 00 10	mov [1000],ax
2006	05 03 00	add ax,3
2009	a9 02 10	mov [1002],ax

Figure 3.10: Compiling, part 4

By the way, don't be misled by this example into thinking that all machine language instructions are 3 bytes in length. It's just a coincidence that all of the ones I've used here are of that length. The actual size of an instruction on the Intel CPUs can vary considerably, from 1 byte to a theoretical maximum of 12 bytes. Most instructions in common use, however, range from 1 to 5 bytes.

Here's the rest of the discussion that we had about this little exercise:

Problem
Algorithms
C++
Executable
Hardware

> **Susan**: In this case mov means add, right?

> **Steve**: No, mov means "move" and add means "add". When we write mov ax,5, it means "move the value 5 into the ax register". The instruction add ax,3 means "add 3 to the current contents of ax, replacing the old contents with this new value".

> **Susan**: So you're moving 5 but adding 3? How do you know when to use mov and when to use add if they both kind of mean the same thing?

> **Steve**: It depends on whether you want to replace the contents of a register without reference to whatever the contents were before (mov) or add something to the contents of the register (add).

> **Susan**: OK, here is what gets me: how do you get from address 1000 and i=5 to ax? No, that's not it; I want you to tell me what is the relationship between ax and address 1000. I see ax as a register and that should contain the addresses, but here you are adding ax to the address. This

doesn't make sense to me. Where are these places? Is address 1000 in RAM?

Steve: The ax register doesn't contain an address. It contains data. After the instruction mov ax,5, ax contains the number 5. After the instruction mov [1000],ax, memory location 1000 contains a copy of the 2-byte value in register ax; in this case, that is the value of the short variable i.

Susan: So do the machine addresses represent actual bytes?

Steve: The machine addresses specify the RAM locations where data (and programs) are stored.

Execution Is Everything

Having examined what the compiler does at **compile time** with the preceding little program fragment, the next question is what happens when the compiled program is executed at **run time**. When we start out, the sections of RAM we're concerned with will look like Figure 3.11.

```
Problem
Algorithms
C++
Executable
Hardware
```

```
Register    Contents

ax          ??
```

Address	Contents		Variable Name
1000	?? ??		i
1002	?? ??		j

Address	Machine Instruction		Assembly Language Equivalent
2000	b8 05 00		mov ax,5
2003	a9 00 10		mov [1000],ax
2006	05 03 00		add ax,3
2009	a9 02 10		mov [1002],ax

Figure 3.11: Before execution

First, a couple of rules for this part of the "game":

1. The bold address in the lower block indicates the next instruction to be executed.
2. We put ?? in the variable and register contents to start out with, to indicate that we haven't stored anything in them yet, and so we don't know what they contain.

Now let's start executing the program. The first instruction, mov ax,5, as we saw earlier, means "set the contents of ax to the value 5". Here's the situation after that instruction is executed:

```
Register   Contents

ax         5
```

Address	Contents	Variable Name
1000	?? ??	i
1002	?? ??	j

Address	Machine Instruction	Assembly Language Equivalent
2000	b8 05 00	mov ax,5
2003	a9 00 10	mov [1000],ax
2006	05 03 00	add ax,3
2009	a9 02 10	mov [1002],ax

Problem
Algorithms
C++
Executable
Hardware

As you can see, we have updated the contents of ax and advanced to the next instruction.

When we have executed the next instruction, mov [1000],ax, the situation looks like this:

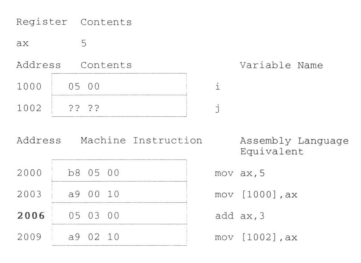

```
Register   Contents

ax         5

Address    Contents                    Variable Name

1000    | 05 00                    |    i

1002    | ?? ??                    |    j


Address    Machine Instruction          Assembly Language
                                         Equivalent

2000    | b8 05 00                 |    mov ax,5

2003    | a9 00 10                 |    mov [1000],ax

2006    | 05 03 00                 |    add ax,3

2009    | a9 02 10                 |    mov [1002],ax
```

This looks just like the previous situation, except that the contents of location 1000 are now known, and of course we have moved to the next instruction.

Here's the result after the next instruction, add ax,3 is executed:

```
Register   Contents

ax         8

Address    Contents                    Variable Name

1000    | 05 00                    |    i

1002    | ?? ??                    |    j


Address    Machine Instruction          Assembly Language
                                         Equivalent

2000    | b8 05 00                 |    mov ax,5

2003    | a9 00 10                 |    mov [1000],ax

2006    | 05 03 00                 |    add ax,3

2009    | a9 02 10                 |    mov [1002],ax
```

As expected, the contents of ax have been increased by the addition of the value 3, leaving the result of 8. Now we're ready for the final instruction.

Problem
Algorithms
C++
Executable
Hardware

Here's the situation after the final instruction, mov [1002],ax, it has been executed:

```
Register   Contents
ax         8
```

Address	Contents		Variable Name
1000	05 00	i	
1002	08 00	j	

Address	Machine Instruction	Assembly Language Equivalent
2000	b8 05 00	mov ax,5
2003	a9 00 10	mov [1000],ax
2006	05 03 00	add ax,3
2009	a9 02 10	mov [1002],ax

As we intended, the variable i has the value 5, and the variable j has the value 8.

A Cast of Characters

This should give you some idea of how numeric variables and values work. But what about nonnumeric ones?

This brings us to the subject of two new variable types and the values they can contain. These are the char (short for "character") and its relative, the string. What are these good for, and how do they work?[20]

A variable of type char corresponds to 1 byte of storage. Since a byte has 8 bits, it can hold any of 256 (2^8) values; the exact values depend on whether it is signed or unsigned, as with the short variables we have seen before. Going strictly according to this description, you might get the idea that a char is just a "really short" numeric variable. A char indeed can be used for this purpose in cases where no more than 256 different numeric values are to be represented. In fact, this explains why you might want a signed char. Such a variable can be used to hold numbers from 128 to +127; an unsigned char, on the

Problem
Algorithms
C++
Executable
Hardware

---

20. In case you were wondering, the most common pronunciation of char has an *a* like the a in "married", while the *ch* sounds like "k".

other hand, has a range from 0 to 255. This facility isn't used very much any more, but in the early days of C, memory was very expensive and scarce, so it was sometimes worth the effort to use a 1-byte variables to hold small values.

However, the main purpose of a char is to represent an individual letter, digit, punctuation mark, "special character" (e.g., $, #, %, and so on) or one of the other "printable" and displayable units from which words, sentences, and other textual data such as this paragraph are composed.[21] The 256 different possibilities are plenty to represent any sentence in English, as well as a number of other European languages, can be represented; in fact, this is one of the main reasons that there are 8 bits in a byte, rather than some other number.

Of course, the written forms of "ideographic" languages such as Chinese and Korean consist of far more than 256 characters, so 1 byte isn't going to do the trick for these languages. While they have been supported to some extent by schemes that switch among a number of sets of 256 characters each, such clumsy approaches to the problem made programs much more complicated and error prone. As the international market for software is increasing rapidly, it has become more important to have a convenient method of handling large *character sets*; as a result, a standard method of representing the characters of such languages by using 2 bytes per character has been developed. It's called the "Unicode standard". There's even a proposed solution that uses 32 bits per character, for the day when Unicode doesn't have sufficient capacity; that should take care of any languages that alien civilizations might introduce to our planet.

Since one char isn't good for much by itself, we often use groups of them, called strings, to make them easier to handle. Just as with numeric values, these variables can be set to literal values, which represent themselves. Figure 3.12 is an example of how to specify and use each of these types we've just encountered. This is the first complete program we've seen, so there are a couple of new constructs that I'll have to explain to you.

By the way, in case the program in Figure 3.12 doesn't seem very useful, that's because it isn't; it's just an example of the syntax of defining and using variables and literal values. However, we'll use these constructs to do useful work later, so going over them now isn't a waste of time.

Problem
Algorithms
C++
Executable
Hardware

---

21. As we will see shortly, not all characters have visible representations; some of these "nonprintable" characters are useful in controlling how our printed or displayed information looks.

```
#include <iostream.h>
#include "string6.h"

int main()
{
    char c1;
    char c2;
    string s1;
    string s2;

    c1 = 'A';
    c2 = c1;

    s1 = "This is a test ";
    s2 = "and so is this.";

    return 0;
}
```

Figure 3.12: Some real characters and strings (code\basic00.cc)

Problem
Algorithms
C++
Executable
Hardware

Why do we need the lines #include <iostream.h> and #include "string6.h"? Because we have to tell the compiler how to manipulate strings. They aren't built in to its knowledge base. For the moment, it's enough to know that the contents of the files iostream.h and string6.h are needed to tell the compiler how to use strings; we'll get into the details of this mechanism later, starting in Chapter 7.

However, since we're already on the subject of files, this would be a good time to point out that the two main types of files in C++ are source files, which in our case have the extension .cc, and header files, which by convention have the extension .h.[22] Source files contain statements that result in executable code, while each header file contains information that allows us to access a set of language features.

The next construct we have to examine is the line int main(), which has two new components. The first is the "return type", which specifies the type of value that will be returned from the program when it ends. In this case, that type is int, which is an integral type exactly like short, except that its size depends on the compiler that you're using. With a 32-bit compiler like the one on the CD-ROM in

---

22. Other compilers sometimes use other extensions for source files, such as .cpp, and for header files, such as .hpp.

this book, an int is 32 bits, or twice the size of a short. With a 16-bit compiler such as Borland C++ version 3.1, an int is the same size as a short. I don't like to use ints, because I want my code to work in the same way on both 16- and 32-bit compilers. However, we don't have much choice here, because the C++ language specifies that main has to have the return type int.

This brings us to the meaning of main(). This tells the compiler where to start executing the code: C++ has a rule that execution always starts at the place called main. We'll get into this in more detail in Chapter 5. For now, you'll just have to take my word that this is necessary; I promise I'll explain what it really means when you have enough background to understand the explanation.

You may also be puzzled by the function of the other statements in this program. If so, you're not alone. Let's see the discussion that Susan and I had about that topic.

> **Susan**: Okay, in the example *why* did you have to write c2 = c1;? Why not B? Why make one thing the same thing as the other? Make it different. Why would you even want c2=c1; and not just say c1 twice, if that is what you want?

Problem
Algorithms
C++
Executable
Hardware

> **Steve**: It's very hard to think up examples that are both simple enough to explain and realistic enough to make sense. You're right that this example doesn't do anything useful; I'm just trying to introduce what both the char type and the string type look like.

> **Susan**: Come to think of it, what does c1='A'; have to do with the statement s1= "This is a test ";? I don't see any relationship between one thing and the other.

> **Steve**: This is the same problem as the last one. They have nothing to do with one another; I'm using an admittedly contrived example to show how these variables are used.

> **Susan**: I am glad now that your example of chars and strings (put together) didn't make sense to me. That is progress; it wasn't supposed to.

What does this useless but hopefully instructive program do? As is always the case, we have to tell the compiler what the types of our variables are before we can use them. In this case, c1 and c2 are of type char, whereas s1 and s2 are strings. After taking care of these formalities, we can start to use the variables. In the first executable statement, c1 = 'A'; we set the char variable c1 to a literal value, in this case a capital *A*; we need to surround this with single quotation marks (') to tell the compiler that we mean the letter *A* rather than a variable named A. In the next line, c2 = c1; we set c2 to the same value as c1 holds, which of course is 'A' in this case. The next executable statement s1 = "This is a test "; as you might expect, sets the string variable s1 to the value "This is a test ",[23] which is a literal of a type called a **C string**. Don't confuse a C string with a string. A C string is a type of literal that we use to assign values to variables of type string; in other words, a string is a variable that can be set to the value of a literal string (C string), but they're not the same type. In the statement s1 = "This is a test "; we use a quotation mark, in this case the double quote ("), to tell the compiler where the literal value starts and ends.

You may be wondering why we need two different kinds of quotes in these two cases. The reason is that there are actually two types of nonnumeric data, *fixed-length data* and *variable-length data*. Fixed-length data are relatively easy to handle in a program, as the compiler can set aside the correct amount of space in advance. Variables of type char are 1 byte long and can thus contain exactly one character; as a result, when we set a char to a literal value, as we do in the line c1 = 'A'; the code that executes that statement has the simple task of copying exactly 1 byte representing the literal 'A' to the address reserved for variable c1.[24]

However, C string literals such as "This is a test " are variable-length data, and dealing with such data isn't so easy. Since there could be any number of characters in a C string, the code that does the assignment of a literal value like "This is a test " to a string variable has to have some way to tell where the literal value ends. One possible way to provide this needed information would be for the compiler to store the length of the C string literal in the memory location immediately before the first character in the literal. I would prefer this method; unfortunately, it is not the method used in the C language (and its descendant the C++ language). To be fair, the inventors of C didn't make an arbitrary choice; they had reasons for

Problem
Algorithms
C++
Executable
Hardware

---

23. Please note that there is a *space* (blank) character at the end of that C string, after the word "test". That space is part of the C string's value.

24. Warning: Every character inside the quotes has an effect on the value of the literal, whether the quotes are single or double; even "invisible" characters such as the *space* (' ') will change the literal's value. In other words, the line c1 = 'A'; is *not* the same as the line c1 = 'A '; The latter statement may or may not be legal, depending on the compiler you're using, but it is virtually certain not to give you what you want, which is to set the variable c1 to the value equivalent to the character 'A'. Instead, c1 will have some weird value resulting from combining the 'A' and the space character. In the case of a string value contained in double quotes, multiple characters are allowed, so "A B" and "AB" both make sense, but the space still makes a difference; namely, it keeps the 'A' and 'B' from being next to one another.

their decision on how to indicate the length of a string. You see, if we were to reserve only 1 byte to store the actual length in bytes of the character data in the string, then the maximum length of a string would be limited to 255 bytes. This is because the maximum value that could be stored in the length byte, as in any other byte, is 255. Thus, if we had a string longer than 255 bytes, we would not be able to store the length of the string in the 1 byte reserved for that purpose. On the other hand, if we were to reserve 2 bytes for the length of each string, then programs that contain many strings would take more memory than they should.

While the extra memory consumption that would be caused by using a 2-byte length code may not seem significant today, the situation was considerably different when C was invented. At that time, conserving memory was very important; the inventors of C therefore chose to mark the end of a C string by a byte containing the value 0, which is called a **null byte**.[25]

This solution has the advantage that only one extra byte is needed to indicate the end of a C string of any length. However, it also has some serious drawbacks. First, this solution makes it impossible to have a byte containing the value 0 in the middle of a C string, as all of the C string manipulation routines would treat that null byte as being the end of the C string. Second, it is a nontrivial operation to determine the length of a C string; the only way to do it is to scan through the C string until you find a null byte. As you can probably tell, I'm not particularly impressed with this mechanism; nevertheless, as it has been adopted into C++ for compatibility with C, we're stuck with it for literal strings in our programs.[26] Therefore, the literal string "ABCD" would occupy 5 bytes, 1 for each character, and 1 for the null byte at the end.[27] But we've skipped one step: How do we represent characters in memory? There's no intuitively obvious way to convert the character 'A' into a value that can be stored in 1 byte of memory.

The answer, at least for our purposes in English, is called the **ASCII code** standard. This stands for American Standard Code for Information Interchange, which as the name suggests was invented

Problem
Algorithms
C++
Executable
Hardware

---

25. I don't want to mislead you about this notion of a byte having the value 0; it is *not* the same as the representation of the decimal digit "0". As we'll see, each displayable character (and a number of invisible ones) is assigned a value to represent it when it's part of a string or literal value (i.e., a C string literal or char literal). The 0 byte I'm referring to is a byte with the binary value 0.

26. Happily, we can toss it overboard in most other circumstances, as you'll see in a future chapter.

27. The compiler adds the null byte automatically when it sees the ending ".

precisely to allow the interchange of data between different programs and makes of computers. Before the invention of ASCII, such interchange was difficult or impossible, since every manufacturer made up its own code or codes. Here are the specific character codes that we have to be concerned with for the purposes of this book:

1. The codes for the capital letters start with hex 41 for 'A', and run consecutively to hex 5a for 'Z'.[28]
2. The codes for the lower case letters start with hex 61 for 'a', and run consecutively to hex 7a for 'z'.
3. The codes for the numeric digits start with hex 30 for '0', and run consecutively to hex 39 for '9'.

Given these rules, the memory representation of the string "ABCD" might look something like Figure 3.13.

```
Address    Hex value

1000       41
1001       42
1002       43
1003       44
1004       00  (null byte; that is, end of C string)
```

Figure 3.13: Yet another small section of RAM

Problem
Algorithms
C++
Executable
Hardware

Now that we see how strings are represented in memory, I can explain why we need two kinds of quotes. The double quotes tell the compiler to add the null byte at the end of the string literal, so that when the assignment statement s1 = "This is a test "; is executed, the program knows when to stop copying the value to the string variable.

A Byte by Any Other Name. . .

Have you noticed that I've played a little trick here? The illustration of the string "ABCD" should look a bit familiar; its memory contents are exactly the same as in Figure 3.2, where we were discussing numeric variables. I did this to illustrate an important point: the

---

28. You may wonder why I have to specify that the codes for the capital letters run consecutively from 'A' to 'Z'; isn't that obvious? Perhaps, but there is a code (or to be more precise, a set of slightly differing codes) called EBCDIC (Extended Binary Coded Decimal Interchange Code), in which this is not true! See Eric Raymond's amusing and interesting book, *The New Hacker's Dictionary*, for details on this and many other historical facts.

contents of memory actually consists of uninterpreted bytes, which have meaning only when used in a particular way by a program. That is, the same bytes can represent numeric data or characters, depending on how they are referred to.

This is one of the main reasons why we need to tell the C++ compiler what types our variables have. Some languages allow variables to be used in different ways at different times, but in C++ any given variable always has the same type; for example, a char variable can't change into a short. At first glance, it seems that it would be much easier for programmers to be able to use variables any way they like; why is C++ so restrictive?

The C++ **type system**, as this feature of a language is called, is specifically designed to minimize the risk of misinterpreting or otherwise misusing a variable. It's entirely too easy in some languages to change the type of a variable without meaning to; the resulting bugs can be very difficult to find, especially in a large program. In C++, the usage of a variable can be checked by the compiler. This **static type checking** allows the compiler to tell you about many errors that otherwise would not be detected until the program is running (**dynamic type checking**). This is particularly important in systems that need to run continuously for long periods of time. While you can reboot your machine if your word processor crashes due to a run-time error, this is not acceptable as a solution for errors in the telephone network, for example.

Of course, you probably won't be writing programs demanding that degree of reliability any time soon, but strict static type checking is still worthwhile in helping eliminate errors at the earliest possible stage in the development of our programs.

Problem
Algorithms
C++
Executable
Hardware

Some Strings Attached

After that infomercial for the advantages of static type checking, we can resume our examination of strings. You may have noticed that there's a **space** character at the end of the string "This is a test ". That's another reason why we have to use a special character like " (the double quote) to mark the beginning and end of a string; how else would the compiler know whether that space is supposed to be part of the string or not? The space character is one of the **nonprinting characters** (or **nondisplay characters**) that controls the format of our displayed or printed information; imagine how hard it would be to read this book without space characters! While we're on the subject, I should also tell you about some other characters that have special meaning to the compiler. They are listed in Figure 3.14.

Name	Graphic	Use
Single quote	'	surrounds a single character value
Double quote	"	surrounds a multi-character value
Semicolon	;	ends a statement
Curly braces	{ }	groups statements together
Parentheses	( )	surrounds part of a statement[29]
Backslash	\	Tells the compiler that the next character should be treated differently from the way that it would normally be treated.[30]

Figure 3.14: Special characters for program text

I compiled this figure at the instigation of guess who:

Susan: How about you line up all your cute little " ' \ ; things and just list their meanings? I forget what they are by the time I get to the next one. Your explanations of them are fine, but they are scattered all over the place; I just want one place that has all the explanations.

Steve: That's a good idea. As usual, you're doing a good job representing the novices; keep up the good work!

Our next task, after a little bit of practice with the memory representation of a C string, will be to see how we get the values of our strings to show up on the screen.

Exercises, Second Set

2. Assume that a C string literal starts at memory location 1001. If the contents of memory are as illustrated in Figure 3.15, what is the value of the C string?

---

29. I'll be more specific later, when we have seen some examples.

30. For example, if you wanted to insert a " in a string, you would have to use \", because just a plain " would indicate the end of the string. That is, if you were to set a string to the value "This is a \"string\".", it would display as: This is a "string".

Problem
Algorithms
C++
Executable
Hardware

```
Address      Hex value

1000         44
1001         48
1002         45
1003         4c
1004         4c
1005         4f
1006         00
```

Figure 3.15: A small section of RAM

In and Out

Most programs need to interact with their users, both to ask them what they want and to present the results when they are available. The computer term for this topic is **I/O** (short for "input/output"). We'll start by getting information from the keyboard and displaying it on the screen; later, we'll go over the more complex I/O functions that allow us to read and write data on the disk.

Figure 3.16 shows how to display the text "This is a test and so is this." as promised:

Problem
Algorithms
C++
Executable
Hardware

```cpp
#include <iostream.h>
#include "string6.h"

int main()
{
    string s1;
    string s2;

    s1 = "This is a test ";
    s2 = "and so is this.";

    cout << s1;
    cout << s2;

    return 0;
}
```

Figure 3.16: Some simple output (code\basic01.cc)

What << means here is suggested by its arrowlike shape. The information on its right is sent to the "output target" on its left. In this case, we're sending the information to one of the predefined destinations, cout, which stands for "character output". Characters sent to cout are displayed on the screen.[31] The result of this operation will be that the following output will appear on the screen:

This is a test and so is this.

So much for (simple) output. Input from the keyboard is just as simple. Let's modify our little sample to use it, as shown in Figure 3.17.

```
#include <iostream.h>
#include "string6.h"

int main()
{
    string s1;
    string s2;

    cin >> s1;
    cin >> s2;

    cout << s1;
    cout << " ";
    cout << s2;

    return 0;
}
```

Problem
Algorithms
C++
Executable
Hardware

Figure 3.17: Some simple input and output (code\basic02.cc)

As you might have guessed, cin (shorthand for "character input") is the counterpart to cout, as >> is the counterpart to <<; cin supplies characters from the keyboard to the program via the >> operator.[32] This program will wait for you to type in the first string, ended by hitting the ENTER key, then do the same for the second string. When you hit ENTER the second time, the program will display the first string, then a blank, and then the second string.

Susan had some questions about these little programs, beginning with the question of case sensitivity:

31. By the way, cout is pronounced "see out".

32. Similarly to cout, cin is pronounced "see in" rather than "sin".

Susan: Are the words such as cout and cin case sensitive? I had capitalized a few of them just out of habit because they begin the sentence and I am not sure if that was the reason the compiler gave me so many error messages. I think after I changed them I reduced a few messages.

Steve: **Everything** in C++ is case sensitive. That includes keywords like if, for, do, and so on, as well as your own variables. That is, if you have a variable called Name and another one called name, those are completely different and unrelated to one another. You have to write cin and cout just as they appear here, or the compiler won't be able to figure out what you mean.

If Only You Knew

In our examples so far, the program always executes the same statements in the same order. However, any real program is going to need to alter its behavior according to the data it is processing. For example, in a banking application, it might be necessary to send out a notice to a depositor whenever the balance in a particular account drops below a certain level; or perhaps the depositor would just be charged some exorbitant fee in that case. Either way, the program has to do something different depending on the balance. This can be accomplished by using an if **statement**, as shown in Figure 3.18.

Problem
Algorithms
C++
Executable
Hardware

```cpp
#include <iostream.h>

int main()
{
    short balance;

    cout << "Please enter your bank balance: ";
    cin >> balance;

    if (balance < 10000)
        cout << "Please remit $20 service charge." << endl;
    else
        cout << "Have a nice day!" << endl;

    return 0;
}
```

Figure 3.18: Using an if statement (code\basic03.cc)

This program starts by displaying the line

Please enter your bank balance:

on the screen. Then it waits for you to type in your balance, followed by the ENTER key (so it knows when you're done). The conditional statement checks whether you're a "good customer". If your balance is less than $10,000, the next statement is executed, which displays the line

Please remit $20 service charge.[33]

The phrase << endl is new here. It means "we're done with this line of output; send it out to the screen". You could also use the special character '\n', which means much the same thing; its official name is "newline".

Now let's get back to our regularly scheduled program. If the condition is false (that is, you have at least $10,000 in the bank), the computer skips the statement that asks you to remit $20; instead, it executes the one after the else, which tells you to have a nice day. That's what else is for, it specifies what to do if the condition specified in the if statement is false (that is, not true). If you typed in a number 10,000 or higher, the program would display

Have a nice day!

Problem
Algorithms
C++
Executable
Hardware

You don't have to specify an else if you don't want to. In that case, if the if condition isn't true, the program just goes to the next statement as though the if had never been executed.

Now you should have enough information to be able to write a simple program of your own. Susan asked for an assignment to do just that:

> **Susan**: Based on what you have presented in the book so far, send me a setup, an exercise for me to try to figure out how to program, and I will give it a try. I guess that is the only way to do it. I can't even figure out a programmable situation on my own. So if you do that, I will do my best with it, and that will help teach me to think. (Can that be?) Now, if you do this, make it simple, and no tricks.

---

33. This explanation assumes that the "10,000" is the balance in dollars. Of course, this doesn't account for the possibility of balances that aren't a whole number of dollars, and there's also the problem of balances greater than $32,767, which wouldn't fit into a short. I'll mention possible solutions to these problems in Appendix A.

Of course, I did give her the exercise she asked for (exercise 3), but also of course, that didn't end the matter. She decided to add her own flourish, which resulted in exercise 4. Here they are, along with some others that fall in the same category.

Exercises, Third Set

3.   Write a program that asks the user to type in the number of people that are expected for dinner, not counting the user. Assuming that the number typed in is n, display a message that says "A table for (n+1) is ready.". For example, if the user types 3, display "A table for 4 is ready.".

4.   Modify the program from exercise 3 to display an error message if the number of guests is more than 20.

5.   Write a program that asks the user to type in his or her name and age. If the age is less than 47, then indicate that the user is a youngster; otherwise, that he or she is getting on in years.

6.   Write a program that asks the user whether Susan is the world's most tenacious novice. If the answer is "true", then acknowledge the user's correct answer; if the answer is "false", then indicate that the answer is erroneous. If neither "true" nor "false" is typed in, chastise the user for not following directions.

7.   Write a program that calculates how much extra allowance a teenager can earn by doing extra chores. Her allowance is calculated as $10 if she does no extra chores; she gets $1 additional for each extra chore she does.

```
Problem
Algorithms
C++
Executable
Hardware
```

While We're on the Subject

The while statement is another way of affecting the order of program execution. This conditional statement executes the statement under its control as long as a certain condition is true. Such potentially repeated execution is called a **loop**; a loop controlled by a while statement is called, logically enough, a while *loop*. Figure 3.19 is a program that uses a while loop to challenge the user to guess a secret number from 0 to 9, and keeps asking for guesses until the correct answer is entered.

```
#include <iostream.h>

int main()
{
     short Secret;
     short Guess;

     Secret = 3;

     cout << "Try and guess my number. Hint: It's from 0 to 9" << endl;
     cin >> Guess;

     while (Guess != Secret)
          {
          cout << "Sorry, that's not correct." << endl;
          cin >> Guess;
          }

     cout << "You guessed right!" << endl;

     return 0;
}
```

Figure 3.19: Using a while statement (code\basic04.cc)

Problem
Algorithms
C++
Executable
Hardware

There are a few wrinkles here that we haven't seen before. Although the while statement itself is fairly straightforward, the meaning of its condition != isn't intuitively obvious. However, if you consider the problem we're trying to solve, you'll probably come to the (correct) conclusion that != means "not equal", since we want to keep asking for more guesses while the Guess is not equal to our Secret number.[34]

You might also be wondering whether an if statement with an else clause would serve as well as the while; after all, if is used to select one of two alternatives, and the else could select the other one. The answer is that this would allow the user to take only one guess before the program ends; the while loop lets the user try again as many times as needed to get the right answer.

---

34. You may be wondering why we need parentheses around the expression Guess != Secret. The conditional expression has to be in parentheses so that the compiler can tell where it ends and the statement to be controlled by the while begins.

Just up the Block

A more significant addition to our arsenal of programming weapons is the ability to group several statements into one logical section of a program. That's the function of the **curly braces**, { and }. The first one of these starts such a section, called a **block**, and the second one ends the block. Because the two statements after the while are part of the same block, they are treated as a unit; both are executed if the condition in the while is true, and neither is executed if it is false. A block can be used anywhere that a statement can be used, and is treated in exactly the same way as if it were one statement.[35]

At the Fair

Now we're ready to write a real, runnable program that vaguely resembles a real solution to a real problem. We'll start with a simple, rural type of programming problem.

Imagine that you are at a county fair. The contest for the heaviest pumpkin is about to get underway, and the judges have asked for your help in operating the "pumpkin scoreboard". This device has a slot for the current pumpkin weight (the CurrentWeight slot), and another slot for the highest weight so far (the HighestWeight slot); each slot can hold three numbers from 0 to 9 and therefore can indicate any weight from 0 to 999. The judges want you to maintain an up-to-date display of the current weight and of the highest weight seen so far. The scale isn't very accurate, so the weights are expressed to the nearest pound. How would you go about this task?

Probably the best way to start is by setting the number in both slots to the weight of the first pumpkin called out. Then, as each new weight is called out, you change the number in the CurrentWeight slot to match the current weight; if it's higher than the number in the HighestWeight slot, you change that one to match as well. Of course, you don't have to do anything to the HighestWeight slot when a weight less than the previous maximum is called out, because that pumpkin can't be the winner. How do we know when we are done? Since a pumpkin entered in this contest has to have a weight of at least 1

```
Problem
Algorithms
C++
Executable
Hardware
```

---

35. If you look at someone else's C++ program, you're likely to see a different style for lining up the {} to indicate where a block begins and ends. As you'll notice, my style puts the { and } on separate lines rather than running them together with the code they enclose, to make them stand out, and indents them further than the conditional statement. I find this the clearest, but this is a matter where there is no consensus. The compiler doesn't care how you indent your code or whether you do so at all; it's a stylistic issue.

pound, the weigher calls out 0 as the weight when the weighing is finished. At that point, the number in the HighestWeight slot is the weight of the winner.

The procedure you have just imagined performing can be expressed a bit more precisely by the following algorithm:

1. Ask for the first weight.
2. Set the number in the CurrentWeight slot to this value.
3. Copy the number in the CurrentWeight slot to the HighestWeight slot.
4. Display both the current weight and the highest weight so far (which are the same, at this point)
5. While the CurrentWeight value is greater than 0 (that is, there are more pumpkins to be weighed), do steps 5a to 5d:

    a. Ask for the next weight.
    b. Set the number in the CurrentWeight slot to this weight.
    c. If the number in the CurrentWeight slot is greater than the number in the HighestWeight slot, copy the number in the CurrentWeight slot to the HighestWeight slot.
    d. Display the current weight and the highest weight so far.

6. Stop. The number in the HighestWeight slot is the weight of the winner.

Problem
Algorithms
C++
Executable
Hardware

You've already seen most of the constructs that the program contains, but let's examine the role of the *preprocessor directive* #include <iostream.h>.[36] This tells the compiler that we want to use the standard C++ I/O library. The term *preprocessor directive* is a holdover from the days when a separate program called the *preprocessor* handled functions such as #include before handing the program over to the compiler; these days, these facilities are provided by the compiler, but the name has stuck.

The #include command has the same effect as copying all of the code from a file called iostream.h into our file; iostream.h defines the I/O functions and variables cout, cin, <<, and >>, along with others that we haven't used yet. If we left this line out, none of our I/O statements would work.

---

36. The other new constructs will be covered in the text after the program listing.

Now let's take a look at the actual pumpkin-weighing program. Figure 3.20 is the translation of our little problem into C++.

English	C++

First, we have to tell the compiler what we're up to in this program

Define the standard input and output functionality	#include <iostream.h>
This is the main part of the program	int main()
Start of program	{
Define variables	short CurrentWeight; short HighestWeight;

Here's the start of the "working" code

Problem
Algorithms
C++
Executable
Hardware

Ask for the first weight	cout << "Please enter the first weight: ";
Set the number in the CurrentWeight slot to the value entered by the user	cin >> CurrentWeight;
Copy the number in the CurrentWeight slot to the HighestWeight slot	HighestWeight = CurrentWeight;
Display the current and highest weights	cout << "Current weight " << CurrentWeight << endl; cout << "Highest weight " << HighestWeight << endl;
While the number in the CurrentWeight slot is greater than 0 (i.e., there are more pumpkins to be weighed)	while (CurrentWeight > 0)
Start repeated steps	{

Figure 3.20: A C++ program (code\pump1.cc)

Ask for the next weight	cout << "Please enter the next weight: ";
Set the number in the CurrentWeight slot to this value	cin >> CurrentWeight;
If the number in the CurrentWeight slot is more than the number in the HighestWeight slot,	if (CurrentWeight > HighestWeight)
then copy the number in the CurrentWeight slot to the HighestWeight slot	HighestWeight = CurrentWeight;
Display the current and highest weights	cout << "Current weight " << CurrentWeight << endl; cout << "Highest weight " << HighestWeight << endl;
End repeated steps in while loop	};

We've finished the job; now to clean up

Tell the rest of the system we're okay	return 0;
End of program	};

Problem
Algorithms
C++
Executable
Hardware

Figure 3.20 continued

We've already covered most of the constructs used in the program in Figure 3.20. However, Susan had some questions about variable names.

Susan: Tell me again what the different shorts mean in this figure. I am confused, I just thought a short held a variable like i. What is going on when you declare HighestWeight a short? So do the "words" HighestWeight work in the same way as i?

Steve: A short is a variable. The name of a short is made up of one or more characters; the first character must be a letter or an underscore (_), while any character after the first must be either a letter, an underscore, or a digit from 0 to 9. To define a short, you write a line that gives the name of the short. This is an example: short HighestWeight;

Susan: OK, but then how does i take 2 bytes of memory and how does HighestWeight take up 2 bytes of memory? They look so different, how do you know that HighestWeight will fit into a short?

Steve: The length of the names that you give variables has nothing to do with the amount of storage that the variables take up. After the compiler gets through with your program, there aren't any variable names; each variable that you define in your source program is represented by the address of some area of storage. If the variable is a short, that area of storage is 2 bytes long; if it's a char, the area of storage is 1 byte long.

Susan: Then where do the names go? They don't go "into" the short?

Steve: A variable name doesn't "go" anywhere; it tells the compiler to set aside an area of memory of a particular length that you will refer to by a given name. If you write short xyz; you're telling the compiler that you are going to use a short (that is, 2 bytes of memory) called xyz.

Susan: If that is the case, then why bother defining the short at all?

Problem
Algorithms
C++
Executable
Hardware

Steve: So that you (the programmer) can use a name that makes sense to you. Without this mechanism, you'd have to specify everything as an address. Isn't it easier to say
    HighestWeight = CurrentWeight;
rather than
    mov ax,[1000]
    mov [1002],ax
or something similar?

Susan also had a question about the formatting of the output statement cout << "Highest weight " << HighestWeight << endl;.

Susan: Why do we need both "Highest weight" and HighestWeight in this line?

Steve: Because "Highest weight" is displayed on the screen to tell the user that the following number is supposed to represent the highest weight seen so far. On the other hand, HighestWeight is the name of the variable that holds that information, so including HighestWeight in the output statement will result in displaying the highest weight we've seen so far on the screen. Of course, the same analysis applies to the next line, which displays the label "Current weight" and the value of the variable CurrentWeight.

The topic of #include **statements** was the cause of some discussion with Susan. Here's the play by play:

Susan: Is the include command the only time you will use the # symbol?

Steve: There are other uses for #, but you won't see any of them for a long time, if ever.

Susan: So #include is a command.

Steve: Right; it's a command to the compiler.

Susan: Then what are the words we have been using for the most part called? Are those just called *code* or just *statements*? Can you make a list of commands to review?

Steve: The words that are defined in the language, such as if, while, for, and the like are called keywords. User defined names such as function and variable names are called identifiers.

Susan: So iostream.h is a header file telling the compiler that it is using info from the iostreams library?

Steve: Essentially correct; to be more precise, when we include iostream.h, we're telling the compiler to look into iostream.h for definitions that we're going to use.

Susan: Then the header file contains the secondary code of machine language to transform cin and cout into something workable?

Steve: Close, but not quite right. The machine code that makes cin and cout do their thing is in the iostreams library; the header file gives the compiler the information it needs to compile your references to cout, cin, <<, and >> into references to the machine code in the library.

Susan: So the header file directs the compiler to that section in the library where that machine code is stored? In other words, it is like telling the compiler to look in section XXX to find the machine code?

Steve: The header file tells the compiler what a particular part of the library does, while the library contains the machine code that actually does it.

Problem
Algorithms
C++
Executable
Hardware

If you're a programmer in some other language than C, you may wonder why we have to tell the compiler that we want to use the standard I/O library. Why doesn't the compiler know to use that library automatically? This seeming oversight is actually the result of a decision made very early in the evolution of C: to keep the language itself (and therefore the compiler) as simple as possible, adding functionality with the aid of standard libraries. Since a large part of the libraries can be written in C, this decision reduces the amount of work needed to "port" the C language from one machine architecture or operating system to another. Once the compiler has been ported, it's not too difficult to get the libraries to work on the new machine. In fact, even the C (or C++) compiler can be written in C (or C++), which makes the whole language quite portable. This may seem impossible. How do you get started? In fact, the process is called *bootstrapping*, from the impossible task of trying to lift yourself by your own bootstraps.[37] The secret is to have one compiler that's already running; then you use that compiler to compile the compiler for the new machine. Once you have the new compiler running, it is common to use it to compile itself, so that you know it's working. After all, a compiler is a fairly complex program, so getting it to compile and execute properly is a pretty good indication that it's producing the right code.

Problem
Algorithms
C++
Executable
Hardware

Most of the rest of the program should be fairly easy to understand, except for the two lines int main() and return 0;, which have related functions. Let's start with the line int main(). As we've already seen, the purpose of the main() part of this line is to tell the compiler where to start execution; the C++ language definition specifies that execution always starts at a block called main. This may seem redundant, as you might expect the compiler to assume that we want to start execution at the beginning of the program. However, C++ is intended to be useful in the writing of very large programs; such programs can and usually do consist of several source code modules, each of which contains some of the functionality of the program. Without such a rule, the compiler wouldn't know which module should be executed first.

The int part of this same line specifies the type of the *exit code* that will be returned from the program by a return statement when the program is finished executing; in this case, that type is int. The exit code can be used by a *batch file* to determine whether our program finished executing correctly; an exit code of 0, by convention, means that it did.

The final statement in the program is return 0;. This is the return statement just mentioned, whose purpose is to return an exit code of

---

37. If this term sounds familiar, we've already seen it in the context of how we start up a computer when it's turned on, starting from a small *boot program* in the *ROM*, or Read-Only Memory.

0 when our program stops running. The value that is returned, 0, is an acceptable value of the type we declared in the line int main(), namely, int; if it didn't match, the compiler would tell us we had made an error.

Finally, the closing curly brace, }, tells the compiler that it can stop compiling the current block, which in this case is the one called main. Without this marker, the compiler would tell us that we have a missing }, which of course would be true.

Novice Alert

Susan decided a little later in our collaboration that she wanted to try to reproduce this program just by considering the English description, without looking at my solution. She didn't quite make it without peeking, but the results are illuminating nevertheless.

> **Susan**: What I did was to cover your code with a sheet of paper and just tried to get the next line without looking, and then if I was totally stumped then I would look. Anyway, when I saw that if statement then I knew what the next statement would be but I am still having problems with writing backwards. For example

```
if (CurrentWeight > HighestWeight)
    HighestWeight = CurrentWeight;
```

> That is just so confusing because we just want to say that if the current weight is higher than the highest weight, then the current weight will be the new highest weight, so I want to write CurrentWeight = HighestWeight. Anyway, when I really think about it I know it makes sense to do it the right way; I'm just having a hard time thinking like that. Any suggestions on how to think backward?

> **Steve**: What that statement means is "*set* HighestWeight *to the current value of* CurrentWeight. The point here is that = does *not* mean "is equal to"; it means "set the variable to the left of the = to the value of the expression to the right of the =". It's a lousy way of saying that, but that's what it means.

> **Susan**: With all the { and } all over the place, I was not sure where and when the return 0; came in. So is it always right before the last }? OK, now that I think about it, I guess it always would be.

> **Steve**: You have to put the return statement at a place where the program is finished whatever it was doing. That's because whenever that statement is executed, the program is going to stop running.

Problem
Algorithms
C++
Executable
Hardware

Usually, as in this case, you want to do that at the physical end of the program.

Susan: Anyway, then maybe I am doing something wrong, and I am tired, but after I compiled the program and ran it, I saw that the HighestWeight label was run in together with the highest number and the next sentence, which said "Please enter the next weight". All those things were on the same line and I thought that looked weird; I tried to fix it but the best I had the stamina for at the moment was to put a space between the " and the P, to at least make a separation.

Steve: It sounds as though you need some endls in there to separate the lines.

Take It for a Spin

Problem
Algorithms
C++
Executable
Hardware

Assuming that you've installed the software from the CD-ROM in the back of this book, you can try out this program. To run it, just change to the normal subdirectory under the main directory where you installed the software, and type pump1. It will ask you for weights and keep track of the highest weight that has been entered. Type 0 and hit ENTER to end the program.

If just running the program normally doesn't give you a good enough feel for how each statement works, you can run it in under control of the gdb debugger, which shows you each statement as it is to be executed along with the contents of all the variables. To run the program under gdb, make sure you are in the normal subdirectory, then type trace pump1. The program will start up and show you the first line of executable code. Type z and hit ENTER to execute each line of the program. The values of CurrentWeight and HighestWeight will be displayed immediately before the execution of each line. When you are asked for a weight, type one in and hit ENTER just as when executing normally.[38] When you enter a 0 weight, the program will stop looping and execution will take the path to the end of the program. At that point, type q (for *quit*) and hit ENTER to exit from the debugger.[39] This "computer's eye" view of the program should

38. The gdb debugger has many commands, but we'll only use a few of them. For more information on gdb, you can type info at a DOS prompt, move down to the entry labeled "GDB", and hit ENTER. Warning: gdb is intended for experienced programmers, so the documentation isn't always as simply written as it might be. If you stick with the gdb commands I've listed here, you shouldn't have any trouble.

39. You can also type q and hit ENTER to leave the debugger at any other point if you get tired of watching the trace.

clear up any confusion on your part as to exactly how it works.[40]
We're almost done with this chapter, but first let's practice a little
more with chars and strings.

Exercises, Fourth Set

8.　Here are four possible versions of an output statement.
Assuming that the value of the string variable called name is
"Joe Smith", what does each one of them do?

　　a.　cout << "That is very old, " << name << ". " << endl;
　　b.　cout << "That is very old, " << name << '. ' << endl;
　　c.　cout << "That is very old, " << name << "." << endl;
　　d.　cout << "That is very old, " << name << '.' << endl;

Now it's time for some review on what we've covered in this
chapter.

Review

We started out by discussing the tremendous reliability of computers;
whenever you hear "it's the computer's fault", the overwhelming
likelihood is that in fact the software is to blame rather than the
hardware. Then we took a look at the fact that, although computers
are calculating engines, many of the functions for which we use them
don't have much to do with numeric calculations; for example, the
most common use of computers is probably word processing, which
doesn't use much in the way of addition or subtraction. Nevertheless,
we started out our investigation of programming with numeric
variables, which are easier to understand than numeric ones. To use
variables, we need to write a C++ program, which consists primarily
of a list of operations to be performed by the computer, along with
directions that influence how these operations are to be translated
into machine instructions.

That led us into a discussion of why and how our C++ program is
translated into machine instructions by a *compiler*. We examined an
example program that contained simple *source code statement*s, both
those that define variables and those that use those variables and
constants to calculate results. We covered the symbols that are used

```
Problem
Algorithms
C++
Executable
Hardware
```

---

40. If you're confused about the seemingly meaningless values that those variables have before
　　the first statement that sets each one to a value, let me assure you that they are indeed
　　meaningless. I'll explain why that is in the next chapter.

to represent the operations of addition, subtraction, multiplication, division, and *assignment*, which are +, −, *, /, and = respectively. While the first four of these should be familiar to you, the last one is a programming notion rather than a mathematical one. This may be confusing because the operation of assignment is expressed by the = sign, but is *not* the same as mathematical equality. For example, the statement x = 3; does *not* mean "*x* is equal to 3", but rather "set the variable x to the value 3.

After this discussion of the structure of statements in C++, we started an exploration of how the CPU actually stores and manipulates data in memory. The topics covered in this section included the order in which multibyte data items are stored in memory and the use of *general register*s to manipulate data efficiently.

Then we spent some time pretending to be a compiler, to see how a simple C++ program looks from that point of view, in order to improve our understanding of what the compiler does with our programs. This exercise involved keeping track of the addresses of variables and instructions and watching the effect of the instructions on the general registers and memory locations. During this exploration of the machine, we got acquainted with the *machine language* representation of instructions, which is the actual form that our executable programs take in memory. After a thorough examination of what the compiler does with our source code at *compile time*, we followed what would happen to the registers and memory locations at *run time* (that is, if the sample program were actually executed).

Then we began to look at two data types that can hold nonnumeric data, namely the char and the string. The char corresponds to 1 byte of storage, and therefore can hold one character of data. Examples of appropriate values for a char variable include letters (a–z, A–Z), digits (0–9), and special characters (e.g., , . ! @ # $ %). A char can also represent a number of other "nonprintable" characters such as the "space", which causes output to move to the next character position on the screen. Actually, a char can also be used as a "really short" numeric variable, but that's mostly a holdover from the days when memory was a lot more expensive, and every byte counted.

One char isn't much information, so we often want to deal with groups of them as a single unit; an example would be a person's name. This is the province of the string variable, which can handle an indefinitely long group of chars.

At the beginning of our sample program for strings and chars, we encountered a new construct, the #include *statement*. This tells the

Problem
Algorithms
C++
Executable
Hardware

compiler where to find instructions on how to handle data types such as strings, about which it doesn't have any built-in knowledge. Then we came across the line int main(), which indicates where we want to start executing our program. A C++ program always starts execution at the place indicated by such a line. We also investigated the meaning of int, which is the *return type* of main. The return type tells the compiler what sort of data this program returns to the operating system when it finishes executing; the return value can be used to determine what action a batch file should take next.

As we continued looking at the sample program for strings and chars, we saw how to assign literal values to both of these types, and noticed that two different types of quotes are used to mark off the literal values: the single quote ('), which is used in pairs to surround a literal char value consisting of exactly one char, such as 'a'; and the double quote ("), which is used in pairs to surround a literal string value of the *C string* type, such as "This is a test". We also investigated the reason for these two different types of literal values, which involves the notion of a *null byte* (a byte with the value 0); this null byte is used to mark the end of a C string in memory.

This led us to the discussion of the *ASCII code*, which is used to represent characters by binary values. We also looked at the fact that the same bytes can represent either a numeric value or a C string, depending on how we use those bytes in our program. That's why it's so important to tell the compiler which of these possibilities we have in mind when we write our programs. The way in which the compiler regulates our access to variables by their type, which is defined at compile time, is called the *type system*; the fact that C++ uses this *static type checking* is one of the reasons that C++ programs can be made more robust than programs written in languages that use *dynamic type checking*, where these errors are not detected until run time.

After a short discussion of some of the special characters that have a predefined meaning to the compiler, we took an initial glance at the mechanisms that allow us to get information into and out of the computer, known as *I/O*. We looked at the << function, which provides display on the screen when coupled with the built-in destination called cout. Immediately afterwards, we encountered the corresponding input function >> and its partner cin, which team up to give us input from the keyboard.

Next, we went over some program organization concepts, including the if statement, which allows the program to choose between two alternatives; the while statement, which causes another statement to be executed while some condition is true; and the *block*,

Problem
Algorithms
C++
Executable
Hardware

which allows several statements to be grouped together into one logical statement. Blocks are commonly used to enable several statements to be controlled by an if or while statement.

At last we were ready to write a simple program that does something resembling useful work, and we did just that. The starting point for this program, as with all programs, was to define exactly what the program should do; in this case, the task was to keep track of the pumpkin with the highest weight at a county fair. The next step was to define a solution to this problem in precise terms. Next, we broke the solution down into steps small enough to be translated directly into C++. Of course, the next step after that was to do that translation. Finally, we went over the C++ code, line by line, to see what each line of the program did.

Now that the review is out of the way, we're about ready to continue with some more C++. First, though, let's step back a bit and see where we are right now.

Conclusion

```
Problem
Algorithms
C++
Executable
Hardware
```

We've come a long way from the beginning of this chapter. Starting from basic information on how the hardware works, we've made it through our first actual, runnable program. By now, you should have a much better idea whether you're going to enjoy programming (and this book). Assuming you aren't discouraged on either of these points, let's proceed to gather some more tools, so we can undertake a bigger project.

Answers to Exercises

1.   3c43. In case you got a different result, here's a little help:
     a. If you got the result 433a, you started at the wrong address.
     b. If you got the result 433c, you have the bytes in the wrong order.
     c. Finally, if you got 3a43, you made both of these mistakes.
     If you made one or more of these mistakes, don't feel too bad; even experienced programmers have trouble with hexadecimal values once in awhile. That's one reason we use compilers and assemblers rather than writing everything in hex!

2. "HELLO". See the previous answer if you couldn't figure out what the "D" at the beginning was for; you started at the wrong place.

3. Figure 3.21 is Susan's answer to this problem, followed by our usual banter.

```
#include <iostream.h>
int main()
{
    short n;
    cout << "Please type in the number of guests ";
    cout << "of your dinner party. ";
    cin >> n;
    cout << "A table for " << n+1 << "is ready. ";
    return 0;
}
```

Figure 3.21: First dinner party program (code\basic05.cc)

Susan: I would have sent it sooner had I not had the last cout arrows going like this >> (details).<G> Also, it just didn't like the use of endl; at the end of the last cout statement. It just kept telling me I had a parse error.

Steve: If you wrote something like

```
cout << "A table for " << n+1 << "is ready. " << "endl;"
```

then it wouldn't work for two reasons. First, "endl;" is just a character string, not anything recognized by <<. Second, you're missing a closing ;, because characters inside quotes are treated as just plain characters by the compiler, not as having any effect on program structure.

The correct way to use endl in your second output statement is as follows:

```
cout << "A table for " << n+1 << "is ready. " << endl;
```

By the way, you might want to add a " " in front of the is in is ready, so that the number doesn't run up against the is. That would make the line look like this:

```
cout << "A table for " << n+1 << " is ready. " << "endl;"
```

Susan: Okay.

Problem
Algorithms
C++
Executable
Hardware

4.　Figure 3.22 is Susan's answer to this problem, followed by our discussion.

```cpp
#include <iostream.h>

int main()
{
    short n;

    cout << "Excluding yourself, please type the ";
    cout << "number of guests in your dinner party.\n";

    cin >> n;

    if (n>20)
        cout << "Sorry, your party is too large. ";
    else
        cout << "A table for " << n+1 << " is ready. ";

    return 0;
}
```

Figure 3.22: Second dinner party program (code\basic06.cc)

Problem
Algorithms
C++
Executable
Hardware

Steve: Congratulations on getting your program to work!

Susan: Now, let me ask you this: can you ever modify else? That is, could I have written else (n>20), or does else always stand alone?

Steve: You can say something like Figure 3.22.

```cpp
if (x < y)
  {
  cout << "x is less than y" << endl;
  else
    {
    if (x > y)
      cout << "x is greater than y" << endl;
    else
      cout << "x must be equal to y!" << endl;
    }
  }
```

In other words, the controlled block of an if statement or an else statement can have another if or else inside it. In fact, you can have as many "nested" if or else statements as you wish; however, it's best to avoid very deep nesting because it tends to confuse the next programmer who has to read the program.

5.   The program should look like Figure 3.23.

```
#include <iostream.h>
#include "string6.h"

int main()
{
    string name;
    short age;

    cout << "What is your name? ";
    cin >> name;

    cout << "Thank you, " << name << endl;

    cout << "What is your age? ";
    cin >> age;

    if (age < 47)
        cout << "My, what a youngster!" << endl;
    else
        cout << "Hi, Granny!" << endl;

    return 0;
}
```

Figure 3.23· Name and age program (code\basic07.cc)

Problem
Algorithms
C++
Executable
Hardware

One point that might be a bit puzzling in this program is why it's not necessary to add an << endl to the end of the lines that send data to cout before we ask the user for input. For example, in the sequence:

```
cout << "What is your name? ";
cin >> name;
```

how do we know that the C string "What is your name? " has been displayed on the terminal before the user has to type in the answer? Obviously, it would be hard for the user to answer our request for information without a clue as to what we're asking for.

As it happens, this is a common enough situation that the designers of the iostreams library have anticipated it and solved it for us. When we use that library to do output to the screen and input from the keyboard, we can be sure that any screen output we have already requested will be displayed before any input is requested from the user via the keyboard.

6.   Figure 3.24 shows Susan's program, which is followed by our discussion.

```
#include <iostream.h>
#include "string6.h"

int main()
{
    string answer;

    cout << "Please respond to the following statement ";
    cout << "with either true or false\n";

    cout << "Susan is the world's most tenacious novice.\n";
    cin >> answer;

    if (answer != "true")
        if (answer != "false")
            cout << "Please answer with either true or false.";

    if (answer == "true")
        cout << "Your answer is correct\n";

    if (answer == "false")
        cout << "Your answer is erroneous\n";

    return 0;
}
```

Problem
Algorithms
C++
Executable
Hardware

Figure 3.24: Novice program (code\basic08.cc)

Susan: Steve, look at this. It even runs!

Also, I wanted to ask you one more question about this program. I wanted to put double quotes around the words true and false in the 3rd output statement because I wanted to emphasize those words, but I didn't know if the compiler could deal with that so I left it out. Would that have worked if I had?

Steve: Not if you just added quotes, because " is a special character that means "beginning or end of C string". Here's what you would have to do to make it work:

```
cout << "Please answer with either \"true\" or \"false\".";
```

The \ is a way of telling the compiler to treat the next character differently from its normal usage. In this case, we are telling the compiler to treat the special character " as "not special"; that is, \" means "just the character double quote, please, and no nonsense". This is called an *escape*, because it allows you to get out of the trap of having a " mean something special. We also use the \ to tell the compiler to treat a "nonspecial" character as "special"; for example, we use it to make up special characters that don't have any visual representation. You've already seen '\n', the "newline" character, which means "start a new line on the screen".

Susan: Another thing I forgot is how you refer to the statements in () next to the "if" keywords; what do you call the info that is in there?

Steve: The condition.

7.   Figure 3.25 is Susan's version of this program. Actually, it was her idea in the first place.

```cpp
#include <iostream.h>
#include "string6.h"

int main()
{

    short x;

    cout << "Elena can increase her $10 allowance each week ";
    cout << "by adding new chores." << endl;

    cout << "For every extra chore Elena does, she gets ";
    cout << "another dollar." <<            endl;

    cout << "State the number of new chores done this week." << endl;
    cin >> x;

    if (x==0)
        {
        cout << "There is no extra allowance for Elena ";
        cout << "this week. " << endl;
        }
    else
        {
        cout << "Elena will now earn " << 10 + x;
        cout << " dollars this week." << endl;
        }

    return 0;
};
```

Problem
Algorithms
C++
Executable
Hardware

Figure 3.25: Allowance program (code\basic09.cc)

8.   You'll be happy (or at least unsurprised) to hear that Susan and I had quite a discussion about this problem.

Susan: Remember on my "test" program how I finally got that period in there? Then I got to thinking that maybe it should have been surrounded by single quotes ' instead of double quotes. It worked with a double quote but since it was only one character it should have been a single quote, so I went back and changed it to a single quote and the compiler *didn't like that at all*. So I put it back to the double. So what is the deal?

Steve: You should be able to use 'x' or "x" more or less interchangeably with <<, because it can handle both of those data types (char and C string, respectively). However, they are indeed different types. The first one specifies a literal char value, whereas the second specifies a literal C string value. A char value can only contain one character, but a C string can be as long as you want, from none to hundreds or thousands of characters.

Susan: Here's the line that gave me the trouble:

```
cout << "That is very old, " << name << ". " << endl;
```

Problem
Algorithms
C++
Executable
Hardware

Remember I wanted to put that period in at the end in that last line? It runs like this but not with the single quotes around it. That I don't understand. This should have been an error. But I did something right by mistake <G>. Anyway, is there something special about the way a period is handled?

Steve: I understand your problem now. No, it's not the period; it's the space after the period. Here are four possible versions of that line:

```
1. cout << "That is very old, " << name << ". " << endl;
2. cout << "That is very old, " << name << '. ' << endl;
3. cout << "That is very old, " << name << "." << endl;
4. cout << "That is very old, " << name << '.' << endl;
```

None of these is exactly the same as any of the others. However, 1, 3, and 4 will do what you expect, whereas 2 will produce weird looking output, with some bizarre number where the . should be. Why is this? It's not because . is handled specially, but because the space (" "), when inside quotes, either single or double, is a character like any other character. Thus, the expression '. ' in line 2 is a "multicharacter constant", which has a value dependent on the compiler; in this case, you'll get a short value equal to (256 * the ASCII value of the period) + the ASCII value of the space. This comes out to 11808, as I calculate it. So the line you see on the screen may look like this:

That is very old, Joe Smith11808

Now why do all of the other lines work? Well, 1 works because a C string can have any number of characters and be sent to cout correctly; 3 works for the same reason; and 4 works because << can also handle a one-character constant such as '.'.

I realize it's hard to think of the space as a character, when it doesn't look like anything; in addition, you can add spaces freely between variables, expressions, and so forth, in the program text. However, once you're dealing with C strings and literal character values, the space is just like any other character.

Susan: So it is okay to use single characters in double quotes? If so, why bother with single quotes?

Steve: Single quotes surround a literal of type char. This is a 1-byte value that can be thought of (and even used) as a very short number. Double quotes surround a literal of type "C string". This is a multibyte value terminated by a 0 byte, which cannot be used or treated as a number.

Susan: I am not too clear on what exactly the difference is between the char and "C string". I thought a char was like a alpha letter, and a string was just a bunch of letters.

Steve: Right. The difference is that a C string is variable length, and a char isn't; this makes a lot of difference in how they can be manipulated.

Susan: Am I right in thinking that a char could also be a small number that is not being used for calculations?

Steve: Or that is used for (very small) calculations; for instance, if you add 1 to the value 'A', you get the value for 'B'. At least that's logical.

Susan: What do you mean by "terminated by a 0 byte"? That sounds familiar; was that something from an earlier chapter which is now ancient history?

Steve: Yes, we covered that some time ago. The way the program can tell that it's at the end of a C string (which is of variable length, remember) is that it gets to a byte with the value 0. This is a crummy way to specify the size of a variable-length string, in my opinion, but it's too late to do anything about it; it's built into the compiler.

Susan: When you say a C string, do you mean the C programming language in contrast to other languages?

Problem
Algorithms
C++
Executable
Hardware

Steve: Yes.

Susan: All right, then the 0 byte used to terminate a C string is the same thing as a null byte?

Steve: Yes.

Susan: Then you mean that each C string must end in a 0 so that the compiler will know when to stop processing the data for the string?

Steve: Yes.

Susan: Could you also just put 0? Hey, it doesn't hurt to ask. I don't see the problem with the word *hello*; it ends with an o and not a 0. But what if you do need to end the sentence with a 0?

Steve: It's not the digit 0, which has the ASCII code 30h, but a byte with a 0 value. You can't type in a null byte directly, although you can create one with a special character sequence if you want to. However, there's no point in doing that usually, because all literal C strings such as "hello" always have an invisible 0 byte added automatically by the compiler. If for some reason you need to explicitly create a null byte, you can write it as '\0', as in

```
char x = '\0';
```

which emphasizes that you really mean a null byte and not just a plain old 0 like this:

```
char x = 0;
```

The difference between these two is solely for the benefit of the next programmer to look at your code; they're exactly the same to the compiler.

Problem
Algorithms
C++
Executable
Hardware

Chapter 4

More Basics

A Modest Proposal

Now that we have seen how to write a simple program in C++, it's time to acquire some more tools. We'll extend our example program from Chapter 3 for finding the heaviest pumpkin. Eventually, we want to provide the weights of the three heaviest pumpkins, so that first, second, and third prizes can be awarded. It might seem that this would require just a minor modification of the previous program, in which we would keep track of the heaviest so far, second heaviest so far, and third heaviest so far, rather than merely the heaviest so far. However, this modification turns out to be a bit more complicated than it seems. Since this book is intended to teach you how to program using C++, rather than just how to use the C++ language, it's worth investigating why this is so. First, though, here are the objectives for this chapter.

Objectives of This Chapter

By the end of this chapter, you should

1. Understand the likelihood of error in even a small change to a program.
2. Be aware that even seemingly small changes in a problem can result in large changes in the program that solves the problem.
3. Have some understanding of the type of thinking needed to solve problems with programming.

4. Understand the selection sorting algorithm for arranging values in order.
5. Understand how to use a vector to maintain a number of values under one name.
6. Be able to use the for statement to execute program statements a (possibly varying) number of times.
7. Be familiar with the arithmetic operators ++ and +=, which are used to modify the value of variables.

Algorithmic Thinking

Let's take our program modification one step at a time, starting with just the top two weights. Figure 4.1 is one possible way to handle this version of the problem.

Problem
Algorithms
C++
Executable
Hardware

```cpp
#include <iostream.h>

int main()
{
    short CurrentWeight;
    short HighestWeight;
    short SecondHighestWeight;

    cout << "Please enter the first weight: ";
    cin >> CurrentWeight;
    HighestWeight = CurrentWeight;
    SecondHighestWeight = 0;
    cout << "Current weight " << CurrentWeight << endl;
    cout << "Highest weight " << HighestWeight << endl;

    while (CurrentWeight > 0)
        {
        cout << "Please enter the next weight: ";
        cin >> CurrentWeight;
        if (CurrentWeight > HighestWeight)
            {
            SecondHighestWeight = HighestWeight;
            HighestWeight = CurrentWeight;
            }
        cout << "Current weight " << CurrentWeight << endl;
        cout << "Highest weight " << HighestWeight << endl;
        cout << "Second highest weight " << SecondHighestWeight << endl;
        };

    return 0;
}
```

Figure 4.1: Finding the top two weights, first try (code\pump1a.cc)

The reasons behind some of the new code should be fairly obvious, but we'll go over them anyway. The new lines are **bold** so you can find them easily. First, of course, we need a new variable, SecondHighestWeight, to hold the current value of the second highest weight we've seen so far. Then, when the first weight is entered, the statement SecondHighestWeight = 0; sets the SecondHighestWeight to 0. After all, there isn't any second-highest weight when we've only seen one weight. The first nonobvious change is the addition of the statement SecondHighestWeight = HighestWeight;, which copies the old HighestWeight to SecondHighestWeight, whenever there's a new highest weight. On reflection, however, this should make sense; when a new high is detected, the old high must be the second highest value (so far). Also, we have to copy the old HighestWeight to SecondHighestWeight before we change HighestWeight. After we have set HighestWeight to a new value, it's too late to copy its old value into SecondHighestWeight.

First, let's see how Susan viewed this solution:

> **Susan**: I noticed that you separate out the main program {} from the other {} by indenting. Is that how the compiler knows which set of {} goes to which statements and doesn't confuse them with the main ones that are the body of the program? Does it just get deeper if you have more modifiers? How do you know how far to indent these {}. Is it two tabs? Are you going to discuss how to physically lay this all out? Obviously I can see how you are doing it, but are there rules for how to do it? I want more rules.

> **Steve**: The compiler doesn't care about indentation at all; that's just for the people reading the program. All the compiler cares about is the number of { it has seen so far without matching }. There aren't any hard rules about this; it's a "religious" issue in C++, where different programmers can't agree on the best way.

> **Susan**: Now on this thing with setting SecondHighestWeight to 0. Is that initializing it? See, I know what you are doing, and yet I can't see the purpose of doing this clearly, unless it is initializing, and then it makes sense.

> **Steve**: That's correct.

> **Susan**: How do you know how to order your statements? For example, why did you put the SecondHighestWeight = HighestWeight;" above the other statement? What would happen if you reversed that order?

> **Steve**: Think about it. Let's suppose that

Problem
Algorithms
C++
Executable
Hardware

CurrentWeight is 40
HighestWeight is 30
SecondHighestWeight is 15

and the statements were executed in the following order:

1. HighestWeight = CurrentWeight
2. SecondHighestWeight = HighestWeight

What would happen to the values? Well, statement 1 would set HighestWeight to CurrentWeight, so the values would be like this:

CurrentWeight is 40
HighestWeight is 40
SecondHighestWeight is 15

Then statement 2 would set SecondHighestWeight to HighestWeight, leaving the situation as follows:

CurrentWeight is 40
HighestWeight is 40
SecondHighestWeight is 40

Problem
Algorithms
C++
Executable
Hardware

This is clearly wrong. The problem is that we need the value of HighestWeight *before* it is set to the value of CurrentWeight, not afterward. After that occurs, the previous value is lost.

Susan: Yes, that is apparent; I was just wondering if the computer had to read it in the order that you wrote it, being that it was grouped together in the {}. For example, you said that the compiler doesn't read the {} as we write them, so I was wondering if it read those statements as we write them. Obviously it has to. So then everything descends in a progression downward and outward, as you get more detailed in the instructions.

To run this program normally, just change to the normal subdirectory under the main directory where you installed the software, and type pump1a. It will ask you for weights and keep track of the highest weight that has been entered. Type 0 and hit ENTER to end the program.

To run the program under gdb, make sure you are in the normal subdirectory, then type trace pump1a. The program will start up and show you the first line of executable code. Type z and hit ENTER to execute each line of the program. The values of CurrentWeight, HighestWeight, and SecondHighestWeight will be displayed below the line that is to be executed next. When you are asked for a weight, type one in and hit ENTER just as when executing normally. When you enter a 0 weight, the program will stop looping and execution will take the path to the end of the program. At that point (or when you're tired of tracing the program), type q (for *quit*) and hit ENTER to exit from the debugger.

A Prize Catch

This program may seem to keep track of the highest and second highest weights correctly, but in fact there's a hole in the logic. To be exact, it doesn't work correctly when the user enters a new value that's less than the previous high value but more than the previous second-high value. In that case, the new value should be the second-high value, even though there's no new high value. For example, suppose that you enter the following weights: 5 2 11 3 7. If we were to update SecondHighestWeight only when we see a new high, our program would indicate that 11 was the high, and 5 the second highest; since neither 3 nor 7 is a new high, SecondHighestWeight would remain as it was when the 11 was entered.

Here's what ensued when Susan tried out the program and discovered this problem:

> **Susan**: Steve, the program! I have been playing with it. Hey this is fun, but look, it took me awhile. I had to go over it and over it, and then I was having trouble getting it to put current weights that were higher than second weights into the second weight slot. For example, if I had a highest weight of 40 and the the second highest weight of 30 and then selected 35 for a current weight, it wouldn't accept 35 as the second-highest weight. It increased the highest weights just fine and it didn't change anything if I selected a lower number of the two for a current weight. Or did you mean to do that to make a point? I am supposed to find the problem? I bet that is what you are doing.

> **Steve**: Yep, and I'm not sorry, either.<G>

> **Susan**: You just had to do this to me, didn't you? OK, what you need to do is to put in a statement that says if the current weight is greater than the second-highest weight, then set the second-highest weight to the current weight, as illustrated in Figure 4.1.

Problem
Algorithms
C++
Executable
Hardware

```
else
   {
   if (CurrentWeight > Second HighestWeight)
      Second HighestWeight = CurrentWeight;
   }
```

I hope you are satisfied.

Steve: Satisfied? Well, no, I wouldn't use that word. How about ecstatic? You have just figured out a bug in a program, and determined what the solution is. Don't tell me you don't understand how a program works.

Now I have to point out something about your code. I understood what you wrote perfectly. Unfortunately, compilers aren't very smart, and therefore have to be extremely picky. So you have to make sure to spell the variable names correctly. This would make your answer like the if clause shown in Figure 4.2.

Congratulations again.

As Susan figured out, we have to add an else clause to our if statement, so that the corrected version of the statement looks like Figure 4.2.

Problem
Algorithms
C++
Executable
Hardware

```
if (CurrentWeight > HighestWeight)
   {
   SecondHighestWeight = HighestWeight;
   HighestWeight = CurrentWeight;
   }
else
   {
   if (CurrentWeight > SecondHighestWeight)
         SecondHighestWeight = CurrentWeight;
   }
```

Figure 4.2: Using an if statement with an else clause

In this case, the condition in the first if is checking whether CurrentWeight is greater than the previous HighestWeight; when this is true, we have a new HighestWeight and we can update both HighestWeight and SecondHighestWeight. However, if CurrentWeight is not greater than HighestWeight, the else clause is executed. It contains another if; this one checks whether CurrentWeight is greater than the old SecondHighestWeight. If so, SecondHighestWeight is set to the value of CurrentWeight.

What happens if two (or more) pumpkins have the same weight and therefore should be tied for first place? In that case, the first one of them to be encountered is going to set HighestWeight, as it will be the highest yet encountered. When the second pumpkin of the same weight is seen, it won't trigger a change to HighestWeight, since it's not higher than the current occupant of that variable. It will pass the test in the else clause, if (CurrentWeight > SecondHighestWeight), however, which will cause SecondHighestWeight to be set to the same value as HighestWeight. This is reasonable behavior, unlikely to startle the (hypothetical) user of the program, and therefore is good enough for our purposes. In a real application program, we'd have to try to determine what the user of this program would want us to do.

Finally, the output is changed to reflect both the highest and second-highest weights, along with the current weight. Figure 4.3 shows the corrected program.

```cpp
#include <iostream.h>

int main()
{
    short CurrentWeight;
    short HighestWeight;
    short SecondHighestWeight;

    cout << "Please enter the first weight: ";
    cin >> CurrentWeight;
    HighestWeight = CurrentWeight;
    SecondHighestWeight = 0;
    cout << "Current weight " << CurrentWeight << endl;
    cout << "Highest weight " << HighestWeight << endl;

    while (CurrentWeight > 0)
        {
        cout << "Please enter the next weight: ";
        cin >> CurrentWeight;
        if (CurrentWeight > HighestWeight)
            {
            SecondHighestWeight = HighestWeight;
            HighestWeight = CurrentWeight;
            }
        else
            if (CurrentWeight > SecondHighestWeight)
                SecondHighestWeight = CurrentWeight;
        cout << "Current weight " << CurrentWeight << endl;
        cout << "Highest weight " << HighestWeight << endl;
        cout << "Second highest weight " << SecondHighestWeight << endl;
        };

    return 0;
}
```

Problem
Algorithms
C++
Executable
Hardware

Figure 4.3: Finding the top two weights (code\pump2.cc)

To run this program normally, just change to the normal subdirectory under the main directory where you installed the software, and type pump2. It will ask you for weights and keep track of the highest weight that has been entered. Type 0 and hit ENTER to end the program.

To run the program under gdb, make sure you are in the normal subdirectory, then type trace pump2. The program will start up and show you the first line of executable code. Type z and hit ENTER to execute each line of the program. The values of CurrentWeight, HighestWeight, and SecondHighestWeight will be displayed below the line that is to be executed next. When you are asked for a weight, type one in and hit ENTER just as when executing normally. When you enter a 0 weight, the program will stop looping and execution will take the path to the end }. At that point (or when you're tired of tracing the program), type q (for *quit*) and hit ENTER to exit from the debugger.

By the way, since we've just been using the if statement pretty heavily, this would be a good time to list all of the conditions that it can test. We've already seen some of them, but it can't hurt to have them all in one place. Figure 4.4 lists these conditions, with translations.

```
Problem
Algorithms
C++
Executable
Hardware
```

Condition Symbol	Controlled block will be executed if:
>	First item is larger than second item
<	First item is smaller than second item
>=	First item is larger than or equal to second item
<=	First item is smaller than or equal to second item
!=	First item differs from second item
==	First item has the same value as the second item

Figure 4.4: What if?

You may wonder why we have to use == to test for equality rather than just =. That's because = means "assign right hand value to variable on left", rather than "compare two items for equality". This is a "feature" of C++ (and C) that allows us to accidentally write if (a

= b) when we mean if (a == b). What does if (a = b) mean? It means the following:

1. Assign the value of b to a.
2. If that value is 0, then the if is false.
3. Otherwise, the if is true.

Some people find this useful; I don't. Therefore, I always enable the compiler warning that tells you when you use a = inside an if statement in a way that looks like you meant to test for equality.

What a Tangled Web We Weave. . .

I hope this excursion has given you some appreciation of the subtleties that await in even the simplest change to a working program; many experienced programmers still underestimate such difficulties and the amount of time that may be needed to ensure that the changes are correct. I don't think it's necessary to continue along the same path with a program that can award three prizes. The principle is the same, although the complexity of the code grows with the number of special cases we have to handle. Obviously, a solution that could handle any number of prizes without special cases would be a big improvement, but it will require some major changes in the organization of the program. That's what we'll take up next.

Problem
Algorithms
C++
Executable
Hardware

You May Already Have Won

One of the primary advantages of the method we've used so far to find the heaviest pumpkin(s) is that we didn't have to save the weights of all the pumpkins as we went along. For simplicity, let's assume that there are only five weights to be read in. If we don't mind saving all five weights, then we can solve the "three prize" problem by the following method:

1. Read in all of the weights.
2. Make a list consisting of the three highest weights in descending order.
3. Award the first, second, and third prizes, in that order, to the three entries in the list of highest weights.

Now let's break those down into substeps which can be more easily translated into C++:

1. Read in all of the weights.

    a. Read first number
    b. Read next number
    c. If we haven't read five weights yet, go back to 1b

Now we have all the numbers; proceed to calculation phase:

2. Make a list consisting of the three highest weights in descending order.

    a. Find the largest number in the original list of weights
    b. Copy it to the sorted list
    c. If we haven't found the three highest numbers, go back to 2a

Problem
Algorithms
C++
Executable
Hardware

Oops. That's not going to work, since we'll get the same number each time.[1]

To prevent that from happening, we have to mark off each number as we select it. Here's the revised version of step 2:

2. Make a list consisting of the three highest weights in descending order.

    a. Find the largest number in the original list of weights
    b. Copy it to the sorted list
    c. Mark it off in the original list of weights, so we don't select it again
    d. If we haven't found the three highest numbers, go back to 2a

Now we're ready for output:

---

1. I realize I'm breaking a cardinal rule of textbooks. Never admit that the solution to a problem is anything but obvious, so the student who doesn't see it immediately feels like an idiot. In reality, even a simple program is difficult to get right, and indicating the sort of thought processes that go into analyzing a programming problem might help demystify this difficult task.

3. Award the first, second, and third prizes, in that order, to the three entries in the list of highest weights.

    a. Write first number
    b. Write another number
    c. If we haven't done them all, go back to 3b

Unlike our previous approach, this obviously can be generalized to handle any number of prizes. However, we have to address two problems before we can use this approach: First, how do we keep track of the weights? And, second, how do we select out the highest three weights? Both of these problems are much easier to solve if we don't have a separate variable for each weight.

Variables, by the Numbers

The solution to our first question is to use a vector.[2] This is a variable containing a number of "sub-variables" that can be addressed by position in the vector; each of these sub-variables is called an **element**. A vector has a name, just like a regular variable, but the elements do not. Instead, each element has a number, corresponding to its position in the vector. For example, we might want to create a vector of short values called Weight, with five elements. To do this, we would write this line: vector<short> Weight(5);.[3]

We haven't heard from Susan for awhile, but the following exchange should make up for that.

> **Susan**: OK, why do we need another header (#include "vector.h")?[4]

> **Steve**: Each header contains definitions for a specific purpose. For example, iostream.h contains definitions that allow us to get information in (I) and out (O) of the computer. On the other hand, vector.h contains definitions that allow us to use vectors.

Problem
Algorithms
C++
Executable
Hardware

---

2. In order to use vectors, we have to #include the header file vector.h; otherwise, the compiler won't understand that type of variable.

3. A vector actually contains some additional information beyond the elements themselves. Unfortunately, how a vector actually works is too complicated to go into in this book.

4. Note that the #include statement for vector.h in Figure 4.5 uses "" rather than <> around the file name. The use of "" tells the compiler to search for vector.h in the current directory first, and then the "normal" places that header files supplied with the compiler are located. This is necessary because vector.h in fact is in the current directory. If we had written #include <vector.h>, the compiler would look only in the "normal" places, and therefore would not find vector.h.

Susan: So then using a vector is just another way of writing this same program, only making it a little more efficient?

Steve: In this case, the new program can do more than the old program could: The new program can easily be changed to handle virtually any number of prizes, whereas the old program couldn't.

Susan: So there is more than one way to write a program that does basically the same thing?

Steve: As many ways as there are to write a book about the same topic.

Susan: I find this to be very odd. I mean, on one hand the code seems to be so unrelentingly exact; on the other, it can be done in as many ways as there are artists to paint the same flower. That must be where the creativity comes in. Then I would expect that the programs should behave in different manners, yet accomplish the same goal.

Steve: It's possible for two programs to produce similar (or even exactly the same) results from the user's perspective and yet work very differently internally. For example, the vectorized version of the weighing program could produce exactly the same final results as the original version, even though the method of finding the top two weights was quite different.

Problem
Algorithms
C++
Executable
Hardware

Now we can refer to the individual elements of the vector called Weight by using their numbers, enclosed in **square brackets** ([ ]); the number in the brackets is called the **index**. Here are some examples:

```
Weight[1] = 123;
Weight[2] = 456;
Weight[3] = Weight[1] + Weight[2];
Weight[i+1] = Weight[i] + 5;⁵
```

As these examples indicate, an element of a vector can be used anywhere a "regular" variable can be used.[6] But the most valuable difference between a regular variable and an element of a vector is that we can vary which element we are referring to in a given statement, by varying its index. Take a look at the last sample line, in which two elements of the vector Weight are used; the first one is element i+1 and the other is element i. As this indicates, we don't

---

5. By the way, if you're wondering how to pronounce Weight[i], it's "weight sub i". "Sub" is short for **subscript**, which is an old term for "index".

6. What I'm calling a *regular variable* here is technically known as a **scalar variable**; that is, one with only one value at any given time.

have to use a constant value for the element number but can calculate it while the program is executing; in this case, if i is 0, the two elements referred to are element 1 and element 0, while if i is 5, the two elements are elements 6 and 5, respectively.

The ability to refer to an element of a vector by number rather than by name allows us to write statements that can refer to any element in a vector, depending on the value of the index variable in the statements. To see how this works in practice, let's look at Figure 4.5, which solves our three-prize problem.

```
#include <iostream.h>
#include "vector.h"

int main()
{
    vector<short> Weight(5);
    vector<short> SortedWeight(3);
    short HighestWeight;
    short HighestIndex;
    short i;
    short k;

    cout << "I'm going to ask you to type in five weights, in pounds." << endl;

    for (i = 0; i < 5; i ++)
        {
        cout << "Please type in weight #" << i+1 << ": ";
        cin >> Weight[i];
        }

    for (i = 0; i < 3; i ++)
        {
        HighestWeight = 0;
        for (k = 0; k < 5; k ++)
            {
            if (Weight[k] > HighestWeight)
                {
                HighestWeight = Weight[k];
                HighestIndex = k;
                }
            }
        SortedWeight[i] = HighestWeight;
        Weight[HighestIndex] = 0;
        }

    cout << "The highest weight was: " << SortedWeight[0] << endl;
    cout << "The second highest weight was: " << SortedWeight[1] << endl;
    cout << "The third highest weight was: " << SortedWeight[2] << endl;

    return(0);
};
```

Problem
Algorithms
C++
Executable
Hardware

Figure 4.5: Using a vector (code\vect1.cc)

To run this program normally, just change to the normal subdirectory under the main directory where you installed the software, and type vect1. It will ask you for 5 weights and display the highest 3 of them.

To run the program under gdb, make sure you are in the normal subdirectory, then type trace vect1. The program will start up and show you the first line of executable code. Type z and hit ENTER to execute each line of the program. The values of k, i, HighestIndex, HighestWeight, Weight, and SortedWeight will be displayed below the line that is to be executed next. When you are asked for a weight, type one in and hit ENTER just as when executing normally. After you've entered 5 weights, the program will start the sorting process. When the sorted results have been displayed (or when you're tired of tracing the program), type q (for *quit*) and hit ENTER to exit from the debugger.

This program uses several new features of C++ which need some explanation. First, of course, there is the line that defines the vector Weight:

```
vector<short> Weight(5);
```

Problem
Algorithms
C++
Executable
Hardware

As you might have guessed, this means that we want a vector of five elements, each of which is a short. As we have already seen, this means that there are five distinct index values each of which refers to one element. However, what isn't so obvious is what those five distinct index values actually are. You might expect them to be 1, 2, 3, 4 and 5; actually, they are 0, 1, 2, 3, and 4.

This method of referring to elements in a vector is called **zero-based indexing**.[7] Although it might seem arbitrary to start

---

7. Here's an interesting side note on a case where the inventors of a commonly used facility should have used zero-based indexing, but didn't. We're still suffering from the annoyances of this one.

Long ago, there was no standard calendar, with year numbers progressing from one to the next, when January 1st came around. Instead, years were numbered relative to the reign of the current monarch; for example, the Bible might refer to "the third year of Herod's reign". This was fine in antiquity, when most people really didn't care what year it was. There were few retirement plans or 50th wedding anniversaries to celebrate anyway. However, it was quite annoying to historians to try to calculate the age of someone who was born in the fourth year of someone's reign and died in the tenth year of someone else's. According to Grolier's Multimedia Encyclopedia:

'About AD 525, a monk named Dionysius Exiguus suggested that years be counted from the birth of Christ, which was designated AD (anno Domini, "the year of the Lord") 1. This proposal came to be adopted throughout Christendom during the next 500 years. The year before AD 1 is designated 1 BC (before Christ).'

The encyclopedia doesn't state when the use of the term BC started, but the fact that its translation is English is a suspicious sign indicating that this was considerably later. In any event, this numbering system made matters considerably easier. Now, you could tell that

counting at 0 rather than at 1, assembly language programmers find it perfectly natural, because the calculation of the address of an element is simpler with such indexing; the formula is "(address of first element) + (element number) * (size of element)".

This bit of history is relevant because C, the predecessor of C++, was originally intended to replace assembly language so that programs could be moved from one machine architecture to another with as little difficulty as possible. One reason for some of the eccentricities of C++ is that it has to be able to replace C as a "portable assembly language" that doesn't depend on any specific machine architecture. This explains, for example, the great concern of the inventor of C++ for run-time efficiency, as he wished to allow programmers to avoid the use of C or assembly language for efficiency.[8] Since C++ was intended to replace C completely, it has to be as efficient as possible; otherwise, programmers might switch back from C++ to C whenever they were concerned about the speed and size of their programs.

The last two lines in the variable definition phase define two variables, called i and k, which have been traditional names for **index variables** (i.e., variables used to hold indexes) since at least the invention of FORTRAN in the 1950s. The inventors of FORTRAN

Problem
Algorithms
C++
Executable
Hardware

---

someone who was born in AD 1200 and died in AD 1250 was approximately 50 years old at death.

Unfortunately, however, there was still a small problem. Zero hadn't yet made it to Europe from Asia when the new plan was adopted, so the new calendar numbered the years starting with 1, rather than 0; that is, the year after 1 BC was 1 AD. While this may seem reasonable, it accounts for a number of oddities of our current calendar:

1. Date ranges spanning AD and BC are hard to calculate, since you can't just treat BC as negative. For example, if someone were born in 1 BC and died in 1 AD, how old was that person? You might think that this could be calculated as 1 – (–1), or 2; however, the last day of 1 BC immediately preceded the first day of 1 AD, so the person might have been only a few days old.
2. The 20th century consists of the years 1901 to 2000; the year numbers of all but the last year of that century actually start with the digits *19* rather than *20*.
3. Similarly, the third millennium starts on January 1, 2001, not 2000.

The reason for the second and third of these oddities is that since the first century started in 1 AD, the second century had to start in 101 AD; if it started in 100 AD, the first century would have consisted of only 99 years (1–99), rather than 100.

If only they had known about the zero. Then the zeroth century would have started at the beginning of 0 AD and ended on the last day of 99 AD. The first century would have started at 100 AD, and so on; coming up to current time, we would be living through the last years of the 19th century, which would be defined as all of those years whose year numbers started with *19*. The second millennium would start on January 1, 2000, as everyone would expect.

8. *Run-time efficiency* means the amount of time a program takes to run, as well as how much memory it uses. These issues are very significant when writing a program to be sold to or used by others, as an inefficient program may be unacceptable to the users.

used a fairly simple method of determining the type of a variable: if it began with one of the letters I through N, it was an integer. Otherwise, it was a **floating-point variable** (i.e., one that can hold values that contain a fractional part, such as 3.876). This rule was later changed so that the user could specify what type the variable was, as we do in C++, but the default rules were the same as in the earlier versions of FORTRAN, to allow programs using the old rules to continue to compile and run correctly.

Needless to say, Susan had some questions about the names of index variables:

> **Susan**: So whenever you see i or k you know you are dealing with a vector?

> **Steve**: Not necessarily. Variables named i and k are commonly used as indexes, but they are also used for other purposes sometimes.

> **Susan**: Anyway, if i and k are sometimes used for other purposes, then the compiler doesn't care what you use as indexes? Again, no rules? Just customs?

> **Steve**: Right.

```
Problem
Algorithms
C++
Executable
Hardware
```

I suspect one reason for the durability of these short names is that they're easy to type, and many programmers aren't very good typists.[9] In C++, the only remnant of this FORTRAN tradition of assigning letters I through N to start the names of integral variables is that i, j, k, m and n are used as indexes.[10]

---

9. I strongly recommend learning how to type (i.e., touch type). I was a professional programmer without typing skills for over 10 years before agreeing to type (someone else's) book manuscript. At that point, I decided to teach myself to touch-type, so I wrote a *Dvorak keyboard* driver for my Radio Shack Model III computer and started typing. In about a month I could type faster than with my previous two finger method and eventually got up to 80+ words per minute on English text. If you've never heard of the Dvorak keyboard, it's the one that has the letters laid out in an efficient manner; the "home row" keys are AOEUIDHTNS rather than the absurd set ASDFGHJKL;. This "new" (1930s) keyboard layout reduces effort and increases speed and accuracy compared to the old QWERTY keyboard, which was invented in the 1880s to prevent people from typing two keys in rapid succession and jamming the typebars together. This problem has been nonexistent since the invention of the Selectric typewriter (which uses a ball rather than type bars) in the 1960s, but inertia keeps the old layout in use even though it is very inefficient.

In any event, since I learned to type, writing documentation has required much less effort. This applies especially to writing articles or books, which would be a painful process otherwise.

10. By the way, the reason that l (the letter "ell") isn't used very much for this purpose is that it looks too much like a 1 (the numeral one); the compiler doesn't get confused by this resemblance, but programmers very well might.

After the variable definitions are out of the way, we can proceed to the executable portion of our program. First, we type out a note to the user, stating what to expect. Then we get to the code in Figure 4.6.

```
for (i = 0; i < 5; i ++)
    {
    cout << "Please type in weight #" << i+1 << ": ";
    cin >> Weight[i];
    }
```

Figure 4.6: Using a for statement (from code\vect1.cc)

The first line here is called a for **statement**, which is used to control a for **loop**; this is a loop control facility similar to the while *loop* we encountered in Chapter 3. The difference between these two statements is that a for loop allows us to specify more than just the condition under which the **controlled block** will be repetitively executed.[11] A for statement specifies three expressions (separated by ";") that control the execution of the for loop: a starting expression, a continuation expression, and a modification expression. In our case, these are i = 0, i < 5, and i ++, respectively. Let's look at the function and meaning of each of these components.

First, the **starting expression**, i = 0. This is executed once before the block controlled by the for statement is executed. In this case, we use it to set our index variable, i, to 0, which will refer to the first element of our Weight vector.

Next, the **continuation expression**, i < 5. This specifies under what conditions the statement controlled by the for will be executed; in this case, we will continue executing the controlled statement as long as the value of i is less than 5. Be warned that the continuation expression is actually executed *before* every execution of the controlled block; thus, if the continuation expression is false when the loop is entered, the controlled block will not be executed at all.

The notion of the continuation expression is apparently confusing to some novices. Susan fell into that group.

> **Susan**: In your definition of for, how come there is no ending expression? Why is it only a modification expression? Is there never a case for a conclusion?

Problem
Algorithms
C++
Executable
Hardware

---

11. You may sometimes see the term *controlled statement* used in place of *controlled block*; since as we have already seen a block can be used anywhere that a single statement can be used, *controlled statement* and *controlled block* are actually just two ways of saying the same thing.

Steve: The "continuation expression" tells the compiler when you want to continue the loop; if the continuation expression comes out false, then the loop terminates. That serves the same purpose as an "ending expression" might, but in reverse.

Finally, let's consider the **modification expression**, i ++.[12] This is exactly equivalent to i = i + 1, which means "set i to one more than its current value", an operation technically referred to as **incrementing a variable**. You may wonder why we need two ways to say the same thing; actually, there are a few reasons. One is that ++ requires less typing, which as we know isn't a strong point of many programmers; also, the ++ (pronounced "plus plus") operator doesn't allow the possibility of mistyping the statement as, for example, i = j + 1; when you really meant to increment i. Another reason why this feature was added to the C language is that, in the early days of C, compiler technology wasn't very advanced, and the ++ operator allowed the production of more efficient programs. You see, many machines can add one to a memory location by a single machine language instruction, usually called something like *increment memory*. Even a simple compiler can generate an "increment memory" instruction as a translation of i ++, while it takes a bit more sophistication for the compiler to recognize i = i + 1 as an increment operation. Since incrementing a variable is a very common operation in C++, this was worth handling specially.[13]

Now that we have examined all the parts of the for statement, we can see that its translation into English would be something like this:

1.   Set the index variable i to 0.
2.   If the value of i is less than 5, execute the following block (in this case, the block with the cout and cin statements). Otherwise, skip to the next statement after the end of the controlled block; that is, the one following the closing }.
3.   Add one to the value of i and go back to step 2.

Susan didn't think these steps were very clear. Let's listen in on the conversation that ensued:

Problem
Algorithms
C++
Executable
Hardware

---

12. You don't need a space between the variable name and the ++ operator; however, I think it's easier to read this way.

13. By the way, the name C++ is sort of a pun using this notation; it's supposed to mean "the language following C". In case you're not doubled over with laughter, you're not alone. I guess you had to be there.

Susan: Where in the for statement does it say to skip to the next statement after the end of the controlled block when i is 5 or more?

Steve: It doesn't have to. Remember, the point of {} is to make a group of statements act like one. A for statement always controls exactly one "statement", which can be a block contained in {}. Therefore, when the continuation expression is no longer true, the next "statement" to be executed is whatever follows the } at the end of the block.

Susan: Okay, now I get it. The {} curly brackets work together with the < 5 to determine that the program should go on to the next statement.

Steve: Right.

Susan: Now, on the "controlled block" — so other statements can be considered controlled blocks too? I mean is a controlled block basically just the same thing as a block? I reviewed your definition of *block*, and it seems to me that they are. I guess it is just a statement that in this case is being controlled by for.

Steve: Correct. It's called a *controlled block* because it's under the control of another statement.

Susan: So if we used while before the {} then that would be a while controlled block?

Steve: Right.

Susan: Then where in step 3 or in i++ does it say to go back to step 2?

Steve: Again, the for statement executes one block (the *controlled block*) repeatedly until the continuation expression is false. Since a block is equivalent to one statement, the controlled block can also be referred to as the *controlled statement*. In the current example, the block that is controlled by the for loop consists of the four lines starting with the opening { on the next line after the for statement itself and ending with the closing } after the line that says cin << Weight[i];.

Susan: Okay. But now I am a little confused about something else here. I thought that cout statements were just things that you would type in to be seen on the screen.

Steve: That's correct, except that cout is a variable used for I/O, not a statement.

Susan: So then why is << i+1 << put in at this point? I understand what it does now but I don't understand why it is where it is.

Problem
Algorithms
C++
Executable
Hardware

Steve: Because we want to produce an output line that varies depending on the value of i. The first time, it should say

    Please enter weight #1:

The second time, it should say

    Please enter weight #2:

and so on. The number of the weight we're asking for is one more than i; therefore we insert the expression << i + 1 << in the output statement so that it will stick the correct number into the output line at that point.

Susan: How does << i+1 << end up as #1 ?

Steve: The first time, i is 0; therefore, i + 1 is 1. The # comes from the end of the preceding part of the output statement.

Now let's continue with the next step in the description of our for loop, the modification expression i ++. In our example, this will be executed five times. The first time, i will be 0, then 1, 2, 3, and finally 4. When the loop is executed for the fifth time, i will be incremented to 5; therefore, step 2 will end the loop by skipping to the next statement after the controlled block.[14] A bit of terminology is useful here: Each time through the loop is called an *iteration*.

Let's hear Susan's thoughts on this matter.

Problem
Algorithms
C++
Executable
Hardware

Susan: When you say that "step 2 will end the loop by skipping to the next statement after the controlled block", does that mean it is now going on to the next for statement? So when i is no longer less than 5, the completion of the loop signals the next controlled block?

Steve: In general, after all the iterations in a loop have been performed, execution proceeds to whatever statement follows the controlled block. In this case, the next statement is indeed a for statement, so that's the next statement that is performed after the end of the current loop.

The discussion of the for statement led to some more questions about loop control facilities and the use of parentheses:

Susan: How do you know when to use () ? Is it only with if and for and while and else and stuff like that, whatever these statements are called? I mean they appear to be modifiers of some sort; is there a special name for them?

---

14. In case you're wondering why the value of i at the end of this loop will be 5, the reason is that at the end of each pass through the loop, the modification expression (i ++) is executed before the continuation expression that determines whether the next execution will take place (i < 5). Thus, at the end of the fifth pass through the loop, i is incremented to 5 and then tested to see if it is still less than 5. Since it isn't, the loop terminates at that point.

Steve: The term **loop control** applies to statements that control loops that can execute controlled blocks a (possibly varying) number of times; these include for and while. The if and else statements are somewhat different, since their controlled blocks are executed either once or not at all. The () are needed in those cases to indicate where the controlling expression(s) end and the controlled block begins. You can also use () to control the order of evaluation of an arithmetic expression: The part of the expression inside parentheses is executed first, regardless of normal ordering rules. For example, 2*5+3 is 13, while 2*(5+3) is 16.

Susan: So then if you just wrote while CurrentWeight > 0 with no () then the compiler couldn't read it?

Steve: Correct.

Susan: Actually it is beginning to look to me as I scan over a few figures that almost everything has a caption of some sort surrounding it. Everything either has a " " or () or {} or [] or <> around it. Is that how it is going to be? I am still not clear on the different uses of () and {}; does it depend on the control loop?

Steve: The {} are used to mark the controlled block, while the () are used to mark the conditional expression(s) for the if, while, for, and the like. Unfortunately, () also have other meanings in C++, which we'll get to eventually. The inventor of the language considers them to have been overused for too many different meanings, and I agree.

Susan: OK, I think I have it: {} define blocks and () define expressions. How am I to know when a new block starts? I mean if I were doing the writing, it would be like a new paragraph in English, right? So are there any rules for knowing when to stop one block and start another?

Steve: It depends entirely on what you're trying to accomplish. The main purpose of a block is to make a group of statements act like one statement; therefore, for example, when you want to control a group of statements by one if or for, you group those statements into a block.

Problem
Algorithms
C++
Executable
Hardware

Now that we've examined the for statement in excruciating detail, what about the block it controls? The first statement in the block:

```
cout << "Please type in weight #" << i+1 << ": ";
```

doesn't contain anything much we haven't seen before; it just displays a request to enter a weight. The only difference from previous uses we've made of the cout facility is that we're inserting a numeric expression containing a variable, i+1, into the output. This causes the expression to be translated into a human-readable form consisting of digits. All of the expressions being sent to cout in one statement are strung together to make one line of output, if we don't specify otherwise. Therefore, when this statement is executed during the first iteration of the loop, the user of this program will see:

Please type in weight #1:

Then the user will type in the first weight. The same request, with a different value for the weight number, will show up each time the user hits ENTER, until five values have been accepted.

The second statement in the controlled block,

cin >> Weight[i];

is a little different. Here, we're reading the number the user has typed in at the keyboard and storing it in a variable. But the variable we're using is different each time through the loop: it's the ith element of the Weight vector. So, on the first iteration, the value the user types in will go into Weight[0]; the value accepted on the second iteration will go into Weight[1]; and so on, until on the fifth and last iteration, the typed-in value will be stored in Weight[4].

Here's Susan's take on this.

Problem
Algorithms
C++
Executable
Hardware

Susan: What do you mean by the ith element? So does Weight[i] mean you are directing the number that the user types in to a certain location?

Steve: Yes, to the element whose number is the current value of i.

Susan: When you say cin >> Weight[i] does that mean you are telling the computer to place that variable in the index? So this serves two functions, displaying the weight the user types in and associating it to the index?

Steve: No, that statement tells the computer to place the value read in from the keyboard into element i of vector Weight.

Susan: What I am confusing is what is being seen on the screen at the time that the user types in the input. So, the user sees the number on the screen but then it isn't displayed anywhere after that number is entered? Then, the statement cin >> weight [i] directs it to a location somewhere in memory with a group of other numbers that the user types in?[15]

---

15. This will be illustrated under the contents of Weight heading in Figure 4.8.

Steve: Correct.

A Sorted Tale

Now that we have stored all of the weights, we want to find the three highest of the weights. We'll use a sorting algorithm called a **selection sort**, which can be expressed in English as follows:

1. Repeat the following steps three times, once through for each weight that we want to select:
2. Search through the list (i.e., the Weight vector), keeping track of the highest weight seen so far in the list and the index of that highest weight.
3. When we get to the end of the list, copy the highest weight we've found to the current element of another list (the "output list", which in this case is the vector SortedWeight). The index i of the current element in the output list is equal to the number of times we have been through the loop before; that is, the true highest weight, which we will identify first, goes in position 0 of the output list, the next highest in position 1, and so forth.
4. Finally, set the highest weight we've found in the original list to 0, so we won't select it as the highest value again on the next pass through the list.

Let's take a look at the portion of our C++ program that implements this sort, in Figure 4.7.

```
for (i = 0; i < 3; i ++)
    {
    HighestWeight = 0;
    for (k = 0; k < 5; k ++)
        {
        if (Weight[k] > HighestWeight)
            {
            HighestWeight = Weight[k];
            HighestIndex = k;
            }
        }
    SortedWeight[i] = HighestWeight;
    Weight[HighestIndex] = 0;
    }
```

Figure 4.7: Sorting the weights (from code\vect1.cc)

Problem
Algorithms
C++
Executable
Hardware

Susan had some interesting comments and questions on this algorithm. Let's take a look at our discussion of the use of the variable i:

Susan: Now I understand why you used the example of i = i + 1; in Chapter 3; before, it didn't make sense why you would do that silly thing. Anyway, now let me get this straight. To say that, in the context of this exercise, means you can keep adding 1 to the value of i? I am finding it hard to see where this works for the number 7, say, or anything above 5 for that matter. So, it just means you can have 4 +1 or + another 1, and so on? See where I am having trouble?

Steve: Remember, a short variable such as i is just a name for a 2-byte area of RAM, which can hold any value between –32768 and +32767. Therefore, the statement i ++; means that we want to recalculate the contents of that area of RAM by adding 1 to its former contents.

Susan: No, that is not the answer to my question. Yes, I know all that<G>. What I am saying is this: I assume that i ++; is the expression that handles any value over 4, right? Then let's say that you have pumpkins that weigh 1, 2, 3, 4, and 5 pounds consecutively. No problem, but what if the next pumpkin was not 6 but say 7 pounds? If at that point, the highest value for i was only 5 and you could only add 1 to it, how does that work? It just doesn't yet have the base of 6 to add 1 to. Now do you understand what I am saying?

Steve: I see the problem. We're using the variable i to indicate which weight we're talking about, not the weight itself. In other words, the first weight is Weight[0], the second is Weight[1], the third is Weight[2], the fourth is Weight[3], and the fifth is Weight[4]. The actual values of the weights are whatever the user of the program types in. For example, if the user types in 3 for the first weight, 9 for the second one, 6 for the third, 12 for the fourth, and 1 for the fifth, then the vector will look like this:

Element	Value
Weight[0]	3
Weight[1]	9
Weight[2]	6
Weight[3]	12
Weight[4]	1

The value of i has to increase by only one each time because it indicates which element of the vector Weight is to store the current value being typed in by the user. Does this clear up your confusion?

Problem
Algorithms
C++
Executable
Hardware

Susan: I think so. Then it can have any whole number value 0 or higher (well, up to 32767); adding the 1 means you are permitting the addition of at least 1 to any existing value, thereby allowing it to increase. Is that it?

Steve: No, I'm not permitting an addition; I'm performing it. Let's suppose i is 0. In that case, Weight[i] means Weight[0], or the first element of the Weight vector. When I add 1 to i, i becomes 1. Therefore, Weight[i] now means Weight[1]. The next execution of i ++; sets i to 2; therefore, Weight[i] now means Weight[2]. Any time an i is used in an expression, for example, Weight[i], i + j, or i + 1 you can replace the i by whatever the current value of i is. The only place where you can't replace a variable such as i by its current value is when it is being modified, as in i ++ or the i in i = j + 1. In those cases, i means the address where the value of the variable i is stored.

Susan: OK, then i is not the number of the value typed in by the user; it is the location of an element in the Weight vector, and that is why it can increase by 1, because of the i ++?

Steve: Correct, except that I would say "that is why it *does* increase by 1". This may just be terminology.

Susan: But in this case it can increase no more than 4 because of the i < 5 thing?

Steve: Correct.

Susan: But it has to start with a 0 because of the i = 0 thing?

Steve: Correct.

Susan: So then cin >> Weight [i] means that the number the user is typing has to go into one of those locations but the only word that says what that location could be is Weight; it puts no limitations on the location in that Weight vector other than when you defined the index variable as short i;. This means the index cannot be more than 32767.

Steve: Correct. The current value of i is what determines which element of Weight the user's input goes into.

Susan: I think I was not understanding this because I kept thinking that i was what the user typed in and we were defining its limitations. Instead we are telling it where to go.

Steve: Correct.

Problem
Algorithms
C++
Executable
Hardware

Having beaten that topic into the ground, let's look at the correspondence between the English description of the algorithm and the code:

1. Repeat the following steps once through for each prize:

    for (i = 0; i < 3; i ++)

    (During this process the variable i is the index into the SortedWeight vector where we're going to store the weight for the current prize we're working on. While we're looking for the highest weight, i is 0; for the second-highest weight, i is 1; finally, when we're getting ready to award a third prize, i will be 2.)

2. Search through the input list. For each element of the list Weight, we check whether that element (Weight[k]) is greater than the highest weight seen so far in the list (HighestWeight). If that is the case, then we reset HighestWeight to the value of the current element (Weight[k]) and the index of the highest weight so far (HighestIndex) to the index of the current element (k).

Problem
Algorithms
C++
Executable
Hardware

3. When we get to the end of the input list, HighestWeight is the highest weight in the list, and HighestIndex is the index of that element of the list that had the highest weight. Therefore, we can copy the highest weight to the current element of another list (the "output list"). As mentioned earlier, i is the index of the current element in the output list. Its value is the number of times we have been through the outer loop before; that is, the highest weight, which we will identify first, goes in position 0 of the output list, the next highest in position 1, and so on:

    SortedWeight[i] = HighestWeight;

4. Finally, set the highest weight in the input list to 0, so we won't select it as the highest value again on the next pass through the list.

    Weight[HighestIndex] = 0;

    This statement is the reason that we have to keep track of the "highest index"; that is, the index of the highest weight. Otherwise, we wouldn't know which element of the original

Weight vector we've used and have to set to 0 to prevent it's being used again.

Here's Susan's rendition of this algorithm:

Susan: OK, let me repeat this back to you in English. The result of this program is that after scanning the list of user input weights the weights are put in another list, which is an ordering list, named k. The program starts by finding the highest weight in the input list. It then takes it out, puts it in k, and replaces that value it took out with a 0, so it won't be picked up again. Then it comes back to find the next highest weight and does the same thing all over again until nothing is left to order. Actually this is more than that one statement. But is this what you mean? That one statement is responsible for finding the highest weight in the user input list and placing it in k. Is this right?

Steve: It's almost exactly right. The only error is that the list that the weights are moved to is the SortedWeight vector, rather than k. The variable k is used to keep track of which is the next entry to be put into the SortedWeight vector.

Susan: OK. There was also something else I didn't understand when tracing through the program. I did see at one point during the execution of the tracing version of this program that i=5. Well, first I didn't know how that could be because i is supposed to be < 5, but then I remembered that i ++ expression in the for loop, so I wondered if that is how this happened. I forgot where I was at that point, but I think it was after I had just completed entering 5 values and i was incrementing with each value. But see, it really should not have been more than 4 because if you start at 0 then that is where it should have ended up.

Steve: The reason that i gets to be 5 after the end of the loop is that at the end of each pass through the loop, the modification expression (i ++) is executed before the continuation expression (i < 5). So, at the end of the fifth pass through the loop, i is incremented to 5 and then tested to see if it is still less than 5. Since it isn't, the loop terminates at that point.

Susan: I get that. But I still have a question about the statement if Weight[k] > highest weight. Well, the first time through, this will definitely be true because we've initialized HighestWeight to 0, since any weight would be greater than 0. Is that right?

Steve: Yes. Every time through the outer (i) loop, as we get to the top of the inner loop, the 0 that we've just put in HighestWeight should be replaced by the first element of Weight; that is, Weight[0], except of course if we've already replaced Weight[0] by 0 during a previous pass. It would also be possible to initialize HighestWeight to Weight[0] and then

Problem
Algorithms
C++
Executable
Hardware

start the loop by setting k to 1 rather than 0. That would cause the inner (k) loop to be executed only four times per outer loop execution, rather than five, and therefore would be more efficient.

Susan: Then HighestIndex=k; is the statement that sets the placement of the highest number to its rank?

Steve: Right.

Susan: Then I thought about this. It seems that the highest weight is set first, then the sorting takes place so it makes four passes (actually five) to stop the loop.

Steve: The sorting is the whole process. Each pass through the outer loop locates one more element to be put into the SortedWeight vector. Is that what you're saying here?

Susan: Then the statement Weight[HighestIndex] = 0; comes into play, replacing the highest number selected on that pass to 0.

Steve: Correct.

Problem
Algorithms
C++
Executable
Hardware

Susan: Oh, when k is going through the sorting process why does i increment though each pass? It seems that k should be incrementing.

Steve: Actually, k increments on each pass through the inner loop, or 15 times in all. It's reset to 0 on each pass through the outer loop, so that we look at all of the elements again when we're trying to find the highest remaining weight. On the other hand, i is incremented on each pass through the outer loop or three times in all, once for each "highest" weight that gets put into the SortedWeight vector.

Susan: OK, I get the idea with i, but what is the deal with k? I mean I see it was defined as a short, but what is it supposed to represent, and how did you know in advance that you were going to need it?

Steve: It represents the position in the original list, as indicated in the description of the algorithm.

Susan: I still don't understand where k fits into this picture. What does it do?

Steve: It's the index in the "inner loop", which steps through the elements looking for the highest one that's still there. We get one "highest" value every time through the "outer loop", so we have to execute that outer loop three times. Each time through the outer loop, we execute the inner loop five times, once for each entry in the input list.

Susan: Too many terms again. Which is the "outer loop" and which was the "inner loop"?

Steve: The outer loop executes once for each "highest" weight we're locating. Each time we find one, we set it to 0 (at the end of the loop) so that it won't be found again the next time through.

Susan: OK, now I am confused with the statement: if (Weight[k] > HighestWeight). This is what gets me: if I understand this right (and obviously I don't) how could Weight[k] ever be greater than HighestWeight, since every possible value of k represents one of the elements in the Weight vector, and HighestWeight is the highest weight in that vector? For this reason I am having a hard time understanding the code for step 2, but not the concept.

Steve: The value of HighestWeight at any time is equal to the highest weight that has been seen *so far*. At the beginning of each execution of the outer loop, HighestWeight is set to 0. Then, every time that the current weight (Weight[k]) is higher than the current value of HighestWeight, we reset HighestWeight to the value of the current weight.

Susan: I still don't understand this statement. Help.

Steve: Remember that HighestWeight is reset to 0 on each pass through the outer loop. Thus, this if statement checks whether the kth element of the Weight vector exceeds the highest weight we've seen before in this pass. If that is true, obviously our "highest" weight isn't really the highest, so we have to reset the highest weight to the value of the kth element; if the kth element isn't the true highest weight, at least it's higher than what we had before. Since we replace the "highest" weight value with the kth value any time that the kth value is higher than the current "highest" weight, at the end of the inner loop, the number remaining in HighestWeight will be the true highest weight left in Weight. This is essentially the same algorithm as we used to find the highest weight in the original version of this program, but now we apply it several times to find successively lower "highest" weights.

Susan: OK, I understand now, i increments to show how many times it has looped through to find the highest number. You are doing a loop within a loop, really, it is not side by side is it?

Steve: Correct.

Susan: So, when you first enter your numbers they are placed in an index called i, then they are going to be cycled through again, placing them in a corresponding index named k, looking for the top three numbers. To start out through each pass, you first set the highest weight

Problem
Algorithms
C++
Executable
Hardware

to the first weight since you have preset the highest weight to 0. But, to find the top three numbers you have to look at each place or element in the index. At the end of each loop you sort out the highest number and then set that removed element to 0 so it won't be selected again. You do this whole thing three times.

Steve: That's right, except for some terminology: where you say "an index called i", you should say "a vector called Weight", and where you say "an index called k", you should say "a vector called SortedWeight". The variables i and k are used to step through the vectors, but they are not the vectors themselves.

Susan: OK, then the index variables just are the working representation of what is going on in those vectors. But are not the numbers "assigned" an index? Let's see; if you lined up your five numbers you could refer to each number as to its placement in a vector. Could you then have the column of weights in the middle of the two indexes of i and k to each side?

Steve: If I understand your suggestion, it wouldn't work, because k and i vary at different speeds. During the first pass of the outer loop, i is 0, while k varies from 0 to 5; on the second pass of the outer loop, i is 1, while k varies from 0 to 5 again, and the same for the third pass of the outer loop. The value of i is used to refer to an individual element of the SortedWeight vector, the one that will receive the next "highest" weight we locate. The value of k is used to refer to an individual element of the Weight vector, the one we're examining to see if it's higher than the current HighestWeight.

Susan: This is what gets me, how do you know in advance that you are going to have to set HighestIndex to k? I see it in the program as it happens and I understand it then, but how would you know that the program wouldn't run without doing that? Trial and error? Experience? Rule books? <G>

Steve: Logic. Let's look at the problem again. The sorting algorithm that we're using here is called *selection sort*, because each time through the outer loop it selects one element out of the input vector and moves it to the output vector. To prevent our selecting the same weight (i.e., the highest one in the original input) every time through the outer loop, we have to clear each weight to 0 as we select it. But, to do that, we have to keep track of which one we selected; that's why we need to save HighestIndex.

Being a glutton for punishment, Susan brought up the general problem of how to create an algorithm in the first place.

Problem
Algorithms
C++
Executable
Hardware

Susan: Do they make instruction sheets with directions of paths to follow? How do you identify problems? I mean, don't you encounter pretty much the same types of problems frequently in programming and can they not be identified some way so that if you knew a certain problem could be categorized as a Type C problem, let's say, you would approach it with a Type C methodology to the solution? Does that make sense? Probably not.

Steve: It does make sense, but for some reason such "handbooks" are rare. Actually, my previous book, *Efficient C/C++ Programming* was designed to provide something like you're suggesting, with solutions to common problems at the algorithmic level. There's also a book called *Design Patterns* that tries to provide tested solutions to common design problems, at a much higher level.

Details, Details

Let's go back and look at the steps of the algorithm more closely.[16] Step 1 should be fairly self-explanatory, once you're familiar with the syntax of the for statement; it causes the statements in its controlled block to be executed three times, with the index variable i varying from 0 to 2 in the process.

Step 2 is quite similar to the process we went through to find the highest weight in our previous two programs; however, the reason for the HighestIndex variable may not be obvious. We need to keep track of which element of the original vector (i.e., Weight) we have decided is the highest so far, so that this element won't be selected as the highest weight on *every* pass through the Weight vector. To prevent this error, step 4 sets each "highest" weight to a value that won't be selected on a succeeding pass. Since we know there should be no 0 weights in the Weight vector, we can set each selected element to 0 after it has been selected, to prevent its reselection. Figure 4.8 shows a picture of the situation before the first pass through the data:[17]

Problem
Algorithms
C++
Executable
Hardware

---

16. They start on page 136.

17. The ??? in SortedWeight indicate that those locations contain unknown data, as they haven't been initialized yet.

Index	contents of Weight	contents of SortedWeight
0	5	???
1	2	???
2	11	???
3	3	
4	7	

Figure 4.8: Initial situation

Here, the highest value is 11 in Weight[2]. After we've located it and copied its value to SortedWeight[0], we set Weight[2] to 0, yielding the situation in Figure 4.9.

Index	contents of Weight	contents of SortedWeight
0	5	11
1	2	???
2	0	???
3	3	
4	7	

Problem
Algorithms
C++
Executable
Hardware

Figure 4.9: After the first pass

Now we're ready for the second pass. This time, the highest value is the 7 in Weight[4]. After we copy the 7 to SortedWeight[1], we set Weight[4] to 0, leaving the situation in Figure 4.10.

Index	contents of Weight	contents of SortedWeight
0	5	11
1	2	7
2	0	???
3	3	
4	0	

Figure 4.10: After the second pass

On the third and final pass, we locate the 5 in Weight[0], copy it to SortedWeight[2], and set Weight[0] to 0. As you can see in Figure 4.11, SortedWeight now has the results we were looking for: the top three weights, in descending order.

Index	contents of Weight	contents of SortedWeight
0	0	11
1	2	7
2	0	5
3	3	
4	0	

Figure 4.11: Final situation

To Err Is Human. . .

That accounts for all of the steps in the sorting algorithm. However, our implementation of the algorithm has a weak spot that we should fix. If you want to try to find it yourself, look at the code and explanation again before going on. Ready?

The key word in the explanation is "should" in the following sentence: "Since we know there *should* be no 0 weights in the Weight vector, we can set each selected element to 0 after it has been selected, to prevent its reselection." How do we *know* that there are no 0 weights? We don't, unless we screen for them when we accept input. In the first pumpkin-weighing program, we stopped the input when we got a 0, but in the programs in this chapter, we ask for a set number of weights. If one of them is 0, the program will continue along happily.[18] Before we change the program, though, let's try to figure out what would happen if the user types in a 0 for every weight.

You can try this scenario out yourself. To run it, just change to the normal subdirectory under the main directory where you installed the software, and type vect1. When it asks for weights, enter a 0 for each of the five weights. In case you're reading this away from your computer, here's what will happen (although the element number in the message may not be the same):

You have tried to use element 51082 of a vector which has only 5 elements.

Why doesn't the program work in this case? Because we have an **uninitialized variable**; that is, one that has never been set to a valid

Problem
Algorithms
C++
Executable
Hardware

---

18. For that matter, what if someone types in a negative weight, such as −5? Of course, this doesn't make any sense, but it's a good idea to try to prevent errors, rather than assuming that users of a program will always act sensibly.

value. In this case, it's HighestIndex. Let's look at the sorting code one more time, in Figure 4.12.[19]

```
for (i = 0; i < 3; i ++)
    {
    HighestWeight = 0;
    for (k = 0; k < 5; k ++)
        {
        if (Weight[k] > HighestWeight)
            {
            HighestWeight = Weight[k];
            HighestIndex = k;
            }
        }
    SortedWeight[i] = HighestWeight;
    Weight[HighestIndex] = 0;
    }
```

Figure 4.12: Sorting the weights, again (from code\vect1.cc)

Problem
Algorithms
C++
Executable
Hardware

It's clear that HighestWeight is **initialized** (i.e., given a valid value) before it is ever used; the statement HighestWeight = 0; is the first statement in the block controlled by the outer for loop. However, the same is not true of HighestIndex. Whenever the condition in the if statement is true, both HighestWeight and HighestIndex will indeed be set to legitimate values: HighestWeight will be the highest weight seen so far on this pass, and HighestIndex will be the index of that weight in the Weight vector. However, what happens if the condition in the if statement never becomes true? In that case, HighestIndex will have whatever random value it started out with at the beginning of the program; it's very unlikely that such a value will be correct or even refer to an actual element in the Weight vector.

Here's the discussion that Susan and I had on this topic:

Susan: You say that HighestIndex isn't initialized properly. But what about when you set k equal to 0 and then HighestIndex is set equal to k? Is that not initialized?

---

19. You may have noticed a slight oddity in this code. The block controlled by the for statement consists of exactly one statement; namely, the if that checks for a new HighestWeight value. According to the rules I've provided, that means we don't have to put curly braces ({}) around it to make it a block. While this is true, long experience has indicated that it's a very good idea to make it a block anyway, as a preventive measure. It's very common to revisit old code to fix bugs or add new functions, and in so doing we might add another statement after the if statement at a later time, intending it to be controlled by the for. The results wouldn't be correct, since the added statement would be executed exactly one time after the loop was finished, rather than once each time through the loop. Such errors are very difficult to find, because the code looks all right when inspected casually; therefore, a little extra caution when writing the program in the first place often pays off handsomely.

Steve: The problem is that the statement HighestIndex = k; is executed only when Weight[k] is greater than HighestWeight. If that never occurs, then HighestIndex is left in some random state.

Susan: OK, then why didn't you say so in the first place? I understand that. However, I still don't understand why the program would fail if all the weights the user typed in were 0. To me it would just have a very boring outcome.

Steve: That's the case in which HighestIndex would never be initialized; therefore, it would contain random garbage and would cause the program to try to display an element at some random index value.

Susan: I traced through the program again briefly tonight and that reminds me to ask you why you put the highest weight value to 1596 and the second-highest weight value to 1614?

Steve: I didn't. Those just happened to be the values that those memory locations had in them before they were initialized.

Susan: I was totally confused right from the beginning when I saw that. But did you do that to show that those were just the first two weights, and that they have not been, how would you say this, "ordered" yet? I don't know the language for this in computerese, but I am sure you know what I am saying.

Steve: Not exactly; they haven't been initialized at that point, so whatever values they might contain would be garbage.

Susan: So at that point they were just the first and second weights, or did you just arbitrarily put those weights in there to get it started? Anyway, that was baffling when I saw that.

Steve: Before you set a variable to a particular value, it will have some kind of random junk in it. That's what you're seeing at the beginning of the program, before the variables have been initialized.

Susan: OK, I am glad this happened, I can see this better, but whose computer did that? Was it yours or mine? I mean did you run it first and your computer did it, or was it my computer that came up with those values?

Steve: It's your computer. The program starts out with "undefined" values for all of the uninitialized variables. What this means in practice is that their values are whatever happened to be left around in memory at those addresses. This is quite likely to be different on your machine from what it is on mine or even on yours at a different time.

Problem
Algorithms
C++
Executable
Hardware

Susan: So something has to be there; and if you don't tell it what it is, the old contents of memory just comes up?

Steve: Right.

Susan: If it had worked out that the higher number had been in first place, then I would have just assumed that you put that there as a starting point. I am really glad that this happened but I was not too happy about it when I was trying to figure it out.

Steve: See, it's all for your own good.

Susan: If that were the case, I would think it nearly impossible that we have the same values at any given address. How could they ever be remotely the same?

Steve: It's very unlikely that they would, unless the address were one that was used by very basic software such as DOS or Windows, which might be the same on our computers.

Susan: Anyway, then you must have known I was going to get "garbage" in those two variables, didn't you? Why didn't you advise me at least about that? Do you know how confusing it was to see that first thing?

Problem
Algorithms
C++
Executable
Hardware

Steve: Yes, but it's better for you to figure it out yourself. Now you really know it, whereas if I had told you about it in advance, you would have relied on my knowledge rather than developing your own.

I hope that has cleared up the confusion about the effect of an uninitialized variable in this example. But, why do we have to initialize variables ourselves? Surely they must have some value at any given time. Let's listen in on the conversation that Susan and I had about this point:

Susan: So, each bit in RAM is capable of being turned on or off by a 1 or a 0? Which one is on and which one is off? Or does that matter? How does this work electronically? I mean how does the presence of a 0 or a 1 throw the RAM into a different electronic state?

Steve: To be more exact, each "switch" is capable of existing in either the "on" or "off" state. The assignment of states to 1s and 0s is our notion, which doesn't affect the fact that there are exactly two distinct states the switch can assume, just like a light switch (without a dimmer). We say that if the switch is off, it's storing a 0, and if it's on, it's storing a 1.

Susan: What is the "normal state" of RAM: on or off?

Steve: It's indeterminate. That's one reason why we need to explicitly set our variables to a known state before we use them.

Susan: That didn't make sense to me originally, but I woke up this morning and the first thing that came to my mind was the light switch analogy. I think I know what you meant by *indeterminate*.

If we consider the light switch as imposed with our parental and financial values, it is tempting to view the "normal state" of a light switch as off. Hey, does the light switch really care? It could sit there for 100 years in the on position as easily as in the off position. Who is to say what is normal? The only consequence is that the light bulb will have been long burned out. So it doesn't matter, it really doesn't have a normal state, unless people decide that there is one.

Steve: What you've said is correct. The switch doesn't care whether it's on or off. In that sense, the "normal" position doesn't really have a definition other than one we give it.

However, what I meant by *indeterminate* is slightly different: When power is applied to the RAM, each bit (or to be more precise, a switch that represents that bit) could just as easily start out on as off. It's actually either one or the other, but which one is pretty much random, so we have to set it to something before we know its value.

Susan: Oh, you broke my heart, when I thought I had it all figured out! Well, I guess it was OK, at least as far as the light switch was concerned, but then RAM and a light switch are not created equal. So RAM is pretty easy to please, I guess. . .

Problem
Algorithms
C++
Executable
Hardware

After that bit of comic relief, let's get back to the analysis of this program. It should be fairly obvious that if the user types in even one weight greater than 0, the if statement will be true when that weight is encountered, so the program will work. However, if the user typed in all 0 weights, the program would fail, as we saw before, because the condition in the if statement would never become true. To prevent this from causing program failure, all we have to do is to add one more line, the one in **bold** in Figure 4.13.

```
for (i = 0; i < 3; i ++)
    {
    HighestWeight = 0;
    HighestIndex = 0;
    for (k = 0; k < 5; k ++)
        {
        if (Weight[k] > HighestWeight)
            {
            HighestWeight = Weight[k];
            HighestIndex = k;
            }
        }
    SortedWeight[i] = HighestWeight;
    Weight[HighestIndex] = 0;
    }
```

Figure 4.13: Sorting the weights, with correct initialization (from code\vect2.cc)

Now we can be sure that HighestIndex always has a value that corresponds to some element of the Weight vector, so we won't see the program fail as the previous one would. To check this, you can run the corrected program by typing vect2 at the DOS prompt in the normal subdirectory. This time, entering five 0 weights will produce the expected result: The top three weights will all be 0.

To run the program under gdb, make sure you are in the normal subdirectory, then type trace vect2. The program will start up and show you the first line of executable code. Type z and hit ENTER to execute each line of the program. The values of k, i, HighestIndex, HighestWeight, Weight, and SortedWeight will be displayed below the line that is to be executed next. When you are asked for a weight, type one in and hit ENTER just as when executing normally. After you've entered 5 weights, the program will start the sorting process. When the sorted results have been displayed (or when you're tired of tracing the program), type q (for *quit*) and hit ENTER to exit from the debugger.

By the way, it's also possible to initialize a variable at the same time as you define it. For example, the statement short i = 12; defines a short variable called i and sets it to the value 12 at the same time. This is generally a good practice to follow when possible; if you initialize the variable when you define it, you don't have to remember to write a separate statement to do the initialization.

To Really Foul Things up Requires a Computer

We should pay some more attention to the notion of program failure, as it's very important. The first question, of course, is what it means to say that a program "fails". The best answer is that it doesn't work correctly, but that isn't very specific.

As you can imagine, this notion was the topic of some discussion with Susan:

> **Susan**: What do you mean by a program failing? I know it means it won't work, but what happens? Do you just get error messages, and it won't do anything? Or is it like the message that you have on page 143?

> **Steve**: In general, a program "failing" means that it does something unexpected and erroneous. Because I have put some safety features into the implementation of vector, you'll get an error message if you misuse a vector by referring to a nonexistent element.

In general, a program failure may or may not produce an error message. In the specific case that we've just seen, we'll probably get an error message while trying to access a nonexistent element of the Weight vector. However, it's entirely possible for a program to just "hang" (run endlessly), "crash" your system, produce an obviously ridiculous answer, or worst of all, provide a seemingly correct but actually erroneous result.

The causes of program failures are legion. A few of the possibilities are these:

Problem
Algorithms
C++
Executable
Hardware

1. Problems isolated to our code

    a. The original problem could have been stated incorrectly.
    b. The algorithm(s) we're using could have been inappropriate for the problem.
    c. The algorithm(s) might have been implemented incorrectly.
    d. The input to the program might be outside the expected range.

    And so on. . .

2. Problems interacting with other programs

a.   We might be misusing a function supplied by the system, like the << operator.
b.   The documentation for a system function might be incorrect or incomplete. This is especially common in "guru"-oriented operating systems, where the users are supposed to know everything.
c.   A system function might be unreliable. This is more common than it should be.
d.   The compiler might be generating the wrong instructions. I've seen this on a few rare occasions.
e.   Another program in the system might be interfering with our program. This is quite common in some popular operating environments that allow several programs to be executing concurrently.[20]

And so on. . .

With a simple program such as the ones we're writing here, errors such as the ones listed under problems with the code are more likely, as we have relatively little interaction with the rest of the system. As we start to use more sophisticated mechanisms in C++, we're more likely to run into instances of interaction problems.

Problem
Algorithms
C++
Executable
Hardware

What, Me Worry?

After that excursion into the sources of program failure, let's get back to our question about about initializing variables. Why do we have to worry about this at all? It would seem perfectly reasonable for the compiler to make sure that our variables were always initialized to some reasonable value; in the case of numeric variables such as a short, 0 would be a good choice. Surely Bjarne Stroustrup, the designer of C++, didn't overlook this.

No, he didn't; he made a conscious decision not to provide this facility. It's not due to cruelty or unconcern with the needs of programmers. On the contrary, he stated in the Preface to the first Edition of *The C++ Programming Language* that "C++ is a general-purpose programming language designed to make programming more enjoyable for the serious programmer".[21] To

---

20. Especially those whose names begin with "W".

21. *The C++ Programming Language, 2nd Edition.* v.

allow C++ to replace C completely, he could not add features that would penalize efficiency for programs that do not use these features. Adding initialization as a built-in function of the language would make programs larger and slower, even if they were already careful to initialize all of their variables. This may not be obvious, but we'll see in a later section why it is so.

Here's Susan's reaction to these points about C++:

Susan: What is run-time efficiency?

Steve: How long it takes to run the program and how much memory it uses up.

Susan: So are you saying that C++ is totally different from C? That one is not based on the other?

Steve: No, C++ is a descendant of C. However, C++ provides much more flexibility to programmers than than C.

Susan: Now, about what Bjarne said back in 1986: Who enjoys this, and if C++ is intended for a serious programmer, why am I reading this book? What is a serious programmer? Would you not think a serious programmer should have at least taken Computer Programming 101?

Steve: This book should be a pretty good substitute for Computer Programming 101. You probably know considerably more than the usual graduate of such a course, although the e-mail tutoring has been a major contributor to your understanding. Anyway, if you want to learn how to program, you have to start somewhere, and it might as well be with the intention of being a serious programmer.

Garbage in, Garbage Out

In the meantime, there's something else we should do if we want the program to work as it should. As the old saying "Garbage in, garbage out" suggests, by far the best solution to handling spurious input values is to prevent them from being entered in the first place. What we want to do is to check the input value and warn the user if it's invalid. Figure 4.14 illustrates a new input routine that looks like it should do the trick.

Problem
Algorithms
C++
Executable
Hardware

```
for (i = 0; i < 5; i ++)
  {
  cout << "Please type in weight #" << i+1 << ": ";
  cin >> Weight[i];
  if (Weight[i] <= 0)
    {
    cout << "I'm sorry, " << Weight[i] << " is not a valid weight.";
    cout << endl;
    }
  }
```

Figure 4.14: Garbage prevention, first attempt (from code\vect2a.cc)

To run this program normally, just change to the normal subdirectory under the main directory where you installed the software, and type vect2a. It will ask you for 5 weights and display the highest 3 of them.

To run the program under gdb, make sure you are in the normal subdirectory, then type trace vect2a. The program will start up and show you the first line of executable code. Type z and hit ENTER to execute each line of the program. The values of k, i, HighestIndex, HighestWeight, Weight, and SortedWeight will be displayed below the line that is to be executed next. When you are asked for a weight, type one in and hit ENTER just as when executing normally. After you've entered 5 weights, the program will start the sorting process. When the sorted results have been displayed (or when you're tired of tracing the program), type q (for *quit*) and hit ENTER to exit from the debugger.

Most of this should be familiar; the only line that has a new construct in it is the if statement. The condition <= means "less than or equal to", which is reasonably intuitive.

Unfortunately, this program won't work as we intended. The problem is what happens after the error message is displayed; namely, the loop continues at the top with the next weight, and we never correct the erroneous input. Susan wanted to know exactly what that last statement meant:

> **Susan**: When you say that "we never correct the erroneous input", does that mean that it is added to the list and not ignored?

> **Steve**: Right.

To fix this problem completely, we need to use the approach shown in the final version of this program (Figure 4.15).

Problem
Algorithms
C++
Executable
Hardware

```
#include <iostream.h>
#include "vector.h"

int main()
{
    vector<short> Weight(5);
    vector<short> SortedWeight(3);
    short HighestWeight;
    short HighestIndex;
    short i;
    short k;

    cout << "I'm going to ask you to type in five weights, in pounds." << endl;

    for (i = 0; i < 5; )
        {
        cout << "Please type in weight #" << i+1 << ": ";
        cin >> Weight[i];
        if (Weight[i] <= 0)
            {
            cout << "I'm sorry, " << Weight[i] << " is not a valid weight.";
            cout << endl;
            }
        else
            i ++;
        }

    for (i - 0; i < 3; i ++)
        {
        HighestIndex = 0;
        HighestWeight = 0;
        for (k = 0; k < 5; k ++)
            {
            if (Weight[k] > HighestWeight)
                {
                HighestWeight = Weight[k];
                HighestIndex = k;
                }
            }
        SortedWeight[i] = HighestWeight;
        Weight[HighestIndex] = 0;
        }

    cout << "The highest weight was: " << SortedWeight[0] << endl;
    cout << "The second highest weight was: " << SortedWeight[1] << endl;
    cout << "The third highest weight was: " << SortedWeight[2] << endl;

    return(0);
};
```

Problem
Algorithms
C++
Executable
Hardware

Figure 4.15: Finding the top three weights using vectors (code\vect3.cc)

To run this program normally, just change to the normal subdirectory under the main directory where you installed the software, and type vect3. It will ask you for 5 weights and display the highest 3 of them.

To run the program under gdb, make sure you are in the normal subdirectory, then type trace vect3. The program will start up and show you the first line of executable code. Type z and hit ENTER to execute each line of the program. The values of k, i, HighestIndex, HighestWeight, Weight, and SortedWeight will be displayed below the line that is to be executed next. When you are asked for a weight, type one in and hit ENTER just as when executing normally. After you've entered 5 weights, the program will start the sorting process. When the sorted results have been displayed (or when you're tired of tracing the program), type q (for *quit*) and hit ENTER to leave the debugger.

Now let's look at the changes that we've made to the program from the last revision. The first change is that the for loop has only two sections rather than three in its control definition (inside the ()). As you may recall, the first section specifies the initial condition of the index variable; in this case, we're starting i out at 0, as is usual in C and C++. The second section indicates when we should continue executing the loop; here, it's as long as i is less than 5. But the third section, which usually indicates what to do to the index variable, is missing. The reason for this is that we're going to adjust the index variable manually in the loop, depending on what the user enters.

In this case, if the user enters an invalid value (i.e., less than or equal to 0), we display an error message and leave i as it was, so that the next time through the loop, the value will go into the same element in the Weight vector. When the user enters a valid value, the else clause increments i so that the next value will go into the next element in the vector. This fixes the error in our previous version that left incorrect entries in the vector.

Now that we have beaten the pumpkin weighing example to a pulp,[22] let's review the mass of information to which I've subjected you so far in this chapter.

Problem
Algorithms
C++
Executable
Hardware

Review

We started out by extending our pumpkin weighing program to tell us the highest two weights rather than just the highest one. During

---

22. Pumpkin pie, anyone?

this exercise, we learned the use of the else clause of an if statement. We also saw that making even an apparently simple change to a working program can introduce an error; in this case we were copying the highest weight to the next highest weight only when a new high weight was detected. This would produce an incorrect result if a value higher than the previous second highest but lower than the current highest weight were entered.

Next we extended the program again, this time to handle any number of prizes to be given to the highest weight, second-highest weight, third-highest weights, and so on. This required a complete reorganization of the program; the new version used the *selection sort* algorithm to produce a list of as many of the highest weights as we need, in descending order. To do this, we had to use a vector, or set of values with a common name, to store all of the weights as they were read in. When they had all been entered, we searched through them three times, once to find each of the top three elements. A vector, just like a regular variable, has a name. However, unlike a regular variable, a vector does not have a single value, but rather consists of a number of *elements*, each of which has a separate value. An element is referred to by a number, called an *index*, rather than by name; each element has a different index. The lowest index is 0, and the highest index is 1 less than than the number of elements in the vector; for example, with a 10 element vector, the legal indexes are 0 through 9. The ability to refer to an element by its index allows us to vary the element we are referring to in a statement by varying the index; we used this facility to good use in our implementation of the selection sort, which we'll review shortly.

Problem
Algorithms
C++
Executable
Hardware

We then added the for statement to our repertoire of loop control facilities. This statement provides more precise control than the while statement. Using for, we can specify a *starting expression*, a *continuation expression*, and a *modification expression*. The starting expression sets up the initial conditions for the loop. Before each possible execution of the controlled block, the continuation expression is checked, and if it is true, the controlled block will be executed; otherwise, the for loop will terminate. Finally, the modification expression is executed after each execution of the controlled block. Most commonly, the starting expression sets the initial value of a variable, the continuation expression tests whether that variable is still in the range we are interested in, and the modification expression changes the value of the variable. For example, in the for statement

```
for (i = 0; i < 5; i ++)
```

the starting expression is i = 0, the continuation expression is i < 5, and the modification expression is i ++. Therefore, the block controlled by the for statement will be executed first with the variable i set to 0; at the end of the block, the variable i will be incremented by 1, and the loop will continue if i is still less than 5.

Then we used the for statement and a couple of vectors to implement a *selection sort*. This algorithm goes through an "input list" of n elements once for each desired "result element". In our case, we want the top three elements of the sorted list, so the input list has to be scanned three times. On each time through, the algorithm picks the highest value remaining in the list and adds that to the end of a new "output list". Then it removes the found value from the input list. At the end of this process, the output list has all of the desired values from the input list, in descending order of size. When going over the program, we found a weak spot in the first version: If all the weights the user typed were less than or equal to 0, the program would fail because one of the variables in the program would never be *initialized*; that is, set to a known value.

This led to a discussion of why variable initialization isn't done automatically in C++. Adding this feature to programs would make them slower and larger than C programs doing the same task, and C++ was intended to replace C completely. If C++ programs were significantly less efficient than equivalent C programs, this would not be possible, so Bjarne Stroustrup (the designer of C++) omitted this feature.

Problem
Algorithms
C++
Executable
Hardware

While it's important to insure that our programs work correctly even when given unreasonable input, it's even better to prevent this situation from occurring in the first place. So the next improvement we made to our pumpkin weighing program was to tell the user when an invalid value had been entered and ask for a valid value in its place. This involved a for loop without a modification expression, since we wanted to increment the index variable i to point to the next element of the vector only when the user typed in a valid entry; if an illegal value was typed in, we requested a legal value for the same element of the vector.

Exercises

So that you can test your understanding of this material, here are some exercises.

1. If the program in Figure 4.16 is run, what will be displayed?

```cpp
#include <iostream.h>
#include "vector.h"
int main()
{
    vector<short> x(5);
    short Result;
    short i;
    for (i = 0; i < 5; i ++)
        {
        x[i] = 2 * i;
        }
    for (i = 0; i < 5; i ++)
        {
        Result = Result + x[i];
        }
    cout << Result << endl;
    return 0;
}
```

Figure 4.16: Exercise 1 (code\morbas00.cc)

2. If the program in Figure 4.17 is run, what will be displayed?

```cpp
#include <iostream.h>
#include "vector.h"
int main()
{
    vector<short> x(4);
    short Result;
    short i;
    x[0] = 3;
    for (i = 1; i < 4; i ++)
        x[i] = x[i-1] * 2;
    Result = 0;
    for (i = 0; I < 4; i ++)
        Result = Result + x[i];
    cout << Result << endl;
    return 0;
}
```

Problem
Algorithms
C++
Executable
Hardware

Figure 4.17: Exercise 2 (code\morbas01.cc)

3. Write a program that asks the user to type in a weight, and display the weight on the screen.
4. Modify the program from exercise 3 to ask the user to type as many weights as desired, stopping as soon as a 0 is entered. Add up all of the weights entered and display the total on the screen at the end of the program.

Answers to exercises can be found at the end of the chapter.

Conclusion

We've covered a lot of material in this chapter in our quest for better pumpkin weighing, ranging from sorting data into order based on numeric value through the anatomy of vectors. Next, we'll take up some more of the language features you will need to write any significant C++ programs.

Answers to Exercises

```
Problem
Algorithms
C++
Executable
Hardware
```

1. The correct answer is: "Who knows?" If you said "30", you forgot that the loop variable values are from 0 through 4, rather than from 1 through 5. On the other hand, if you said "20", you had the right total of the numbers 0, 2, 4, 6, and 8, but didn't notice that the variable Result was never initialized. Of course, adding anything to an unknown value makes the final value unpredictable. Most current compilers, including the one on the CD-ROM in the back of this book, are capable of warning you about such problems; if you compiled the program with this warning turned on, you'd see a message something like this:

    morbas00.cc:7: warning: 'short result' may be used uninitialized in this function.

    This is the easiest way to find such errors, especially in a large program. Unfortunately, the compiler may produce such warnings even when they are not valid, so the final decision is still up to you.

      Running this program normally isn't likely to give you much information. To run the program under gdb, make sure you are in the normal subdirectory, then type trace morbas00. The program will start up and show you the first line of executable code. Type z and hit ENTER to execute each line of the program; the values of x[i], i, and Result will be displayed immediately before the execution of each line. When the results have been displayed (or when you're tired of tracing the program), type q (for *quit*) and hit ENTER to exit from the debugger.

2. The correct answer is 45. In case this isn't obvious, consider the following:

    a. The value of x[0] is set to 3.
    b. In the first for loop, the value of i starts out at 1.
    c. Therefore, the first execution of the assignment statement x[i] = x[i−1] * 2; is equivalent to x[1] = x[0] * 2;. This clearly sets x[1] to 6.
    d. The next time through the loop i is 2, so that same assignment statement x[i] = x[i−1] * 2; is equivalent to x[2] = x[1] * 2;. This sets x[2] to 12.
    e. Finally, on the last pass through the loop, the value of i is 3, so that assignment statement x[i] = x[i−1] * 2; is equivalent to x[3] = x[2] * 2; This sets x[3] to 24.
    f. The second for loop just adds up the values of all the entries in the x vector; this time, we remembered to initialize the total, Result, to 0, so the total is calculated and displayed correctly.

    Problem
    Algorithms
    C++
    Executable
    Hardware

    Running this program normally isn't likely to give you much information, but you might want to run it under control of the gdb debugger. You can do this in exactly the same way as you did the previous program, except that you would type trace morbas01 rather than trace morbas00.

3. Let's start with Susan's proposed solution to this problem, in Figure 4.18, and the questions that she came up during the process.

```
#include <iostream.h>

int main()
{
    short weight;

    cout << "Please write your weight here. "\n;
    cin >> weight

    return 0;
};
```

Figure 4.18: Weight requesting program, first try (code\morbas02.cc)

Susan: Would this work? Right now by just doing this it brought up several things that I have not thought about before.

First, is the # standard for no matter what type of program you are doing?

Steve: The iostream.h header file is needed if you want to use <<, >>, cin and cout, which most programs do, but not all.

Susan: Ok, but I meant the actual pound sign (#), is that always a part of iostream.h?

Steve: It's not part of the filename, it's part of the #include command, which tells the compiler that you want it to pretend that you've just typed in the entire iostream.h file in your program at that point.

Susan: So then this header is declaring that all you are going to be doing is input and output?

Steve: Not exactly. It tells the compiler how to understand input and output via << and >>. Each header tells the compiler how to interpret some type of library functions; iostream.h is the one for input and output.

Problem
Algorithms
C++
Executable
Hardware

Susan: Where is the word iostream derived from? (OK, io, but what about stream?)

Steve: A stream is C++ talk for "a place to get or put characters". A given stream is usually either an istream (input stream) or an ostream (output stream). As these names suggest, you can read from an istream or write to an ostream.

Susan: Second, is the \n really necessary here, or would the program work without it?

Steve: It's optional; however, if you want to use it, the \n should be inside the quotes, since it's used to control the appearance of the output. It can't do that if it's not sent to cout. Without the \n, the user would type the answer to the question on the same line as the question; with the \n, the answer would be typed on the next line, as the \n would cause the active screen position to move to the next line at the end of the question.

Susan: OK, that is good, since I intended for the weight to be typed on a different line. Now I understand this much better. As far as why I didn't include the \n inside the quotes, I can't tell you other than the time of night I was writing or it was an oversight or a typo. I was following your examples and I am not a stickler for details type person.

Now that that's settled, I have another question: Is "return 0" the same thing as an ENTER on the keyboard with nothing left to process?

Steve: Sort of. It means that you're done with whatever processing you were doing and are returning control to the operating system (the C: prompt).

Susan: How does the program handle the ENTER? I don't see where it comes into the programs you have written. It just seems that at the end of any pause that an ENTER would be appropriate. So is the ENTER something that is part of the compiler that it just knows that by the way the code is written an ENTER will necessarily come next?

Steve: The istream input mechanism lets you type until you hit an ENTER, then takes the result up to that point.
   One more point. We never tell the user that we have received the information. I've added that to your example.

Figure 4.19 illustrates the compiler's output for that erroneous program:

```
morbas02.cc: In function 'int main()':
morbas02.cc:7: stray '\' in program
morbas02.cc:11: parse error before 'return'
```

Problem
Algorithms
C++
Executable
Hardware

Figure 4.19: Error messages from the erroneous weight program (code\morbas02.cc)

And Figure 4.20 shows the corrected program.

```
#include <iostream.h>

int main()
{
    short weight;

    cout << "Please write your weight here.\n ";
    cin >> weight;
    cout << "I wish I only weighed " << weight << " pounds.\n";

    return 0;
};
```

Figure 4.20: The corrected weight program (code\morbas03.cc)

4.   This was an offshoot of the previous question, which occurred when Susan wondered whether the program in Figure 4.20 would terminate. Let's start from that point in the conversation:

Susan: Would this only run once? If so how would you get it to repeat?

Steve: We could use a for loop controlled only by a continuation expression. Let's suppose that we wanted to add up all the weights that were entered. Then the program might look like Figure 4.21.

```
#include <iostream.h>
main()
{
    short weight;
    short total;

    total = 0;
    for (; weight > 0; )
        {
        cout << "Please type in your weight, typing 0 to end:";
        cin >> weight;
        total += weight;
        }

    cout << "The total is: " << total << endl;
    return 0;
}
```

Figure 4.21: The weight totalling program (code\morbas04.cc)

Problem
Algorithms
C++
Executable
Hardware

Susan: But wouldn't for (;Weight > 0;) mean it is a partial vector? Since you didn't declare a vector, I don't understand how this works. I would understand if you wrote while (weight > 0) now (so this is how you repeat, only with loops?) but writing for like this confuses me.

Steve: The statement for (; weight > 0;) means exactly the same as while (weight > 0). That is, there's no initial expression and no modification expression; therefore, the loop will continue as long as weight > 0. See, you only thought you didn't understand this.

There's only one other thing about this program that you haven't seen before: the += operator. This is a relative of ++, the increment operator, and means "add what's on the *right* to what's on the *left*". In this case, result += input[i]; means exactly the same as result = result + input[i];. The motivation for this shortcut, as you might imagine, is the same as that for ++: It requires less typing, is more likely to be correct, and is easier to compile to efficient code. Just like the "increment memory" instruction, many machines have an "add (something) to memory" instruction, and it's easier to figure out that such an instruction should be used for an expression like x += y than in the case of the equivalent x = x + y.

Let's see what Susan has to say about this notation:

Susan: Now I did find something that was very confusing. You say that += means to "add what's on the right to what's on the left" but your example shows that it is the other way around. Unless this is supposed to be mirror imaged or something, I don't get it.

Steve: No, the example is correct. total += weight; is the same as total = total + weight;, so we're adding the value on the right of the += (i.e., weight) to the variable on the left (i.e., total). Is that clearer now?

Susan: OK, I think I got it now, I guess if it were more like an equation, you would have to subtract total from the other side when you moved it. Why is it that the math recollection that I have instead of helping me just confuses me?

Steve: Because, unfortunately, the = is the same symbol used to mean "is equal to" in mathematics. The = in C++ means something completely different: "set the thing on the left to the value on the right".

Running this program normally isn't likely to give you much information, so you might want to run it under control of the gdb debugger. You can do this in exactly the same way as you did the previous two programs, except that you would type trace moibas04 to start.

Problem
Algorithms
C++
Executable
Hardware

Chapter 5

Functional Literacy

Form Follows Function

C++ was intended to be useful in writing large programs. Such programs are usually composed of many source code files, or *source code modules*, as I mentioned in Chapter 3.

In such a case, we must have some way of creating an executable program (sometimes abbreviated to just an *executable*) from a number of source code modules. We also need some way for code in one module to refer to code in another one. Similarly, we have to be able to specify where execution of our program should start; this is taken care of by the C++ rule that execution always starts at the block called main.

As we've already seen, the computer can't execute source code. Therefore, any source code modules we write have to be translated into object code; the result of such translation is an object code module. One other kind of module we're interested in is the library module, which contains the object code from several source code modules. Here's a list of these different kinds of modules, with a little more detail:

1. A **source code module** is a file that contains source code for a program. Almost every part of every program starts out as a source code module.
2. Compilation of a source code module produces a file called an **object code module** (or **object file**), which contains object (machine) code.
3. Several object code modules of a generally useful nature can be combined to make a file called a **library module**, usually abbreviated to **library**.

The idea of various types of modules led to the following discussion with Susan:

Susan: So an object file is like some kind of interface between your code and the binary numbers of the machine? I am confused. Is this describing how a compiler works? I was wondering about that.

Steve: Each source code file is translated by the compiler into one object file. Then these object files will be combined along with some previously prepared library files, to make an executable program.

Susan: iostreams is a library? So are these like already written programs that you can refer to like a real library?

Steve: Yes.

Susan: The libraries contain code segments that are generalized, and the other modules contain code segments that are program specific?

Steve: Right, except that a library contains object code, not source code.

Susan: Where is the library? I am serious.

```
Problem
Algorithms
C++
Executable
Hardware
```

Steve: You can have more than one library, including ones written for more specialized purposes by different companies. The main library for the djgpp compiler is in a file called libgpp.a. However, the name of the main library file is dependent on which compiler you're using; in some cases, the library code is broken down into more than one file.

Susan: So what is a "source code module"? Is it a set of code written by the programmer?

Steve: It's a file containing part of a program, in source code. Most significant programs consist of a number of modules, rather than one big one (file), partly because it's easier to find and edit one logical segment of a program than a whole bunch of code all in one big file.

Susan: Okay then, so a module is just a big logical segment? How is it delineated from the rest of the program? Is it named? How do you find it? Can you just tell by looking where a module starts and ends?

Steve: A module, in C++ terminology, is a file. Therefore, a source code module is a source code file, which contains program statements. It has a name, which is the name of the file. I think the rest of the answers to your questions on this topic should be obvious from this definition; if not, please let me know.

Susan: So a source code module is like a library, only as we have discussed it is more specific than a library; it is for the program that you are working on?

Steve: Right.

Susan: Where are these modules and how do they get there?

Steve: Wherever you (or whoever wrote the code) put them. In the case of your "weight-writing" program, the code you wrote is in a source code module. That module is compiled to make an object code module, which is then combined with other object code modules that I have written, and library module(s) that come with the compiler, to make an executable file that can be run.

Susan: So then the source code module is a "miniprogram" within a program that holds the source code to be later compiled?

Steve: It contains part of the source code of a program, which needs to be compiled and combined with other previously compiled code before it can be used. I think that's the same as what you're saying.

Actually, I've misused C++ terminology a little here in the interests of comprehensibility. The term *block* isn't quite correct as applied to main(); the correct term is *function*. Let's take a look at the difference between these two concepts, some other related definitions, and the objectives for this chapter.

Problem
Algorithms
C++
Executable
Hardware

Definitions

A *block* is a section of code that acts like one statement, as far as the language is concerned; that is, wherever a statement can occur, a block can be substituted, and it will be treated as one statement for the purposes of program organization.

A **function** is also a section of code, but its characteristics are different from those of a block. For one thing, you can't substitute a function for a statement; also, a function has a name, whereas blocks are anonymous. This name enables one function to start execution of another one.

A **function call** (or just "call" for short) causes execution to be transferred temporarily from the current function to the one named in the call.

A **called function** is a function that starts execution as a result of a function call.

A **calling function** is a function that suspends execution as a result of a function call.

A return **statement** is the mechanism used by a called function to return to the calling function, which picks up just where it left off.

Objectives of This Chapter

By the end of this chapter, you should

1. Understand how and when to use functions to reduce the amount of code you have to write,
2. Understand what software really is,
3. Understand how your source code is turned into an executable program,
4. Understand how storage is assigned to different types of variables,
5. Understand how functions can call one another.

Functioning Normally

```
Problem
Algorithms
C++
Executable
Hardware
```

Susan had a question about this new notion of a function, as related to modules:

Susan: So a module has nothing to do with blocks and functions? If a function only "calls" another function, then how do you call a module?

Steve: The main idea of a module is to keep related functions together so they are easier to find and modify together. Some language features apply to modules rather than functions but they don't amount to much.

When we call a function, we usually have to provide it with input (for example, some values to be averaged) and it usually produces output which we use in further processing (for example, the average of the input values). Some functions, though, have only one or the other. For example, some pairs of functions consist of one **storage function** and one **retrieval function**; the first stores data for the second to retrieve later. In that case, the storage function may not give us anything back when we call it, and the retrieving function may not need any input from us.

To see how and why we might use a function, let's take a look at a program having some duplicated code (Figure 5.1).

```
#include <iostream.h>

int main()
{
    short FirstWeight;
    short SecondWeight;
    short FirstAge;
    short SecondAge;
    short AverageWeight;
    short AverageAge;

    cout << "Please type in the first weight: ";
    cin >> FirstWeight;

    cout << "Please type in the second weight: ";
    cin >> SecondWeight;

    AverageWeight = (FirstWeight + SecondWeight) / 2;

    cout << "Please type in the first age: ";
    cin >> FirstAge;

    cout << "Please type in the second age: ";
    cin >> SecondAge;

    AverageAge = (FirstAge + SecondAge) / 2;

    cout << "The average weight was: " << AverageWeight << endl;
    cout << "The average age was: " << AverageAge << endl;

    return(0);
};
```

```
Problem
Algorithms
C++
Executable
Hardware
```

Figure 5.1: A sample program with duplicated code (code\nofunc.cc)

I'd like you to look particularly at this line,

```
    AverageWeight = (FirstWeight + SecondWeight) / 2;
```

and this one,

```
    AverageAge = (FirstAge + SecondAge) / 2;
```

These two lines are awfully similar; the only difference between them is that one of them averages two weights and the other averages two ages. While this particular example doesn't take too much code to duplicate, it may not be too difficult for you to imagine the inefficiency and nuisance of having to copy and edit many lines of code every time we want to do exactly the same thing with different data. Instead of copying the code and editing it to change the name of the variables, we can write a function that averages whatever data we give it.

Figure 5.2 is a picture of a function call.

```
short Average(short First, short Second)        (3)

{

    short Result;

    Result = (First + Second) / 2;

    return Result;                               (4)

}
```

```
                                                (1)
int main()

{

    short i;

    short j;

    short k;

    i = 5;

    j = 6;

    k = Average(i,j);                           (2)

    cout << k << endl;                          (5)

    return 0;

}
```

Problem
Algorithms
C++
Executable
Hardware

Figure 5.2: A function call

The calling function **(1)** is main; the function call is at position **(2)**. The called function is Average **(3)**, and the return is at position **(4)**; the returned value is stored in the variable k, as indicated by the assignment operator = in the statement k = Average(i,j); and the calling function, main, resumes execution at line **(5)**.[1]

In case you're wondering why we started the example at the beginning of main, it's because every C++ program starts executing at that point. When the main function calls another function, such as Average, then main is suspended until Average is finished. When Average finishes, main resumes where it left off.

This isn't limited to one "level" of calls. The same thing can happen if Average (for example) calls another function, let's say Funcx; Average will wait until Funcx returns before continuing. Then when Average finishes, it will return to main, which will take up where it left off.

This idea of calling and returning from functions led to the following discussion with Susan:

> **Susan**: So if you wanted to be really mean you could get into someone's work in progress and stick a return somewhere in the middle of it and it would end the program right there? Now that I am thinking about it, I am sure you could do a whole lot worse than that. Of course, I would never do such a thing, but what I am saying is that whatever you are doing when the program gets to the return statement, then it is *the end*? Next stop, C:\?

> **Steve**: If you're in the main program, then a return statement means "back to the C:\ prompt". If you're in a function other than main, it means "back to the function that called this function". In the case of a function that returns a value, the expression in the return statement tells the compiler what value to use in place of the function call. For example, the statement x = Average(i,j); sets x to the result in the return statement of the function Average. As you can see by looking at that function, the returned value is the average of the two input values, so that is the value that x is set to by this statement.

> **Susan**: OK, but what about the return 0; at the end of the main program? Why should it be 0?

Problem
Algorithms
C++
Executable
Hardware

---

1. If you provide no return statement, then the called function will just return to the calling function when it gets to its closing }. However, this is not legal for a function that is defined to return a value and is considered to be poor form even for those functions that return no value. This of course leads to the question of why we'd call a function that doesn't return a value. One possibility is that the function exists only to produce output on the screen, rather than to return any results. The actions that a function performs other than returning a value are called **side effects**.

Steve: The return statement in the main program can return a different value if you wish. However, the custom is to return 0 from the main program to mean "everything went well" and some value greater than 0 to mean "there's a problem". This isn't entirely arbitrary. A batch file can test that return value and use it to alter the flow of execution of commands in the batch file.

Susan: OK, let's see if I have this right: The return statement has to match the main statement. This is so confusing. Look, when you say "The value that is returned, 0, is an acceptable value of the type we declared in the line int main () — since I see no 0 anywhere around int main () — you are referring to the int. An int can have a value of 0, right?

Steve: Right, the 0 has to match the int. That's because a function can have a return type, just like the type of a variable. In this case, int is the type of the main function, and the value is filled in by the return statement.

Susan: OK, then all this is saying is that the value that is produced is the same type as that declared at the beginning of a program. Since we declared the type of main as an int, if the value produced were a letter or a picture of a cow, then you would get an error message?

Problem
Algorithms
C++
Executable
Hardware

Steve: Well, actually a letter (i.e., a char) would be acceptable as an int, due to rules left over from C. Otherwise, you're exactly correct.

Susan: Hey, where is the 0 coming from to be returned?

Steve: It's specified as a literal value in the return statement; you could put any legal int value in there instead, if you wanted to.

Susan: So the return value doesn't have to be a 0?

Steve: Right.

Susan: So 0 could be another int value, but it can't be a variable? Even I don't know what I am talking about now!

Steve: I think I've confused you unnecessarily. You can certainly return a value that is specified as a variable, such as return i;. What I meant was that the 0 we're returning in this case is a constant, not a variable.

Susan: The picture helps with the calling confusion. But I don't understand why int main is the calling function if the calling function suspends execution. How can you initiate a function if it starts out suspended? But I am serious.

Steve: The main function starts execution as the first function in your program. Therefore, it isn't suspended unless and until it calls another function.

Above Average

I think it's time for a more detailed example of how we would use a function. Suppose we want to average sets of two numbers and we don't want to write the averaging code more than once. The Average function just illustrated provides this service; its input is the two numbers we want to average, and its output is the average. Figure 5.3 shows the code for the function Average without all the lines and arrows:

```
short Average(short First, short Second)
{
      short Result;

      Result = (First + Second) / 2;

      return Result;
}
```

Figure 5.3: A function to average two values

If you want to see this function used in a running program, you can.[2] For the normal version, change to the normal subdirectory and type func1; when it asks you to type a number in, type one in and hit ENTER. To run it under gdb, make sure you are in the normal subdirectory, then type trace func1. The program will start up and show you the first line of executable code. Type z and hit ENTER to execute each line. The values of all the variables in main will be displayed immediately before the execution of each line in that function. When you get to the end of the program (or when you're tired of tracing), type q (for *quit*) and hit ENTER to exit from the debugger.[3]

Problem
Algorithms
C++
Executable
Hardware

---

2. If you want to see the whole program that this function is used in, it's in Figure 5.5.

3. Please don't be confused by the seemingly random values that all of the variables start out with when tracing the program. These are just the garbage values that happen to be lying around in memory where those variables reside; as we've already seen, variables that haven't yet been assigned a value are called *uninitialized variables*. The variables in this program are all initialized before they are used, but the tracing program starts to display them before the initializing statements have been executed; therefore, they appear uninitialized at the

As had become routine, I couldn't sneak this idea (of writing a function) past Susan without a discussion.

> **Susan:** Where you say "and we don't want to write the averaging code more than once." Are you just saying if you didn't do the Average function thing then you would have to write this program twice? I mean for example would you have to write a program separately for weights and then another one from the beginning for ages?
>
> **Steve:** We wouldn't have to write an entirely separate program; however, we would have to write the averaging code twice. One of the main purposes for writing a function is so that we don't have to repeat code.

To analyze this piece of code, let's start at the beginning. Every function starts with a **function declaration**, which tells the compiler some vital statistics of the function. The function declaration consists of three parts:

1. A return type;
2. The function's name;
3. An argument list.

In the case of our Average function, the function declaration is short Average(short First, short Second). The return type is short, the name of the function is Average, and the argument list is (short First, short Second). Let's take these one at a time.

```
Problem
Algorithms
C++
Executable
Hardware
```

Return to Sender

The first part of the function declaration is the **return type**, in this case short. This indicates that the function Average will provide a value of type short to the calling function when the Average function returns. Looking at the end of the function, you will see a statement that says return Result;. Checking back to the variable definition part of the function, we see that Result is indeed a short, so the value we're returning is of the correct type. If that were not the case, the compiler would tell us that we have a discrepancy between the declared return type of our function and the type actually returned in the code. This is another example where the compiler helps us out with static type

beginning of the trace. We'll see later in this chapter exactly why we have to initialize all of our variables before we use them.

checking, as mentioned in Chapter 3; if we say we want to return a short and then return some other incompatible type such as a string, we've made a mistake.[4] It's much easier for the compiler to catch this and warn us than it is for us to locate the error ourselves when the program doesn't work correctly.

Susan wanted to know more about the return type. Here's the conversation that ensued:

> **Susan**: This return type thing — it will have to be the same type of value as the output is?

> **Steve**: For our purposes here, the answer is yes. As I've already mentioned, there are exceptions to this rule, but we won't need to worry about them.

> **Susan**: Is the word return always a part of the code when you use a function?

> **Steve**: Yes, except that some functions have no return value. They don't have to have an explicit return statement, but can just "fall off the end" of the function, which acts like a return; statement. This is considered poor form, though; it's better to have a return statement.

The function name (in this case, Average) follows the same rules as a variable name. This is not a coincidence, because both function names and variable names are identifiers, which is a fancy word for "user defined names". The rules for constructing an identifier are pretty simple, as specified in the *C++ Draft Standard*: "An identifier is an arbitrarily long sequence of letters and digits. The first character is a letter; the underscore _ counts as a letter. Upper- and lower-case letters are different. All characters are significant." In other words:

1. Your identifiers can be as long as you wish,[5]

Problem
Algorithms
C++
Executable
Hardware

---

4 What do I mean by an *incompatible type*? C++ has rules that, for example, allow us to return a char variable where a short (or an int) is expected; the compiler will convert the char into either of those types for us automatically. This is convenient sometimes, but it reduces the chances of catching an error of this kind, and therefore is less safe than it could be. This practice is a legacy from C, which means that it can't be changed for practical reasons, even though it is less than desirable theoretically.

5. You don't have to worry about wasting space in your program by using long identifiers. They go away when your program is compiled and are replaced by addresses of the variables or functions to which they refer.

2.   They can be made of any combination of letters and digits, as long as the first character is a letter. For historical reasons, the underscore character _ counts as a letter,[6]

3.   The upper and lower case version of the same character aren't considered equal as far as names are concerned; that is, the variable xyz is a different variable from Xyz, while XYZ is yet another variable. Of course, *you* may get confused by having three variables with those names, but the compiler considers them all distinct,

4.   The compiler is required to distinguish between two identifiers, no matter how many identical characters they contain, as long as at least one character is different in the two names.

By the way, the reason that first character of an identifier can't be a digit is to make it easier for the compiler to figure out what's a number and what isn't. Another rule is that user defined names cannot conflict with names defined by the C++ language (keywords); some examples of keywords that we've already seen are if, for, and short.

Problem
Algorithms
C++
Executable
Hardware

Finally, we have the **argument list**. In this case, it contains two arguments, a short called First, which holds the first number that our Average function uses to calculate its result; the second argument (also a short) is called Second, which of course is the other number needed to calculate the average. In other cases, there might be several entries in the argument list, each of which provides some information to the called function. But what exactly *is* an argument?

For the Sake of Argument

The question of what is an argument is more subtle than it may appear. An argument is a value that is supplied by a function (the *calling function*) that wishes to use the services of another function (the *called function*). In this case, the calling function will be our main function, and the called function is our Average function, while the arguments are two short values to be averaged. Arguments like the ones here are actually copies of values from the calling function; that is, the compiler will set the variable named in the argument list of the called function to the value supplied by the calling function.

---

6. You should avoid starting your variable or function names with an underscore, as such names are "reserved" for use by compiler writers and other language implementers.

This process of making a copy of the calling function's argument is referred to as *call by value*, and the resulting copy is called a **value argument**.[7]

Figure 5.4 is an example of this argument passing mechanism at work with only one argument.

```
#include <iostream.h>

short Birthday(short age)
{
    age ++;
    return age;
}

int main()
{
    short x;
    short y;

    x = 46;
    y = Birthday(x);

    cout << "Your age was: " << x << endl;
    cout << "Happy Birthday: your age is now " << y << endl;

    return 0;
}
```

Problem
Algorithms
C++
Executable
Hardware

Figure 5.4: Argument passing with one argument (code\birthday.cc)

In this program, main sets x to 46 and then calls Birthday with x as the argument. When Birthday starts, a new variable called age is created, and set to 46, because that's the value of x, the argument with which main called Birthday. Birthday adds one to its variable age, and then returns the new value of that variable to main. What will be printed by the line cout << x << endl;? Answer: 46, because the variable age in Birthday was a *copy* of the value of the argument from main, not the actual variable x named in the call to Birthday. On the other hand, the value of y in the main program will be 47, because that is the return value from Birthday.

---

7. This discussion might make you wonder whether there's another type of argument besides a value argument. There is, and we'll find out about it in Chapter 7.

As you might have guessed, the notion of copying the argument when a function is called occasioned an intense conversation with Susan.

Susan: This is tough. I don't get it at all. Does this mean the value of the short named x will then be copied to another location in the function named Birthday?

Steve: Yes, the value in the short named x will be copied to another short called age before the execution of the first line in the function Birthday. This means that the original value of x in main won't be affected by anything that Birthday does.

Susan: Now for the really confusing part. I don't understand where you say "An argument like the one here (short age) is actually a copy of a value in the calling function". Now, I have read this over and over and nothing helped. I thought I understood it for a second or two and then I would lose it; finally I have decided that there is very little in this section that I do understand. Help.

Steve: When you write a function, the normal behavior of the compiler is to insert code at the beginning of the function to make a copy of the data that the calling function supplies. This copy of the data is what the called function actually refers to, not the original. Therefore, if you change the value of an argument, it doesn't do anything to the original data in the calling function.

Problem
Algorithms
C++
Executable
Hardware

If you (the programmer of the function) actually want to refer to the data in the calling function and not a copy of it, you can specify this when you write the function. There are cases in which this makes sense, and we'll see some of them in Chapter 7.

Susan: I don't understand why it is a copy of the calling function and not the called function.

Steve: It's not a copy of the calling function; it's a copy of the value from the calling function, for the use of the called function. In the sample program, main sets x to 46 and then calls Birthday with x as the argument. When Birthday starts, a new variable called age is created, and set to 46, because that's the value of x, the argument with which main called Birthday. Birthday adds 1 to its variable age, and returns the new value of age to main. What will be printed by the line "cout << x << endl;"? Answer: 46, because the variable age in Birthday was a *copy* of the value of the argument from main, not the actual variable (x) specified in the call to Birthday. Does this explanation clarify this point?

Susan: I still don't understand the program. It doesn't make any sense. If x = 46, then it will always be 46 no matter what is going on in the called function. So why call a function? You know what, I think my biggest problem is that I don't understand the argument list. I think that is where I am hung up on this.

Steve: The arguments to the function call (x, in the case of the function call Birthday(x)) are transferred to the value of the argument in the function itself (the short variable age, in the case of the function Birthday(short age)).

Susan: In that case, why bother putting an x there, why just not put 46? Would it not do the same thing in the called function, since it is already set to 46?

Steve: Yes, but what if you wanted to call this function from another place where the value was 97 rather than 46? The reason that the argument is a variable is so you can use whatever value you want.

Susan: If we called Birthday with the value 46, then the 46 would be 46++, right?

Steve: 46++ is a syntax error, because you can't change the value of a literal constant. Only a variable can be modified.

Susan: So if you want to state a literal value, do you always have to declare a variable first and then set a variable to that literal value?

Steve: No, sometimes you can use a literal value directly without storing it in a variable. For example,

cout << 15;

or

cout << "Hello, my name is Steve Heller";

What I was trying to say is that you can't *change* a literal value. Thus, 15++; is not legal because a literal value such as 15 represents itself, that is, the value 15. If you could write 15++;, what should it do? Change all occurrences of 15 to 16 in the program?

Susan: I get that. Now, how does age get initialized to the value of x?

Steve: The compiler does that when it starts the function, because you have declared in the function declaration that the argument to the function is called age, and you have called the function with an argument called x. So the compiler copies the value from x into age right before it starts executing the function.

Problem
Algorithms
C++
Executable
Hardware

Susan: Oh, OK. That makes sense, because maybe later on you want to call the same function again and change only a little part of it, but you still need the original to be the same, so you can just change the copy instead of the original. Is that the purpose?

Steve: The reason that the called function gets a copy of data rather than the original is so that the person writing the calling function knows that the original variable hasn't been changed by calling a function. This makes it easier to create programs by combining your own functions with functions that have already been written (such as in the library). Is that what you meant?

Susan: So is everything copied? I am getting confused again, are you going to talk a little more about copying in the book? Have I just not gotten there? Anyway, if you haven't mentioned this more, I think you should, it explains hidden stuff.

Steve: Don't worry, we're going to go into *much* more detail about how this works. It's a major topic in Chapter 7.

General Delivery

```
Problem
Algorithms
C++
Executable
Hardware
```

The same analysis that we have just applied to the Birthday function applies also to the Average function that we started out with; the arguments First and Second are copies of the values specified in the call to Average.

Now that we have accounted for the Average function's input and output, we can examine how it does its work. First, we have a variable definition for Result, which will hold the value we will return to the calling function; namely, the average of the two input values.

Then we calculate that average, with the statement Result = (First + Second) / 2;. Once the average has been calculated, we're ready to return it to the calling program, which is accomplished by the line return Result;. Finally, we reach the closing }, which tells the compiler that the function is done.

Using a Function

Now that we have seen how to write the Average function, let's see how to use it. The program in Figure 5.5 uses our Average function twice, once to average two weights, and once to average two ages.

```
#include <iostream.h>

short Average(short First, short Second)
{
    short Result;

    Result = (First + Second) / 2;

    return Result;
}

int main()
{
    short FirstWeight;
    short SecondWeight;
    short FirstAge;
    short SecondAge;
    short AverageWeight;
    short AverageAge;

    cout << "Please type in the first weight: ";
    cin >> FirstWeight;

    cout << "Please type in the second weight: ";
    cin >> SecondWoight;

    AverageWeight = Average(FirstWeight, SecondWeight);

    cout << "Please type in the first age: ";
    cin >> FirstAge;

    cout << "Please type in the second age: ";
    cin >> SecondAge;

    AverageAge = Average(FirstAge, SecondAge);

    cout << "The average weight was: " << AverageWeight << endl;
    cout << "The average age was: " << AverageAge << endl;

    return(0);
};
```

Problem
Algorithms
C++
Executable
Hardware

Figure 5.5: Using the Average function (code\func1.cc)

As before, calling a function requires specifying its name and its
argument(s) and doing something with the return value, if any. In this
case, we call Average with the arguments FirstWeight and
SecondWeight, and store the result in AverageWeight. This is
accomplished via the line AverageWeight = Average(FirstWeight,
SecondWeight);. Later, we call Average with the arguments FirstAge

and SecondAge, and store the result in AverageAge. We do this via the line AverageAge = Average(FirstAge, SecondAge);.

The value of writing a function to average two numbers wasn't obvious to Susan at first. After some discussion, however, she agreed that it was valuable. Here's the conversation that convinced her:

> **Susan**: In general, I just don't understand why you even need to call the Average function in the first place; it looks like extra steps to me. It seems to me that all you need are your two input values, which end up just giving you the results right there for weight and age. I think that this is what bothers me the most. For example, when you get done with the set of weights, you should just have your results right then and there instead of calling the function of Average.

> **Steve**: But what is the result you want? You want the average of the weights. Where is that calculated?

> **Susan**: After you are done with that, then you already have written a set of ages so you can just use the result of that. It just seems like you are going in circles unnecessarily with this program. That is why I don't understand it.

> **Steve**: Again, just because you have a set of ages doesn't mean that you have the average age; some code somewhere has to calculate that average.

Problem
Algorithms
C++
Executable
Hardware

Susan still had a lot of trouble with visualizing the way this function worked. However, running it in "trace" mode got her moving again, resulting in the following discussion:

> **Susan**: Why does everything starts out initialized to 0 except Result, which appears to hold an address in memory?

> **Steve**: The values of uninitialized variables are not reliable. In this case, I'm getting a similar value of Result to the one you're getting; however, you cannot count on this. There's also no reason to think that the contents of Result are a memory address; they're just garbage until the variable is initialized.

> **Susan**: Steve, I don't understand this; first you tell me that those numbers are garbage but represent addresses in memory and now you tell me that they are just garbage, but that they are not reliable. I don't understand, if they are uninitialized, how they ever *could* be reliable. This implies that at some time you could get an expected value even if they are uninitialized. They should always be garbage. So, when do those numbers represent memory addresses and when not?

Steve: Apparently I've confused you unnecessarily again. Here are the facts:

1. The contents of an uninitialized variable are garbage.
2. Since they are garbage, they represent nothing.
3. Since they are garbage, they can have any value, which may or may not appear to have meaning. Regardless of appearances, the value of an uninitialized variable is meaningless.

Then our discussion returned to the topic of how the main program works:

Susan: Oh, OK, so AverageWeight = Average(FirstWeight, SecondWeight); is the part that starts the Average function running?

Steve: Right.

Susan: Then after averaging the weights, why does Result go to 0? It looks to me that Result has no value at these points and I don't understand why.

Steve: Because you're looking at the next call to Average, where its variable Result is uninitialized again. By default, variables are uninitialized whenever they are created, which occurs each time the function where they "live" is entered. The "old" Result from the first call to Average died when the first call to Average was finished, and the new Result that is created on the second call is uninitialized until we set it to some known value.

Problem
Algorithms
C++
Executable
Hardware

The next topic we discussed was how to create a new program and get it to run.

Susan: Now when you start out a new program; are all the new source code files named with a .cc extension?

Steve: Yes.

Susan: So this code in Average is where the real averaging takes place, right? Is this the "Average command"? I thought Average meant to average, so what is the deal?

Steve: The deal is that something has to do the averaging; rather than writing the same code every time we need to average another set of two numbers, we put that code in one place (the Average function) and call it whenever we need its assistance. I've updated the text to explain this motivation for using functions.

Susan: OK, then this brings up another one of my questions. How come you write the Average function before the main function?

Steve: So that the main function knows how to call the Average function. There's another way to allow a function to call another one that doesn't come before it in the file, but I thought it was easier to show it this way at first.

Susan: If the main function is going to be executed first, then how come the Average function is written first? Does the compiler always look for main first?

Steve: Yes.

Susan: Yeah, but could the Average function then just be written after main instead of before it? Just to be there when it is needed, instead of before it is needed? Am I right that you still would not have to write it twice; it would still be there for the next time it is needed, right?

Problem
Algorithms
C++
Executable
Hardware

Steve: The Average function can be anywhere, even in a different module, but at the point that you try to use it, the compiler has to know about it; to be precise, you have to specify its return type and what arguments it takes. Otherwise, the program won't compile. On the other hand, the compiled version of the Average function doesn't have to be available until the executable is created; if it's not available at that point, you'll get an error saying that you have referenced an undefined function.

Susan: So does that mean you could put the Average function anywhere you want? Then could it or any "subfunction" be put anywhere you want because the main function would always be executed first? Or could you mess up the code if you put it in a really ridiculous place like inside an output or input statement. . . or could the compiler be able to ignore something like that and go about business as usual? I guess because of the brackets it should ignore such a thing but I am not sure. See, these are the things that we novices are obliged to ponder.

Steve: You can't start a function definition in the middle of another function. That's called a *nested function* and it's not allowed in C++. The rule can be stated approximately as "You can start a function definition anywhere except in the middle of another definition."

Susan: So then the "cue" for the Average function to begin is the word Average (weight) or (age), when the compiler sees that word it just begins that separate function to start its little calculation.

Steve: That's right, except that it needs two arguments, not just one.

Susan: And that function since it was named Average causes the averaging function to work. Is that how it goes?

Steve: If I understand your question, it's not the name that makes the Average function do the averaging, it's the code that adds up the two values and divides by 2. We could replace all the references to Average with the word Glorp and the compiler wouldn't care; however, a future programmer trying to read the program probably wouldn't be amused by that name.

Susan: Oh, so there is nothing magical about the word Average, I thought it might trigger a function of averaging. Well, that sounds reasonable; it's more for us humans than the computer. And then that brings up another question, along the same line of thinking. After the Average function has done its thing, how does the program go from return Result; to the next output statement that asks for the ages? What triggers that change? I am not seeing this in the code.

Steve: The return keyword tells the compiler to hand back control to the function that called the one where the return is, as indicated in Figure 5.2.

Problem
Algorithms
C++
Executable
Hardware

This discussion didn't slake her thirst for knowledge about how to write a program. Here is how we continued:

Susan: Can I mix shorts with strings using the headers that are already stated in the test program?

Steve: Mixing shorts with strings is a dubious proposition, sort of like asking a desk to make you lunch; could you be more specific about what you're trying to do?

Susan: What if you wanted to add a numerical value to your program such as test: You have to put in a short, right? So if you added a short, what else would you have to do to make it work? Or would you have to start over with another main function after the first part and then declare new variables? I tried that too, and the compiler did not like that either. Very inflexible it is. I will tell you after one more try what I am doing. This will keep you in suspense.

Steve: It depends on what you're trying to do with the short. It's usually best to have a specific problem in mind that you're trying to solve by writing a program. Then you can see how to use these facilities (shorts, strings, vectors, etc.) to solve your problem; if not, you can ask me how they would fit into the solution.

As for your second suggestion, you're not allowed to have more than one main function in a program, because the compiler wouldn't know which one to use as the starting address for the program.

Susan: I am not really trying to solve anything, I just want to have the user type in more info and that info is a number — wait!! That is it, in that case it will be like an ASCII character and it doesn't need a short, right? That's right. I can still use a string. We are not crunching any numbers with this.

Steve: As long as you don't try to do any calculations, you can read the data into a string, even data that looks like a number; of course, that data entry method is pretty loose, since if the user types "abc" as an age, the program will accept it.

Susan: Can you define a string without a word but with just a wildcard type of variable like when we use i in shorts? In other words, does it matter what we call a variable?

```
Problem
Algorithms
C++
Executable
Hardware
```

Steve: A variable is always a "wildcard", whether it's a short or a string. For example, a short variable always has a name, such as i, or index, or whatever makes sense to you, and a value, which is a number such as 14 or 99. A string variable also has a name, such as FirstName, or street, or whatever makes sense to you, and a value, which consists of characters rather than a number, such as "Susan" or "Wesley".

A Convincing Argument

As you can see, using a function isn't very difficult. We have to provide it with the material to work on (its input arguments) and can store its return value in a variable for further processing (or use it directly, if we wish). But there's a little more here than meets the eye. How does the variable FirstWeight, for example, get transformed into the variable First that we used when writing the function?

This explanation requires us to to look at some more underlying software technology: To be precise, we're going to spend some time examining the infrastructure that makes computers usable for programmers. First, though, we have to consider a more general notion, that of a "virtual computer".

The Man behind the Curtain

Unlike many words in the vocabulary of computing, *virtual* has more or less retained its standard English definition: "That is so in essence or effect, although not formally or actually; admitting of being called by the name so far as the effect or result is concerned."[8] In other words, a virtual computer would be something that acts just like a computer, but really isn't one. Who would want such a thing?

Apparently everyone, since *virtual computer* is just another name for what we have been calling *software*. This may seem a rash statement, but it really isn't. One of the most important mathematical discoveries (inventions?) of the twentieth century was Alan Turing's demonstration that it was possible to create a fairly simple computing device (called a *Turing machine* for some reason) that could imitate *any* other computing device. This machine works in the following way: You provide it with a description of the other computer you want it to imitate, and it follows those directions. Suppose we want a computer that calculates only trigonometric functions. Then we could theoretically write a set of instructions as to how such a computer would behave, feed it into a Turing machine, and have the Turing machine imitate the behavior of this theoretical "trigonometric computer".

This is undoubtedly interesting, but you may be wondering what it has to do with programming. Well, what do we do when we write a program? In the case of our pumpkin weighing program, we're describing the actions that would be taken by a hypothetical "pumpkin weighing computer". When we run the program, the real computer simulates these actions. In other words, we have created a virtual pumpkin weighing computer.

The same analysis applies to any program. A program can most fundamentally be defined as instructions to a "universal computer", telling it how to simulate the specialized computer you actually want to use. When the universal computer executes these instructions, it behaves exactly as the hypothetical specialized computer would behave.

Of course, real computers aren't really universal; they have limits in the amount of memory or disk space they contain and the speed of their execution. However, for problems that can be solved within those limits, they are truly universal computing devices that can be tailored to a particular problem by programming.

```
Problem
Algorithms
C++
Executable
Hardware
```

---

8. *Oxford English Dictionary*, first current definition (4).

The Object of My Affections

Now let's take a look at one of these areas of software technology. We've already seen that the function of a compiler is to convert our human-readable C++ program into machine instructions that can be executed by the computer. As we've already seen, the compiler doesn't actually produce an executable program that can stand by itself; instead, it translates each source code module into a machine language file called an *object code module* (or *object file*). This file contains the instructions that correspond to the source code statements you've written, but not the "infrastructure" needed to allow them to be executed. We'll see what that infrastructure does for us shortly.

Problem
Algorithms
C++
Executable
Hardware

The creation of an object file rather than a complete executable program isn't a universal characteristic of compilers, dictated by nature. In fact, one of the most popular compilers in the early history of the PC, the Turbo Pascal™ compiler, did create an executable file directly from source code. This appears much simpler, so we have to ask why this approach has been abandoned with C++. As I've mentioned before, C++ was intended to be useful in writing large programs. Such programs can consist of hundreds or even thousands of modules (sections of source code) each containing hundreds or thousands of lines of code. Once all the modules are compiled, the object files resulting from the compilation are run through a program called the *linker*. The linker combines information from all of the object files, along with some previously prepared files called *library modules* (or *libraries*), to produce an executable program; this is called **linking** the program. One reason for this two-step approach is that we wouldn't want to have to recompile every module in a large program every time we made a change in one section; therefore, only those modules that have been affected are recompiled.[9] When all of the affected modules have been recompiled, the program is relinked to produce an updated executable.

To make such a system work, it's necessary to set up conventions as to which parts will be executed first, where data needed by more than one module will be stored, and so on. Also, a lot of operations aren't supplied as part of the language itself but are very handy in

---

9. The alert reader may wonder why I said "those modules that have been affected" rather than "those modules that have been changed". The reason is that even if we don't change a particular module, we will have to recompile it if a header file that it uses is changed. This can be a serious maintenance problem in large systems; there are special programming methods used to alleviate it, which are outside the scope of this book.

writing programs, such as the I/O functions that we've already seen. These make up the infrastructure needed to execute C++ programs.

Figure 5.6 is a picture of the process of turning your source code into an executable file.

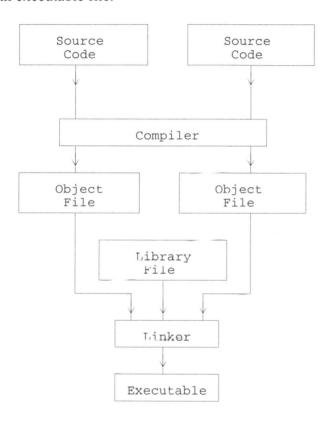

Figure 5.6: Making an executable

Susan found this explanation and diagram to be helpful.

Susan: This is beginning to come into focus. So you write your source code, it has a middle man called a object file and that just passes the buck over to a linker, which gathers info the program may need from the libraries, and then the program is ready to be read by the machine. Close?

Steve: Very close; in fact, exactly correct except for some nomenclature that isn't very important at this point.

Operating Systematically

As is often the case in programming, this infrastructure is divided into several layers. The higher ones depend on the lower ones for more fundamental services. The lowest level of the infrastructure is supplied by the **operating system**, a program that deals with the actual hardware of your computer. By far the most common operating system for Intel CPUs, as this is written, is MS-DOS, followed by OS/2 and Windows NT. All of these provide some of the same facilities; for example, you are accustomed to dealing with files and directories when using application programs such as word processors and spreadsheets. However, the disk drive in your computer doesn't know anything about files or directories. As we have seen in Chapter 2, all it can do is to store and retrieve fixed-size pieces of data called *sectors*, given an absolute address on the disk described by a platter, track number, and sector number. Files are a creation of the operating system, which keeps track of which parts of which files are stored where on the disk.[10]

```
Problem
Algorithms
C++
Executable
Hardware
```

A modern operating system provides many more facilities than just keeping track of file storage. For example, it arranges for code and data to be stored in separate areas of RAM with different *access rights*, so that code can't be accidentally overwritten by a runaway program; that is, one that writes outside the memory areas it is supposed to use. This is a valuable service, as errors of this kind are quite difficult to find and can cause havoc when they occur.

That's the good news. The bad news is that MS-DOS was created before the widespread availability of reasonably priced CPUs with memory protection facilities and therefore doesn't take advantage of these facilities. Under MS-DOS, it's entirely possible for a runaway program to destroy anything else in memory. Theoretically, we should all be running "real" operating systems by the time you read this; so far, though, the rumors of the demise of MS-DOS have been greatly exaggerated.

This notion intrigued Susan. Here's how that conversation went:

Susan: What is a runaway program?

---

10. You might say that files are "virtual"; that is, they're a figment of the operating system's imagination. Nonetheless, they are quite useful. This reminds me of the story about the man who went to a doctor, complaining that his brother had thought he was a hen for many years. The doctor asked why the family hadn't tried to help the brother before, and the man replied, "We needed the eggs".

Steve: One that is writing in areas that it shouldn't, thus destroying data or programs outside its assigned memory areas.

Susan: How would an operating system actually separate code from data areas? Would it be a physical thing?

Steve: What makes this possible are certain hardware mechanisms built into all modern CPUs, so that certain areas of memory can be assigned to specific programs, for use in predefined ways. When these mechanisms are used, a program can't write (or read, in some cases) outside its assigned area. This prevents one program from interfering with another.

Using Your Library Card

The next level of the infrastructure is supplied by the aforementioned library modules, which contain standardized segments of code that can perform I/O, mathematical functions, and other commonly used operations. So far, we have used the iostreams library, which provided the keyboard input and screen output in our example programs. We've also relied implicitly on the "startup" library, which sets up the conditions necessary for any C++ program to execute properly.[11]

Susan wasn't going to let me get away with this nonsense about the startup library without an explanation:

> **Susan**: I don't know what you are talking about when you say that we have also used a startup library. When did we do that? At startup? Well, is it something that you are actually using without knowing you are using it?

> **Steve**: Yes. It initializes the I/O system, and generally makes the environment safe for C++ programs; they're more fragile than assembly language programs and have to have everything set up for them before they can venture out.

To understand the necessity for the startup library, we have to take a look at the way variables are assigned to memory locations. So far, we have just assumed that a particular variable had a certain address, but how is this address determined in the real world?

There are several possible ways for this to occur; the particular one employed for any given variable is determined by the variable's **storage class**. The simplest storage class is the static **storage class**;

```
Problem
Algorithms
C++
Executable
Hardware
```

---

11. Two other libraries that we've used are the string and vector libraries.

variables of this class are assigned memory addresses in the executable program when the program is linked. The most common way to put a variable in the static storage class is to define it outside any function.[12] Such a variable will be initialized only once before main starts executing. We can specify the initial value if we wish; if we don't specify it, a default value (0 for numeric variables) will be assigned. An example of such a definition would be writing the line short x = 3; outside any function; this would cause x to be set to 3 before main starts executing. We can change the value of such a variable whenever we wish, just as with any other variable. The distinction I'm making here is that a static variable is always initialized before main begins executing. As you will see, this seemingly obvious characteristic of static variables is not shared with variables of all other storage classes.

This idea of assigning storage at link time led to the following discussion with Susan:

> **Susan**: If you declare a variable with only one value then it isn't a variable anymore, is it?

Problem
Algorithms
C++
Executable
Hardware

> **Steve**: A static variable can have its value changed, so it's a genuine variable. I was saying that it's possible to specify what its initial value should be before main starts executing.

> **Susan**: Are you trying to say where in memory this variable is to be stored? Isn't the compiler supposed to worry about that?

> **Steve**: I'm not specifying a location, but rather an attribute of the variable. A static variable behaves differently from the "normal" variables that we've seen up till now. One difference is that a static variable is always initialized to a known value before main starts executing.

Automatic Pilot

The notion of storage classes is essential to the solution of another mystery. You may recall that I mentioned some time ago that C++ doesn't provide automatic initialization of all variables because that facility would make a program bigger and slower. I'll admit that the truth of this isn't intuitively obvious to the casual observer; after all,

---

12. Another way to make a variable static is to state explicitly that the variable is static. However, this only works for variables defined inside functions. For the time being, we'll restrict the discussion to statically allocated variables defined outside any function.

a variable (or more exactly, the storage location it occupies) has to have *some* value, so why not something reasonable? As we have just seen, this *is* done for static variables. However, there is another storage class for which such a facility isn't quite as easy or inexpensive to implement;[13] that's the auto (short for "automatic") **storage class**, which is the default class used for variables defined in functions. An auto variable is not initialized until the function in which it is defined starts execution and even then has no known value until we specifically assign a value to it.[14]

This notion led to a fair amount of discussion between Susan and me.

Susan: Then so far I know about two types of variables, static and auto, is this correct?

Steve: Right, those are the two "storage classes" that we've used so far.

Susan: The auto variables are made up of garbage and the static variables are made up of something understandable, right?

Steve: The auto variables are uninitialized by default, and the static variables are initialized to 0 (if they're numeric, at least).

Susan: When you say that the auto class is used for functions by default does this mean you don't use static ones ever?

Steve: *Default* means "what you get if you don't specify otherwise". For example, these days, if you buy almost any type of car and don't specify that you want a manual transmission, you will get an automatic.

Susan: So, since we have used auto variables up to this point, then I am confused when we initialize them to a value. If we do, would that not make them static?

Steve: This is a difficult topic, so it's not surprising that you're having trouble. I didn't realize quite how difficult until I tried to answer your question and ended up with the essay found under the heading "Static Cling".

Problem
Algorithms
C++
Executable
Hardware

---

13. "Inexpensive", in programming parlance, means "not using up much time and/or space".

14. I'm oversimplifying a bit here. Variables can actually be declared inside any block, not just any function. An auto variable that is declared inside a block is born when the block is entered and lives until that block is finished executing. A static variable that is declared inside a block is initialized when that block is entered for the first time. It retains its value from that point on unless it is explicitly changed, as with any other statically declared variable.

Susan: How do you know what the address will be to assign to a variable? OK, I mean this makes it sound like you, the programmer, know exactly which address in memory will be used for the variable and you assign it to that location.

Steve: You don't have to know the address; however, you do have to know that the address is fixed at link time. That's what makes it possible to initialize a static variable before main starts (if outside all functions) or just once when the function starts (if inside a function). On the other hand, auto variables can't be initialized until their functions start, because their addresses can change between executions of the function.

Susan: I am having a hard time trying to figure out what you mean by using static variables outside functions. If most of what we have been doing up to this point has been outside a function then why did you say that every variable we have used up to this point is auto? Or, I have meant to ask you this, is main really a function even if you don't have anything to call? For example, in the first pumpkin weighing program, we didn't have to call another function but I have been wondering if main is really a function that just has nothing to call? So in that case, the variables used in main would be auto?

Problem
Algorithms
C++
Executable
Hardware

Steve: You are correct that main is a function. To be precise, it's the first function executed in any C++ program. If it calls other functions, that's fine, but it doesn't have to. As with any other function, the variables used in main are auto by default; in the case of the pumpkin weighing program, since we didn't make any of them static, they're all auto in fact.

So far, all of our variables have been auto, and in most programs the vast majority of all variables are of this class.[15] Why should we use these variables when static ones have that handy initialization feature built in?

The first clue to this mystery is in the name auto. When we define a variable of the auto class, its address is assigned *auto*matically when its function is entered; the address is valid for the duration of that function.[16] Since the address of the variable isn't known until its function is entered, it can't be initialized until then, unlike the case with static variables. Therefore, every function would have to start

---

15. You may have noticed that we haven't defined any variables as auto. That's because, while auto and static are both storage classes and are equivalent in that regard, there's almost never any reason to explicitly mark a variable as auto; instead, any variables defined within a function and not marked as static are set to the default class, auto.

16. This is why variables defined outside a function are static rather than auto; if they were auto, when would their addresses be assigned?

with some extra code to initialize every auto variable, which would make the program both slower and larger. Since Bjarne Stroustrup's design goals required that a C++ program should have the same run-time performance as a C program and as little space overhead as possible, such a feature was unacceptable. Luckily, forgetting to initialize an auto variable is something that can be detected at compile time, so it's possible for the compiler to warn us if we make this error. In general, it's a good idea to tell the compiler to warn you about dubious practices. Although not all of them may be real errors, some will be, and this is by far the fastest and best way to find them.[17]

Now we've seen why auto variables aren't initialized by default: Their addresses aren't known until entering the function in which they're defined. But that doesn't explain the advantage of assigning the addresses then. Wouldn't it be simpler (and faster) to assign them all during the linking process, as is done with static variables?

Stacking the Deck

To understand why auto variables aren't assigned addresses during the linking process, we have to look at the way functions relate to one another. In particular, it is very common for a statement in one function to call another function; this is called *nesting* functions, and can continue to any number of levels.

```
Problem
Algorithms
C++
Executable
Hardware
```

Susan explained this in her inimitable way.

> **Susan**: Nesting of functions—does that mean a whole bunch of functions calling each other?

> **Steve**: Yes.

Although functions can call one another, it is very unlikely that every function in a large program will be in the midst of execution at any given time. This means that reserving space in the executable program for all of the variables in all of the functions will make that executable considerably larger than it otherwise would be.

If we had only static variables, this wasteful situation would indeed occur. The alternative, of course, is to use auto variables, which as we have just noted are assigned storage at run time. But where is that storage assigned, if not in the executable program?

---

17. There are also commercial tools that help locate errors of this type, as well as others that can be found by analyzing the source code for inconsistencies.

While all static variables are assigned storage when the executable program is linked, auto variables are instead stored in a data structure called a **stack**; the name is intended to suggest the notion of stacking clean plates on a spring-loaded holder such as you might see in a cafeteria. The last plate deposited on the stack of plates will be the first one to be removed when a customer needs a fresh plate. Back in the world of programming, a stack with one entry might look something like Figure 5.7.[18]

TOP | 1234 |

Figure 5.7: A stack with one entry

If we add (or **push**) another value on to the stack, say 999, the result would look like Figure 5.8.

TOP | 999 |

2nd | 1234 |

Problem
Algorithms
C++
Executable
Hardware

Figure 5.8: A stack with two entries

If we were to push one more item, this time with the value 1666, the result would look like Figure 5.9.

TOP | 1666 |

2nd | 999 |

3rd | 1234 |

Figure 5.9: A stack with three entries

Now, if we retrieve (or **pop**) a value, we'll get the one on top; namely 1666. Then the stack will look like it did in Figure 5.8. The

---

18. The actual memory locations used to hold the items in the stack are just like any other locations in RAM. What makes them part of the stack is how they are used. Of course, as always, one memory location can hold only one item at a given time, so the locations used to hold entries on the stack cannot be simultaneously used for something else like machine instructions.

next value to be popped off the stack will be the 999, leaving us with the situation in Figure 5.7 again. If we continue for one more round, we'll get the value 1234, leaving us with an **empty stack**.

The reason that stacks are used to store auto variables is that the way items are pushed onto or popped off a stack exactly parallels what happens when one function calls another. Let's look at this stack idea again, but this time from the point of view of keeping track of where we are in one function when it calls another one, as well as allocating storage for auto variables.

Don't Call Me, I'll Call You

In Figure 5.5, there are two calls to the function Average: The first one is used to average two weights and the other to average two ages. One point I didn't stress was exactly how the Average function "knew" which call was which; that is, how did Average return to the right place after each time it was called? In principle, the answer is fairly simple: The calling function somehow notifies the called function of the address of the next instruction that should be executed after the called function is finished (the **return address**). There are several possible ways to solve this problem. The simplest solution is to store the return address at some standardized position in the code of the called function; at the end of the called function, that address is used to get back to the caller. While this used to be standard practice, it has a number of drawbacks that have relegated it to the history books. A major problem with this approach is that it requires changing data that are stored with the code of the called routine; as we've already seen, when running a program on a modern CPU under a modern operating system, code and data areas of memory are treated differently, and changing the contents of code areas at run time is not allowed.

Luckily, there is another convenient place to store return addresses: on the stack. This is such an important mechanism that all modern CPUs have a dedicated register, usually called the **stack pointer**, to make it easy and efficient to store and retrieve return addresses and other data of interest only when we're executing a function. In the case of the Intel CPUs, the stack pointer's name is esp.[19] A machine instruction named call is designed to push the return address on the stack and jump to the beginning of the function being

Problem
Algorithms
C++
Executable
Hardware

---

19. That's the 32-bit stack pointer; as in the case of the other registers, there's a 16-bit stack pointer called sp, which consists of the 16 lower bits of the "real" stack pointer esp.

called.[20] The call **instruction** isn't very complex in its operation, but before going into that explanation, you'll need some background information about the working of the CPU when it executes instructions.

How does the CPU "know" what instruction is the next to be executed? By using another dedicated register that we haven't discussed before, the **program counter**, which holds the address of the next instruction to be executed. Normally, this is the instruction physically following the one currently being executed; however, when we want to change the sequence of execution, as in an if statement or a function call, the program counter is loaded with the address of the instruction that *logically* follows the present one. Whatever instruction is at the address specified in the program counter is by definition the next instruction that will be executed; therefore, changing the address in the program counter to the address of any instruction causes that instruction to be the next one to be executed.

Here are the actual steps that the call instruction performs:

Problem
Algorithms
C++
Executable
Hardware

1. It saves the contents of the program counter on the stack.
2. Then it loads the program counter with the address of the first instruction
    of the called function.

What does this sequence of events achieve? Well, since the program counter always points to the next instruction to be executed, the address stored on the stack by the first step is the address of the next instruction after the call. Therefore, the last instruction in the called function can resume execution of the calling function by loading the program counter with the stored value on the stack. This will restart execution of the calling function at the next instruction after the call, which is exactly what we want to achieve.

The effect of the second step is to continue execution of the program with the first instruction of the called function; that's because the program counter is the register that specifies the address of the next instruction to be executed.

---

20. That is, its name is call on Intel machines and many others; all modern CPUs have an equivalent instruction, although it may have a different name.

How It All Stacks Up

As we'll see, the actual way that a stack is implemented is a bit different than is suggested by the "stack of plates" analogy, although the effect is exactly the same. Rather than keeping the top of the stack where it is and moving the data (a slow operation), the data are left where they are and the address stored in the stack pointer is changed, which is a much faster operation. In other words, whatever address the stack pointer is pointing to is by definition the "top of the stack".[21]

For example, suppose that we start with an empty stack, with the stack pointer at 20001ffe. Thus, the stack will look like Figure 5.10.

```
Address              Contents            Meaning
20001ffe        ┌─────────────────┐
                │      ????       │      (none)
                └─────────────────┘
```

Figure 5.10: An empty stack

Then, the user types in the two values "2" and "4" as the values of FirstWeight and SecondWeight, and the first call to Average occurs; let's suppose that call is at location 10001000.[22] The actual sequence of events is something like this:[23]

1. The address of the next instruction to be executed (say, 10001005) is pushed onto the stack, along with the values for the arguments First and Second, which are copies of the arguments FirstWeight and SecondWeight. In the process, the CPU will subtract eight (the size of one address added to the size of two shorts, in bytes) from the stack pointer (which is then 20001ff6) and store the return address at the address currently pointed to by the stack pointer. Thus, the stack looks like Figure 5.11.[24]

Problem
Algorithms
C++
Executable
Hardware

---

21. Please note that the address that the stack occupies in these diagrams is arbitrary. The actual address where the stack is located in your program is determined by the linker and the operating system.

22. As usual, all addresses are in hexadecimal.

23. The details will vary with the compiler, but the principles are as illustrated here.

24. The "Top of Stack" address, that is, the address where the stack pointer is pointing, will be **bold**. Also note that when we push items on the stack the stack pointer will move upward in the diagram. That's because lower addresses appear first in the diagram, and new items pushed onto the stack go at lower addresses. Anything in the diagram "above" the stack

Address	Contents	Meaning
20001ff2	????	(none)
20001ff4	????	(none)
20001ff6	10001005	return address in main
20001ffa	0004	Second
20001ffc	0002	First
20001ffe	????	(none)

Figure 5.11: The stack immediately after the call to Average

2. Execution starts in the Average function. However, before the code we write can be executed, we have to reserve space on the stack for the auto variable(s) defined in Average (other than the arguments First and Second, which have already been allocated); in this case, there is only one, namely Result. Since this variable is a short, it takes 2 bytes, so the stack pointer has to be reduced by 2. After this operation is completed, the stack will look like Figure 5.12.

Problem
Algorithms
C++
Executable
Hardware

Address	Contents	Meaning
20001ff2	????	(none)
20001ff4	????	Result
20001ff6	10001005	return address in main
20001ffa	0004	Second
20001ffc	0002	First
20001ffe	????	(none)

Figure 5.12: The stack after auto variable allocation

Wait a minute. What are those ???? doing at location 20001ff4? They represent an uninitialized memory location. We don't know what's in that location, because that depends on what it was used for previously, which could be almost anything. The C++ compiler uses stack-based addressing for auto variables, as well as copies of

pointer (i.e., at a lower address than the stack pointer's current value) is not a meaningful value, as indicated in the "meaning" column.

arguments passed in from the calling function; that is, the addresses of such variables are relative to the stack pointer, rather than being fixed addresses. In this case, the address of Result would be [esp], or the current value of the stack pointer; Second would be referred to in the object file as [esp+6] (i.e, 6 more than the current value of the stack pointer, to leave room for the return address and Result). Similarly, the address of First would be [esp+8], or 8 more than the current value of the stack pointer.[25] Since the actual addresses occupied by these variables aren't known until the setup code at the beginning of the function is actually executed, there's no way to clear the variables out before then. That's why auto variables aren't automatically initialized.

As you might have guessed, Susan and I went over this in gory detail. Here's the play by play.

Susan: Yes, I think this is what has confused me in the past about functions. I never fully understood how the mechanism worked as how one function calls another. I still don't. But I guess it is by the position of the next address in a stack?

Steve: The stack is used to pass arguments and get return values from functions, but its most important use is to keep track of the return address where the calling function is supposed to continue after the called function is done.

Susan: This is how I am visualizing the use of the stack pointer. In one of my other books it showed how the clock worked in the CPU and it seemed to cycle by pointing in different directions as to what was to happen next in a program. So it was sort of a pointer. Is this how this pointer works? So let me get this straight. All CPUs have some kind of stack pointer, but they are used only for calling functions? Exactly where is the instruction call? It sounds to me like it is in the hardware, and I am having a very difficult time understanding how a piece of hardware can have an instruction.

Steve: All of the instructions executed in a program are executed by the hardware. The call instruction, in particular, does two things:

1. It saves the address of the next instruction (the contents of the program counter) on the stack.

Problem
Algorithms
C++
Executable
Hardware

---

25. The actual mechanism used to refer to variables on the stack in a real compiler is likely to be different from this one, and indeed can vary among compilers. However, this implementation would work.

2.   It changes the program counter to point to the first instruction of the called function.

The return instruction is used to return to the calling function. It does this by the following steps:

1.   It retrieves the saved value of the program counter from the top of the stack;

2.   It sets the program counter back to that value.

The result of this is that execution of the program continues with the next instruction in the calling function.

Susan: Are you saying that, rather than the pointer of a stack actually pointing to the top of the physical stack, wherever it points to by definition will be the top of the stack, even if it really doesn't look like it?

Steve: Exactly.

Susan: Now I see why we have to know what a short is. So then the pointer is pointing to 20001ff4 as the top of the stack even though it doesn't look like it?

Steve: Absolutely correct.

```
Problem
Algorithms
C++
Executable
Hardware
```

Scoped Out

This is a good place to mention another related but distinct way to categorize variables, by their scope; the **scope** of a variable is the part of the program in which it can be accessed. The scopes we are concerned with here are *local scope* and *global scope*. Variables with **global scope** are called *global variables*. These variables are defined outside any function and, therefore by default can be accessed from any function.[26] These must be static, as we have already seen.[27] Variables with **local scope** are called *local variables*. These variables are defined in a function and are accessible only while that function is executing; they can be either static or auto and are auto by default.

---

26. Variables can be defined either inside a function (local variables) or outside a function (global variables); by contrast, code must always be inside a function.

27. However, do **not** use the keyword static when defining global variables that you want to be statically allocated. That keyword, when applied to a global variable, means something else entirely.

Figure 5.13 is a table of the allowable combinations of scope and storage class:

		Storage class	
		static	auto
Scope	local	Y	Y
	global	Y	N

Figure 5.13: Scope vs. storage class

Susan had some comments on this topic.

> **Susan**: On this scope stuff; I think you are going to have to help me understand exactly what is inside a function and what is outside a function. I am not too sure I know what the difference is.

> **Steve**: All code is inside a function. However, some variables (global variables) are outside all functions and therefore shareable by all functions. Variables that are defined inside functions are called *local*, because they are available only to the code that's in that function.

> **Susan**: I am validating this with you now. Please correct any misconceptions.

> - Only variables are declared outside functions.
> - No code is written outside functions.
> - Up to this point I am not to be aware of anything else going on outside a function.

> **Steve**: Correct.

Before we get deeper into the notion of scope, I think we should revisit the question of variable initialization in the light of the notion of global and local variables. This is a difficult topic, so it wouldn't be surprising if you don't find it obvious; Susan didn't. I wrote the next section to explain this topic to her.

Static Cling

What makes a variable static or auto is when its storage is assigned, and therefore when its address is known. In the case of a static

Problem
Algorithms
C++
Executable
Hardware

variable, this happens at link time. In the case of an auto variable it happens when the function where it is defined is entered.[28]

This distinction affects initialization because it's impossible to initialize something until you know where it is. Therefore, an auto variable cannot be initialized until the function where it is defined is entered. This also means that it is impossible for an auto variable to retain its value from one execution of the function where it's defined to the next execution of that function, because the variable might be at a different location the next time.

These rules do not apply to static variables, because their addresses are known at link time and don't change thereafter. A variable defined outside all functions (a *global* variable) is automatically in the static storage class, because otherwise its address would never be assigned.[29] Since its address is known at link time, the initialization of such a variable is performed before the start of main.

A static variable that is defined inside a function is different from one defined globally, in that it is not initialized until the function where it is defined is entered for the first time. However, its value is retained from one execution of its function to another, because its address is fixed rather than possibly varying from one call of the function to the next, as is the case with an auto variable. For this property to be of use, the initialization of a static variable in a function must be performed only once; if it were performed on each entry to the function, the value from the previous execution would be lost. Therefore, that initialization is done only once, when the function is first entered.

Susan wanted some more explanation of what happens at link time, and the related question of why we would want to use static variables.

> **Susan**: Will you tell me again what happens at link time? Let's see, I think it goes like this: The source code is translated into an object file and then the object file is linked to the hardware to make executable code. Is that how it goes?
>
> **Steve**: Not quite. The object file is linked with library files containing predefined functions in compiled form.

---

28. By the way, if you were worried about keeping track of the address of every variable, that's the compiler's problem, not yours. The important distinction between a static and an auto variable is *when* the address is assigned, not what the actual address is.

29. Since all global variables are already in the static storage class, you don't have to (and *shouldn't*) use the keyword static when declaring a global variable. In another confusing legacy from C, the word static has an entirely different and unrelated meaning when used for a global variable.

Problem
Algorithms
C++
Executable
Hardware

Susan: Now, tell me again why you would want a variable to be static? What is the advantage to that? Does it just take up less room and be more efficient?

Steve: The advantage is that a static variable keeps its value from one function call to the next. For example, suppose you wanted to count the number of times that a function was called. You could use a static variable in the function, initialize it to 0, and add 1 to it every time the function was called. When the program was done, the value of that variable would be the number of times the function was called. Obviously, we couldn't use an auto variable to do that, as it would have to be initialized every time the function started or we'd have an uninitialized variable.

Susan: I can see how using a static variable would work but I don't see why an auto variable couldn't do the same thing. Well, I guess it would change each time the function would be used. Are you saying in this case that the variable has to be global?

Steve: Not exactly. Although we could use a global variable, we could also use a static local variable. Figures 5.14 through 5.18 are some sample programs to illustrate the situation.

```cpp
#include <iostream.h>

short counter()
{
    short count = 0;

    count ++;

    cout << count << " ";

    return 0;
}
int main()
{
    short i;

    for (i = 0; i < 10; i ++)
        counter();

    return 0;
}
```

Problem
Algorithms
C++
Executable
Hardware

Figure 5.14: Using an auto variable and initializing it (code\count1.cc)

```cpp
#include <iostream.h>

short counter()
{
    short count;

    count ++;

    cout << count << " ";

    return 0;
}

int main()
{
    short i;

    for (i = 0; i < 10; i ++)
        counter();

    return 0;
}
```

Figure 5.15: Using an auto variable and not initializing it (code\count2.cc)

Problem
Algorithms
C++
Executable
Hardware

```cpp
#include <iostream.h>

short counter()
{
    static short count = 0;

    count ++;

    cout << count << " ";

    return 0;
}

int main()
{
    short i;

    for (i = 0; i < 10; i ++)
        counter();

    return 0;
}
```

Figure 5.16: Using a local static variable and initializing it (code\count3.cc)

```
#include <iostream.h>

short counter()
{
    static short count;

    count ++;

    cout << count << " ";

    return 0;
}

int main()
{
    short i;

    for (i = 0; i < 10; i ++)
        counter();

    return 0;
}
```

Figure 5.17: Using a local static variable and not initializing it (code\count4.cc)

```
#include <iostream.h>

short count;

short counter()
{
    count ++;

    cout << count << " ";

    return 0;
}

int main()
{
    short i;

    for (i = 0; i < 10; i ++)
        counter();

    return 0;
}
```

Problem
Algorithms
C++
Executable
Hardware

Figure 5.18: Using a global variable and not initializing it (code\count6.cc)

What will each of these programs do when run?

Susan: Now, let me think about this. Variables are: static or auto, global or local.

   Local is for use only within functions. These variables are mostly auto, and will be auto by default, but they can be static; in the latter case, they will be initialized to 0.

Steve: Correct; a static numeric variable is initialized to 0 if no other provision is made by the programmer to initialize it.

Susan: Global variables are declared only outside functions. They are always allocated storage at link time, like static local variables.

Steve: Correct.

Susan: Variables with static allocation are fixed because they are initialized at link time and thus are done just once and never change. But they can be local or global.

Steve: The address of a statically allocated variable is set once and never changes; its value can change just like an auto variable can.

Susan: That's what I had mixed up. I was confusing addresses with values.

```
Problem
Algorithms
C++
Executable
Hardware
```

Steve: OK, as long as you're straightened out now.

Susan: An auto variable is assigned an address when the function where it is defined is entered. All auto variables are local.

Steve: Correct.

Susan: Now, here is where I am confused. What is the difference between *at link time* and *when the function where it is defined is entered*? Does *at link time* mean when you are done with your source code and you are making an executable?

Steve: Yes.

Susan: And does *when the function where it is defined is entered* mean when the program is already made into an executable and you are running the program?

Steve: Yes.

Susan: I am confused about what we mean by *initialization*. I am confusing declaring a value for a variable and the designation of an address for a variable. It almost seems as if we are using these two meanings for the same term. I always thought that *initializing a variable* meant just assigning a value to it.

Steve: Initializing a variable means assigning an initial value to it. In the case of an auto variable, this must be done every time the function where it is declared is entered, whereas with a static variable it is done once.

Susan: OK, this is what I imagined this to mean<?>. Then how come, in your figure of a stack, you have values assigned to the places where the variables are?

Steve: Those values are present only *after* the variables to which they correspond have been initialized. In Figure 5.12, for example, the contents of the address corresponding to Result are shown as ???, rather than as a valid value, whereas the values of First and Second are shown as initialized, because they have already been set to values equal to the input arguments provided by the caller.

Susan: Remember when I started the "tracing" program? It had random numbers in the places where numbers are supposed to go, and when I actually entered a value then those random numbers were replaced by that value. And is that why you put ??? there, because you know that something is there but you don't know exactly what? It is just whatever until you can put a real value into those slots.

Steve: Right.

Susan: So if you leave it alone by not initializing it, then it keeps the last value it had each time it goes through the loop and therefore the count goes up?

Steve: Yes, except that the initial value isn't reliable in that case. In the case of the example count programs, that value happened to be 0, but there's no reason to expect that in general.

Susan: I want you to know that it was not immediately apparent to me just what the code in the example programs was doing; it really does look kinda strange. Then I noticed that this code called a function named counter. Why? Couldn't this work without using a function call?

Steve: No, it wouldn't work without a function call, because the whole point is that when a function is called, the auto variables defined in that function have unknown values. How would I show that without a function call?

Susan: I see that. One more point, there was no 5, which I assumed you to mean to be a global initialized variable, so I made one myself by just

Problem
Algorithms
C++
Executable
Hardware

copying 6 and assigning the value of 0 to count. So this is just about all this exercise did for me. . . . I still don't get it. Why? Because they all did the same thing except 1.The results for that were the following: 1 1 1 1 1 1 1 1 1 1. The results for the rest of the programs were all the same, being 1 2 3 4 5 6 7 8 9 10. So, if they all do the same thing, then what is the point? Now, what really makes me mad about this is why 1 has that result. This bothers me. Obviously it is not incrementing itself by 1 after the first increment, it is just staying at one. Oh, wait, okay, okay, maybe. . . how about this: If you initialize it to 0 then each time it comes up through the loop it is always 0 and then it will always add 1 to 0 and it has to do that 10 times.

Steve: Right. By the way, Figure 5.19 is the missing example.

```
#include <iostream.h>

short count = 0;

short counter()
{
    count ++;

    cout << count << " ";

    return 0;
}

int main()
{
    short i;

    for (i = 0; i < 10; i ++)
        counter();

    return 0;
}
```

Problem
Algorithms
C++
Executable
Hardware

Figure 5.19: Using a global variable and initializing it (code\count5.cc)

Susan: Then on the initialized local static variable, why does it work? Because it is static, and because its address is one place and won't budge; that means its value can increment. Well, would that mean it isn't written over in its location every time the function is called so we can add a value to it each time through?

Steve: Right.

Susan: And then the uninitialized static one works for the same reason the auto uninitialized one works.

Steve: Not quite. A static local variable is *always* initialized to something, just like a global variable is. If you don't specify an initial value for a static local numeric variable, it will be initialized to 0 during the first execution of the function where it is defined.

Susan: Now as for global, this is hard. Let me guess. Do the global initialized and uninitialized work for the same reasons I said earlier?

Steve: The global variables are always initialized, whether you specify an initial value or not; if you don't specify one, it will be 0.

Susan: That's what you said about static numeric variables. Are they the same? Well, they have to be the same because only static variables can be global, right?

Steve: Correct. Global variables are always statically allocated.

Susan: So if you don't initialize it then it can become any number unless it is a static numeric without explicit initialization and then it will be 0 by default?

Steve: Correct.

Susan: OK, let me see if I have this. All static really means is that the variable is put in an address of memory that can't be overwritten by another memory address but can be overwritten when we change the variable's value?

Steve: Right.

Susan: These are tricks, and you know I don't like tricks. If they are global numeric variables, whether explicitly initialized or not, they are static; therefore they will at least have a value of 0. In example 5 this is stated explicitly but not in example 6, so the variable also will take the value of 0 by default, therefore these two programs are effectively identical, just like 3 and 4. That is why examples 3, 4, 5, and 6 have the same results.

Steve: Well, obviously the trick didn't work; you got the answers right.

Let's pause here to look at a sample program that has examples of all the types of variables and initialization states we've just discussed. These are:[30]

Problem
Algorithms
C++
Executable
Hardware

---

30. Remember, there aren't any global auto variables, because they would never be initialized.

1.   global, not explicitly initialized
2.   global, explicitly initialized
3.   auto, uninitialized
4.   auto, initialized
5.   local static, not explicitly initialized
6.   local static, explicitly initialized

Careful examination of the sample program, shown in Figure 5.20, will help you to visualize how and where each of these variables might be used.

```cpp
#include <iostream.h>

short count1; // A global variable, not explicitly initialized
short count2 = 5; // A global variable, explicitly initialized

short func1()
{
    short count3; // A local auto variable, not explicitly initialized
    short count4 = 22; // A local auto variable, explicitly initialized
static short count5; // A local static variable, not explicitly initialized
static short count6 = 9; // A local static variable, explicitly initialized

    count1 ++; // Incrementing the global variable count1.
    count2 ++; // Incrementing the global variable count2.
    count3 ++; // Incrementing the local uninitialized auto variable count3.
    count4 ++; // Incrementing the local auto variable count4.
    count5 ++; // Incrementing the local static variable count5.
    count6 ++; // Incrementing the local static variable count6.

    cout << "count1 = " << count1 << endl;
    cout << "count2 = " << count2 << endl;
    cout << "count3 = " << count3 << endl;
    cout << "count4 = " << count4 << endl;
    cout << "count5 = " << count5 << endl;
    cout << "count6 = " << count6 << endl;
    cout << endl;

    return 0;
}

int main()
{
    func1();
    func1();

    return 0;
}
```

Problem
Algorithms
C++
Executable
Hardware

Figure 5.20: Using variables of different scopes and storage classes
(code\scopclas.cc)

Figure 5.21 is the output that results from running this program normally. To run it under gdb, make sure you are in the normal subdirectory, then type trace scopclas. The program will start up and show you the first line of executable code. Type z and hit ENTER to execute each line. The values of all the variables in main will be displayed immediately before the execution of each line in that function, and the variables in func1 will be displayed as they are when the program is run normally. When you get to the end of the program (or when you're tired of tracing), type q (for *quit*) and hit ENTER to exit from the debugger.

```
count1 = 1
count2 = 6
count3 = -32768
count4 = 23
count5 = 1
count6 = 10

count1 = 2
count2 = 7
count3 = -32767
count4 = 23
count5 = 2
count6 = 11
```

> Problem
> Algorithms
> **C++**
> Executable
> Hardware

Figure 5.21: The results of using variables of different scopes and storage classes (code\scopclas.out)

The results shown should help to answer the question of when we would want to use a static variable rather than an auto variable: whenever we need a variable that keeps its value from one execution of a function to another. You may be wondering where that weird value for count3 came from. Since we never initialized it, we can't complain when its value is meaningless. Although the compiler can warn us about such problems in some cases, they are still a significant source of errors in C++ programs, so it's worthwhile doing some additional exercises to help drive the point home.

Exercises, First Set

1. What will each of the programs in Figures 5.22 through 5.27 do when run?

```
//auto local variable, initialized

#include <iostream.h>

short mess()
{
    short xyz;

    xyz = 5;

    return 0;
}

short counter()
{
    short count = 0;

    count ++;

    cout << count << " ";

    return 0;
}

int main()
{
    short i;

    for (i = 0; i < 10; i ++)
        {
        mess();
        counter();
        }

    cout << endl;

    return 0;
}
```

Problem
Algorithms
C++
Executable
Hardware

Figure 5.22: Exercise 1a (code\inita.cc)

```
//auto local variable, uninitialized

#include <iostream.h>

short mess()
{
   short xyz;

   xyz = 5;

   return 0;
}

short counter()
{
   short count;

   count ++;

   cout << count << " ";

   return 0;
}

int main()
{
   short i;

   for (i = 0; i < 10; i ++)
     {
     mess();
     counter();
     }

   cout << endl;

   return 0;
}
```

Problem
Algorithms
C++
Executable
Hardware

Figure 5.23: Exercise 1b (code\initb.cc)

```
//static local variable, explicitly initialized

#include <iostream.h>

short mess()
{
    short xyz;

    xyz = 5;

    return 0;
}

short counter()
{
    static short count = 0;

    count ++;

    cout << count << " ";

    return 0;
}

int main()
{
    short i;

    for (i = 0; i < 10; i ++)
        {
        mess();
        counter();
        }

    cout << endl;

    return 0;
}
```

Problem
Algorithms
C++
Executable
Hardware

Figure 5.24: Exercise 1c (code\initc.cc)

```
//static local variable, not explicitly initialized

#include <iostream.h>

short mess()
{
   short xyz;

   xyz = 5;

   return 0;
}
short counter()
{
   static short count;

   count ++;

   cout << count << " ";

   return 0;
}
int main()
{
   short i;

   for (i = 0; i < 10; i ++)
      {
      mess();
      counter();
      }

   cout << endl;

   return 0;
}
```

Problem
Algorithme
C++
Executable
Hardware

Figure 5.25: Exercise 1d (code\initd.cc)

```
//global variable, explicitly initialized

short count = 0;

#include <iostream.h>

short mess()
{
   short xyz;

   xyz = 5;

   return 0;
}
short counter()
{
   count ++;

   cout << count << " ";

   return 0;
}
int main()
{
   short i;

   for (i = 0; i < 10; i ++)
      {
      mess();
      counter();
      }

   cout << endl;

   return 0;
}
```

Problem
Algorithms
C++
Executable
Hardware

Figure 5.26: Exercise 1e (code\inite.cc)

```
//global variable, not explicitly initialized

short count;

#include <iostream.h>

short mess()
{
   short xyz;

   xyz = 5;

   return 0;
}
short counter()
{
   count ++;

   cout << count << " ";

   return 0;
}
int main()
{
   short i;

   for (i = 0; i < 10; i ++)
      {
      mess();
      counter();
      }

   cout << endl;

   return 0;
}
```

Problem
Algorithms
C++
Executable
Hardware

Figure 5.27: Exercise 1f (code\initf.cc)

Answers to exercises can be found at the end of the chapter.

Think Globally?

Now that, I hope, we've cleared up the question of when different types of variables are initialized, let's continue with the distinction between global and local variables. You may be surprised that a programmer would accept the limitation of allowing certain variables to be accessed only in certain functions. Surely it's more powerful to be able to access anything anywhere. Isn't it?

Let me tell you a little story about the "power" of global variables. Unlike the one about the funny odometers, this one is true.

A BASIC Difficulty

In the late 1970s, I worked for a (very) small software house that was developing a database program for the Radio Shack TRS-80 Model III computer. This computer was fairly powerful for the time; it had two 79K floppy disks and a maximum of 48K memory. The database program had to be able to find a subset of the few thousand records in the database in a minute or so. The speed of the floppy drive was the limiting factor. The only high-level language that was available was a BASIC interpreter clearly related by ancestry to QBASIC, the BASIC that comes with MS-DOS, but much more primitive; for example, variable names were limited to 2 characters.[31] There was also an assembler, but even at that time I wasn't thrilled with the idea of writing a significant application program in assembly language. So we were stuck with BASIC.

```
Problem
Algorithms
C++
Executable
Hardware
```

Actually, that wasn't so bad. BASIC then, as now, had pretty good string manipulation functions,[32] and the file access functions, although primitive, weren't too hard to work with for the application in question. You could read or write a fixed number of bytes anywhere in a disk file, and since all of the records in a given database were in fact the same length, that was good enough for our purposes. However, there were a couple of (related) glaring flaws in the language: there were no named subroutines (analogous to functions in C++), and all variables were global.

Instead of names, subroutines were addressed by line number. In TRS-80 BASIC, each line had a number, and you could call a subroutine that started at line 1000 by writing "GOSUB 1000". At the end of the subroutine, a "RETURN" statement would cause control to return to the next statement after the GOSUB.

While this is functional in a moronic way, it has some serious drawbacks. First, of course, a number isn't as mnemonic as a name. Remembering that line 1000 is the beginning of invoice printing

---

31. That is, two significant characters; you could have names as long as you wanted, but any two variables that had the same first two characters were actually the same variable.

32. Much better than the ones that come with C!

routine, for example, isn't as easy as remembering the name PrintInvoice. In addition, if you "renumbered" the program to make room for inserting new lines between previously existing lines, the line numbers would change. The second drawback is that, as the example suggests, there was no way to pass arguments to a subroutine when it was called. Therefore, the only way for a subroutine to get input or produce output was by using and changing global variables. Yet another problem with this line-numbered subroutine facility was that you could call any line as a subroutine; no block structure such as we have in C++ was available to impose some order on the flow of control.

With such an arrangement, it was almost impossible to make a change anywhere in even a moderately large program without breaking some subroutine. One reason for this fragility was that a variable could be used or changed anywhere in the program; another was that it was impossible to identify subroutines except by adding comments to the program, which could be out of date. For both these reasons, almost any change could have effects throughout the program.

I Say "Live It, or Live with It"

After some time struggling with this problem, I decided to end it, once and for all, by adding named subroutines with arguments and local variables to the language. This made it possible to maintain the program, and we ended up selling several hundred copies of it over the course of a couple of years. Besides, fixing the language was fun.[33]

The moral? There's almost always a way around a limitation of a computer language, although it may not be worth the effort to find it. Luckily, with C++, adding functionality is a bit easier than patching BASIC in assembly language.

Nesting Instinct

After that (theoretically) instructive anecdote, it's time to get back to our regularly scheduled text, where we were examining the function of the stack in storing information needed during execution of a

Problem
Algorithms
C++
Executable
Hardware

---

33. Unfortunately, the details of this adventure are both too technical and not very relevant to the task at hand. Also, I've forgotten exactly how I did it; after all, it was over 15 years ago.

function. The next statement in our example program (Figure 5.5) is Result = (First + Second) / 2;. Since we've assumed that First is 2, and Second is 4, the value of Result will be (4+2)/2, or 3. After this statement is executed, the stack looks like Figure 5.28.

Address	Contents	Meaning
20001ff2	????	(none)
20001ff4	0003	Result
20001ff6	10001005	return address in main
20001ffa	0004	Second
20001ffc	0002	First
20001ffe	????	(none)

Figure 5.28: The stack after the initialization of Result

Problem
Algorithms
C++
Executable
Hardware

Finally, at the end of the function, the stack pointer will be incremented to point to the stored return address. Then the return instruction will reload the program counter with the stored return address, which in this case is 10001005. Then the value of Result will be made available to the calling function and the stack pointer will be adjusted so the stack looks as it did before we called Average.

After the return, the stack will be empty, as we no longer need the arguments, the auto variable Result, or the return address from the Average function. Figure 5.29 shows what the stack looks like at this point.

Address	Contents	Meaning
20001ff2	????	(none)
20001ff4	0003	(none)
20001ff6	10001005	(none)
20001ffa	0004	(none)
20001ffc	0002	(none)
20001ffe	????	(none)

Figure 5.29: The stack after exiting from Average

Do not be fooled by the casual statement "the stack is empty". That means only that the stack pointer (esp) is pointing to the same place it was when we started our excursion into the Average function; namely, 20001ffe. The values that were stored in the memory locations used by Average for its auto variables haven't been erased by changing the stack pointer. This illustrates one very good reason why we can't rely on the values of auto variables until they've been initialized; we don't know how those memory locations on the stack have been used previously.

The previous discussion of how arguments are copied into local variables when a function is called applies directly to our Average function; if we try to change the input arguments, we will change only the copies of those arguments, and the corresponding variables in the calling function won't be altered. That's perfectly acceptable here, since we don't want to change the values in the calling function; we just want to calculate their average and provide the result to the calling function. An argument that is handled this way is called a *value argument*, as its value is copied into a newly created variable in the called function, rather than allowing us access to the "real" argument in the calling function.[34]

One thing we haven't really discussed here is how the return value gets back to the caller. In the cases we've examined so far, using the compiler that accompanies this book, it's stored in a register (eax, to be precise), which is then available to the calling routine after we get back.[35] This is a very easy and fast way to pass return values back to the caller. However, it has a drawback: a register can only hold one value of 32 bits. Sometimes this is not enough, in which case another mechanism will have to be used; unfortunately, we won't get a chance to cover it in this book. In any event, it's time to go over the material we've covered in this chapter.

Problem
Algorithms
C++
Executable
Hardware

Review

First, we added the fundamental programming concept of the *function*. A function is a piece of code that can "stand alone"; it can

---

34. It's also possible to define a function that has access to an actual variable in the calling function; we'll see how and when to do that at the appropriate time.

35. In case you're wondering how I know which register is used to pass back the return value, it's simple. I cheated by examining the compiled code with a utility program. Different compilers do this differently, but luckily you don't have to worry about this detail when writing C++ programs.

be compiled separately from other functions, and provides some service that we can use by a mechanism known as a *function call*. The function that makes the call is known as the *calling function*, and the one it calls is known as the *called function*. Before we can call a function, we need to know what input values it needs and what it returns. This information is provided by a *function declaration* at the beginning of each function. This includes an *argument list*, which specifies input values that the called function uses (if any), and a *return type*, which specifies the type of the value that it produces when it's finished (if any). When we call a function, it executes until it reaches the end of its code or reaches a return statement, whichever comes first. When either of these events occurs, the program continues execution in the calling function immediately after the function call statement. Ordinarily, as in our example, an argument to a function is actually a copy of the variable in the calling program, so that the called function can't modify the "real" value in the caller. Such an argument is called a *value argument*.[36]

We also saw that function and variable names can be of any length, consisting of upper or lower case characters (or both), digits, and the special character underscore (_). To make it easier for the compiler to distinguish numbers from variable names, the first character can't be a digit. Also, a variable name can't be the same as a *keyword*, or name defined by the language; examples of keywords we've seen so far include if, for, and short.

After finishing the construction of our Average function, we saw how to use it by making a function call. Then we launched into an examination of the way that values in the calling function are converted into arguments in the called function, which required a detour into the software infrastructure.

We started this excursion by looking at the *linker*, which is used to construct programs from a number of functions compiled into separate *object file*s. Next, we explored the notion of *storage class*, which determines the working lifetime of a variable. The simplest storage class is static. Variables of this class, which includes all variables defined outside any function, have storage assigned to them by the linker and retain the same address during the lifetime of the program. On the other hand, auto (for "automatic") variables are always defined in a function and are assigned storage on the *stack* when that function starts execution. The stack is the data structure that stores function arguments and *return addresses* during the execution of a function; it's called that because it behaves like a

Problem
Algorithms
C++
Executable
Hardware

---

36. As this might suggest, there is another type of argument, which we'll get to in Chapter 6.

spring-loaded stack of plates in a cafeteria, where the last one put on the top is the first one to be removed. Don't take this analogy too literally; most of the diagrams in this chapter show adding and removing data at the bottom rather than the top, but that doesn't affect the functioning of the stack.

Then we noted that each variable, in addition to a storage class, has a *scope*, which is the part of a program in which the variable can be accessed. At this point, the scopes that are important to us are *local scope* and *global scope*. As you might guess, a global variable can be referred to anywhere, while a local variable can be accessed only in the function where it is defined. Although it may seem limiting to use local variables rather than global ones, programs that rely on global variables are very difficult to maintain, as a change anywhere can affect the rest of the program. Programs that limit the scope of their variables, on the other hand, minimize the amount of code that can be affected by a change in one place. Because local variables are only usable while in the function where they are defined, they can be stored on the stack; therefore, they don't occupy memory during the entire lifetime of the program.

Of course, local variables take up room while they're being used, which means that the stack has to have enough storage to hold all of the local variables for the current function and all of the functions that haven't finished executing. That is, the stack has to have enough room for all of the variables in the current function, the function that called the current function, the one that called that one, and so on up to the main function. which is always the top-level function in a C++ program. Since the amount of memory that is allocated to the stack is not unlimited, it's possible to run out of space, in which case your program will stop working. This is called a *stack overflow*, by analogy with what happens if you put too many plates on the cafeteria plate stack: It falls over and makes a mess. When using the GNU compiler that comes with this book, it's unlikely that you'll ever run out of stack space unless you have a bug in your program. Other compilers aren't as generous in their space allotments, so the likelihood of a stack overflow is less remote. The solution to this problem, should it arise, is to use another kind of storage allocation called *dynamic storage*; we'll see an example of this mechanism in Chapter 7.

Now that we've gone through that review, it's time to do another exercise to drive home some points about scope and storage classes.

Problem
Algorithms
C++
Executable
Hardware

Exercises, Second Set

2. If the program in Figure 5.30 is run, what will be displayed?

```cpp
#include <iostream.h>

short i;

short Calc(short x, short y)
{
static short j = 0;

    cout << "The value of j in Calc is: " << j << endl;

    i ++;

    j = x + y + j;

    return j;
};
```

```
Problem
Algorithms
C++
Executable
Hardware
```

```cpp
int main()
{
    short j;

    for (i = 0; i < 5; i ++)
        {
        j = Calc(i + 5, i * 2) + 7;
        cout << "The value of j in main is: " << j << endl;
        }

    return(0);
};
```

Figure 5.30: Exercise 2 (code\calc1.cc)

Answers to exercises can be found at the end of the chapter.

Conclusion

We've covered a lot of material in this chapter, ranging from the anatomy of functions through a lot more information on what's going on "underneath the covers" of even a fairly simple C++ program. Next, we'll see how to write a realistic, although simplified, application program using some more advanced concepts in C++.

Answers to Exercises

1.   Here are the answers for each of the programs in Figures 5.22 through 5.27, problems 1a–1f:

   a.   1 1 1 1 1 1 1 1 1 1

   b.   6 6 6 6 6 6 6 6 6 6

   c.   1 2 3 4 5 6 7 8 9 10

   d.   1 2 3 4 5 6 7 8 9 10

   e.   1 2 3 4 5 6 7 8 9 10

   f.   1 2 3 4 5 6 7 8 9 10

Why are these the way they are? Well, let's take them in order, except for b, which I'll take up last.

   a.   The reason for the results from a should be fairly obvious; since we set the variable count to 0 every time we enter the counter function, incrementing it always gives the answer 1.

Problem
Algorithms
C++
Executable
Hardware

As for c–f, they all produce the same answer; namely, the output value starts at 1 and increments by 1 each time. This is because the variable named count is statically allocated in each of these cases, which has two consequences: The initialization of the variable is done only once and it retains its value from one call of the counter function to the next. However, the reason for this behavior differs slightly in each of these cases, as follows:

   c.   In initc.cc, count is a static variable defined in the counter function, which is explicitly initialized to 0.
   d.   In initd.cc, count is a static variable defined in the counter function, which is not explicitly initialized. Statically allocated numeric variables are initialized to 0 if no other initial value is specified.[37]

---

37. You can count on this, because it's part of the language definition; although it's nicer for the next programmer if you specify what you mean rather than leaving it to the compiler.

e.   In inite.cc, count is a global variable explicitly initialized to 0. Note that the keyword static is **not** used to specify that this variable is statically allocated; since globals are always statically allocated, the keyword static means something different when applied to a global variable or function. Even though we won't be using static for global variables or functions, it's possible that you will run into it in other programs, so it might be useful for you to have some idea of its meaning in those situations. An approximate translation of static for global functions or variables is that the function or variable is available for use only in the same file where it is defined, following the point of its definition.

f.   In initf.cc, count is a global variable not explicitly initialized. As in initd.cc, this will work because the default value of a statically allocated numeric variable is 0.

```
Problem
Algorithms
C++
Executable
Hardware
```

Now let's see why b is different.

b.   In initb.cc, count is a local *uninitialized variable*. Here's where we see the reason for the mess function, which apparently does nothing useful; that function is there solely to supply a value that will use the same memory location as the counter function will use to store its count variable after the mess function returns to the main program. In other words, in the GNU compiler that comes with this book, the variable xyz in the mess function happens to land in the same memory location that the variable count occupies in the counter function. Therefore, whatever value happened to be in xyz at the end of the mess function will appear as if by magic in count when counter starts. If we were to initialize count before we used it in counter, we would never see this leftover value, but since we just use count without initializing it, we get whatever value that memory location had left in it from before.

In case this point isn't yet apparent to you, I've drawn a set of pictures that might help clear it up. At the point in main where mess is about to be called, let's suppose that the stack is empty, with the stack pointer pointing to 20001ffe. The call instruction is at location 10001000, and is 5 bytes long, so the next instruction after the call starts at location 10001005. Before the call to mess occurs, the stack looks like Figure 5.31.[38]

```
Address          Contents        Meaning

20001ff2    ┌──────────────┐     (none)
            │     ????     │
20001ff4    ├──────────────┤     (none)
            │     ????     │
20001ff6    ├──────────────┤     (none)
            │     ????     │
20001ff8    ├──────────────┤     (none)
            │     ????     │
20001ffa    ├──────────────┤     (none)
            │     ????     │
20001ffe    ├──────────────┤     (none)
            │     ????     │
            └──────────────┘
```

Figure 5.31: The stack immediately before the call to mess

Then the call to mess occurs, which leaves the stack looking like Figure 5.32.

```
Address          Contents        Meaning

20001ff2    ┌──────────────┐     (none)
            │     ????     │
20001ff4    ├──────────────┤     (none)
            │     ????     │
20001ff6    ├──────────────┤     (none)
            │     ????     │
20001ff8    ├──────────────┤     (none)
            │     ????     │
20001ffa    ├──────────────┤     return address in main
            │   10001005   │
20001ffe    ├──────────────┤     (none)
            │     ????     │
            └──────────────┘
```

Figure 5.32: The stack immediately before the execution of the first instruction in mess

Problem
Algorithms
C++
Executable
Hardware

---

38. As usual, the **bold** address indicates the current value of the stack pointer.

Then mess declares a variable called xyz, which is an auto variable and therefore has to be stored on the stack. Since xyz is a short, it occupies 2 bytes on the stack, so the stack now looks like Figure 5.33.

Address	Contents	Meaning
20001ff2	????	(none)
20001ff4	????	(none)
20001ff6	????	(none)
20001ff8	????	xyz (uninitialized)
20001ffa	10001005	return address in main
20001ffe	????	(none)

Figure 5.33: The stack after mess has declared the auto variable xyz

So far, so good. Now xyz is assigned the value 5, which leaves the stack looking like Figure 5.34.

Problem
Algorithms
C++
Executable
Hardware

Address	Contents	Meaning
20001ff2	????	(none)
20001ff4	????	(none)
20001ff6	????	(none)
20001ff8	0005	xyz
20001ffa	10001005	return address in main
20001ffe	????	(none)

Figure 5.34: The stack after the auto variable xyz in mess is assigned the value 5

Then mess returns to main, so the stack is empty again. But here's the tricky part: to say "the stack is empty" merely means that the stack pointer has been reset back to 20001ffe. The data stored in locations 20001ff8-20001ffc have not been changed in any way.[39] So, before counter is called, the situation looks like Figure 5.35.

Address	Contents	Meaning
20001ff2	????	(none)
20001ff4	????	(none)
20001ff6	????	(none)
20001ff8	0005	(none)
20001ffa	10001005	(none)
20001ffe	????	(none)

Figure 5.35: The stack before counter is called

When counter is called, let's assume the return address in main is now 10001013. After this is stored on the stack, we have the situation illustrated in Figure 5.36 upon entry to counter.

Address	Contents	Meaning
20001ff2	????	(none)
20001ff4	????	(none)
20001ff6	????	(none)
20001ff8	0005	(none)
20001ffa	10001013	return address in main
20001ffe	????	(none)

Figure 5.36: The stack immediately before the execution of the first instruction in counter

The first thing that counter does is to allocate storage for its one auto variable, i, by subtracting 2 from the stack pointer. After this is done, the situation is as illustrated in Figure 5.37.

Problem
Algorithms
C++
Executable
Hardware

---

39. This statement is true when running the DJGPP compiler on an Intel machine; it may not be true on other systems. However, that possibility only reinforces the point that you should not rely on such behavior, as it is outside the definition of the C++ language.

```
Address              Contents           Meaning

20001ff2              ????              (none)

20001ff4              ????              (none)

20001ff6              ????              (none)

20001ff8              0005              i (uninitialized)

20001ffa            10001013           return address in main

20001ffe              ????              (none)
```

Figure 5.37: The stack when counter is entered

That is, the variable i is assigned the storage location that previously held the value of xyz; this storage location (20001ff8) still has the value 5 left over from xyz. Of course, if we initialize i as we should, we'll never see that old value. However, this program doesn't initialize i; thus, i starts out with the leftover value 5 from xyz before counter increments i.

Problem
Algorithms
C++
Executable
Hardware

The moral of the story is "always initialize your auto variables before use"; otherwise, you'll get whatever junk happens to be lying around in memory at the location where they are assigned when the function starts.

As you might guess, this set of problems led to a discussion with Susan.

> **Susan**: Steve, what I don't get is what does the function called mess (aptly named) do? See, since I am still sketchy on function calls this really bothers me. Am I to assume that the mess function call comes first and then the counter function call comes second, and what does one have to do with the other?

> **Steve**: As we've discussed before, all the lines in a given function (like main) are executed in sequential order from top to bottom, unless you use a flow control construct like if, while, or for, to change that order.

> **Susan**: If it weren't for problem 1b, I would think that you were playing a trick on me and that this call was just a distraction and not utilized at all but I see it does do something, but what I am not sure.

> **Steve**: You're correct that it does do something. One of the rules in figuring out a program is that everything does something; the question is

often exactly what it is doing. Once you have that figured out, the rest is often pretty easy to determine.

2.　　If you got this one right, congratulations! It's just *filled* with tricks, but they're all things that you might run into in a real (poorly written) program. Here's the answer:

```
The value of j in Calc is: 0
The value of j in main is: 12
The value of j in Calc is: 5
The value of j in main is: 23
The value of j in Calc is: 16
The value of j in main is: 40
```

Let's see how this came about. The first question is why there are only three values displayed by each output statement. The for loop that calls the Calc routine and displays the results should execute 5 times, shouldn't it?

This is the first trick. Since i is a global variable, the statement i ++; in the Calc function affects its value. Therefore, i starts out at 0 in the main function, as usual, but when the Calc function is called, i is incremented to 1. So the next time the modification expression i ++ in the for statement is executed, i is already 1 and is changed to 2. Now the controlled block of the for statement is executed again, with i set to 2. Again, the call to Calc results in i being incremented an extra time, to 3, so the next execution of the for loop sets i to 4. The final call to Calc increments the value of i to 5, so the for loop terminates, having executed only three times rather than the five you would expect by looking at it. Now you can see why global variables are dangerous!

Now what about the values of j? Well, since the j in Calc is a static variable, it is initialized only once. Because it is a local static variable, that initialization is performed when Calc is called for the first time. So the first time Calc is called, j is set to 0. The arguments specified by main on the first call to Calc are 5 and 0; this means that, inside Calc, x and y have those values, respectively. Then the new value of j is calculated by the statement j = x + y + j;, or 5 in total. The return j; statement specifies this as the return value of Calc; this value is then added to 7 as specified by the assignment statement j = Calc(i + 5, i * 2) + 7; in main. That explains why the output statement in main displays the value of j as 12 the first time.

It's very important to note that the variable j in main is completely unrelated to the variable j in Calc. Since they are local variables, they

Problem
Algorithms
C++
Executable
Hardware

have nothing in common but their names. There is no risk of confusion (at least on the compiler's part), since we can access a local variable only in the function in which it is defined. Therefore, when we refer to j in main, we mean the one defined there; and when we refer to j in Calc, we mean the one defined there.

Next, we call Calc again with the arguments 7 and 4. To compute these arguments from the expressions i + 5 and i * 2, you have to remember that i has been modified by Calc and is now 2, not 1 as we would expect normally. When we get to Calc, it displays the old value of j (5), left over from the previous execution of this function. This is because j is a local static variable; thus, the initialization statement static short j = 0; is executed only once, upon the first call to the function where it is defined. Once j has been set to a value in Calc, it will retain that value even in a subsequent call to Calc; this is quite unlike a normal auto variable, which has no known value at the beginning of execution of the function where it is defined. A new value of j is now calculated as 7 + 4 + 5, or 16, and returned to main.

On return from Calc, the value of j in main is 23, as set by the assignment statement j = Calc(i + 5, i * 2) + 7;. We also don't want to forget that i is now 3, having been changed in Calc.

Exactly the same steps occur for the last pass through the for loop: we call Calc with the new values of i + 5 and i * 2, which are 9 and 8, respectively, since i has been incremented to 4 by the for statement's modification expression i ++. Then Calc displays the old value of j, which is 16, and calculates the new value, which is 33. This is added to the literal value 7 and stored in j in main, resulting in the value 40, which is then displayed by the output statement.

Don't get discouraged if you didn't get this one, especially the effects caused by a global i. Even experienced programmers can be taken by surprise by programs that use global variables in such error-prone ways.

Problem
Algorithms
C++
Executable
Hardware

Chapter 6

Taking Inventory

A class Act

Now we have enough of the fundamentals of programming under our belts to look at some of the more powerful features of C++. As I've mentioned before, C++ is the successor to C. What I haven't told you is *why* it was invented. One of the main reasons was to improve on C's support for user defined data types. What are these, and why are they so important?

As is the case with C++, the data types available in C are divided into two groups: **native** (i.e., defined in the language itself) and **user defined** (i.e., defined by the programmer).[1] However, there is a major difference between C and C++ in the support provided to user defined types. In C, variables of the native types are fully supported by the language, while variables of user defined types are not; the native types that we've been using are char, short, and unsigned short (and int, but only for the return type of main), all of which have been inherited from C.[2]

By fully supported, I mean that native variables in both C and C++ can be defined, initialized, assigned values, passed as arguments and return values, and compared to other values of the same type. Such a variable can be assigned storage in either the static or auto storage

---

1. In this case, *user* means "programmer"; i.e., the user of the language itself, rather than the user of a program written in the language.

2. There are actually several other native C++ types that we haven't used: long, float, double, and bool. The long type is useful for storing whole-number values that are larger than will fit into a short (hence the name), while float and double are able to store values that have fractional parts as well as integral values. These are useful in scientific and engineering calculations; I'll go into these types in somewhat more detail in Appendix A. The bool type, recently added to C++, is useful for keeping track of a true/false condition. We'll see how to use this variable type later in this chapter.

classes: If a variable is auto, the storage is assigned at entry to the function where it is defined, and released automatically at exit from that function; if it is static, it is initialized to some reasonable value either at link time (for a *global* variable) or upon the first entry to the function where it is defined (for a *local* variable).[3] However, most of these facilities aren't available to user defined data types in C. For example, they can't be compared; of course, this limitation is understandable, since the compiler has no idea how to compare two variables of a type that you define. Similarly, what is a reasonable default value for a variable of a user defined type? Presumably, the user (i.e., the programmer) knows, but the compiler doesn't.

In this chapter, we'll see how to give the compiler enough information to allow data types that we define to behave just like the native types. Let's start out with some definitions and objectives. Susan had a revealing question here:

> **Susan**: I think I need to find out something here. I am getting the impression that what is "native" is C and what is "user defined" is C++. Is that right? And if so, why?

> **Steve**: Pretty much so. As to why, the answer is pretty simple: the reason that C++ was invented in the first place was to add good support for user defined types to the efficiency of C.

Problem
Algorithms
C++
Executable
Hardware

Definitions

A class is a user defined type.

A class **interface** tells the compiler what facilities the class provides. This interface is usually found in a header file, which by convention has the extension .h.

A class **implementation** tells the compiler how to implement the facilities defined in the class interface. This is usually found in a source code file, which in the case of the compiler on the CD-ROM in the back of this book usually has the extension .cc.

An **object** is a variable of a class type. Its behavior is defined by the code that implements the class.

A **member function** is a function that is part of the definition of a class.

---

3. Please note that the terms class and *storage class* have nothing to do with one another. This is another case where C++ reuses the same word for different concepts.

A **member variable** is a variable that is part of the definition of a class.

Objectives of This Chapter

By the end of this chapter, you should

1. Understand what a user defined type (a class) is, and how it is defined.
2. Understand how variables of some simple classes are created, destroyed, and copied.
3. Understand how and why access to the internals of a class is controlled.

Pay Some Attention to the Man Behind the Curtain

In C++, a user defined variable is called an *object*. Each object has a type, just like variables of native types (short, char, etc.). For example, if we define a class called StockItem (as we will do in this chapter), then an object can be of type StockItem, just as a native variable can be of type short. However, an additional step is required when we want to use user defined types. Since the compiler has no intrinsic knowledge of these types, we have to tell it exactly what they are and how they work. We do this by defining a class, which specifies both the data contained in the user defined variable and what operations can be performed on these data.

Problem
Algorithms
C++
Executable
Hardware

This may be too abstract to be very clear or helpful to you if you're not familiar with this idea of making up your own data types, which you probably aren't. Here's how Susan put it upon her first encounter with this idea.

> **Susan**: I can tell that there is only one thing that I think that I understand about this. That is, that C++ is not a language. You have to *make it up* as you go along. . . .

That may be overdoing it a bit, but there is a grain of truth in her observation: C++ is more of a "language kit" than it is a language. What do I mean by this?

I mean that to use C++ in the most effective way, rather than merely as a "better C", it is necessary to make up data types and tell the compiler how to treat them as though they were native data types. So far in this book, we have been using data types that were previously defined, either by the compiler and language (*native* types, e.g., short, char) or by libraries (class types, e.g., string). Now we're going to actually make up our own types that will be usable just like those of a native type; the difference between using variables and making up new variable types is analogous to the difference between using a program and writing a program, but carried to the next higher level.

In the event that you find this notion hard to understand, you're not alone; neither did Susan.

> **Susan**: This is an outrage! I didn't understand one other word as I was far beyond anything that could even be described as shock. I think I did faint. I may as well have been in a coma.

Interestingly enough, she did in fact understand this idea of making up our own data types, so perhaps she was overestimating the degree of her shock.

Before we get back to the technical explanation of how we create new data types, I'm sure one more question is burning in your mind: *Why* should we do this? What's wrong with the native types like char and short? The answer is simple: We make up types so that we can match the language to the needs of the problem we're trying to solve. For example, suppose we want to write a program to do inventory control for a small business like a grocery store. Such a program needs objects representing items in the store, which have prices, names, and so on. We'd need to define each of these types of objects so that it can display the behavior appropriate to the thing it represents. The availability of objects that have relevance to the problem being solved makes it much easier to write (and *read*) a program to handle inventory than if everything has to be made of shorts and chars.

I suspect that the advantages of making up one's own data types may still not be apparent to some of you, so let me make an analogy with natural languages. Making up new data types in C++ is in some ways quite similar to making up new words in English (for example). You might think that if everyone made up new words, the result would be chaos. Actually, this is correct, with the very important exception of technical jargon and other vocabularies that are shared by people who have more in common than simply being speakers of English. For example, physicians have their own "language" in the form of medical terminology. Of course, a cynical observer might

Problem
Algorithms
C++
Executable
Hardware

conclude that the reason for such specialized vocabulary is to befuddle or impress the naive listener, and of course it can be used for that purpose. However, there is also a much more significant and valid reason: The ability of experts in a field to communicate with one another quickly and precisely. The same is true of creating our own data types; they enable us to write programs more easily and more understandably to those who are conversant with the problems being solved. It's much easier to talk to a store owner about inventory objects than about shorts and chars!

Here's the discussion that Susan and I had on this topic:

Susan: Why should we have user defined data types?

Steve: So that you can match the language to the needs of the problem you're trying to solve. For example, if you were writing a nurse's station program in C++, you would want to have objects that represented nurses, doctors, patients, various sorts of equipment, and so on. Each of these objects would display the behavior appropriate to the thing or person it was representing.

Susan: Why do you need that? What if each individual who spoke English made up a unique version of English (well, it is user defined, right?), how can we communicate? This is garbage.

Steve: We need user defined types for the same reason that specialists need jargon in their technical fields. For example, why do you health-care professionals need words like tachycardia? Why don't you just say "a fast heartbeat" in simple English?

Hey, that's not a bad way to explain this: Adding classes is like adding specialized vocabulary to English. I don't remember ever seeing that explanation before; what do you think of it?

Susan: Huh? Then you are saying that, by defining a class of objects, they can take on more realistic qualities than just abstract notions? That is, if I wanted to define *nurse* in a program, then I would do it with a class named nurse and then I can define in that program the activities and functions that the nurse objects would be doing. Is this how you keep everything straight, and not mix them up with other objects?

Steve: Yes, that's one of the main benefits of object-oriented programming. You might be surprised how hard it is to teach an old-line C programmer the importance of this point.

Susan: So is this what object-oriented programming is? I have heard of it, but never knew what it meant. Could it also be described as user defined programming? I guess there are advantages to teaching a novice;

Problem
Algorithms
C++
Executable
Hardware

you don't have to undo old ideas to make way for newer ones. It is just that little matter of total bewilderment that you must deal with.

Steve: Yes, but I'm getting used to that.

Susan: So, anything that is user defined is a class? That is, native variables are not classes?

Steve: Every user defined type is a class; data items of a class type are called *objects*. Variables of native types are not objects in the strict sense.

Susan: OK, so if I want to make up something, then what I make up is called a class as opposed to the other type of stuff that isn't made up and is really C++; that is called *native*. That is intuitive, thank you. Then the stuff I put in the made up stuff (you realize you are reading at a sixth grade level here?) are all data items? And that data is called an *object*, or only the variables of made up stuff are called *objects*? I guess just the variables of the class are called *objects* because I just made an effort to move and read your definition for *object*. So native variables are not objects, they are just variables. Am I am talking in circles again?

```
Problem
Algorithms
C++
Executable
Hardware
```

Steve: No, you're not; you're making perfect sense. The only point you have missed is that there are functions in the objects, as well as data items. We'll get into that shortly.

Susan: So Steve, tell me this: What have I been doing up to this point? How does this new stuff compare to the old stuff and which one is it that the programmer really uses? (Let's see, do I want curtain 1 or 3; which one holds the prize?) I just want to get a little sense of direction here; I don't think that is a whole lot to ask, do you?

Steve: What you've been doing up to this point is *using* classes (string, vector) as well as native types like short and char. This new stuff shows how to *create* classes like string, rather than just using them.[4]

Assuming that I've sold you on the advantages of making up our own data types, let's see how we can actually do it. Each data type is represented by a class, whose full definition is composed of two parts: the **interface** definition (usually contained in a file with the extension .h), and the **implementation** definition (usually contained in a file with the extension .cc). The interface definition tells the compiler (and the class user) *what* the class does, while the implementation definition tells the compiler *how* the objects of that

---

4. In case you were wondering, you can't create new native types.

class actually perform the functions specified in the interface definition. Let's take a look at a step-by-step description of how to create and use a class.

1.   Write the class interface definition, which will be stored in a file with the extension .h. In our example of a StockItem class, we'll use item1.h to hold our first version of this interface definition. This definition tells the compiler the names and types of the member functions and variables that make up the objects of the class. This gives the compiler enough information that objects of this class can be created in a user's program.

2.   Write the class implementation definition, which will be stored in a file with the extension .cc; in our example, the first one of these will be stored in the file item1.cc. This definition is the code that tells the compiler how to perform the operations that the interface definition refers to. The implementation definition file must #include the interface definition file (item1.h, in this case) so that the compiler can tell what the interface is that is being implemented.

3.   Write the program that uses objects in the class to do some work; the first such program we'll write will be itemtst1.cc. This program also needs to #include the interface definition file, so that the compiler can tell how to create objects of this class.

4.   Compile the class implementation definition to produce an object file (item1.o). This makes the class available for use by the user program.

5.   Compile the user program to produce an object file (itemtst1.o).

6.   Link the object file from the user program, the object file from the class implementation definition, and the standard libraries together to form a finished executable; our first sample will be called itemtst1.exe.

```
Problem
Algorithm
C++
Executable
Hardware
```

A couple of items in this list need some more discussion. Let's see how Susan brought them to my attention.

Susan: I have a problem here. First under section 2, you put "The class implementation definition file must #include"; excuse me, but that doesn't make sense. What do you mean by #include? How do you say that, "pound include"?

Steve: Yes, that's how it's pronounced. You could also leave off the "pound" and just say "include", and every C and C++ programmer would understand you.

Susan: Section 6 that stuff with the linking. . .isn't that done by the compiler; if not, how do you do it?

Steve: The linker does it, but the compiler is generally capable of calling the linker automatically for you; that's why we haven't needed to worry about this before.

Susan: OK, where is the linker? Is it not part of the compiler software? If not, where does it come from?

Steve: Every compiler comes with one, but you can also buy one separately if you prefer.

Susan: Who puts it in your computer? Also, how do you "call" the linker if you have always had the compiler do it for you?

Problem
Algorithms
C++
Executable
Hardware

Steve: It is installed along with the compiler. You can tell the compiler not to call it automatically if you prefer to do it manually; there are reasons to do that sometimes. For example, when you're making a change that affects only one module in a large program, you recompile only that one module, then relink all the object files again to make the executable.

Susan: How do you do that manually?

Steve: This varies according to what compiler you're using. With the DJGPP compiler, you use the compiler to compile one file and then tell the compiler separately to use the linker to link all the object files. If you want to run the linker directly, you can use the gxx command instead of the usual gcc command that runs the compiler.

Taking Stock

Now let's start on our first class definition, which is designed to help solve the problem of maintaining inventory in a small grocery store. We need to keep track of all the items that we carry, so we're going to define a class called StockItem. The StockItem class, like other classes, is composed of a number of functions and variables. As I suggested to Susan earlier, to make this more concrete, think of something like Lego blocks, which you can put together to make parts that can in turn be used to build bigger structures. The smallest

Legos are the native types, and the bigger, composite ones are class types.

For the compiler to be able to define an object correctly, we'll have to tell it the names and types of the member variables that will be used to store the information about each StockItem; this enables the compiler to allocate memory for a StockItem.

So how do we identify these member variables? By considering what member variables each StockItem object will need to keep track of its corresponding item in the stock of the store. After some thought, I've come up with the following list of member variables:

1. The name of the item (m_Name),
2. The number in stock (m_InStock),
3. The distributor that we purchase it from (m_Distributor),
4. The price we charge (m_Price), and
5. The item number, or UPC (m_UPC).

What I mean by *an item* is actually something like "chunky chicken soup, 16 oz.", rather than a specific object like a particular can of soup. In other words, every can of soup with the same item number is considered equivalent to every other can of soup with the same item number, so all we have to keep track of for each item can be described by the above data. For the item number, we'll use the Universal Product Code (UPC), which is printed as a bar code on almost every product other than fresh produce; it's a 10-digit number, which we'll represent as a string for convenience. As is appropriate for a class, every StockItem object has the same member variables associated with it.

Susan took me to task about the notion of a StockItem object vs. a specific object like a particular can of soup. It didn't take too long to clear this one up:

> **Susan**: When you say "rather than a specific object like a particular can of soup". How much more specific can you get than "chunky chicken soup, 16 oz."?

> **Steve**: Each can of chunky chicken soup is at least slightly different from every other one; at the very least, they occupy different volumes of space.

> **Susan**: So by *specific object* you mean an individual can of soup, even though it may be identical to all the others, just one of many of the same type. Is that it?

Problem
Algorithm
C++
Executable
Hardware

Steve: Exactly.

Let's recap what we know about a StockItem so far. We know that we need a member variable in the class definition for each value in the above description. Each StockItem object will store the name of the item (m_Name), its price (m_Price), the number of items in stock (m_InStock), the name of the distributor (m_Distributor), and the UPC (m_UPC) of the item.

Of course, merely storing these data isn't very useful unless we can do something with them. Therefore, objects of the StockItem class also need to be able to perform several operations on their data; we'll start by giving them the ability to display their contents. Figure 6.1 illustrates a very simple way that this class might be used.

```
#include <iostream.h>
#include "string6.h"
#include "item1.h"

int main()
{
    StockItem soup;

    soup = StockItem("Chunky Chicken",32,129,
    "Bob's Distribution","123456789");

    soup.Display();

    return 0;
}
```

```
Problem
Algorithms
C++
Executable
Hardware
```

Figure 6.1: The initial sample program for the StockItem class
(code\itemtst1.cc)

This program defines a StockItem named soup, assigns it some data, displays it on the screen via a function called Display, and finally terminates normally. By the time we're done with this chapter, you'll understand exactly how every operation in this program is performed by the StockItem class. Before we get too deeply into this particular class, however, we should look at the functions that almost all classes have in common. First, we'll need some more definitions to clarify the terms that we'll need for the discussion.

More Definitions

A **concrete data type** is a class whose objects behave like variables of native data types. That is, the class gives the compiler enough information that its objects can be created, copied, assigned, and automatically destroyed just as native variables are. The StockItem class that we will construct in this chapter is a concrete data type.

A **constructor** is a member function that creates new variables of the class type. All constructors have the same name as the class for which they are constructors; therefore, the constructors for StockItem variables also have the name StockItem.

A **default constructor** is a constructor that is used when no initial value is specified for an object. Because it is a constructor, it has the same name as the class; since it is used when no initial value is specified, it has no arguments. Thus, StockItem() is the default constructor for the StockItem class.

A **copy constructor** makes a new object with the same contents as an existing object of the same type.

An **assignment operator** is a member function that sets a pre-existing object to the same value as another object of the same type.

A **destructor** is a member function that cleans up when an object expires; for a local object, this occurs at the end of the function where that object is defined.

Problem
Algorithms
C++
Executable
Hardware

Common Behavior

While different classes vary considerably in the facilities that they provide, there are significant benefits to a class whose objects behave like those of native types. As I've just mentioned, such a class is called a *concrete data type*. To make a class a concrete data type, we must define certain member functions that allow creation, copying, and deletion to behave as with a native variable.

Susan wanted to see a chart illustrating the correspondence between what the compiler does for a native type and what we have to do to supply the same functionality to allow a new data type that we define to behave in the same way as a native data type; that is, to make our new type a concrete data type. Of course, I complied with her request: the result is Figure 6.2.

The Native Problem	A Concrete Plan
Here are the essential facilities that the compiler provides for every native type:	To make a concrete data type, we have to provide each of these facilities for our new type. By no coincidence, there is a specific type of member function to provide each of them. Here are the official names and descriptions of each of these four functions:
1. The ability to create a variable with no specified initial value (an uninitialized variable), e.g., short x;.	**1**. A *default constructor* that can create an object when there is no initial value specified for the object.
2. The ability to pass a variable as an argument to a function; in this case, the compiler has to make a copy of the variable so that the called function doesn't change the value of the variable in the calling function.	**2**. A *copy constructor* that can make a new object with the same contents as an existing object of the same type.
3. The ability to assign a value of an appropriate type to a variable that already exists, such as x = 22; or x = z;.	**3**. An *assignment operator* that is used to set an existing object to the value of another object of the same type.
4. Reclaiming the storage assigned to a variable when it ceases to exist, so that those memory addresses can be reallocated to other uses. In the case of auto variables, this is at the end of the function where they were created; with static variables, it's at the end of execution of the program.	**4**. A *destructor* that cleans up when an object expires, including releasing the memory that the object has occupied; for a local object, this occurs at the end of the function where the object was created.

```
Problem
Algorithms
C++
Executable
Hardware
```

Figure 6.2: Comparison of native and class types

Because these member functions are so fundamental to the proper operation of a class, the compiler will generate a version of each of them for us if we don't write them ourselves, just as the corresponding behavior is automatically supplied for the native types. As we will see in Chapter 7, the compiler-generated functions are sometimes too simplistic to be used in a complex class, so we need to create our own versions of these functions. I'll illustrate how to do that at the appropriate time. However, with a simple class such as the one we're creating here, the compiler-generated versions of the assignment operator, copy constructor, and destructor are perfectly adequate, so we won't be creating our own versions of these functions for StockItem.

Susan was a bit confused about the distinction between the compiler-generated versions of these essential functions and the compiler's built-in knowledge of the native types:

> **Susan**: Aren't the compiler-generated versions the same thing as the native versions?

> **Steve**: No, they're analogous but not the same. The compiler-generated functions are created only for objects, not for native types. The behavior of the native types is implemented directly in the compiler, not by means of functions.

> **Susan**: I'm confused. Maybe it would help if you explained what you mean by "implemented directly in the compiler". Are you just saying that objects are implemented only by functions, whereas the native types are implemented by the built-in facilities of the compiler?

> **Steve**: You're not confused, you're correct.

> **Susan**: OK, here we go again. About the assignment operator, what is this "version"? I thought you said earlier that if you don't write your own assignment operator it will use the native operator. So I don't get this.

> **Steve**: There is no native assignment operator for any class type; instead, the compiler will generate an assignment operator for a class if we don't do it ourselves.

> **Susan**: Then how can the compiler create an assignment operator if it doesn't know what it is doing?

> **Steve**: All the compiler-generated assignment operator does is to copy all of the members of the right-hand variable to the left-hand variable.

Problem
Algorithms
C++
Executable
Hardware

This is good enough with the StockItem class. We'll see in Chapter 7 why this isn't always acceptable.

Susan: Isn't a simple copy all that the native assignment operator does?

Steve: The only native assignment operators that exist are for native types. Once we define our own types, the compiler has to generate assignment operators for us if we don't do it ourselves; otherwise, it would be impossible to copy the value of one variable of a class type to another without writing an assignment operator explicitly.

Susan: OK, this is what confused me, I just thought that the natives would be used as a default if we didn't define our own in the class type, even though they would not work well.

Steve: They will. That's what the compiler-generated assignment operator does. I think we have a semantic problem here, not a substantive one.

Susan: Why doesn't it default to the native assignment operator if it doesn't have any other information to direct it to make a class type operator? This is most distressing to me.

Problem
Algorithms
C++
Executable
Hardware

Steve: There isn't any native assignment operator for a StockItem. How could there be? The compiler has never heard of a StockItem until we define that class.

Susan: So it would be a third type of assignment operator. At this point, I am aware of the native type, the user defined type and a compiler-generated type.

Steve: Right. The native type is built into the compiler, the user defined type is defined by. . . the user, and the compiler-generated type is created by the compiler for user defined types where the user didn't define his own.

Susan: Then the native default and the compiler-generated assignment operator are the same? If so, why did you agree with me that there must be three different types of assignment operators? In that case there would really only be two.

Steve: No, there is a difference. Here is the rundown:

   1.   (Native assignment) The knowledge of how to assign values of every native type is built into the compiler; whenever such an assignment is needed, the compiler emits prewritten code

that copies the value from the source variable to the destination variable.

2. (Compiler-generated assignment) The knowledge of how to create an assignment operator for any class type is built into the compiler; the compiler generates code for an assignment operator that merely copies all of the members of the source variable to the destination variable. Note that this is slightly different from 1, where the compiler writes the instructions directly into the object file whenever the assignment is done; here, it generates an assignment operator and then uses that operator whenever an assignment is done.

3. (User defined assignment) This does exactly what we define it to do.

Susan: Did you ever discuss the source variable and the destination variable? I don't recall that concept in past discussions. I like this. All I remember is when you said that = means to set the variable on the left to the value on the right. Does this mean that the variable on the left is the destination variable and the value on the right is the source variable?

Steve: Yes, if the value on the right is a variable; it could also be an expression such as "x + 2".

Susan: But how could it be a variable if it is a known value?

Steve: It's not its value that is known, but its name. Its value can vary at run time, depending on how the program has executed up till this point.

Susan: So the main difference is that in 1 the instructions are already there to be used. In 2 the instructions for the assignment operator have to be "called up" to be used.

Steve: That's a good explanation.

Problem
Algorithms
C++
Executable
Hardware

After my explanation of the advantages of a concrete data type, Susan became completely convinced, so much so that she wondered why we would ever want anything else.

Susan: On your definition for concrete data types. . . this is fine, but what I am thinking is that if something *wasn't* a concrete data type, then it wouldn't work, that is unless it was native. So what would a workable alternative to a concrete data type be?

Steve: Usually, we do want our objects to be concrete data types. However, there are times when, say, we don't want to copy a given object. In the case of an object representing a window on the screen, copying such an object would cause another window to be displayed, which is probably not what we would want to happen.

Susan: OK, so what would you call an object that isn't of a concrete data type?

Steve: There's no special name for an object that *isn't* of a concrete data type.

Susan: So things that are not of a concrete data type have no names?

Steve: No, they have names; I was just saying that there's no term like *non-concrete data type*, meaning one that doesn't act like a native variable. There is a term *abstract data type*, but that means something else.

Susan: See, this is where I am still not clear. Again, if something is *not* a concrete data type, then what is it?

Problem
Algorithms
C++
Executable
Hardware

Steve: There's no special term for a class that doesn't act like a native variable type. If something isn't a concrete data type, then you can't treat it like a native variable. Either you can't copy it, or you can't assign to it, or you can't construct it by default, or you can't destruct it automatically at the end of the function (or some combination of these). The lack of any of those features prevents a class from being a concrete data type.

Susan: Of what use would it be to have a class of a non-concrete data type? To me, it just sounds like an error.

Steve: Sometimes it does make sense. For example, you might want to create a class that has no default constructor; to create an element of such a class, you would have to supply one or more arguments. This is useful in preventing the use of an object that doesn't have any meaningful content; however, the lack of a default constructor does restrict the applicability of such a class, so it's best to provide such a constructor if possible.

Before we can implement these member functions for our StockItem class, we have to define what a StockItem is in more detail than my previous sketch.[5] Let's start with the simplified version of the interface specification for that class in Figure 6.3, which includes

---

5. By the way, in using a functional class such as StockItem to illustrate these concepts, I'm violating a venerable tradition in C++ tutorials. Normally, example classes represent zoo animals, or shapes, or something equally useful in common programming situations.

the specification of the default constructor, the display function, and another constructor that is specific to the StockItem class.

```
class StockItem
{
public:
    StockItem();

    StockItem(string Name, short InStock, short Price,
    string Distributor, string UPC);

    void Display();

private:
    short m_InStock;
    short m_Price;
    string m_Name;
    string m_Distributor;
    string m_UPC;
};
```

Figure 6.3: The initial interface of the StockItem class (code\item1.h)

Problem
Algorithms
C++
Executable
Hardware

Your first reaction is probably something like "What a bunch of malarkey!" Let's take it a little at a time, and you'll see that this seeming gibberish actually has a rhyme and reason to it. First we have the line class StockItem. This tells the compiler that what follows is the definition of a class interface, which as we have already seen is a description of the operations that can be performed on objects of a given user defined type;[6] in this case, the type is StockItem. So that the compiler knows where this description begins and ends, it is enclosed in {}, just like any other block of information that is to be treated as one item.

After the opening {, the next line says public:. This is a new type of declaration called an **access specifier**, which tells the compiler the "security classification" of the item(s) following it, up to the next

---

6. For the implementation of the functions in this interface specification, see the following figures:

    1.   For StockItem(), see Figure 6.4.
    2.   For StockItem(string Name, short InStock, short Price, string Distributor, string UPC), see Figure 6.6.
    3.   For Display(), see Figure 6.7.

access specifier. This particular access specifier, public, means that any part of the program, whether it is defined in this class or not, can use the items starting immediately after the public declaration, and continuing until there is another access specifier.[7] In the current case, all of the items following the public specifier are operations that we wish to perform on StockItem objects. Since they are public, we can use them anywhere in our programs. You may be wondering why everything isn't public; why should we prevent ourselves (or users of our classes) from using everything in the classes? It's not just hardheartedness; it's actually a way of improving the reliability and flexibility of our software, as I'll explain later.

As you might imagine, this notion of access specifiers didn't get past Susan without a battle. Here's the blow-by-blow account.

Susan: So, is public a word that is used often or is it just something you made up for this example?

Steve: It's a keyword of the C++ language, which has intrinsic meaning to the compiler. In this context, it means "any function, inside or outside this class, can access the following stuff, up to the next access specifier (if any)." Because it is a keyword, you can't have a variable named public, just as you can't have one named if.

Problem
Algorithms
C++
Executable
Hardware

Susan: These access specifiers: What are they, anyway? Are they always used in classes?

Steve: Yes.

Susan: Why aren't they needed for native variables?

Steve: Because you can't define access specifiers for native types; their interface and implementation are all predefined in the compiler.

Susan: What does *internals* mean? Do you mean stuff that is done by the compiler rather than stuff that can be done by the programmer?

Steve: Yes, in the case of native data types. In the case of class types, *internals* means the details of implementation of the type rather than what it does for the user.

Susan: You know, I understand what you are saying about *internals*; that is, I know what the words mean, but I just can't picture what you

---

7. By the way, public is a keyword in C++; that is, it is defined in the language. This means that you cannot have a function or variable called public.

are doing when you say *implementation*. I don't see what is actually happening at this point.

Steve: The implementation of a class is the code that is responsible for actually doing the things that the interface says the objects of the class can do. All of the code in the item1.cc file is part of the implementation of StockItem. In addition, the private member variables in the header file are logically part of the implementation, since the user of the class can't access them directly.

Susan: Why is a class function called a *member function*? I like class function better; it is more intuitive.

Steve: Sorry, I didn't make up the terminology. However, I think *member function* is actually more descriptive, because these functions are members (parts) of the objects of the class.

Susan: So on these variables, that m_ stuff; do you just do that to differentiate them from a native variable? If so, why would there be a confusion, since you have already told the compiler you are defining a class? Therefore, all that is in that class should already be understood to be in the class rather than the native language. I don't like to look at that m_ stuff; it's too cryptic.

Steve: It's true that the compiler can tell whether a variable is a member variable or a global variable. However, it can still be useful to give a different name to a member variable so that the *programmer* can tell which is which. Remember, a member variable looks like a global variable in a class implementation, because you don't declare it as you would an argument or a local variable.

Problem
Algorithms
C++
Executable
Hardware

Now we're up to the line that says StockItem();. This is the declaration for a function called a *constructor*, which tells the compiler what to do when we define a variable of a user defined type, since as we have already seen, there's no way for it to know this otherwise. This particular constructor is the *default constructor* for the StockItem class. It's called the "default" constructor because it is used when no initial value is specified by the user; the empty parentheses after the name of the function indicate the lack of arguments to the function. The name of the function is the clue that it's a constructor; the name of a constructor is always the same as the name of the class for which it's a constructor, to make it easier for the compiler to identify constructors among all of the possible functions in a class.

This idea of having variables and functions "inside" objects wasn't intuitively obvious to Susan:

Susan: Now, where you talk about mixing a string and a short in the same function, can this not be done in the native language?

Steve: It's not in the same function but in the same variable. We are creating a user defined variable that can be used just like a native variable.

Susan: OK, so you have a class StockItem. And it has a function called StockItem. But a StockItem is a variable, so in this respect a function can be inside a variable?

Steve: Correct. A StockItem is a variable that is composed of a number of functions and other variables.

Susan: OK, I think I am seeing the big picture now. But you know that this seems like such a departure from what I thought was going on before, where we used native types in functions rather than the other way around. Like when I wrote my little program, it would have shorts in it but they would be in the function main. So this is a complete turnabout from the way I used to think about them; this is hard.

Problem
Algorithms
C++
Executable
Hardware

Steve: Yes, that is a difficult transition to make. Interestingly enough, experience isn't necessarily an advantage here; you haven't had as much trouble with it as some professional programmers who have a lot more experience in writing functions as "stand-alone" things with no intrinsic ties to data structures. However, it is one of the essentials in object-oriented programming; most functions live "inside" objects, and do the bidding of those objects, rather than being wild and free.

Why do we need to write our own default constructor? Well, although we have already specified the member variables used by the class, so that the compiler can assign storage as with any other static or auto variable, that isn't enough information for the compiler to know how to initialize the objects of the class correctly.[8] Unlike a native variable, the compiler can't set a newly created StockItem to a reasonable value, since it doesn't understand what the member variables of a StockItem are used for. That is, it can't do the initialization without help from us. In the code for our default constructor, we will set the member variables to legitimate values, so

---

8. In case it isn't obvious how the compiler can figure out the size of the object, consider that the class definition specifies all of the variables that are used to implement the objects of the class; since the compiler already knows the definitions of all of these components, it can calculate the size of our class variables based on the sizes and types of those components. By the way, the size of our object isn't necessarily the sum of the sizes of its components; the compiler often has to add some space to the objects for reasons that are, unfortunately, beyond the scope of this book.

that we don't have to worry about having an uninitialized StockItem lying around as we did with a short in a previous example. Figure 6.4 shows what the code to our first default constructor looks like.

```
StockItem::StockItem()
{
     m_InStock = 0;
     m_Price = 0;
     m_Name = "";
     m_Distributor = "";
     m_UPC = "";
};
```

Figure 6.4: The default constructor for the StockItem class (from code\item1.cc)

Let's use this example of a StockItem class to illuminate the distinction between interface and implementation. As I've already mentioned, the implementation of a class is the code that is responsible for actually doing the things promised by the interface of that class. The interface was laid out in Figure 6.3. With the exception of the test program that illustrates the use of the StockItem class, all of the code that we will examine in this chapter is part of the implementation: This includes the constructors and the Display member function.

So you can keep track of where this fits into the "big picture", the code in Figure 6.4 is the implementation of the function StockItem::StockItem() (i.e., the default constructor for the class StockItem), whose interface was defined in Figure 6.3.

Now, how does it work? Actually, this function isn't all that different from a "regular" function, but there are some important differences. First of all, the name looks sort of funny: Why is StockItem repeated?

The answer is that, unlike "regular" (technically, *global*) functions, a *member function* always belongs to a particular class. That is, such a function has special access to the data and other functions in the class. To mark its membership, its name consists of the name of the class (in this case, StockItem), followed by the class *membership* operator ::, followed by the name of the function (which in this case, is also StockItem); as we have already seen, the name of a constructor is always the same as the name of its class. Figure 6.5 shows how each component of the function declaration contributes to the whole.[9]

Problem
Algorithms
C++
Executable
Hardware

---

9. By the way, spaces between components of the name aren't significant; that is, we can have them, as in Figure 6.5, or leave them out, as we did in Figure 6.4.

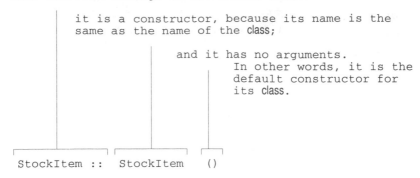

This function belongs to the StockItem class;

    it is a constructor, because its name is the
    same as the name of the class;

        and it has no arguments.
           In other words, it is the
           default constructor for
           its class.

```
StockItem ::   StockItem    ()
```

Figure 6.5: The declaration of the default constructor for the StockItem class

If you've really been paying attention, there's one thing that you may have noticed about this declaration as compared with the original declaration of this function in the class interface definition for StockItem (Figure 6.3). In that figure, we declared this same function as StockItem();, without the additional StockItem:: on the front. Why didn't we need to specify the StockItem:: class membership in the class interface definition? Because inside the declaration of a class, we don't have to specify what class the member functions belong to; by definition, they belong to the class we're defining. Thus, StockItem() in the class interface declaration means "the member function StockItem, having no arguments"; i.e., the default constructor for the StockItem class.

Susan didn't have any trouble with this point, which was quite a relief to me, as I was dreading a big argument.

> **Susan**: Oh, so you don't have to write StockItem::StockItem in the interface definition because it is implied by the class StockItem declaration?
>
> **Steve**: Right.

Now let's look at the executable part of the function (Figure 6.4), which initializes the member variables of the StockItem class; to be more specific, it sets m_InStock and m_Price to 0, and the string variables m_Name, m_Distributor, and m_UPC to "" (that is, an empty C string).

Susan had an objection to my cavalier use of the empty C string "":

Problem
Algorithms
C++
Executable
Hardware

Susan: Excuse me, but what kind of value is " " ? Do you know how annoying it is to keep working with nothing?

Steve: It's not " ", but "". The former has a space between the quotes, and the latter does not; the former is a one-character C string consisting of one space, while the latter is a zero-character C string.

Susan: OK, so the "" is an empty C string, but could you please explain how this works?

Steve: The "" means that we have a C string with no data in it. The compiler generates a literal C string consisting of just the terminating null byte.

Susan: What good does that do? I don't get it.

Steve: Well, a string has to have some value for its char* to point to; if we don't have any real data, then using an empty C string for that purpose is analogous to setting a numeric value to 0.

Susan: OK, so this is only setting the strings in the default constructor to a value that the compiler can understand so you don't get an error message, although there is no real data. We're trying to fool the compiler, right?

Steve: Close, but not quite. Basically, we want to make sure that we know the state of the strings in a default StockItem. We don't want to have trouble with uninitialized variables; remember how much trouble they can cause?

Susan: Yes, I remember. So this is just the way to initialize a string when you don't know what real value it will end up having?

Steve: Right.

Problem
Algorithms
C++
Executable
Hardware

Now let's get back to the member variables of StockItem. One important characteristic of any variable is its scope, so we should pay attention to the scope of these variables. In Chapter 5, we saw two scopes in which a variable could be defined: *local* (i.e., available only within the function where it was defined) and *global* (i.e., available anywhere in the program). Well, these variables aren't arguments (which have local scope) since they don't appear in the function's header, and they aren't defined in the function; therefore, they aren't local variables. Surely they can't be global variables, after I showed you how treacherous those can be.

Go to the Head of the class

I haven't misled you on that point; there is another scope called class **scope**, which applies to all member variables of a class.[10] Class scope means that each object of a given class has one set of member variables. In the case of StockItem, this set of variables consists of m_InStock, m_Price, m_Name, m_Distributor, and m_UPC. Member functions of a class can access member variables of that class without defining them, as though they were global variables.

In addition to scope, each member variable has another attribute we have already encountered: an access specifier. The access of nonmember functions to any member variable or member function depends on the access specifier in effect when the member variable or function was defined. If you look back at Figure 6.3, you'll see that the line private: precedes the definition of the member variables in the StockItem class. The keyword private is an access specifier, like public; however, where a public access specifier allows any function to access the items that follow it, a private access specifier allows only member functions to access items that follow it.[11]

Susan had some more questions about access specifiers, including this new one, private:

> **Susan**: It seems to me that the access specifiers act more like scope than anything. Are they about the same?
>
> **Steve**: Yes, the difference between public and private is somewhat analogous to the difference between global and local variables, but the latter distinction affects where a variable is stored and when it is initialized, whereas an access specifier controls what functions can

---

10. Actually, I'm describing "normal" member variables here. There is another kind, which we won't be covering.

11. Although scope rules and access specifiers are similar in some ways, in that they affect where a variable can be used, they aren't exactly the same. Scope defines where a variable is visible, whereas access specifiers control where a variable (or function) is accessible. That is, if you write a program that tries to read or modify a private variable from outside the class implementation, the compiler knows what you're trying to do but won't let you do it. On the other hand, if you try to access a local variable from a function where it isn't defined, the compiler just tells you it never heard of that variable, which indeed it hasn't in that context. For example, let's suppose that the local variable x defined in function abc has no existence in any other function; in that case, if you try to access a variable named x in another function, say def, where it hasn't been defined, you'll get an error message from the compiler telling you that there is no variable x in function def. However, if there is a a private member variable called x defined in class ghi, and you try to access that member variable from a nonmember function, the compiler will tell you that you're trying to do something illegal. It knows which x you mean, but it won't let you access it because you don't have permission.

access the variable. However, because member variables are defined inside classes, they can't be global, nor can they be local in the sense that a "regular" (i.e., nonmember) variable can be; a member variable must always live inside a single occurrence of an object of its class.

Susan: Are they necessary for every class?

Steve: Pretty much. The default specifier for a class is private; that is, everything you declare in a class interface before the first explicit access specifier is private. Of course, this also means that if you don't ever provide an explicit access specifier in a given class, then everything declared in that class will be private. This isn't usually very useful, because without any public functions it's hard to use a class at all.

Susan: There is a default? Then why would the default be the least useful?

Steve: To make the programmer specify what should be publicly accessible rather than have it happen automatically. In general, it's best to keep as much as possible private, to reduce the dependency of external code on the internal implementation of the class. This makes it easier to change that implementation without causing trouble for the users of the class.

Susan: OK, that makes sense now. Are there any other kinds of access specifiers or are these the only two?

Steve: Actually, there's one more, but it applies only in cases that we won't get to.

Susan: OK, it's good to know that there won't be any more surprises later on.

Steve: I aim to please.

Susan also wanted some more details about this new class scope.

Susan: How about explaining the difference between a class scope and a public access specifier?

Steve: Variables declared in a class always have class scope; that means that they live as long as the object that contains them. The access specifier determines who can access these variables, but does not affect their lifetime.

At the moment, it's not important that that private member variables aren't accessible outside the class, since we're looking at a member function; namely, the constructor StockItem::StockItem(); by virtue of being a member function, it has access to all member variables. So now we can see exactly what this function does; it sets the member variables to 0 or "", whichever is appropriate to their types.

That's all very well, but it doesn't answer a very important question: What exactly do these member variables do? The answer is that they don't do anything by themselves; rather, they are the "raw material" the member functions use to implement the behavior that we want a StockItem to display. If you recall the discussion of interface vs. implementation, then you'll appreciate that the private member variables are also essentially part of the implementation and not part of the interface: Even though they are defined in the interface file, the user of the class can't access them directly.

That's why we call these variables that are declared inside the class definition *member variables*, and the functions that are declared inside the class definition *member functions*; They "belong" to the class that we're defining. The member functions set, change, and use the values of the member variables in the course of implementing the behaviors that the StockItem class interface definition promises.[12]

Susan wasn't buying all this malarkey about member variables without a fight. Here's how it went.

Problem
Algorithms
C++
Executable
Hardware

Susan: What do m_InStock and m_Price and the others actually do? It seems we are missing a verb here.

Steve: They don't do anything by themselves. They are the member variables used to store the count and price of the goods described by a StockItem object, respectively. In the default constructor, they are both set to 0, indicating a StockItem with no content. This is the equivalent of the value 0 that is used to initialize statically allocated numeric variables and is used in the same way; that is, any StockItem that is created without a value is set to this empty state. Notice that this doesn't apply only to statically allocated StockItems, but to all StockItems; this is an example where a user defined type is superior to a native type. That is, we don't have to worry about having an uninitialized StockItem, because the default constructor ensures that every StockItem is set to a known value when it is created.

Susan: Ugh. Don't remind me about uninitialized variables. Okay, that makes more sense now.

---

12. The special status of member functions and variables as implementation aids explains why you cannot apply an access specifier such as public to data or functions declared outside a class, since the purpose of access specifiers is to specify "outside" access to variables and functions used to implement a class. In particular, you can't apply access specifiers to native types, because the way they are implemented is not accessible to the programmer.

So much for the "high-altitude" description of what a class does. Now let's get back to the details that make it work, starting with a little puzzle: figuring out where the StockItem::StockItem() function is used in the test program in Figure 6.1. Believe it or not, this constructor is actually used in that program: To be exact, the line StockItem soup; calls it. Remember that the basic idea of constructing a class is to add data types to the language that aren't available "out of the box". One of the functions that we have to help the compiler with is initialization; a main purpose for the StockItem::StockItem() constructor is to initialize variables of the StockItem type when they are defined to have "default" values (i.e., no values explicitly assigned to them). In other words, this constructor is called when no values are specified; as we've already seen, that's why it's called a *default constructor*.

Susan didn't immediately cotton to the idea of calling a default constructor by simply defining a variable of that class.

> **Susan**: Sure, defining an object is simple if you don't lose your mind defining the classes first.
>
> **Steve**: It *is* simple for the application programmer (the user of the class). We're doing the hard part so he can just use the objects without having to worry about any of this stuff.
>
> **Susan**: Huh? Isn't the the "user of the class" always the same as the "writer of the class"?
>
> **Steve**: Not necessarily. You've been using strings (and vectors, for that matter) for some time now without having to be concerned about how they work. This is not unusual.
>
> **Susan**: Yeah, but if you are a programmer you will be a class writer, not just a user.
>
> **Steve**: Not necessarily, and certainly not with respect to all the classes. You may very well write your own application-specific classes but use the ones from the standard library for all of the low-level stuff like vectors, strings, etc.

```
Problem
Algorithms
C++
Executable
Hardware
```

You should generally write a default constructor for every class you define, so that the state of any "default constructed" variable will be known.[13]

___

13. If you don't define a default constructor, the compiler will supply one for you; however, since it doesn't know much about your class, it won't be able to guarantee very much about

Susan thought that the idea of having to define a default constructor for each class was a bit off the wall.

> **Susan**: When you say that "you should define one of these (default constructors) for every class you define..." my question is how? What are you talking about? I thought a default meant just that, it was a default, you don't have to do anything with it, it is set to a preassigned value.

> **Steve**: It's true that the class user doesn't have to do anything with the default constructors. However, the class writer (that's us, in this case) has to define the default constructor, so when the class user defines an object without providing an initial value, the new object has a reasonable state for an "empty" object. This prevents the problems with uninitialized variables that we've seen crop up with native types.

Shop till You Drop

Problem
Algorithms
C++
Executable
Hardware

Now let's continue with our analysis of the class interface (Figure 6.3, on page 251). Before we can do anything with an inventory record, we have to enter the inventory data. This means that we need another constructor that actually sets the values into the object. We also need some way to display the data for a StockItem on the screen, which means writing a Display function.

The next line of that figure is the declaration of the constructor that creates an object with actual data:

StockItem(string Name, short InStock, short Price, string Distributor, string UPC);

We can tell that this function is a constructor because its name, StockItem, is the same as the name of the class. If you're a C programmer, you may be surprised to see two functions that have the same name, differing only in the types of their arguments. This is not legal in C, but it is in C++; it's called **function overloading**, and as

---

the initial state of one of your variables. The moral is that you should define your own default constructor. As you can see from our example, it's not much work.

So why did I say "generally", rather than "always"? Because there are some times when you don't want to allow an object to be created unless the "real" data for it are available. As with the copy constructor, the compiler will generate a default constructor for you automatically; to prevent this, you can declare a private default constructor, which will cause a compiler error in any user code that tries to define an object of that class without specifying any initial values. You don't actually have to implement this private constructor, because a program that tries to use it will fail in the compile stage; thus, the link phase won't ever be executed.

you'll see, it's a very handy facility that isn't limited to constructors. The combination of the function name and argument types is called the **signature** of a function; two functions that have the same name but differ in the type of at least one argument are distinct functions.[14] In the case of the default constructor, there are no arguments, so that constructor is used where no initial data are specified for the object. The statement StockItem soup; fits that description, so the default constructor is used. However, in the next line of the sample program, we have the expression:

StockItem("Chunky Chicken",32,129,"Bob's Distribution","123456789");

This is clearly a call to a constructor, because the name of the function is the name of a class, StockItem. Therefore, the compiler looks for a constructor that can handle the set of arguments in this call, and finds:

StockItem(string Name, short InStock, short Price, string Distributor, string UPC);

The first argument to the constructor is a string, the second is a short, the third is another short, the fourth is a string, and the fifth is another string; these types all match those specified in the expression in the sample program. Therefore, the compiler can translate that expression into a call to this constructor.

Problem
Algorithms
C++
Executable
Hardware

Figure 6.6 shows the code for that constructor.

```
StockItem::StockItem(string Name, short InStock, short Price,
string Distributor, string UPC)
{
        m_InStock = InStock;
        m_Price = Price;
        m_Name = Name;
        m_Distributor = Distributor;
        m_UPC = UPC;
};
```

Figure 6.6: Another constructor for the StockItem class (from code\item1.cc)

---

14. Note that the names of the arguments are not part of the signature; in fact, you don't have to specify them in the function declaration at all. However, I strongly recommend that you use the same argument names in the function declaration and in the function implementation; this makes it easier for the user of the function to understand what the arguments to the function are. After all, the declaration Stockitem(string,short,short,string,string); doesn't provide much information on what those arguments represent.

As you can see, nothing about this constructor is terribly complex; it merely copies the values of the arguments into the member variables of the object being constructed.

But why do we need more than one constructor? Susan had that same question, and I had some answers for her.

Susan: How many constructors do you need to say the same thing?

Steve: They don't say exactly the same thing. It's true that every constructor in the StockItem class makes a StockItem; however, each argument list varies. The default constructor makes an empty StockItem and therefore doesn't need any arguments, whereas the constructor StockItem::StockItem(string Name, short InStock, short Price, string Distributor, string UPC) makes a StockItem with the values specified by the Name, InStock, Price, Distributor, and UPC arguments in the constructor call.

Susan: Are you saying that in defining a class you can have two functions that have the same name, but they are different in only their arguments and that makes them unique?

Steve: Exactly. This is the language feature called *function overloading*.

Susan: So StockItem soup; is the default constructor in case you need something that can create uninitialized objects?

Steve: Not quite; the default constructor for the StockItem class is StockItem::StockItem(), which doesn't need any arguments, because it constructs an empty StockItem. The line StockItem soup; causes the default constructor to be called to create an empty StockItem.

Susan: And the line StockItem("Chunky Chicken",32,129,"Bob's Distribution","123456789"); is a constructor that finally gets around to telling us what we are trying to accomplish here?

Steve: Again, not quite. That line causes a StockItem with the specified contents to be created, by calling the constructor StockItem::StockItem(string Name, short InStock, short Price, string Distributor, string UPC);.

Susan: Sorry, I was not able to decode your header. Steve, this is too new to me. I need to have more familiarity with this stuff other than a mere definition, to know it better. So are you saying that for every new StockItem you have to have a new constructor for it?

Steve: No, there's one constructor for each way that we can construct a StockItem. One for situations where we don't have any initial data (the

Problem
Algorithms
C++
Executable
Hardware

default constructor), one for those where we're copying one StockItem to another (the compiler-generated copy constructor), and one for those where we are supplying the data for a StockItem. There could be other ones too, but those are all we have right now.

Once that expression has been translated, the compiler has to figure out how to assign the result of the expression to the StockItem object called soup, as requested in the whole statement:

```
soup = StockItem("Chunky Chicken",32,129,"Bob's
Distribution","123456789");
```

Since the compiler has generated its own version of the assignment operator = for the StockItem class, it can translate that part of the statement as well, which results in the StockItem object named soup having the value specified by the call to the constructor.

Finally, we have the line soup.Display(); which displays the value of soup on the screen. Figure 6.7 shows the code for that function.

```
void StockItem::Display()
{
    cout << "Name: ";
    cout << m_Name << endl;
    cout << "Number in stock: ";
    cout << m_InStock << endl;
    cout << "Price: ";
    cout << m_Price << endl;
    cout << "Distributor: ";
    cout << m_Distributor << endl;
    cout << "UPC: ";
    cout << m_UPC << endl;

    return;
};
```

Problem
Algorithms
C++
Executable
Hardware

Figure 6.7: Display member function for the StockItem class (from code\item1.cc)

This is also not very complicated; it just uses << to copy each of the parts of the StockItem object to cout, along with some identifying information that makes it easier to figure out what the values represent.

Susan wanted to know how we could use << without defining a special version for this class.

Susan: Hey, how come you don't have to define << as a class operator? Does the compiler just use the native <<? And that works OK?

Steve: We're using << only for types that already have it defined, which includes all of the native types, as well as the one I provided as part of the string class. If we wanted to apply << to a StockItem, we'd have to write our own version; you'll see how we do that when we go into the implementation of string.

Susan: Then please explain to me why << is being used in Figure 6.7, which is for the StockItem class.

Steve: It's being used for strings and shorts, not objects of the StockItem class. The fact that the strings and shorts are inside the StockItem class is irrelevant in this context; they're still strings and shorts, and therefore can be displayed by the << operators that handle strings and shorts.

Susan: So the stuff you get out of the standard library is only for the use of class types? Not native?

Steve: The iostreams library is designed to be able to handle both native types and class types; however, the latter use requires the class writer to do some extra work, as we'll see when we add these functions to the string class in Chapter 8.

Susan: So that means that the library is set up to understand things we make up for our class types?

Steve: That's right; if we follow the library's rules when creating our own versions of << and >>, then we'll be able to use those operators to read and write our data as though the ability to handle those types was built into the library.

Problem
Algorithms
C++
Executable
Hardware

That should clear up most of the potential problems with the meaning of this Display function. However, it does contain one construct that we haven't seen before: void. This is the return type of the Display function, as might be apparent from its position immediately before the class name StockItem. But what sort of return value is a void? In this context, it means simply that this function doesn't supply a return value at all.

You won't be surprised to learn that Susan had a few questions about this idea of functions that return no value.

Susan: How can a function not return a value? Then what is the point? Then would it "have no function"?

Steve: Now you're telling programming jokes? Seriously, though, the point of calling a function that returns no value is that it causes something to happen. The Display function is one example; it causes the value of a StockItem object to be displayed on the screen. Another example is a "storage function"; calling such a function can cause it to modify the value of some piece of data it is maintaining, so when you call the corresponding "retrieval function", you'll get back the value the "storage function" put away. Such lasting effects of a function call (other than returning a value) are called *side effects*.

Susan: But even a side effect is a change, so then it does do something after all, right?

Steve: Sure, it does something; every function should do something, or you wouldn't write (or call) it. However, some functions don't return any value to the calling program, in which case we specify their return type as void.

Price Fixing

That takes care of the public part of the class definition. Now what about the private part?

As I mentioned before in the discussion of how a class is defined, the access specifier private means that only member functions of the class can access the items after that specifier. It's almost always a good idea to mark all the member variables in a class as private, for two good reasons.

Problem
Algorithms
C++
Executable
Hardware

1. If we know that only member functions of a class can change the values of member data, then we know where to look if the values of the data are incorrect. This can be extremely useful when debugging a program.

2. Marking member variables as private simplifies the task of changing or deleting those member variables should that become necessary. You see, if the member variables are public, then we have no idea what functions in what programs are relying on their values. That means that changing or deleting these member variables can cause havoc anywhere in the system. Limiting access to member functions means that we can make changes freely as long as all of the member functions are kept up to date.

There's only one more point about the member variables in the StockItem class that needs clarification; surely the price of an object in the store should be in dollars and cents, and yet we have only a short to represent it. As you know by now, a short can only hold a whole number from −32768 to 32767. What's going on here?

Not much; I've just decided to store the price in cents rather than dollars and cents. That is, when someone types in a price, I'll assume that it's in cents, so "246" would mean 246 cents, or $2.46. This would of course not be acceptable in a real program, but for now it's OK.

This allows prices up to $327.67 (as well as negative numbers for things like coupons), which should be acceptable for a grocery store. In a big hardware store that sells items like diesel generators and expensive plumbing fixtures, this wouldn't be a big enough range. In Appendix A, I'll give you some tips on how to solve that problem by using a different kind of numeric variable that can hold a greater variety of values. For now, though, let's stick with the short.

Now that we've covered all of the member functions and variables of the StockItem class, Figure 6.8 shows the interface for the StockItem class again.[15]

Problem
Algorithms
C++
Executable
Hardware

```
class StockItem
{
public:
        StockItem();

        StockItem(string Name, short InStock, short Price,
        string Distributor, string UPC);

        void Display();

private:
        short m_InStock;
        short m_Price;
        string m_Name;
        string m_Distributor;
        string m_UPC;
};
```

Figure 6.8: The initial interface of the StockItem class (code\item1.h)

---

15. The test program for this class, itemtst1.cc, is shown in Figure 6.1.

Figure 6.9 shows the implementation for the StockItem class.

```
#include <iostream.h>
#include "string6.h"
#include "item1.h"

StockItem::StockItem()
{
     m_InStock = 0;
     m_Price = 0;
     m_Name = "";
     m_Distributor = "";
     m_UPC = "";
};

StockItem::StockItem(string Name, short InStock, short Price,
string Distributor, string UPC)
{
     m_InStock = InStock;
     m_Price = Price;
     m_Name = Name;
     m_Distributor = Distributor;
     m_UPC = UPC;
};

void StockItem::Display()
{
     cout << "Name: ";
     cout << m_Name << endl;
     cout << "Number in stock: ";
     cout << m_InStock << endl;
     cout << "Price: ";
     cout << m_Price << endl;
     cout << "Distributor: ";
     cout << m_Distributor << endl;
     cout << "UPC: ";
     cout << m_UPC << endl;

     return;
};
```

```
Problem
Algorithms
C++
Executable
Hardware
```

Figure 6.9: The initial implementation of the StockItem class (code\item1.cc)

Susan had a few questions about the way that we specified the header files in this program:

Susan: Where did the #include "string6.h" come from?

Steve: I wrote it; it's the final version of the string header file as defined in Chapter 8.

Susan: So then it has not been covered up to this point? Then you might have to explain how it mysteriously appears in this code.

Steve: I'll tell the reader to expect a nauseatingly detailed description later on.

Susan: Oh, and how come this and the #include item1.h are in "" instead of <>? I thought all header files are in <>?

Steve: Putting an include file name in "" tells the compiler to start looking for the file in the current directory, and then search the "standard places"; using the <> tells the compiler to skip the current directory and start with the "standard places"; that is, where the header files are that come with the compiler. What the "standard places" are depends on the compiler.

Problem
Algorithms
C++
Executable
Hardware

Susan: I know I have not been the most focused test reader in the last week, but did I miss something here? Did you explain way back in an earlier chapter and I just forgot? I want to make sure that you have explained this in the book, and even if you had earlier it would not be a bad idea to remind the reader about this.

Steve: No, I believe it was my omission. Actually, you've been quite focused, although not in quite the same area.

If you run this program by changing to the normal subdirectory, typing itemtst1, and hitting ENTER, you'll see that it indeed prints out the information in the StockItem object.

That's good as far as it goes, but how do we use this class to keep track of all of the items in the store? Surely we aren't going to have a separately named StockItem variable for each one.

Vectoring In

This is another application for our old friend the vector. What we need is a vector of StockItems, which we can use to store the data for all the StockItems in the store. In a real application we would need to be able to vary the number of elements in the vector, unlike our previous use of vectors. After all, the number of items in a store can vary from time to time. However, in our example program we'll ignore this complication and just use a vector that can hold 100 StockItems. Even with this limitation, we will have to keep track of the number of items that are in use, so that we can store each new StockItem in its own vector element and keep track of how many items we may have to search through to find a particular StockItem. Finally, we need something to read in each StockItem from the inventory file where it's stored when we're not running the program.

Susan had some questions about these details of the test program:

Susan: In the paragraph when you are talking about the number of items, I am a little confused. That is, do you mean the number of different products that the store carries or the quantity of an individual item available in the store at any given time?

Steve: The number of different products, which is the same as the number of StockItems. Remember, each StockItem represents any number of objects of that exact description.

Susan: So what you're referring to is basically all the inventory in the store at any given period of time?

Steve: Exactly.

Susan: What do you mean by "need something to read in" and "where it's stored when we're not running the program." I don't know what you are talking about, I don't know where that place would be.

Steve: Well, where are the data when we're not running the program? The disk. Therefore, we have to be able to read in the information for the StockItems from the disk when we start the program.

Susan: Okay, that makes sense now.

Steve: I'm glad to hear it.

Figure 6.10 is a little program that shows the code necessary to read the data for the StockItem vector into memory when the program starts up.

Problem
Algorithms
C++
Executable
Hardware

```
#include <iostream.h>
#include <fstream.h>
#include "vector.h"
#include "string6.h"
#include "item2.h"

int main()
{
    ifstream ShopInfo("shop2.in");
    vector<StockItem> AllItems(100);
    short i;
    short InventoryCount;

    for (i = 0; i < 100; i ++)
        {
        AllItems[i].Read(ShopInfo);
        if (ShopInfo.fail() != 0)
             break;
        }

    InventoryCount = i;

    for (i = 0; i < InventoryCount; i ++)
        {
        AllItems[i].Display();
        }

    return 0;
}
```

```
Problem
Algorithms
C++
Executable
Hardware
```

Figure 6.10: Reading and displaying a vector of StockItems
(code\itemtst2.cc)

This program has a number of new features that need examination. First, we've had to add the "file stream" header file fstream.h to the list of include files, so that we will be able to read data in from a file. The way we do this is to create an ifstream object that is "attached" to a file when the object is constructed. In this case, the line ifstream ShopInfo("shop2.in"); creates an ifstream object called ShopInfo, and connects it to the file named shop2.in. Then we pass this ShopInfo object to a new member function called Read, which uses ShopInfo to get data from the file and store it into our vector. This was anything but obvious to Susan.

Susan: How does just adding the header file fstream.h, enable you to read data in from a file?

Steve: The file fstream.h contains the declaration of the ifstream class.

Susan: Where did the ifstream class come from?

Steve: From the standard library that comes with the compiler.

Susan: Where did it come from and how did it get there? Who defined it and when was it written? Your only reference to this is just "The way we do this is to create an ifstream object that is 'attached' to a file when the object is constructed". If this is just something that you wrote to aid this program that we don't have to worry about at this time, then please mention this.

Steve: I didn't write it, but we don't have to worry about it. I'll explain it to the minimum extent necessary.

After that bit of comic relief, let's get back to reality. Figure 6.11 is the new interface to the StockItem class, showing the declaration of the new Read member function.[16]

```
class StockItem
{
public:
        StockItem();

        StockItem(string Name, short InStock, short Price,
        string Distributor, string UPC);

        void Display();
        void Read(ifstream& s);

private:
        short m_InStock;
        short m_Price;
        string m_Name;
        string m_Distributor;
        string m_UPC;
};
```

Problem
Algorithms
C++
Executable
Hardware

Figure 6.11: The second version of the interface for the StockItem class
(code\item2.h)

---

16. For the implementation of the functions in this interface specification, see the following figures:

1. For StockItem(), see Figure 6.4.
2. For StockItem(string Name, short InStock, short Price, string Distributor, string UPC), see Figure 6.6.
3. For Display(), see Figure 6.7.
4. For Read(ifstream& s), see Figure 6.12.

And Figure 6.12 is the implementation of the new Read function:

```
void StockItem::Read(ifstream& s)
{
     s >> m_Name;
     s >> m_InStock;
     s >> m_Price;
     s >> m_Distributor;
     s >> m_UPC;
}
```

Figure 6.12: The Read function for the StockItem class (from code\item2.cc)

As you can see, this is pretty simple; it just reads the data for one StockItem in from the file by way of the ifstream object s, using one >> expression to read in each member variable's value. However, there's one construct here we haven't seen before: the & in ifstream&. What does that mean?

The &, in this context, means that the argument to which it refers is a **reference argument**, rather than a "normal" argument. It's important to understand this concept thoroughly, so let's go into it in detail.

Problem
Algorithms
C++
Executable
Hardware

References Required

As you may recall from Chapter 5, when we call a function, it doesn't ordinarily operate on actual variables in the calling function; instead, a new local variable is created and initialized to the value of each expression from the calling function and the called function works on that local variable. Such a local variable is called a *value argument*, because it is a new variable with the same value as the caller's original argument. There's nothing wrong with this in many cases; sometimes, though, as in the present case, we have to do it a bit differently. A reference argument, such as the ifstream& argument to Read, is *not* a copy of the caller's argument, but another name for the actual argument passed by the caller.

Reference arguments are more efficient than value arguments, because the overhead of making a copy for the called function is avoided. Another difference is that any changes made to a reference argument change the caller's argument as well, which in turn means that the caller's actual argument must be a variable, not an expression like x + 3; changing the value of such an expression wouldn't make much sense. This characteristic of reference arguments can confuse the readers of the calling function; there's no way to tell just by looking at the calling function that some of its variables can be changed by calling another function. This means that we should limit the use of reference arguments to those cases where they are necessary.

In this case, however, it *is* necessary to change the ifstream object that is the actual argument to the Read function, so that we don't get the same input every time we try to read from it. Therefore, we have to use a reference argument.

The complete decoding of the function declaration void StockItem::Read(ifstream& s) is shown in Figure 6.13.

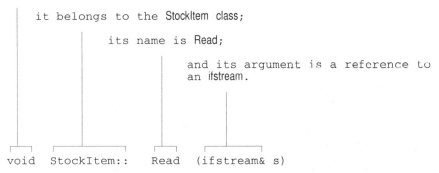

```
This means that the function we're defining doesn't return
anything;

    it belongs to the StockItem class;

            its name is Read;

                    and its argument is a reference to
                    an ifstream.




void   StockItem::    Read   (ifstream& s)
```

Problem
Algorithms
C++
Executable
Hardware

Figure 6.13: The declaration of the function StockItem::Read in code\item2.h

Putting it all together: we're defining a void function (one that doesn't return a value), called Read, which belongs to class StockItem. This function takes an argument named s that's a reference to an ifstream. That is, the argument s is another name for the ifstream passed to us by the caller, not a copy of the caller's ifstream.

As you probably have guessed, Susan had some questions about this whole concept.

Susan: How does Read make Shopinfo go get data?

Steve: Well, the argument s is a reference to the ifstream object provided by the caller; in this case, the ifstream object to which s refers is Shopinfo. That ifstream is connected to the file shop2.in.

Susan: How does Read do the reading? How come you are using >> without a cin statement?

Steve: cin isn't a statement, but a stream that is created automatically whenever we #include iostream.h in our source file. Therefore, we can read from it without connecting it to a file. In this case, we're reading from a different stream, namely s.

Susan: How come this is a void type? I would think it would return data being read from a file.

Steve: You would think so, wouldn't you? I love it when you're logical. However, what it actually does is to read data from a file into the object for which it was called. Therefore, it doesn't need a return value.

Susan: So the ifstream object is a transfer mechanism? That is, ifstream s; would read data from a file named s?

Steve: Yes, it's a transfer mechanism. However, ifstream s; would create an ifstream called s, that was not connected to any file; the file could be specified later. If we wanted to create an ifstream called s that was connected to a file called xyz, then we would write ifstream s("xyz");

Susan: OK. An ifstream just reads data from a file. It doesn't care which file, until you specify it?

Problem
Algorithms
C++
Executable
Hardware

Steve: Right.

Susan: What does this mean without cin? Is it just the same thing, only you can't call it cin because cin is for native use and this is a class? How come the >> is preceded by the argument s?

Steve: The s takes the place of cin, because we want to read from the stream s, not the stream cin.

Susan: Tell me what you mean by just a *stream*.

Steve: Think of it like a real stream, and the bytes are little barges that float downstream. Isn't that poetic? Anyway, there are three predefined streams that we get automatically when we #include <iostream.h>: cin, cout, and cerr. The first two we've already seen, and the last one is where error messages are sent.

There is one point that we haven't examined yet, though: how this routine determines that it's finished reading from the input file. With keyboard input, we process each line separately when it's typed in, but that won't do the job with a file, where we want to read all the items in until we get to the end of the file.

We actually handle this detail in the main program itemtst2.cc, by asking ShopInfo whether there is any data left in the file; to be exact, we call the ifstream member function fail() to ask the ShopInfo ifstream whether we have tried to read past the end of the file. If we have, then the result of that call to ShopInfo.fail() will be nonzero (which signifies true). If we haven't yet tried to read past the end of the file, then the result of that call will be 0 (which signifies false). How do we use this information?

We use it to decide whether to execute a break **statement**. This is a loop control device that interrupts processing of a loop whenever it is executed. The flow of control passes to the next statement after the end of the controlled block of the for statement.[17]

The loop will terminate in one of two ways. Either 100 records have been read, in which case i will be 100; or the end of the file is reached, in which case i is the number of records that have been read in successfully.

Susan had some questions about the implementation of this program.

Susan: What is fail()?

Steve: It's a member function of the ifstream class.

Susan: Where did it come from?

Steve: From the library that defines that class.

Susan: But it could be used in other classes, right?

Steve: Not unless they define it as well.

Susan: How does all the data having been read translate into "nonzero"? What makes a "nonzero" value true?

Steve: That's a convention used by that function.

Susan: So anything other than 0 is considered true?

Steve: Yes.

Susan: Where did break come from?

Problem
Algorithms
C++
Executable
Hardware

---

17. The break statement can also terminate execution of a while loop, as well as some other types of control mechanisms that we won't get to.

Steve: It's another keyword like for; it means to terminate the loop that is in progress.

Susan: I do not understand what is actually happening with the program at this time. When is break implemented? Is it just to end the reading of the entire file?

Steve: We have to stop reading data when there is no more data in the file. The break statement allows us to terminate the loop when that occurs.

Susan: What do you mean that the loop will terminate either by 100 records being read or when the end of the file is reached? Isn't that the same thing?

Steve: It's the same thing only if there are exactly 100 records in the file.

Susan: So you mean when there are no more records to be read? So that the loop won't continue on till the end with nothing to do?

Steve: Exactly.

Problem
Algorithms
C++
Executable
Hardware

Susan: So does i just represent the number of records in the file?

Steve: Actually, it's the number of records that we've read.

Susan: Does this library have a card catalogue? I would like to know what else is in there.

Steve: There is a library reference manual for most libraries. If you get a library with a commercial compiler, that manual comes with the compiler documentation; otherwise, it's usually an on-line reference (that is, a help file).

Susan: A novice would not know this. Put it in the book.

Steve: Done.

Susan: Well, the program sounded like that indeed there were 100 records in the file. However, I see that in practice that might change, and why you would therefore need to have a break.

Steve: You obviously understand this.

Whether there are 100 records in the file or fewer than that number, obviously the number of items in the vector is equal to the current value of i. Or is it?

Don't Fence Me In

Let's examine this a bit more closely. It's actually quite easy to make a mistake in counting objects when writing a program. It's quite common to make the mistake of thinking you have one more or one less than the actual number of objects. In fact, this error is common enough to have a couple of widely known nicknames: an **off by one error**, also known as a **fencepost error**. The former name should be fairly evident, but the latter name may require some explanation. First, let's try it as a "word problem". If you have to put up a fence 100 feet long, and each section of the fence is 10 feet long, how many sections of fence do you need? Obviously, the answer is 10. Now how many fenceposts do you need? 11. The confusion caused by counting fenceposts when you should be counting segments of the fence (and vice-versa) is the cause of a fencepost error.

That's fine as a general rule, but what about this specific example? Well, let's start out by supposing that we have an empty file, so the sequence of events in the upper loop is as follows:

Problem
Algorithms
C++
Executable
Hardware

1. Set i to 0.
2. Is i less than 100? If not, exit. If so, continue.
3. Use the Read function to try to read a record into the ith element of the AllItems vector.
4. Call ShopInfo.fail() to find out whether we've tried to read past the end of the file.
5. If so, execute the break statement to exit the loop.

The answer to the question in step 4 is that in fact nothing was read, so we do execute the break and leave the loop. The value of i is clearly 0 here, because we never went back to the top of the loop; since we haven't read any records, setting count to i works in this case.

Now let's try the same thing, but this time assuming that there is one record in the file. Here's the sequence of events:

1. Set i to 0.
2. Is i less than 100? If not, exit. If so, continue.
3. Use the Read function to try to read a record into the ith element of the AllItems vector.

4.   Call ShopInfo.fail() to find out whether we've tried to read past the end of the file.

5.   If so, execute the break statement to exit the loop. In this case, we haven't run off the end of the file, so we go back to the top of the loop, and continue as follows:

6.   Increment i to 1.

7.   Is i less than 100? If not, exit. If so, continue.

8.   Use the Read function to try to read a record into the AllItems vector.

9.   Call ShopInfo.fail() to find out whether we've tried to read past the end of the file.

10. If so, execute the break statement to exit the loop.

The second time through, we do execute the break. Since i is 1, and the number of elements read was also 1, it's correct to set the count of elements to i.

It should be pretty clear that this same logic applies to all the possible numbers of elements up to 99. But what if we have 100 elements in the file? Relax, I'm not going to go through these steps 100 times, but I think we should start out from the situation that would exist after reading 99 elements, and see if we get the right answer in this case too. After the 99th element has been read, i will be 99; we know this from our previous analysis that indicates that whenever we start executing the statements in the controlled block of the loop, i is always equal to the number of elements previously read. So here's the 100th iteration of the loop:

Problem
Algorithms
C++
Executable
Hardware

1.   Increment i to 100.

2.   Is i less than 100? If not, exit. If so, continue.

Since i is not less than 100, we exit.

At this point, we've read 100 records and i is 100, so these two numbers are still the same. Therefore, we can conclude that setting count equal to i when the loop is finished is correct; we have no fencepost error here.

Susan wasn't sure why I was hammering this fencepost thing into the ground:

> **Susan**: Why are you always saying that "it's correct to set the count of elements to i"?

> **Steve**: Because I'm showing how to tell whether or not we have a fencepost error. That requires a lot of analysis.

Now that we have made sure that we're counting the number of items in the file correctly,[18] you might want to run the itemtst2 program, by changing to the normal subdirectory, typing itemtst2, and hitting ENTER. You'll see that it indeed prints out each StockItem object read in from the file.

Can I Help You?

Of course, this isn't all we want to do with the items in the store's inventory. Since we have a working means of reading and displaying the items, let's see what else we might want to do with them. Here are a few possible transactions at the grocery store:

1. George comes in and buys 3 bags of marshmallows. We have to adjust the inventory for the sale.
2. Sam wants to know the price of a can of string beans.
3. Judy comes in looking for chunky chicken soup; there's none on the shelf where it should be, so we have to check the inventory to see if we're supposed to have any.

All of these scenarios require the ability to find a StockItem object given some information about it. Let's start with the first example, which we might state as a programming task in the following manner: "Given the UPC from the bag of marshmallows, and the number of bags purchased, adjust the inventory by subtracting the number purchased from the previous quantity on hand."

To break this down further, the steps should look something like this:

1. Take the UPC from the item.
2. For every item in the inventory list, check whether its UPC is the same as the one from the item.
3. If it doesn't match, go back to step 2.
4. If it does match, subtract the number purchased from the inventory.

Problem
Algorithms
C++
Executable
Hardware

Figure 6.14 is a program that looks as though it should solve this problem. Does it?

---

18. This whole procedure we've just been through reminds me of the professor who claimed that some point he was making was obvious. This was questioned by a student, so the professor spent 10 minutes absorbed in calculation and finally emerged triumphantly with the news that it was indeed obvious.

```
#include <iostream.h>
#include <fstream.h>
#include "vector.h"
#include "string6.h"
#include "item2.h"

int main()
{
    ifstream ShopInfo("shop2.in");
    vector<StockItem> AllItems(100);
    short i;
    short InventoryCount;
    string PurchaseUPC;
    short PurchaseCount;
    bool Found;

    for (i = 0; i < 100; i ++)
        {
        AllItems[i].Read(ShopInfo);
        if (ShopInfo.fail() != 0)
            break;
        }

    InventoryCount = i;

    cout << "What is the UPC of the item?" << endl;
    cin >> PurchaseUPC;
    cout << "How many items were sold?" << endl;
    cin >> PurchaseCount;

    Found = false;
    for (i = 0; i < InventoryCount; i ++)
        {
        if (PurchaseUPC == AllItems[i].m_UPC)
            {
            Found = true;
            break;
            }
        }

    if (Found == true)
        {
        AllItems[i].m_InStock -= PurchaseCount;
        cout << "The inventory has been updated." << endl;
        }
    else
        cout << "Can't find that item. Please check UPC" << endl;

    return 0;
}
```

Problem
Algorithms
C++
Executable
Hardware

Figure 6.14: First attempt to update inventory of StockItems
(code\itemtst3.cc)

There's nothing really new here except for the bool variable type, which we'll get to in a moment, and the -= operator that the program uses to adjust the inventory; -= is just like +=, except that it subtracts the right-hand value from the left-hand variable, while += adds.

The bool variable type is a new addition to C++. Expressions and variables of this type are limited to the two values true and false.[19] This is a new data type that was added to C++ in the draft standard, and should be available on any compiler that conforms to the actual standard. We've been using the terms true and false to refer to the result of a logical expression such as if (x < y); similarly, a bool variable or function return value can be either true or false.

However, if you compile this program, you'll find that it is not valid. The problem is that we're trying to access private member variables of the StockItem class, namely m_UPC and m_InStock, from function main. Since main is not a member function of StockItem, this is not allowed. The error message from the compiler should look something like this:

```
itemtst3.cc: In function 'int main()':
itemtst3.cc:19: no match for 'operator >>(class ifstream, class StockItem)'
itemtst3.cc:34: member 'm_UPC' is a private member of class 'StockItem'
itemtst3.cc:43: member 'm_InStock' is a private member of class 'StockItem'
```

Problem
Algorithms
C++
Executable
Hardware

Does this mean that we can't accomplish our goal of updating the inventory? Not at all. It merely means that we have to do things "by the book" rather than going in directly and reading or changing member variables that belong to the StockItem class. Of course, we could theoretically "solve" this access problem by simply making these member variables public rather than private. However, this would allow anyone to mess around with the internal variables in our StockItem objects, which would defeat one of the main purposes of using class objects in the first place: that they behave like native types as far as their users are concerned. We want the users of this class to ignore the internal workings of its objects and merely use them according to their externally defined interface; the implementation of the class is our responsibility, not theirs.

This notion of implementation being separated from interface led to an excellent question from Susan:

> **Susan**: Please explain to me why you needed to list those member variables as private in the interface of StockItem. Actually, why do they

---

19. The type bool is short for "boolean", which means "either true or false". The derivation of the term "boolean" is interesting but not relevant here.

even need to be there at all? Well, I guess you are telling the compiler that whenever it sees the member variables that they will always have to be treated privately?

Steve: They have to be there so that the compiler can figure out how large an object of that class is. Many people, including myself, consider this a flaw in the language design, because private variables should really be private, not exposed to the class user's view.

Obviously, she'd lost her true novice status by this point. Six months after finding out what a compiler is, she was questioning the design decisions made by the inventor of C++; what is more, her objections were quite well founded.

As it happens, we can easily solve our access problem without exposing the implementation of our class to the user. All we have to do is to add a couple of new member functions called CheckUPC and DeductSalesFromInventory to the StockItem class; the first of these allows us to check whether a given UPC belongs to a given StockItem, and the second allows us to adjust the inventory level of an item.

Susan had another suggestion as to how to solve this problem, as well as a question about why I hadn't anticipated it in the first place:

Problem
Algorithms
C++
Executable
Hardware

Susan: Hey, wouldn't it be easier to write a special main that is a member function to get around this?

Steve: That's an interesting idea, but it wouldn't work. For one thing, main is never a member function; this is reasonable when you consider that you generally have quite a few classes in a program. Which one would main be a member function of?

Susan: So then all these new member functions do is to act as a gobetween linking the StockItem class and the inventory update program to compare data that is privately held in the StockItem class?

Steve: Yes, the new entries in the interface are designed to make the private data available in a safe manner. I think that's the same as what you're saying.

Susan: If you wanted to change the program, why didn't you just do it in the first place instead of breaking it down in parts like this?

Steve: Because that's not the way it actually happens in real life.

Susan: Do you think it less confusing to do that, and also does this act as an example of how you can modify a program as you see the need to do it?

Steve: Right on both counts.

Figure 6.15 shows the new, improved interface definition. The declarations of the two new functions CheckUPC and DeductSalesFromInventory should be pretty easy to figure out: CheckUPC takes the UPC that we want to find and compares it to the UPC in its StockItem, then returns true if they match and false if they don't. Here's another good use for the bool data type; the only possible results of the CheckUPC function are that the UPC in the StockItem matches the one we've supplied (in which case we return true) or it doesn't match (in which case we return false). DeductSaleFromInventory takes the number of items sold and subtracts it from the previous inventory. But where did those other two member functions GetInventory and GetName come from?

```
class StockItem
{
public:
    StockItem();

    StockItem(string Name, short InStock, short Price,
    string Distributor, string UPC);

    void Display();
    void Read(ifstrcam& s);

    bool CheckUPC(string ItemUPC);
    void DeductSaleFromInventory(short QuantitySold);
    short GetInventory();
    string GetName();

private:
    short m_InStock;
    short m_Price;
    string m_Name;
    string m_Distributor;
    string m_UPC;
};
```

Problem
Algorithms
C++
Executable
Hardware

Figure 6.15: An enhanced interface for the StockItem class (code\item4.h)

The Customer Is Always Right

I added those functions because I noticed that the "itemtst" program wasn't very user-friendly. Originally it followed these steps:

1. Ask for the UPC.
2. Ask for the number of items purchased.
3. Search through the list to see whether the UPC is legitimate.
4. If so, adjust the inventory.
5. If not, give an error message.
6. Exit.

What's wrong with this picture? Well, for one thing, why should the program make me type in the number of items sold if the UPC is no good? Also, it never told me the new inventory or even what the name of the item was. It may have known these things, but it never bothered to inform me. So I changed the program to work as follows:

Problem
Algorithms
C++
Executable
Hardware

1. Ask for the UPC.
2. Search through the list to see whether the UPC was legitimate.
3. If not, give an error message and exit.
4. If the UPC was OK, then

   a. Display the name of the item, and the number in stock.
   b. Ask for the number of items purchased.
   c. Adjust the inventory.
   d. Display a message with the name of the item and number of remaining units in inventory.

5. Exit.

To do this, I needed those two new functions GetInventory and GetName, so as you've seen, I added them to the class declaration. Figure 6.16 shows the implementation of all of these new functions.

```
bool StockItem::CheckUPC(ItemUPC)
{
      if (m_UPC == ItemUPC)
            return true;
      else
            return false;
}

void StockItem::DeductSaleFromInventory(short QuantitySold)
{
      m_InStock -= QuantitySold;
      return;
}

short StockItem::GetInventory()
{
      return m_InStock;
}

string StockItem::GetName()
{
      return m_Name;
}
```

Figure 6.16: Some new functions for the StockItem class (from
code\item4.cc)

Our current itemtst example is getting to be enough like a real
program that I'm going to start using the term *application program*
(or equivalently, *application*) to refer to it sometimes. As is generally
true of C++ programs, the responsibility for doing the user's work is
divided up into a main program (or application program) and a set of
classes (sometimes called *infrastructure*) used in the application. In
this case, itemtst4.cc is the main program, or application program,
whereas the other two files (item4.h and item4.cc) are the
infrastructure. Figure 6.17 shows the new, improved version of our
application, which updates the inventory and actually tells the user
what it's doing. This code should be pretty easy to follow; it simply
implements the first item purchase scenario I outlined in the list on
page 281.

Problem
Algorithms
C++
Executable
Hardware

```
#include <iostream.h>
#include <fstream.h>
#include "vector.h"
#include "string6.h"
#include "item4.h"

int main()
{
    ifstream ShopInfo("shop2.in");
    vector<StockItem> AllItems(100);
    short i;
    short InventoryCount;
    short OldInventory;
    short NewInventory;
    string PurchaseUPC;
    string ItemName;
    short PurchaseCount;
    bool Found;

    for (i = 0; i < 100; i ++)
        {
        AllItems[i].Read(ShopInfo);
        if (ShopInfo.fail() != 0)
            break;
        }
```

Problem
Algorithms
C++
Executable
Hardware

```
    InventoryCount = i;
    cout << "What is the UPC of the item? ";
    cin >> PurchaseUPC;
    Found = false;

    for (i = 0; i < InventoryCount; i ++)
        {
        if (AllItems[i].CheckUPC(PurchaseUPC) == true)
            {
            Found = true;
            break;
            }
        }

    if (Found == true)
        {
        OldInventory = AllItems[i].GetInventory();
        ItemName = AllItems[i].GetName();

        cout << "There are currently " << OldInventory << " units of "
        << ItemName << " in stock." << endl;
        cout << "How many items were sold? ";
        cin >> PurchaseCount;

        AllItems[i].DeductSaleFromInventory(PurchaseCount);
        cout << "The inventory has been updated." << endl;
```

Figure 6.17: Updating StockItem inventory (code\itemtst4.cc)

```
        NewInventory = AllItems[i].GetInventory();
        cout << "There are now " << NewInventory << " units of "
        << ItemName << " in stock." << endl;
        }
    else
        cout << "Can't find that item. Please check UPC" << endl;

    return 0;
}
```

Figure 6.17 continued

You can run this program normally by changing to the normal subdirectory, typing itemtst4, and hitting ENTER. To run it under gdb, make sure you are in the normal subdirectory, then type trace itemtst4 and hit ENTER. The program will start up and ask you for the UPC; you can use 8144976072, which is the (made-up) UPC for "antihistamines". Type in that number and hit ENTER. Then the program will stop at the line that determines whether the UPC has been found, if (Found == true). Type z and hit ENTER to execute each line from then on. The values of the relevant variables will be displayed immediately before the execution of each remaining line in main.[20] When you get to the end of the program (or when you're tired of tracing), type q (for *quit*) and hit ENTER to exit from the debugger.

Problem
Algorithms
C++
Executable
Hardware

Next Customer, Please?

Now let's consider what might be needed to handle some of the other possibilities, starting with the second scenario in that same list. To refresh your memory, here it is again: "Sam wants to know the price of a can of string beans".

How would this be expressed as a programming task? Perhaps in this way: "Given a UPC, look up the price of the item in the inventory".

Here is a set of steps to solve this problem:

1. Ask for the UPC.
2. Search through the list to see whether the UPC is legitimate.
3. If not, give an error message and exit.
4. If the UPC is OK, then display the name and price of the item.

---

20. Note that the Found variable will be displayed as 0 for false and 1 for true, due to limitations of gdb.

5.   Exit.

Have you noticed that this solution is very similar to the solution to the first problem? For example, the search for an item with a given UPC is exactly the same. It seems wasteful to duplicate code rather than using the same code again, and in fact we've seen how to avoid code duplication by using a function. Now that we're doing "object-oriented" programming, perhaps this new function should be a member function instead of a global one.

This is a good idea, except that the search function can't be a member function of StockItem, because we don't have the right StockItem yet; if we did, we wouldn't need to do the search. Therefore, what we have to do is to create a new class that contains a member variable that is a vector of StockItems and write the search routine as a member function of this new class; the new member function would look through its vector to find the StockItem we want. Then we can use the member functions of StockItem to do the rest of the work. Figure 6.18 shows the interface (class declaration) for this new class, called Inventory.[21]

Problem
Algorithms
C++
Executable
Hardware

```
#include "vector.h"

class Inventory
{
public:
    Inventory();

    short LoadInventory(ifstream& InputStream);
    StockItem FindItem(string UPC);
    bool UpdateItem(StockItem Item);

private:
    vector<StockItem> m_Stock;
    short m_StockCount;
};
```

Figure 6.18: Interface of Inventory class (code\invent1.h)

---

21. For the implementation of the functions in this interface specification, see the following figures:

    1.   For Inventory(), see Figure 6.19.
    2.   For LoadInventory(ifstream& InputStream), see Figure 6.20.
    3.   For FindItem(string UPC), see Figure 6.22.
    4.   For UpdateItem(StockItem Item), see Figure 6.23.

Susan was somewhat surprised that I would even consider writing a global function to find a StockItem:

> **Susan**: What do you mean by making this a member function instead of a global function? When was it ever a global function?
>
> **Steve**: It wasn't any kind of function before; we were just duplicating code. However, making it a function would make sense; the question is what kind of function, global or member?
>
> **Susan**: I am not sure if I truly understand the problem as to why you can't search StockItem as a member function.
>
> **Steve**: A member function of StockItem always accesses a particular StockItem. However, our problem is that we don't know which StockItem we want; therefore, a member function, which necessarily applies to a particular StockItem, won't solve our problem.
>
> **Susan**: OK, Stevie, here is the deal. Why would you even consider making this a global function? Of course it is a member function. We are doing object oriented programming aren't we?
>
> **Steve**: My, aren't we knowledgeable all of a sudden? Who was that person who was completely ignorant of programming eight months ago?
>
> **Susan**: You've got me there. But seriously, what would be the advantage of making it a global function rather than a member function? This is what has me bothered about the whole thing.
>
> **Steve**: There wouldn't be any advantage. I just wanted to point out that it clearly can't be a member function of StockItem, and indicate the possible alternatives.
>
> **Susan**: Oh, then so far that is all our program is able to do? It is unable to locate one item of all possible items and display it just from the UPC code? In fact that is what we are trying to accomplish, right?
>
> **Steve**: Exactly.

Susan also wasn't sure what the purpose of the LoadInventory function was.

> **Susan**: What does the code short LoadInventory (ifstream& InputStream); do? Does it just give you an object named LoadInventory that reads a file that has a reference argument named InputStream? I don't get this.

Problem
Algorithms
C++
Executable
Hardware

Steve: That's quite close. The line you're referring to is the declaration of a function named LoadInventory, which takes a reference to an ifstream. The implementation of the function, as you'll see shortly, reads StockItem records from the file connected to the ifstream.

Once that was cleared up, she had some questions about the way the FindItem function works, including its interface.

Susan: Is the argument UPC to the FindItem function a string because it is returning the name of a stock item?

Steve: That's the input to the FindItem function, not its output; therefore, it's not "returning" anything. Or did I misunderstand your question?

Susan: Let's see if I even know what I was asking here. OK, how about this: I wanted to know why UPC was a string and not a short, since a UPC is usually a number. In this case, it will be returning a name of a "found item" so that is why it is a string, right?

Steve: No, it's because the UPC won't fit in any of the types of numbers we have available. Thus, the most sensible way to store it is as a string. Since we don't use it in calculations anyway, that's not much of a restriction.

Susan: Oh. OK. So a string is more useful for storing numbers that are somewhat lengthy as long as you don't calculate with those numbers. They are nothing more than "numerical words"?

Steve: Exactly.

Problem
Algorithms
C++
Executable
Hardware

Most of this should be fairly self-explanatory by this point. We start out with the default constructor which makes an empty Inventory.[22] Figure 6.19 has the implementation for the default constructor.

```
Inventory::Inventory()
{
        m_Stock = vector<StockItem>(100);
        m_StockCount = 0;
}
```

Figure 6.19: Default constructor for Inventory class (from code\invent1.cc)

---

22. As before, we can count on the compiler to supply the other three standard member functions needed for a concrete data type: the copy constructor, the assignment operator =, and the destructor.

There's nothing complex here; all we're doing is setting the m_Stock variable to a newly constructed vector of 100 StockItems, and we're setting the number of active StockItems to 0, because we haven't yet read any data in from the file.

Then we have a couple of handy functions. The first is LoadInventory, which will take data from an ifstream and store it in its Inventory object, just as we did directly in our application itemtst4.cc.

Susan had a question about this:

> **Susan**: How did you know that you were going to need to use an ifstream again?

> **Steve**: Because we're reading data from a file into a vector of StockItems, and reading data from a file is what ifstreams are for.

Figure 6.20 shows the implementation of LoadInventory.

```
short Inventory::LoadInventory(ifstream& InputStream)
{
      short i;

      for (i = 0; i < 100; i ++)
          {
          m_Stock[i].Read(InputStream);
          if (InputStream.fail() != 0)
                break;
          }

      m_StockCount = i;
      return m_StockCount;
}
```

Problem
Algorithms
C++
Executable
Hardware

Figure 6.20: LoadInventory function for Inventory class (from code\invent1.cc)

Now we come to the FindItem member function. Its declaration is pretty simple: It takes an argument of type string which contains the UPC that we're looking for. Its implementation is pretty simple, too: It will search the Inventory object for the StockItem that has that UPC and return a copy of that StockItem, which can then be interrogated to find the price or whatever other information we need.

However, there's a serious design issue here: What should this function return if the UPC doesn't match the UPC in any of the StockItem entries in the Inventory object? The application program has to be able to determine whether or not the UPC is found. In the original program this was no problem, because the main program maintained that information itself. But in this case, the member function FindItem has to communicate success or failure to the caller somehow.

Of course, we could use a return value of true or false to indicate whether the UPC is found, but we're already using the return value to return the StockItem to the calling function. We could add a reference argument to the FindItem function and use it to set the value of a variable in the caller's code, but that's very nonintuitive; functions that use arguments only for input are easier to use and less likely to cause surprises.

Nothing Ventured, Nothing Gained

There's one more possibility. We can return a **null object** of the StockItem class; that is, an object that exists solely to serve as a placeholder, representing the desired object that we couldn't find.

Problem
Algorithms
C++
Executable
Hardware

I like this solution, because when the member function terminates, the application program has to test something anyway to see if the desired StockItem was found; why not test whether the returned object is a null StockItem? This solution, while quite simple, requires a minor change to our implementation of StockItem: We have to add an IsNull member function to our StockItem class so that we can tell whether the returned StockItem is a null StockItem or a "normal" one. We have to add the line bool IsNull(); to the class interface needed to provide this new function, and provide the implementation as shown in Figure 6.21.

```
bool StockItem::IsNull()
{
     if (m_UPC == "")
          return true;
     return false;
};
```

Figure 6.21: The implementation of IsNull (from code\item5.cc)

As you can see, not much rocket science is involved in this member function: all we do is check whether the UPC is the null string "", and if so, return true. Otherwise, we return false. Since no real item can have a UPC of "", this should work well. Let's hear from Susan on the topic of this function (and function return values in general).

Susan: This is something I have not thought about before: When you call a function where does the return value go?

Steve: Wherever you put it. If you say x = sum(weight);, then the return value goes into x. If you just say sum(weight);, then it is discarded.

Susan: Why is it discarded?

Steve: Because you didn't use it; therefore, the compiler assumes you have no further use for it.

Susan: So the return value can be used in only one place?

Steve: Yes, unless you save it in a variable, in which case you can use it however you like.

Figure 6.22 shows the implementation of FindItem, which uses CheckUPC to check whether the requested UPC is the one in the current item and returns a null StockItem if the desired UPC isn't found in the inventory list.

```
StockItem Inventory::FindItem(string UPC)
{
    short i;
    bool Found = false;

    for (i = 0; i < m_StockCount; i ++)
        {
        if (m_Stock[i].CheckUPC(UPC) == true)
            {
            Found = true;
            break;
            }
        }

    if (Found == true)
        return m_Stock[i];

    return StockItem();
}
```

Problem
Algorithms
C++
Executable
Hardware

Figure 6.22: FindItem function for Inventory class (from code\invent1.cc)

Here's my interchange with Susan on the implementation of this function:

Susan: About the first if statement, if (m_Stock[i].CheckUPC(UPC) == true): does that mean if you find the UPC you are looking for then the program breaks and you don't need to continue looking? In that case, what does the statement Found = true; do? It looks as if you are setting Found to the value true.

Steve: That's right. If we've actually found the item we're looking for, then Found will have been set to true, so we'll return the real item; otherwise, we'll return a null StockItem to indicate that we couldn't find the one requested.

After we get a copy of the correct StockItem and update its inventory via DeductSaleFromInventory, we're not quite done; we still have to update the "real" StockItem in the Inventory object. This is the task of the last function in our Inventory class: UpdateItem. Figure 6.23 shows its implementation.

```
bool Inventory::UpdateItem(StockItem Item)
{
    string UPC = Item.GetUPC();

    short i;
    bool Found = false;

    for (i = 0; i < m_StockCount; i ++)
        {
        if (m_Stock[i].CheckUPC(UPC) == true)
            {
            Found = true;
            break;
            }
        }

    if (Found == true)
        m_Stock[i] = Item;

    return Found;
}
```

Problem
Algorithms
C++
Executable
Hardware

Figure 6.23: UpdateItem function for Inventory class (from code\invent1.cc)

This function needs another function in the StockItem class to get the UPC from a StockItem object, so that UpdateItem can tell which object in the m_Stock vector is the one that needs to be updated. This additional function, GetUPC, is shown in Figure 6.24.

```
string StockItem::GetUPC()
{
    return m_UPC;
}
```

Figure 6.24: The implementation of GetUPC (from code\item5.cc)

The application program also needs one more function to be added to the interface of StockItem, to retrieve the price from the object once we have found it. This additional function, GetPrice(), is shown in Figure 6.25.

```
short StockItem::GetPrice()
{
     return m_Price;
};
```

Figure 6.25: The implementation of GetPrice (from code\item5.h)

We're almost ready to examine the revised test program. First, though, let's take a look at the complete interfaces and implementations of the StockItem and Inventory classes all in one place. Figure 6.26 shows the interface for StockItem.

```
class StockItem
{
public:
     StockItem();

     StockItem(string Name, short InStock, short Price,
     string Distributor, string UPC);

     void Display();
     void Read(ifstream& s);

     bool CheckUPC(string ItemUPC);
     void DeductSaleFromInventory(short QuantitySold);
     short GetInventory();
     string GetName();
     bool IsNull();
     short GetPrice();
     string GetUPC();

private:
     short m_InStock;
     short m_Price;
     string m_Name;
     string m_Distributor;
     string m_UPC;
};
```

Problem
Algorithms
C++
Executable
Hardware

Figure 6.26: Current interface for StockItem class (code\item5.h)

The implementation for StockItem is in Figure 6.27.

```cpp
#include <iostream.h>
#include <fstream.h>
#include "string6.h"
#include "item5.h"

StockItem::StockItem()
{
    m_InStock = 0;
    m_Price = 0;
    m_Name = "";
    m_Distributor = "";
    m_UPC = "";
};

StockItem::StockItem(string Name, short InStock, short Price,
string Distributor, string UPC)
{
    m_InStock = InStock;
    m_Price = Price;
    m_Name = Name;
    m_Distributor = Distributor;
    m_UPC = UPC;
};

void StockItem::Display()
{
    cout << "Name: ";
    cout << m_Name << endl;
    cout << "Number in stock: ";
    cout << m_InStock << endl;
    cout << "Price: ";
    cout << m_Price << endl;
    cout << "Distributor: ";
    cout << m_Distributor << endl;
    cout << "UPC: ";
    cout << m_UPC << endl;
    cout << endl;

    return;
};

void StockItem::Read(ifstream& s)
{
    s >> m_Name;
    s >> m_InStock;
```

Problem
Algorithms
C++
Executable
Hardware

Figure 6.27: Current implementation for StockItem class (code\item5.cc)

```
    s >> m_Price;
    s >> m_Distributor;
    s >> m_UPC;
}

bool StockItem::CheckUPC(string ItemUPC)
{
    if (m_UPC == ItemUPC)
        return true;

    return false;
}

void StockItem::DeductSaleFromInventory(short QuantitySold)
{
    m_InStock -= QuantitySold;
}

short StockItem::GetInventory()
{
    return m_InStock;
}

string StockItem::GetName()
{
    return m_Name;
}


bool StockItem::IsNull()
{
    if (m_UPC == "")
        return true;

    return false;
};

short StockItem::GetPrice()
{
    return m_Price;
};

string StockItem::GetUPC()
{
    return m_UPC;
}
```

Problem
Algorithms
C++
Executable
Hardware

Figure 6.27 continued

Figure 6.28 contains the interface for the Inventory class.

```
#include "vector.h"

class Inventory
{
public:
    Inventory();

    short LoadInventory(ifstream& InputStream);
    StockItem FindItem(string UPC);
    bool UpdateItem(StockItem Item);

private:
    vector<StockItem> m_Stock;
    short m_StockCount;
};
```

Figure 6.28: Current interface for Inventory class (code\invent1.h)

And Figure 6.29 contains the implementation for Inventory.

Problem
Algorithms
C++
Executable
Hardware

```
#include <iostream.h>
#include <fstream.h>
#include "vector.h"
#include "string6.h"
#include "item5.h"
#include "invent1.h"

Inventory::Inventory()
{
    m_Stock = vector<StockItem>(100);
    m_StockCount = 0;
}

short Inventory::LoadInventory(ifstream& InputStream)
{
    short i;

    for (i = 0; i < 100; i ++)
        {
        m_Stock[i].Read(InputStream);
        if (InputStream.fail() != 0)
            break;
        }

    m_StockCount = i;
    return m_StockCount;
}
```

Figure 6.29: Current implementation for Inventory class (code\invent1.cc)

```
StockItem Inventory::FindItem(string UPC)
{
    short i;
    bool Found = false;

    for (i = 0; i < m_StockCount; i ++)
        {
        if (m_Stock[i].CheckUPC(UPC) == true)
            {
            Found = true;
            break;
            }
        }

    if (Found == true)
        return m_Stock[i];

    return StockItem();
}
bool Inventory::UpdateItem(StockItem Item)
{
    string UPC = Item.GetUPC();

    short i;
    bool Found = false;

    for (i = 0; i < m_StockCount; i ++)
        {
        if (m_Stock[I].CheckUPC(UPC) == true)
            {
            Found = true;
            break;
            }
        }

    if (Found == true)
        m_Stock[i] = Item;

    return Found;
}
```

Problem
Algorithms
C++
Executable
Hardware

Figure 6.29 continued

Testing, 1, 2, 3...

To finish this stage of the inventory control project, Figure 6.30 is the revised test program that uses the Inventory class rather than doing its own search through a vector of StockItems.

```
#include <iostream.h>
#include <fstream.h>
#include "string6.h"
#include "item5.h"
#include "invent1.h"

int main()
{
    ifstream InputStream("shop2.in");
    string PurchaseUPC;
    short PurchaseCount;
    string ItemName;
    short OldInventory;
    short NewInventory;
    Inventory MyInventory;
    StockItem FoundItem;
    string TransactionCode;

    MyInventory.LoadInventory(InputStream);

    cout << "What is the UPC of the item? ";
    cin >> PurchaseUPC;

    FoundItem = MyInventory.FindItem(PurchaseUPC);
    if (FoundItem.IsNull() == true)
        {
        cout << "Can't find that item. Please check UPC." << endl;
        return 0;
        }

    OldInventory = FoundItem.GetInventory();
    ItemName = FoundItem.GetName();

    cout << "There are currently " << OldInventory << " units of "
    << ItemName << " in stock." << endl;

    cout << "Please enter transaction code as follows:\n";
    cout << "S (sale), C (price check): ";
    cin >> TransactionCode;

    if (TransactionCode == "C" || TransactionCode == "c")
        {
        cout << "The name of that item is: " << ItemName << endl;
```

Figure 6.30: Updated inventory application (code\itemtst5.cc)

```
            cout << "Its price is: " << FoundItem.GetPrice();
            }
    else if (TransactionCode == "S" || TransactionCode == "s")
            {
            cout << "How many items were sold? ";
            cin >> PurchaseCount;

            FoundItem.DeductSaleFromInventory(PurchaseCount);
            MyInventory.UpdateItem(FoundItem);

            cout << "The inventory has been updated." << endl;

            FoundItem = MyInventory.FindItem(PurchaseUPC);
            NewInventory = FoundItem.GetInventory();

            cout << "There are now " << NewInventory << " units of "
            << ItemName << " in stock." << endl;
            }

        return 0;
}
```

Figure 6.30 continued

Problem
Algorithms
C++
Executable
Hardware

This program can perform either of two operations, depending on
what the user requests. Once the UPC has been typed in, the user is
prompted to type either "C" for price check or "S" for sale. Then an if
statement selects which of the two operations to perform. The code
for the S (i.e., "sale") operation is the same as it was in the previous
version of this application, except that, of course, at that time it was
the only possible operation, so it wasn't controlled by an if statement.
The code for the C (i.e., price check) operation is new, but it's very
simple. All it does is to display both the item name and the price.

The only part of the program that might not be obvious at this
point is the expression in the if statement that determines whether the
user wants to enter a price check or sale transaction. The first part of
the test is if (TransactionCode == "C" || TransactionCode == "c"). The || is
the "logical or" operator. It can be translated as "if at least one of the
two expressions on its right or left is true, then produce the result true;
if they're both false, then produce the result false". In this case, this
means that the if statement will be true if the TransactionCode variable
is either C or c. Why do we have to check for either a lower- or

upper-case letter, when the instructions to the user clearly state that the choices are C or S?

This is good practice because users generally consider upper and lower case letters to be equivalent. Of course, as programmers, we know that the characters c and C are completely different; however, we should humor the users in this harmless delusion. After all, they're our customers!

Susan had a couple of questions about this program.

> **Susan**: What do the following output statements mean: cout << S (sale); and cout << C (price check);? I am not clear as to what they are doing.

> **Steve**: Nothing special; the prompts S (sale) and C (price check) are just to notify the user what his or her choices are.

> **Susan**: OK, so the line with the || is how you tell the computer to recognize upper case as well as lower case to have the same meaning?

> **Steve**: Yes, that's what we're doing here.

> **Susan**: So what do you call those || thingys?

Problem
Algorithms
C++
Executable
Hardware

> **Steve**: They're called "vertical bars". The operator that is spelled || is called a "logical OR" operator, because it results in the value true if either the left-hand **or** the right-hand expression is true (or if both are true).

> **Susan**: What do you mean by using else and if in the line else if (TransactionCode == "S" || TransactionCode == "s")? I don't believe I have seen them used together before.

> **Steve**: I think you're right. Actually, it's not that mysterious: As always, the else means that we're specifying actions to be taken if the original if isn't true. The second if merely checks whether another condition is true and executes its controlled block if that is the case.

You can run this program normally by changing to the normal subdirectory, typing itemtst5, and hitting ENTER. To run it under gdb, make sure you are in the normal subdirectory, then type trace itemtst5 and hit ENTER. The program will start up and show you the first line of executable code. Type z and hit ENTER to execute each line from then on; when the program asks for a UPC, you can use 8144976072, which is the (made-up) UPC for "antihistamines". The values of the relevant variables will be displayed immediately before the execution of each remaining line in main. When the program asks you for a transaction code, type S for "sale" or P for "price check", and then hit ENTER. When you get to the end of the program (or when you're tired of tracing), type q (for *quit*) and hit ENTER to exit from the debugger.

Paging Rosie Scenario

By this point, you very understandably might have gotten the notion that we have to make changes to our classes every time we need to do anything slightly different in our application program. In that case, where's the advantage of using classes instead of just writing the whole program in terms of shorts, chars, and so on?

Well, this is your lucky day. It just so happens that the next (and last) scenario we are going to examine requires no more member functions at all; in fact, we don't even have to change the application program. Here it is, for reference: "Judy comes in looking for chunky chicken soup; there's none on the shelf where it should be, so we have to check the inventory to see if we're supposed to have any".

The reason we don't have to do anything special for this scenario is that we're already displaying the name and inventory for the item as soon as we find it. Of course, if we hadn't already handled this issue, there are many other ways that we could solve this same problem. For example, we could use the Display member function of StockItem to display an item as soon as the UPC lookup succeeds, rather than waiting for the user to indicate what operation our application is supposed to perform.

Problem
Algorithms
C++
Executable
Hardware

For that matter, we'd have to consider a number of other factors in writing a real application program, even one that does such a simple task as this one. For example, what would happen if the user indicated that 200 items had been sold when only 100 were in stock? Also, how would we find an item if the UPC isn't available? The item might very well be in inventory somewhere, but the current implementation of Inventory doesn't allow for the possibility of looking up an item by any information other than the UPC.

Although these topics and many others are essential to the work of a professional programmer, they would take us too far afield from our purpose in this book, which is to teach you how to program using C++. Therefore, we will leave them for another day (and another book). Now let's review what we've covered in this chapter.

Review

The most important concept we covered in this chapter is the idea of creating user defined data types. In C++, this is done by defining a class for each such data type. Each class has both a class *interface*, which describes the behavior that the class displays to the "outside world" (i.e., other, unrelated functions), and a class *implementation*, which tells the compiler how to perform the behaviors promised in the interface definition. A variable of a class type is called an *object*. With proper attention to the interface and the details of implementation, it is possible to make objects behave just like native variables; that is, they can be initialized, assigned, compared, passed as function arguments, and returned as function return values.

Both the interface and the implementation of a class are described in terms of the functions and variables of which the class is composed; these are called *member functions* and *member variables*, because they belong to the class rather than being "free-floating" like the *global* functions and variables we encountered earlier.

Of course, one obvious question is why we need to make up our own variable types. What's wrong with char, short, and the rest of the native types that C++ has inherited from C? The answer is that it's easier to write an inventory control program, for example, if we have data types representing items in the stock of a store, rather than having to express everything in terms of the native types. An analogy is the universal preference of professionals to use technical jargon rather than "plain English": Jargon conveys more information, more precisely, in less time.

Problem
Algorithms
C++
Executable
Hardware

The idea of using objects rather than functions as the fundamental building blocks of programming is the basis of the "object-oriented programming" paradigm.[23]

Then we examined how creating classes differs from using classes, as we have been doing throughout the book. A fairly good analogy is that creating your own classes is to using classes as writing a program is to using a program.

Next, we went through the steps needed to actually create a new class; our example is the StockItem class, which is designed to allow tracking of inventory for a small grocery store. These steps include writing the interface definition, writing the implementation, writing

---

23. Purists may not approve of this use of the term *object-oriented programming*, as I'm not using this term in its strictest technical sense. However, since we are using objects and classes as our central organizing ideas, using the term *object-oriented* programming seems reasonable to me in this context.

the program that uses the class, compiling the implementation, compiling the program that uses the class, and linking the object files resulting from these compilation steps together with the standard libraries to produce the final executable program.

Then we moved from the general to the specific, analyzing the particular data and functions that the StockItem class needed to perform its duties in an application program. The member variables needed for each StockItem object included the name, count, distributor, price, and UPC. Of course, merely having these member variables doesn't make a StockItem object very useful, if it can't do anything with them. This led us to the topic of what member functions might be needed for such a class.

Rather than proceed immediately with the specialized member functions that pertain only to StockItem, however, we started by discussing the member functions that nearly every class needs to make its objects act like native variables. A class that has (at least) the capabilities of a native type is called a *concrete data type*. Such a class requires the following member functions:

1. A *default constructor*, which makes it possible to create an object of that class without supplying any initial data,
2. A *copy constructor*, which makes it possible to create a new object of this type with the same contents as an existing object of the same type,
3. An *assignment operator*, which copies the contents of one object of this type to another object of the same type,
4. A *destructor*, which performs whatever cleanup is needed when an object of this type "dies".

Problem
Algorithms
C++
Executable
Hardware

Since these member functions are so important to the proper functioning of a class, the compiler will create a version of each of them for us if we don't write them ourselves. In the case of StockItem, these compiler-generated member functions are perfectly acceptable, with the exception of the default constructor. The compiler-generated default constructor doesn't initialize a new StockItem object to a valid state, so we had to write that constructor ourselves to be sure of what a newly created StockItem contains.

Next, we looked at the first version of a class interface specification for StockItem (Figure 6.3), which tells the user (and the compiler) exactly what functions objects of this class can perform. Some items of note in this construct are these:

1. The *access specifiers* public and private, which control access to the implementation of a class by functions not in the class (*nonmember function*s). Member variables and functions in the public section are available for use by nonmember functions, whereas member variables and functions in the private section are usable only by member functions.

2. The declarations of the *constructor* functions, which construct a new object of the class. The first noteworthy point about constructors is that they have the same name as the class, which is how the compiler identifies them as constructors. The second point of note is that there can be more than one constructor for a given class; all constructors have the same name, and are distinguished by their argument lists. This facility, called *function overloading*, to C++ functions in general, not just constructors. That is, you can have any number of functions with the same name; as long as they have different argument lists, the compiler considers them different functions. In this case, we have written two constructors: the default constructor, which is used to create a StockItem when we don't specify an initial value, and a constructor that has arguments to specify values for all of the member variables.[24]

Problem
Algorithms
C++
Executable
Hardware

3. The declaration of a "normal" member function (that is, not a constructor or other predefined function) named Display, which as its name indicates, is used to display a StockItem on the screen.

4. The declaration of the member variables of StockItem, which are used to keep track of the information for a given object of the StockItem class.

Once we'd defined the class interface, we started on the class implementation by writing the default constructor for the StockItem class: StockItem::StockItem(). The reason for the doubled name is that when we write the implementation of a member function, we have to specify what class that member function belongs to; the first StockItem is the name of the class, whereas the second StockItem is the name of the function, which, as always with constructors, has the same name as the class. By contrast, we didn't have to specify the class name when declaring member functions in the interface

---

24. The compiler has also supplied a copy constructor for us, so that we can use StockItem objects as function arguments and return values.

definition, because all functions defined there are automatically member functions of that class.

The next topic we visited was the scope of member variables, which is class scope. Each object of a given class has one set of member variables, which live as long as the object does. These member variables can be accessed from any member function as though they were global variables.

Then we examined how the default constructor was actually used in the example program, discovering that the line StockItem soup; was enough to cause it to be called. This is appropriate because one of the design goals of C++ was to allow a class object to be as easy to use as a native variable. Since a native variable can be created simply by specifying its type and name, the same should be true of a class object.

This led to a discussion of the fact that the person who writes a class isn't always the person who uses it. One reason for this is that the skills required to write a program using a class are not the same as those required to create the class in the first place.

Next, we covered the other constructor for the StockItem class. This one has arguments specifying the values for all of the member variables that make up the data part of the class.

Then we got to the final function of the first version of the StockItem class: the Display function, which as its name indicates is used to display the contents of a StockItem on the screen. This function uses the pre-existing ability of << to display the shorts and strings that hold the contents of the StockItem. The return type of this function is a type we hadn't seen before, void, which simply means that there is no return value from this function. We don't need a return value from the Display function because we call it solely for its *side effect*: displaying the value of its StockItem on the screen.

Next, we took up the private part of the StockItem class definition, which contains the member variables. We covered two reasons why it is a good idea to keep the member variables private: First, it makes debugging easier, because only the member functions can modify the member variables; second, we can change the names or types of our member variables or delete them from the class much more easily if we don't have to worry about what other functions might be relying on them. While we were on the subject of the member variables of StockItem, I also explained how we could use a short to store a price: By expressing the price in cents, rather than dollars and cents, any price up to $327.67 could be stored in such a variable.

As we continued with the analysis of how the StockItem objects would be used, we discovered that we actually needed a vector of

Problem
Algorithms
C++
Executable
Hardware

such objects, one for each different item in the stock. We also needed some way to read the information for these StockItem objects from a disk file, so we wouldn't have to type it in every time we started the program up. So the next program we examined provided this function via a C++ library class we hadn't seen before: ifstream (for input from a file). We also added a new function called Read to use this new class to read information for a StockItem from the file containing that information.

While looking at the implementation of the new Read member function, we ran into the idea of a *reference argument*, an argument that is another name for the caller's variable, rather than a copy of that variable (a *value argument*). This makes it possible to change the caller's variable by changing the value of the argument in the function. In most cases, we don't want to be able to change the caller's variable, but it is essential when reading from a stream, because otherwise we'd get the same data every time we read something from the stream. Therefore, we have to use a reference argument in this case, so that the stream's internal state will be updated correctly when we retrieve data from it.

Problem
Algorithms
C++
Executable
Hardware

Then we got to the question of how we could tell when there was no data left in the input file; the answer was to call the ifstream member function fail, which returns zero if some data remain in the stream, and nonzero if nothing is left. We used a nonzero return value from fail to trigger a break statement, which terminates whatever loop contains the break. In this case, the loop was the one that read in data from the input file, so the loop would stop whenever we got to the end of the input file or when we had read 100 records, whichever came first.

This led to a detailed investigation of whether the number of records read in was always calculated correctly. The problem under discussion was the potential for a *fencepost error*, also known as an *off by one error*. After careful consideration, I concluded that the code as written was correct.

Having cleared up that question, we proceeded to some other scenarios that might occur in the grocery store for which this program theoretically was being written. All of the scenarios we looked at had a common requirement: to be able to look up a StockItem, given some information about it. We first tried to handle this requirement by reading the UPC directly from each StockItem object in the vector. When we found the correct StockItem, we would display and update the inventory for that StockItem. However, this didn't compile, because we were trying to access private member variables of a StockItem object from a nonmember function, which is illegal. While we could have changed those variables from private to public, that would directly contradict the reason that we made them private in the first place; that is, to prevent external functions from interfering in the inner workings of our StockItem objects. Therefore, we solved the problem by adding some new member functions (CheckUPC and DeductSalesFromInventory) to check the UPC of a StockItem and manipulate the inventory information for each StockItem. At the same time, we examined a new data type, bool, which is limited to the two values true and false; it is handy for keeping track of information such as whether we have found the StockItem object we are looking for, and communicating such information back to a calling function.

While I was making these changes, I noticed that the original version of the test program wasn't very helpful to its user; it didn't tell the user whether the UPC was any good, the name of the item, or how much inventory was available for sale. So I added some more member functions (GetInventory and GetName) to allow this more "user-friendly" information to be displayed.

Then we progressed to the second of the grocery store scenarios, in which the task was to find the price of an item, given its UPC. This turned out to be very similar to the previous problem of finding an item to update its inventory. Therefore, it was a pretty obvious step to try to make a function out of the "find an item by UPC" operation, rather than writing the code for the search over again. Since we're doing "object-oriented" programming, such a function should probably be a member function. The question was "of which class?" It couldn't be a member function of StockItem, because the whole idea of this function was to locate a StockItem. A member function of StockItem needs a StockItem object to work on, but we didn't have the StockItem object yet.

Problem
Algorithms
C++
Executable
Hardware

The solution was to make another class, called Inventory, which had member functions to load the inventory information in from the disk file (LoadInventory) and search it for a particular StockItem (FindItem). Most of this class was pretty simple, but we did run into an interesting design question: What should the FindItem function return if the UPC didn't match anything in the inventory? After some consideration, I decided to use a *null object* of the class StockItem; that is, one that exists solely to serve as a placeholder representing a non-existent object. This solution required adding an IsNull member function to the StockItem class, so that the user of FindItem could determine whether the returned object was "real" or just an indication of an incorrect UPC.

Then we updated the test program to use this new means of locating a StockItem. Since the new version of the test program could perform either of two functions (price check or sale), we also added some output and input statements to ask the user what he wanted to do. To make this process more flexible, we allowed the user to type in either an upper or lower case letter to select which function to perform. This brought up the use of the "logical OR" operator || to allow the controlled block of an if statement to be executed if either (or both) of two expressions is true. We also saw how to combine an else with a following if statement, when we wanted to select among more than two alternatives.

We needed two more functions to make this new version of the application program work correctly: one to update the item in the inventory (Inventory::UpdateItem(StockItem item)) and one to get the UPC of a StockItem (StockItem::GetUPC()). The reason that we had to add these new functions to the interfaces of Inventory and StockItem, respectively, is that we were no longer operating on the "real" StockItem, as we had been when we accessed the inventory vector directly in the previous version of the application program. Instead, we were getting a copy of the StockItem from the Inventory object and changing that copy; thus, to have the final result put back into the Inventory object, we had to add the UpdateItem member function of Inventory, which overwrote the original StockItem with our changed version. The GetUPC function's role in all this was to allow the UpdateItem function to look up the correct StockItem to be replaced without the main program having to pass the UPC in explicitly; instead, the GetUPC function allowed the UpdateItem function to retrieve the correct UPC from the updated object provided by the application program.

This brought us to the final scenario, which required us to look up the inventory for an item, given its UPC. As it happened, we had already solved that problem by the simple expedient of displaying the name and inventory of the StockItem as soon as it was located.

Finally, I mentioned a few other factors, such as alternative means of looking up an item without knowing its UPC, that would be important in writing a real application program and noted that we couldn't go into them here due to space limitations.

```
Problem
Algorithms
C++
Executable
Hardware
```

Exercises

1. In a real inventory control program, we would need to do more than merely read the inventory information in from a disk file, as we have done in this chapter. We'd also want to

be able to write the updated inventory back to the disk file via an ofstream object, which is exactly like an ifstream object except that it allows us to write to a file rather than reading from one. Modify the header files item5.h and invent1.h to include the declarations of the new functions StockItem::Write and Inventory::StoreInventory, needed to support this new ability.

2. Implement the new functions that you declared in exercise 1. Then update the test program to write the changed inventory to a new file. To connect an ofstream called OutputStream to a file named "test.out", you could use the line:
ofstream OutputStream("test.out");.

Conclusion

In this chapter, we've delved into the concepts and implementations of classes and objects, which are the constructs that make C++ an object-oriented language. Of course, we have only scratched the surface of these powerful topics; in fact, we'll spend the rest of this book on the fundamentals of classes and objects. Unfortunately, it's impossible to cover these constructs and all of their uses in any one book, no matter how long or detailed it may be, and I'm not going to try to do that. Instead, we'll continue with our in-depth examination of the basics of object-oriented programming. In the next chapter, we'll start on the task of creating a string class like the one that we've been using so far in this book.

```
Problem
Algorithms
C++
Executable
Hardware
```

Answers to Exercises

1. Here is the new function declaration that needs to be added to the StockItem interface definition (from code\item6.h):

void Write(ofstream& s);

and the one to be added to the Inventory interface definition, (from code\invent2.h):

void StoreInventory(ofstream& OutputStream);

2. Figure 6.31 shows the implementation of the Write member function for StockItem.

```
void StockItem::Write(ofstream& s)
{
        s << m_Name << endl;
        s << m_InStock << endl;
        s << m_Price << endl;
        s << m_Distributor << endl;
        s << m_UPC << endl;
}
```

Figure 6.31: The Write member function for the StockItem class
(from code\item6.cc)

and Figure 6.32 is the implementation of the StoreInventory
member function of the Inventory class.

```
void Inventory::StoreInventory(ofstream& OutputStream)
{
        short i;

        for (i = 0; i < m_StockCount; i ++)
                m_Stock[i].Write(OutputStream);

        return;
}
```

```
Problem
Algorithms
C++
Executable
Hardware
```

Figure 6.32: The StoreInventory member function for the Inventory
class (from code\invent2.cc)

As you can see, neither of these is tremendously complex
or, for that matter, very different from its counterpart used to
read the data in from the file in the first place.

Finally, Figure 6.33 shows the changes needed to the
application program to write the updated inventory back to a
new file:

```
ofstream OutputStream("shop2.out");
MyInventory.StoreInventory(OutputStream);
```

Figure 6.33: The changes to the application program (from
code\itemtst6.cc)

Of course, in a real program, it would probably be better to
write the updated inventory back to the original file, so that
the next time we ran the program, the updated inventory
would be read in. However, in the case of a test application,

it's simpler to avoid modifying the input file so we can run the same test again if necessary.

You can run this program normally by changing to the normal subdirectory, typing itemtst6, and hitting ENTER. To run it under gdb, make sure you are in the normal subdirectory, then type trace itemtst6 and hit ENTER. The program will start up and show you the first line of executable code. Type z and hit ENTER to execute each line from then on; when the program asks for a UPC, you can use 8144976072, which is the (made-up) UPC for "antihistamines". The values of the relevant variables will be displayed immediately before the execution of each remaining line in main. When you get to the end of the program (or when you're tired of tracing), type q (for *quit*) and hit ENTER to exit from the debugger.

```
Problem
Algorithms
C++
Executable
Hardware
```

Chapter 7

Stringing Along

You may recall the discussion near the beginning of Chapter 6 of *native* vs. *user defined* variable types. I provided a list of native C++ variable types; namely, char, short, long, float, double, bool, and int. We've already created several classes for our inventory control project, and now it's time to apply what we've learned to a more basic type, the string. We've been using strings for a long time, and now it's time to see exactly how the string class works.

Objectives of This Chapter

By the end of this chapter, you should

1. Understand how variables of the string class are created, destroyed, and copied.
2. Understand how to assign memory to variables where the amount of memory needed is not known until the program is running.
3. Understand how literal C strings can be assigned to variables of the string class.

Playing out the string

Susan had some questions about these objectives. Here's the discussion.

> **Susan**: What is the difference between literal C strings and variables of the string class?

317

Steve: A variable of the string class is what you've been using to store variable-length alphanumeric data. You can copy them, input them from the keyboard, assign values to them, and the like. By contrast, a literal C string is just a bunch of characters in a row; all you can do with it is display it or assign it to a string variable.

Susan: OK, then you are saying that variables of the string class are what I am used to working with, but I just didn't know that they were part of a class because you were *keeping this all a big secret*. On the other hand, a literal C string is just some nonsense that you want me to learn to assign to something that might make sense? OK, this is great; sure, this is logical<?>. Hey, a literal C string must be a part of the native language?

Steve: Right all the way along.

Susan: Yes, but why would something so basic as string not be part of the native language? This is what I don't understand. And vectors too; even though they are gross, I can see that they are a very necessary evil. So tell me why those basic things would not be part of the native language?

```
Problem
Algorithms
C++
Executable
Hardware
```

Steve: That's a very good question. In fact, both strings and vectors are going to be supplied by the "standard library" that will be part of the C++ standard, which should take effect about the time this book comes out (mid-1996). They still won't be part of the language itself, because that would make the compiler even more complicated than it already is. However, the user will still be able to use them without having to make them up, so the fact that they aren't part of the language will be of mostly theoretical interest.

Before we get into how to create the string class we've been using in this book, I should expand on the answer I gave Susan as to why string isn't a native type in the first place: To keep the C++ language itself as simple as possible. One of the design goals of C++, as of C, was to allow the language to be moved from one machine type to another as easily as possible ("ported", in the jargon). Since strings, vectors, and so on can be written in C++ (i.e., created out of the more elementary parts of the language), they don't have to be built in. This reduces the amount of effort needed to port C++. In addition, some applications don't need and can't afford anything but the barest essentials; "embedded" CPUs such as those in cameras, VCRs, elevators, or microwave ovens, are probably the most important users of such CPUs, and they're much more common than "real" computers. However, this still leaves the question of why these data types haven't been in a standard library that can be used when necessary. Bjarne says in his book *Design and Evolution of C++* that it might very well have been a mistake to have released C++ to the general public without this library; I tend to agree. In any event, this situation will be remedied when the C++ standard is adopted, which as mentioned is scheduled to occur sometime this year (1996).

Even though strings aren't native, we've been using them for some time already without realizing that they're not native variables, so it should be fairly obvious that this class has to provide the facilities of a concrete data type; that is, one whose objects can be created, copied, assigned, and destroyed as though they were native variables. You may recall from the discussion starting on page 245 in Chapter 6 that we need a default constructor, a copy constructor, an assignment operator, and a destructor. To refresh your memory, here's the description of each of these member functions:

1. A *default constructor* creates an object when there is no initial value specified for the object.
2. A *copy constructor* makes a new object with the same contents as an existing object of the same type.
3. An *assignment operator* sets an existing object to the value of another object of the same type.
4. A *destructor* cleans up when an object expires; for a local object, this occurs at the end of the block where it was created.

Problem
Algorithms
C++
Executable
Hardware

In our StockItem and Inventory class definitions, the compiler-generated versions of these functions were fine for all but the default constructor. In the case of the string class, though, we're going to have to create our own versions of all four of these functions, for reasons that will become apparent as we examine their implementations in this chapter and the next one.

Before we can implement these member functions for our string class, though, we have to define exactly what a string is. The string class is a data type that gives us the following capabilities in addition to those facilities that every concrete data type provides:

1. We can set a string to a literal value like "abc".
2. We can display a string on the screen with the << operator.
3. We can read a string in from the keyboard with the >> operator.
4. We can compare two strings to find out whether they are equal.

5.   We can compare two strings to find out which is "less than" the other; that is, which one would come first in the dictionary.

We'll see how all of these capabilities work sometime in this chapter or the next one, but for now let's start with Figure 7.1, a simplified version of the interface specification for the string class, which includes the specification of the four member functions needed for a concrete data type, as well as a special constructor that is specific to the string class.[1]

```
class string
{
public:
        string();
        string(const string& Str);
        void operator = (const string& Str);
        ~string();

        string(char* p);

private:
        short m_Length;
        char* m_Data;
};
```

Problem
Algorithms
C++
Executable
Hardware

Figure 7.1: The string class interface, initial version (code\string1.h)

The first four member functions in that interface are the standard concrete data type functions. In order, they are

1.   The *default constructor*
2.   The *copy constructor*
3.   The *assignment operator*, operator =
4.   The *destructor*

---

1. For the implementation of the functions in this interface specification, see the following figures:

1.   For string(), see Figure 7.3.
2.   For string(const string& Str), see Figure 8.6.
3.   For operator = (const string& Str), see Figure 7.15.
4.   For ~string(), see Figure 7.17.
5.   For string(char* p), see Figure 7.6.

I've been instructed by Susan to let you see all of the code that implements this initial version of our string class at once before we start to analyze it. Of course, I've done so, and Figure 7.2 is the result.

```cpp
#include <string.h>
#include "string1.h"

string::string()
{
    m_Length = 1;
    m_Data = new char [m_Length];
    memcpy(m_Data,"",m_Length);
};

string::string(char* p)
{
    m_Length = strlen(p) + 1;
    m_Data = new char [m_Length];
    memcpy(m_Data,p,m_Length);
};

void string::operator = (const string& Str)
{
    if (&Str != this)
        {
        delete [] m_Data;
        m_Length = Str.m_Length;
        m_Data = new char [m_Length];
        memcpy(m_Data,Str.m_Data,m_Length);
        }
    return;
};

string::~string()
{
    delete [] m_Data;
};
```

Problem
Algorithms
C++
Executable
Hardware

Figure 7.2: The initial implementation for the string class (code\string1.cc)

Now let's start by looking at the default constructor. Figure 7.3 shows its implementation.

```
string::string()
{
    m_Length = 1;
    m_Data = new char [m_Length];
    memcpy(m_Data,"",m_Length);
};
```

Figure 7.3: The default constructor for the string class (from code\string1.cc)

The first statement here, m_Length = 1; isn't very complicated at all. It simply sets the length of our new string to 1. However, this may seem a bit odd: Why do we need any characters at all for a string that has no value? The answer to this riddle is quite simple: To make our strings as compatible as possible with pre-existing C functions that work on C strings, we need to include the null byte that terminates all C strings, so we need to reserve one more byte of memory for a string's data than the length of the C string. In the current case of a zero-character string, this means that we need one byte of storage for the null byte.

Before proceeding to the next statement, let's take a look at the characteristics of the variables that we're using here. The scope of these variables, as we know from our previous discussion of the StockItem class, is class scope; therefore, each object of the string class has its own set of these variables, and they are accessible from any member functions of the class as though they were global variables.

However, an equally important characteristic of each of these variables is its data type. The type of m_Length is short, which is a type we've encountered before, a 16-bit integer variable that can hold a number between -32768 and 32767. But what about the type of the other member variable, m_Data, which is listed in Figure 7.1 as char*? We know what a char is, but what does that * mean?

**Problem
Algorithms
C++
Executable
Hardware**

Passing Along a Few Pointers

The star means **pointer**, which is just another term for a memory address. In particular, char* (pronounced "char star") means "pointer to a char".[2] This is considered one of the most difficult concepts for beginning programmers to grasp, but you shouldn't have any trouble understanding its definition if you've been following the discussion

---

2. By the way, char* can also be written as char *, but I find it clearer to attach the * to the data type being pointed to.

so far: A pointer is the address of some data item in memory. That is, to say "a variable points to a memory location" is almost exactly the same as saying "a variable's value is the address of a memory location". In the specific case of a variable x of type char*, for example, to say "x points to a C string" is exactly the same as saying "x contains the address of the first byte of the C string."[3] The m_Data variable is used to hold the address of the first char of the data that a string contains; the rest of the characters follow the first character at consecutively higher locations in memory.

If this sounds familiar, it should; a literal C string like "hello" (Chapter 3) consists of a number of chars in consecutive memory locations; it should come as no surprise then when I tell you that a literal C string has the type char*.

As you might infer from these cases, our use of one char* to refer to multiple chars isn't an isolated example. Actually, it's quite a widespread practice in C++, which brings up an important point: A char*, or any other type of pointer for that matter, has two different possible meanings in C++.[4] One of these meanings is the obvious one of signifying the address of a single item of the type the pointer points to. In the case of a char*, that means the address of a char. However, in the case of a literal C string, as well in the case of our m_Data member variable, we use a char* to indicate the address of the first char of an indeterminate number of chars; any chars after the first one occupy consecutively higher addresses in memory. Most of the time, this distinction has little effect on the way we write programs, but sometimes we have to be sensitive to this "multiple personality" of pointers; we'll run across one of these cases later in this chapter.

Susan had some questions (and I had some answers) on this topic of the true meaning of a char*:

> **Susan**: What I get from this is that char* points to a char address either singularly or as the beginning of a string of multiple addresses. Is that right?

> **Steve**: Yes, except that it's a string of several characters, not addresses.

Problem
Algorithms
C++
Executable
Hardware

---

3. C programmers are likely to object that a pointer has some properties that differ from those of a memory address. Technically, they're right, but in the specific case of char* the differences between a pointer and a memory address will never matter. Since we aren't going to be using any other types of pointers in this book, we can avoid adding yet another source of complexity to this discussion.

4. As this implies, it's possible to have a pointer to any type of variable, not just to a char. For example, a pointer to a short would have the type short*, and similarly for pointers to any other data type. However, we won't need to use pointers to any other type of variables in this book.

Susan: Oh, here we go again; this is so confusing. So if I use a string "my name is" then char* points to the address that holds the string of all those letters. But if the number of letters exceeds what the address can hold, won't it take up the next available address in memory and char* point to it after it points to the first address?

Steve: Each memory address can hold 1 byte; in the case of a string, that byte is the value of one char of the string's data. So a char*, as we use it, will always point to the first char of the chars that hold our string's value; the other chars follow that one immediately in memory.

Susan: Let me ask this: When you show an example of a string with the value "Test" (Figure 7.10), the pointer at address 12340002 containing the address 1234febc is really pointing at the T as that would be the first char and the rest of the letters will actually be in the other immediately following bytes of memory?

Steve: Absolutely correct.

Problem
Algorithms
C++
Executable
Hardware

While we're on the subject of that earlier discussion of literal C strings, you may recall that I bemoaned the fact that such literal C strings use a 0 byte to mark the end of the literal value, rather than keeping track of the length separately. Nothing can be done about that decision now, at least as it applies to literal C strings. In the case of the string class, however, the implementation is under our control rather than the language designer's; therefore, I've decided to use a length variable (m_Length) along with the variable that holds the address of the first char of the data (m_Data).

In other words, what we're doing in this exercise is synthesizing a new data type called string. A string needs a length and a set of characters to represent the actual data in the string. The short named m_Length is used in the string class to keep track of the number of characters in the data part of the string; the char* named m_Data is used to hold the address of the first character of the data part of the string.

The next statement, m_Data = new char [m_Length]; takes us on another of our side trips. This one has to do with the dreaded topic of dynamic memory allocation.

The Dynamic Duo, new and delete

So far, we've encountered two storage classes: static and auto. As you might recall from the discussion in Chapter 5, static variables are allocated memory when the program is linked, while the memory for auto variables is assigned to them at entry to the block where they are defined. However, both mechanisms have a major limitation: The amount of memory needed is fixed when the program is compiled. In the case of a string, we need to allocate an amount of memory that cannot be known until the program is executed, so we need another storage class.

As you will be happy to learn, there is indeed another storage class, called **dynamic storage**, which enables us to decide the amount of memory to allocate at run time.[5] To allocate memory dynamically, we use the new operator, specifying the data type of the memory to be allocated and the number of elements that we need. In our example, m_Data = new char [m_Length]; the type is char and the count is m_Length. The result of calling new is a *pointer* to the specified data type; in this case, since we want to store chars, the result of calling new is a pointer to a char, that is, a char*. This is a good thing, because char* is the type of the variable m_Data to which we're assigning the address that is returned from new. So the result of the line we're examining is to set m_Data to the value returned from calling new; that value is the address of a newly assigned block of memory that can hold m_Length chars, which is just what we need to hold the contents of the zero-length C string that represents the value of our empty string.

It may not be obvious why we need to call new to get the address where we will store our data. Doesn't a char* always point to a byte in memory? Yes, it does; the problem is *which* byte. We can't use static (link time) or auto (function entry time) allocation for our string class, because each string can have a different number of characters. Therefore, we have to assign the memory when we find out how many characters we need to store the value of the string. What new does is to get some memory for us and return the address of the beginning of that memory. In this case, we assign that address to our char* variable called m_Data. An important point to note here is that in addition to giving us the address of some memory, new also gives us the right to use that memory for our own purposes. That same memory area will not be made available for any other use until we say we're done with it by calling another operator called delete.

Susan had some questions about how (and why) we use new. Here's the discussion:

Problem
Algorithms
C++
Executable
Hardware

---

5. This terminology doesn't exactly match the official nomenclature used by Bjarne Stroustrup to describe dynamic memory allocation. However, every C and C++ programmer will understand you if you talk about dynamic storage, and I believe that this terminology is easier to understand than the official terminology.

Susan: OK, so all Figure 7.3 does is lay the foundation to be able to acquire memory to store the C string "" and then copy that information that will go into m_Data that starts at a certain location in memory?

Steve: Right; Figure 7.6 is the code for the constructor that accomplishes that task.

Susan: When you say that "the amount of memory needed is fixed when the program is compiled" that bothers me. I don't understand that in terms of auto variables, or is this because that type is known such as a short?

Steve: Right. As long as the types and the quantity of the data items in a class definition are known at compile time, as is the case with auto and static variables, the compiler can figure out the amount of memory they need. The addresses of auto variables aren't known at compile time, but how much space they will take up is.

Susan: OK, I understand the types of the data items. However, I am not sure what you mean by the quantity; can you give me an example?

Problem
Algorithms
C++
Executable
Hardware

Steve: Sure. You might have three chars and four shorts in a particular class definition; in that case, the compiler would add up three times the length of a char and four times the length of a short and allocate that much memory (more or less). Actually, some other considerations affect the size of a class object that aren't relevant to the discussion here, but they can all be handled at compile time and therefore still allow the compiler to figure out the amount of memory needed to store an object of any class.

The final statement in the default constructor, memcpy(m_Data,"",m_Length); is responsible for copying the null byte from the C string "" to our newly allocated area of memory. The function memcpy (short for "memory copy") is one of the C *standard library* functions for C string and memory manipulation. As you can see, it takes three arguments. The first argument is a pointer to the destination, that is, the address that will receive the data. The second argument is a pointer to the source of the data; this, of course, is the address that we're copying from (i.e., the address of the null byte in the "", in our example). The last argument is the number of bytes to copy.

In other words, memcpy reads the bytes that starts at the address specified by its input argument ("") and writes a copy of those bytes to addresses starting at the address specified by its output argument (m_Data). The amount copied is specified by the length argument (m_Length). Effectively, therefore, memcpy copies a certain amount of data from one place in memory to another; in this case, it copies 1 byte from the address of the literal C string "" to the address pointed to by m_Data (that is, the place where we're storing the characters that make up the value of our string).

This notion of dynamic allocation was the subject of some more discussion with Susan.

Susan: This stuff with operator new: I have no idea what you are talking about. I am totally gone, left in the dust. *What* is this stuff? Why do you need new to point to memory locations, I thought that is what char* did?

Steve: You're right that char* points to a memory location. But which one? The purpose of new is to get some memory for us from the operating system and return the address of the first byte of that memory. In this case, we assign that address to our char* variable called m_Data. Afterward, we can store data at that address.

Susan: I am not getting this because I just don't get the purpose of char*, and don't just tell me that it points to an address in memory. I want to know why we need it to point to a specific address in memory rather than let it take on just any random address in memory.

Steve: Because then there would be no way of guaranteeing that the memory that it points to won't be used by some other part of the program or indeed some other program entirely in a multitasking system like Windows. We need to claim ownership of some memory by calling new before we can use it.

Susan: I think I understand now why we need to use new, but why should the result of calling new be a pointer? I am missing this completely. How does new result in char*? Some steps are not obvious here.

Steve: Because that's how new is defined: it gives you an address (pointer) to a place where you can store some chars (or whatever type you requested).

Susan: OK, but in the statement m_Data = new char [m_Length], why is char in this statement not char*? I am getting so confused on this.

Steve: Because you're asking for an address (pointer) to a place where you can store a bunch of chars.

Susan: But then wouldn't it be necessary to specify char* rather than char in the statement?

Problem
Algorithms
C++
Executable
Hardware

Steve: I admit that I find that syntax unclear as well. Yes, in my opinion, it should be stated as char*, but apparently Bjarne thought otherwise.

Susan: OK, so then m_Data is the pointer address where new (memory from the heap) is going to store char data of m_Length. Right?

Steve: Yes, the value assigned to m_Data in the constructor is the value returned from new; this value is the address of an area of memory allocated to this use. The area of memory is of length m_Length.

Susan: Well, I thought that the address stored in m_Data was the first place where you stored your chars. So is new just what goes and gets that memory to put the address in m_Data?

Steve: Exactly.

Susan: Here's what I understand about the purpose of char*. It functions as a pointer to a specific memory address. We need to do that because the computer is stupid and doesn't know where to put the char data, therefore we need char* to say "hey you, computer, look over here, this is where we are going to put the data for you to find and use".

Problem
Algorithms
C++
Executable
Hardware

Steve: That's fine.

Susan: We need to use char* for variable length memory. This is because we don't know how much memory we will need until it is used. For this we need the variable m_Data to hold the first address in memory for our char data. Then we need the variable m_Length that we have set to the length of the C string that will be used to get the initial data for the string. Then we have to have that nifty little helper guy new to get some memory from the heap for the memory of our C string data.

Steve: Sounds good to me.

Susan: Now about memcpy: This appears to be the same thing as initializing the variable. I am so confused.

Steve: That's exactly correct. Maybe you shouldn't get unconfused!

The call to memcpy is the last statement in the constructor. Now let's see what we have accomplished. The constructor has initialized a string by

1. Setting the length of the string to the effective length of a null C string, "", including the terminating null byte (i.e., 1 byte).

2.   Allocating memory for a copy of the null C string.
3.   Copying the contents of the null C string to the allocated memory.

Now let's continue with our examination of the string::string() constructor. Its final result is a string with the value "", whose memory layout might look like Figure 7.4.[6]

```
Address    Name                  string n

12340000   m_Length        ┌──────────────────────┐
                           │         0001         │
                           ├──────────────────────┤
12340002   m_Data          │       1234febc       │──┐
                           └──────────────────────┘  │
                                                      │
                            ┌──────────────────────┐  │
1234febc   (none)          │          00          │←─┘
                            └──────────────────────┘
```

Figure 7.4: An empty string in memory

Using the default constructor is considerably easier than defining it. As we have seen in Chapter 6, the default constructor is called whenever we declare an object without specifying any data to initialize it with; for example, in the line string s; in Figure 7.5, which is the first test program that we will use to illustrate the functioning of the string class.

Problem
Algorithms
C++
Executable
Hardware

```
#include "string1.h"

int main()
{
    string s;
    string n("Test");
    string x;

    s = n;
    n = "My name is: ";

    x = n;
    return 0;
}
```

Figure 7.5: Our first test program for the string class (code\strtst1.cc)

---

6. The reason for the different numbers of digits in the representations of m_Length, m_Data, and the data for the null C string is to indicate how long those data items are.

In case it's still not clear why the line string s; calls the default constructor string::string(), here's the detailed explanation:

1. The compiler knows that we want to create a string because we've defined a variable called s with the type string; that's what string s; means.
2. Therefore, since string is not a native data type, the compiler looks for a function called string::string, which would create a string. It finds one because we've included the file string1.h in our example program; the contents of that file are listed in Figure 7.1.
3. However, we can have several functions named string::string, with different argument lists, because there are several possible ways to supply the initial data for a string we're creating. In this case, we aren't supplying any initial data, so the default constructor string::string() is the only possible choice.
4. Since that function string::string() is declared in the header file, the line string s; is translated to a call to that function.

Problem
Algorithms
C++
Executable
Hardware

I should point out here that the only file that the compiler needs to figure out how to compile the line string s; is the interface file, string1.h. The actual implementation of the string class in string1.cc isn't required, because all the compiler cares about when compiling a program using classes is the contract between the class implementer and the user; that is, the interface file. The actual implementation in string1.cc that fulfills this contract isn't needed until the program is linked to make an executable; at that point, the linker will complain if the compiled versions of the implementation files are not supplied.

Caution: Construction Area

Now that we've disposed of the default constructor, let's take a look at the line in the string interface definition (Figure 7.1) that says string(char* p);.[7] This is the declaration for another constructor; unlike the default constructor we've examined, this one has an argument, char* p.[8]

---

7. I know we've skipped the copy constructor, the assignment operator, and the destructor. Don't worry, we'll get to them later.

8. There's nothing magical about the name p for a pointer. You could call it George if you wanted to, but it would just confuse people. The letter p is often used for pointers, especially by programmers who can't type, which unfortunately is fairly common.

As we saw in Chapter 6, the combination of the function name and argument types is called the *signature* of a function. Two functions that have the same name but differ in the type of at least one argument are distinct functions, and the compiler will use the difference(s) in the type(s) of the argument(s) to figure out which function with the same name should be called in any given case. Of course, this leads to the question of why we would need more than one string constructor; they all make strings, don't they?

Yes, they do, but not from the same "raw material". It's true that every constructor in the string class makes a string, but each constructor has a unique argument list, which determines exactly how the new string will be constructed. The default constructor always makes an empty string (like the C string ""), whereas the constructor string(char* p) takes a C string and makes a string that has the same value as the C string does.

Susan wasn't going to accept this without a struggle.

> **Susan**: I don't get "whereas the string(char* p) constructor takes a C string and makes a string that has the same value as the C string does."

> **Steve**: Well, when the compiler looks at the statement string n("Test"); it has to follow some steps to figure it out.

> 1. The compiler knows that you want to create a string because you've defined a variable called n with the type string; that's what string n means.
> 2. Therefore, since string is not a native data type, the compiler looks for a function called string::string, which would create a string.
> 3. However, there can be several functions named string::string, with different argument lists, because there are several possible ways to get the initial data for the string you're creating. In this case, you are supplying data in the form of a literal C string, whose type is char*; therefore, a constructor with the signature string::string(char*) will match.
> 4. Since a function with the signature string::string(char*) has been declared in the header file, the line string n("Test"); is translated to a call to that function.

> **Susan**: So string(char* p) is just there in case you need it for "any given situation"; what situation is this?

> **Steve**: It depends on what kind of data (if any) we're supplying to the constructor. If we supply no data, then the default constructor is used. If

Problem
Algorithms
C++
Executable
Hardware

we supply a C string (such as a literal C string), then the constructor that takes a char* is used, because the type of a C string is char*.

Susan: So string s; is the default constructor in case you need something that uses uninitialized objects?

Steve: Not quite; the default constructor for the string class is string::string(), which doesn't need any arguments, because it constructs an empty string.

Susan: And the string n ("Test"); is a constructor that finally gets around to telling us what we are trying to accomplish here?

Steve: Again, not quite. The line string n("Test"); causes a string with the value "Test" to be created, by calling the constructor string::string(char* p);.

Susan: See, you are talking first about string n("Test"); in Figure 7.5 and then you get all excited that you just happen to have string::string(char* p) hanging around which is way over in Figure 7.1.

Steve: Now you know that a literal C string such as "Test" has the data type char*. Does this make sense?

Problem
Algorithms
C++
Executable
Hardware

Susan: OK, I think this helped. I understand it better. Only now that I do, it raises other questions that I accepted before but now don't make sense due to what I do understand. Does that make sense to you? I didn't think so.

Steve: Sure, why not? You've reached a higher level of understanding, so you can now see confusions that were obscured before.

Susan: So this is just the constructor part? What about the default constructor, what happened to it?

Steve: We can't use it here, because we have some data to assign to the string when the string is created. A default constructor is used only when there is no initial value for a variable.

Susan: So was the whole point of discussion about default constructors just to let us know that they exist even though you aren't really using them here?

Steve: We are using them to create strings with no initial value, as discussed before.

Susan wasn't clear on why the C string "Test" would be of type char*, which is understandable because that's anything but obvious. Here's the discussion we entered into on this point.

> **Susan**: When you say "Test" is a literal C string of type char* and that the compiler happily finds that declaration, that is fine. But see, it is not obvious to me that it is type char*; I can see char but not char*. Something is missing here so that I would be able to follow the jump from char to char*.

> **Steve**: A literal C string isn't a single char, but a bunch of chars. Therefore, we need to get the address of the first one; that gives us the addresses of the ones after it.

Now that the reason why a literal C string is of type char* is a bit clearer, Figure 7.6 shows the implementation for the constructor that takes a char* argument.

```
string::string(char* p)
{
      m_Length = strlen(p) + 1;
      m_Data = new char [m_Length];
      memcpy(m_Data,p,m_Length);
};
```

Figure 7.6: The char* constructor for the string class (from code\string1.cc)

Problem
Algorithms
C++
Executable
Hardware

You should be able to decode the header string::string(char* p): This function is a constructor for class string (because its class is string and its name is also string); its argument, named p, is of type char*. The next statement is m_Length = strlen(p) + 1;. This is obviously setting the string's length (m_Length) to something, but what?

As you may recall, C strings are stored as a series of characters terminated by a null byte (i.e., one with a 0 value). Therefore, unlike the case with our strings, where the length is available by looking at a member variable (m_Length), to find the length of a C string it is necessary to search from the beginning of the C string until you get to a null byte. Since this is such a common operation in C, the C *standard library* provides the function strlen (short for "string length") to do that search; it returns a result indicating the number of characters in the C string, *not* including the null byte. So the statement m_Length = strlen(p) + 1; sets our member variable m_Length to the length of the C string p, which we compute as the length reported by strlen (not including the terminating null byte) + 1 for the terminating null byte.[9] We need this information because we've decided to store the length explicitly in our string class rather than relying solely on a null byte to mark the end of the string, as is done in C.[10]

Susan had some questions about the implementation of this function, and I supplied some answers.

Susan: What is strlen?

Steve: A function left over from C; it tells us how long a C string is.

Susan: Where did it come from?

Steve: It's from the standard C library, which is part of C++.

Susan: What are you using it for here?

Steve: Finding out how long the C string is that we're supposed to copy into our string.

Susan: Is this C or C++?

Problem
Algorithms
C++
Executable
Hardware

Steve: Both.

Susan: Why is char* so special that it deserves a pointer? What makes it different?

Steve: The * means "pointer". In C++, char* means "pointer to a char".

---

9. This is probably a good place to clear up any confusion you might have about whether there are native and user defined functions; there is no such distinction. However, the reason might not be what you expect; rather than there being no user defined functions, it's just the opposite. That is, functions are never native in the way that variables are: built into the language. Quite a few functions such as strlen and memcpy come *with* the language; that is, they are supplied in the standard libraries that you get when you buy the compiler. However, these functions are not privileged relative to the functions you can write yourself, unlike the case with native variables in C. In other words, you can write a *function* in C or C++ that looks and behaves exactly like one in the library, whereas it's impossible in C to add a type of *variable* that has the same appearance and behavior as the native types; the knowledge of the native variable types is built into the C compiler and cannot be changed by the programmer.

But *why* aren't there any native functions? Because the language was designed to be easy to move from one machine to another. This is easier if the compiler is simpler; so, most of the functionality of the language is provided by functions that can be written in the "base language" the compiler knows about. This includes basic functions such as strlen and memcpy, which can be written in C. For purposes of performance, they are often written in assembly language instead, but that's not necessary to get the language running on a new machine.

10. You may wonder why we even need to include the null byte if we're going to store the length also. Isn't this redundant? Yes, it is, but if we ever want to be able to use any of the C string functions on our strings, we have to include that null byte at the end. Otherwise, the C string functions won't work correctly.

Susan: I just don't understand the need for the pointer in char. See when we were using it (char) before, it didn't have a pointer, so why now? Well, I guess it was because I thought it was native back then when I didn't know that there was any other way. So why don't you have a pointer to strings then? Are all variables in classes going to have to be pointed to? I guess that is what I am asking.

Steve: We need pointers whenever we want to allocate an amount of memory that isn't known until the program is executing. If we wanted to have a rule that all strings could be only 10 characters in length (for example), then we could allocate the space for those characters in the string. However, we want to be able to handle strings of any length, so we have to decide how much space to allocate for the data when the constructor string::string(char* p) is called; the only way to do that is to use a pointer to memory that is allocated at run time, namely m_Data. Then we can use that memory to hold a copy of the C string pointed to by the parameter p.

Susan: Oh, no! Here we go again. Is m_Data a pointer? I thought it was just a variable that held an address.

Steve: Those are equivalent statements.

Susan: Why does it point? (Do you know how much I am beginning to hate that word?) I think you are going to have to clarify this.

Steve: It "points" in a metaphorical sense, but one that is second nature to programmers in languages like C. In fact, it merely holds the address of some memory location. Is that clearer?

Susan: So the purpose of m_Data is just a starting off point in memory?

Steve: Right. It's the address of the first char used to store the value of the string.

Susan: So the purpose of m_Length is to allot the length of memory that starts at the location where m_Data is?

Steve: Close; actually, it's to keep track of the amount of memory that has been allocated for the data.

Susan: But I see here that you are setting m_Length to strlen, so that in effect makes m_Length do the same thing?

Steve: Right; m_Length is the length of the string because it is set to the result returned by strlen (after adding 1 for the null byte at the end of the C string).

Problem
Algorithms
C++
Executable
Hardware

Susan: Why would you want a string with no data, anyway? What purpose does that serve?

Steve: So you can define a string before knowing what value it will eventually have. For example, the statement string s; defines a string with no data; the value can be assigned to the string later.

Susan: Oh yeah, just as you would have short x;. I forgot.

Steve: Yep.

Susan: Anyway, the first thing that helped me understand the need for pointers is variable-length data. I am sure that you mentioned this somewhere, but I certainly missed it. So this is a highlight. Once the need for it is understood then the rest falls in place. Well, almost; it is still hard to visualize, but I can.

Steve: I'll make sure to stress that point until it screams for mercy.

Susan: I think you might be able to take this information and draw a schematic for it. That would help. And show the code next to each of the steps involved.

Problem
Algorithms
C++
Executable
Hardware

Steve: Don't worry, we'll see lots of diagrams later.

Susan: So strlen is a function like any member function?

Steve: Yes, except that it is a global function rather than a member function belonging to a particular class. That's because it's a leftover from C, which doesn't have classes.

Susan: So it is what I can consider as a native function? Now I am getting confused again. I thought that just variables can be either made up (classes) or native. Why are we talking about functions in the same way? But then I remember that, in a backward way, functions belong to variables in classes rather than the other way around. This is just so crazy.

Steve: Functions are never native in the way that variables are; that is, built into the language. A lot of functions come with the language, in the form of the libraries, but they have no special characteristics that make them "better" than ones you write yourself. However, this is not true of variables; in C, it's impossible to add variable types that have the appearance and behavior of the native types.

Susan: You see I think it is hard for me to imagine a function as one word, because I am so used to main() with a bunch of code following it and I think of that as the whole function; see where I am getting confused?

Steve: When we call a function like strlen, that's not the whole function, it's just the name of the function. This is exactly like the situation where we wrote Average and then called it later to average some numbers.

Susan: A function has to "do something", so you will have to define what the function does; then when we use the function, we just call the name and that sets the action in gear?

Steve: Exactly.

Susan: Now, about this char* thing. . . (don't go ballistic, please) . . . exactly what is it? I mean it is a pointer to char, so what is *? Is it like an assignment operator? How is it classified?

Steve: * means "pointer to the type preceding". So char* means "pointer to char", short* means "pointer to short", and so on.

Susan: So that would be for a short with variable-length data? And that would be a different kind of short than a native short?

Steve: Almost, but not quite, correct. It would be for variable-length data consisting of one or more shorts, just as a literal C string is variable-length data consisting of one or more chars.

Susan: So it would be variable by virtue of the number of shorts?

Steve: Actually, by virtue of the *possibility* of having a number of shorts other than exactly one. If you *might* need two or three (or 100, for that matter) shorts (or any other type), and you don't know how many when the program is compiled, then you pretty much have to use a pointer.

Susan: OK, yes, you said that about * and what it means to use a char*, but I thought it would work only with char so I didn't know I would be seeing it again with other variable types. I can't wait.

Steve: Luckily, it appears that we will avoid pointers to types other than char, due to space constraints. I'll bet you're terribly disappointed.

Problem
Algorithms
C++
Executable
Hardware

    The next line in the constructor, m_Data = new char [m_Length]; is the same as the corresponding line in the default constructor; in this case, of course, the amount of memory being allocated is equal to the length of the input C string (including its terminating null byte), rather than the fixed value 1.

Now that we have the address of some memory that belongs to us, we can use it to hold the characters that make up the value of our string. The literal value that our test program uses to call this constructor is "Test", which is four characters long, not counting the null byte at the end; since we have to make room for that null byte, the total is 5 bytes, so that's what we'd ask for from new. Assuming that the return value from new was 1234febc, Figure 7.7 illustrates what our new string looks like at this point.

Address	Name	string n
12340000	m_Length	0005
12340002	m_Data	1234febc
1234febc	(none)	????

Figure 7.7: string n during construction

Problem
Algorithms
C++
Executable
Hardware

The reason for the ???? is that we haven't set the data at that location to any value yet, so we don't know what it contains. Actually, this brings up a point we've skipped so far, where new gets the memory it allocates. The answer is that all of the "free" memory in your machine (i.e., memory that isn't used to store the operating system, the code for your program, statically allocated variables, and the stack) is lumped into a large area called the **heap**. This is where dynamically allocated memory "lives".[11] That's a loose way of stating what actually happens, which is that new cordons off part of the heap as being "in use" and returns a pointer to that portion.

It's possible that the idea of a variable that holds a memory address but which is itself stored in memory isn't that obvious. It wasn't to Susan:

---

11. This is a bit of an oversimplification. In a "real" operating system, the heap will occupy most or all of the free memory in your computer. However, in MS-DOS, this is not true; the problem is that MS-DOS was devised to run on a very limited processor called the 8088, which had a maximum of 640K of available memory for programs. As a result of this historical limitation, a program that runs under MS-DOS can't access most of the memory in today's machines. Even if you have 32 MB of RAM, you'll run out of memory if you try to allocate more than a few hundred KB from the heap under MS-DOS. You'll be happy to know that the programs you compile with the compiler on the CD-ROM in the back of this book don't have this limitation, as they run under a "DOS extender", an operating system extension which was invented largely to solve this problem.

Susan: I don't get this stuff about a pointer being stored in a memory address and having a memory address in it. So what's the deal?

Steve: Here's an analogy that might help. Have you ever seen a set of mailboxes for an apartment building? The regular mailboxes are pretty small, but what do they do when you get something that is too big to fit into your regular mailbox? One solution is to put the larger object into one of a few large mailboxes, and leave the key to the larger mailbox in your regular mailbox.

So at this point, we have allocated m_Length bytes of memory, which start at the address in the pointer variable m_Data. Now we need to copy the current value of the input C string (pointed to by p) into that newly allocated area of memory. This is the job of the next statement, memcpy(m_Data,p,m_Length); which copies the data from the C string pointed to by p to our newly allocated memory.

The final result is that we have made (constructed) a string variable and set it to a value specified by a C string. To see what our string might look like in memory, see Figure 7.10. But how would this function operate in a program? To answer that question, Figure 7.8 gives us another look at our sample program.

```
#include "string1.h"

int main()
{
    string s;
    string n("Test");
    string x;

    s = n;
    n = "My name is: ";

    x = n;
    return 0;
}
```

Problem
Algorithms
C++
Executable
Hardware

Figure 7.8: A simple test program for the string class (code\strtst1.cc)

Constructive Criticism?

How does the compiler interpret the line string n("Test");? First, it determines that string is the name of a class. A function with the name of a class, as we have already seen, is always a constructor for that class. The question is which constructor to call; the answer is determined by the type(s) of the argument(s). In this case, the argument is a literal C string, which has the type char*; therefore, the compiler looks for a constructor for class string that has an argument of type char*. Since there is such a constructor, the one we have just examined, the compiler generates a call to it. Figure 7.9 shows it again for reference while we analyze it.

```
string::string(char* p)
{
        m_Length = strlen(p) + 1;
        m_Data = new char [m_Length];
        memcpy(m_Data,p,m_Length);
};
```

Figure 7.9: The char* constructor for the string class, again (from code\string1.cc)

When the program executes, string::string(char* p) is called with the argument "Test". Let's trace the execution of the constructor.

Problem
Algorithms
C++
Executable
Hardware

1.   The first line is m_Length = strlen(p) + 1;. This sets the member variable m_Length to the length of the C string whose address is in p, including the null byte that terminates the string. In this case, the C string is "Test", and its length, including the null byte, is 5.
2.   Next, the line m_Data = new char [m_Length]; is executed. This allocates m_Length (5, in this case) bytes of memory from the heap and sets the variable m_Data to the address of that memory.
3.   Finally, the line memcpy(m_Data,p,m_Length); copies m_Length bytes (5, in this case) of data from the C string pointed to by p to the memory pointed to by m_Data.

When the constructor is finished, the string variable n has a length, 5, and contents, "Test". It's now ready for use in the rest of the program.

After all the discussion, Susan provided this rendition of the char* constructor for the string class.

Susan: So first we define a class. This means that we will have to have one or more constructors, which is a function with the same name as the class, used to create objects of that class. The char* constructor we're dealing with here goes through three steps, as follows: Step 1 sets the length of the string; step 2 gets the memory to store the data, and provides the address of that memory; step 3 does the work; it copies what you want.

Steve: Right.

Tricky Assignment

Now, let's look at the next line: s = n;. That looks harmless enough; it just copies one string, n, to another string, s.[12] But wait a second; how does the compiler know how to assign a value to a variable of a type we've made up?

Just as the compiler will generate a version of the default constructor if we don't define one, because every object has to be initialized somehow, the ability to assign one value of a given type to a variable of the same type is essential to being a data type; therefore, the compiler will supply a version of operator =, the *assignment operator*, if we don't define one ourselves. In Chapter 6, we were able to rely on the compiler-generated operator =, which simply copies every member variable from the source object to the target object. That was perfectly fine for our StockItem and Inventory objects, so wouldn't it do the job here?

Unfortunately, no. The reason is that the member variable m_Data isn't really the data for the string; it's a pointer to (i.e., the address of) those data. The compiler-generated =, however, doesn't know how we're using m_Data, so it copies the pointer rather than the data. In our example, s = n;, the member variable m_Data in s would end up pointing to the same place in memory as the member variable m_Data in n. Thus, if either s or n did something to change "its" data, both strings would have their values changed, which isn't how we expect variables to behave.

As you might suspect, Susan didn't think the need for us to define our own operator = was obvious at all. Here's how I started talking her into it.

> **Susan**: On operator =, up to this point it has been OK to use the compiler-generated operator =, right?

> **Steve**: Right.

Problem
Algorithms
C++
Executable
Hardware

---

12. By the way, in case you're wondering what useful function this statement serves in the sample program, the answer is none. It's just to illustrate how operator = works.

Susan: I have a little note to you off to the side in the margins about this operator =, it says "If it was good enough for native data then why not class data?" I think that is a very good question, and I don't care about that pointy thing. This is ridiculous. I don't understand why m_Data isn't really data for the string; it is part of the string, so why isn't it part of its data?

Steve: It *points* to the data for the string, which is a bunch of characters. It isn't the characters itself, but their address.

As Susan has found, the problem we have to deal with may not be easy to visualize without a diagram, so I've drawn one for her (and your) elucidation. Let's suppose that our string object n looks like Figure 7.10 in memory.

```
Address      Name                    string n

12340000    m_Length        ┌─────────────────────────┐
                            │          0005           │
                            ├─────────────────────────┤
12340002    m_Data          │        1234febc         │──┐
                            └─────────────────────────┘  │
                                                         │
                                                         │
Problem                                      ┌─────────┐ │
Algorithms  1234febc    (none)               │   "T"   │◄┘
C++                                          └─────────┘
Executable  1234febd    (none)               ┌─────────┐
Hardware                                     │   "e"   │
                                             └─────────┘

            1234febe    (none)               ┌─────────┐
                                             │   "s"   │
                                             └─────────┘

            1234febf    (none)               ┌─────────┐
                                             │   "t"   │
                                             └─────────┘

            1234fec0    (none)               ┌─────────┐
                                             │    0    │
                                             └─────────┘
```

Figure 7.10: string n in memory

So far, so good. We have an object of type string, which contains a length and a pointer to a dynamically allocated memory area where its actual data are stored. However, if we use the compiler-generated operator = to execute the statement s = n;, the result looks like Figure 7.11.

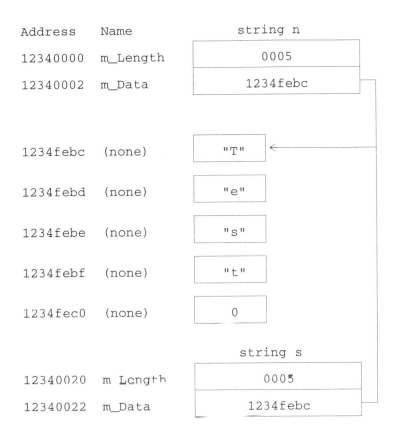

Address   Name   string n

12340000   m_Length | 0005 |

12340002   m_Data | 1234febc |

1234febc   (none) | "T" |

1234febd   (none) | "e" |

1234febe   (none) | "s" |

1234febf   (none) | "t" |

1234fec0   (none) | 0 |

                                 string s

12340020   m_Length | 0005 |

12340022   m_Data | 1234febc |

Problem
Algorithms
C++
Executable
Hardware

Figure 7.11: strings n and s in memory after compiler-generated =

In other words, the two strings s and n are like Siamese twins; whatever affects one of them affects the other, since they share one copy of the data "Test". What we really want is two strings that are independent of one another, so that we can change the contents of one without affecting the other one. Very shortly, we'll see how to accomplish this.

Susan still wasn't convinced, so we discussed this issue further.

Susan: Actually, looking at these figures makes this whole idea more understandable. Yes, I see somewhat your meaning in Figure 7.11; that pointy thing is pointing all over the place. Oh no, I don't want to see how to make two independent strings! Just eliminate the pointy thing and it will be all better. OK?

Steve: Sorry, that isn't possible. You'll just have to bear with me until I can explain it to you better.

Susan: Well, let me ask you this: Is the whole point of writing the statement s=n just to sneak your way into this conversation about this use of operator =? Otherwise, I don't see where it would make sense for the sample program.

Steve: Yes, that's correct.

Susan: And the chief reason for creating a new = is that the new one makes a copy of the data using a new memory address off the heap, rather than having the pointer pointing to the same address while using the compiler-generated operator =? If so, why? Getting a little fuzzy around that point. With StockItem, the compiler-generated operator = was good enough. Why not now?

Steve: Yes, that's why we need to create our own operator =. As for why we didn't need one before: Since the components of a StockItem are all concrete data types, we don't have to worry about "sharing" the data as we do with the string class, which contains a char*.

Susan: So when you use char* or anything with a pointer, that is outside the realm of concrete data types?

Problem
Algorithms
C++
Executable
Hardware

Steve: Right. However, the reason that we can't allow pointers to be copied as with the compiler-generated operator = isn't that they aren't concrete data types, but that they aren't the actual data of the strings. They're the *address* of the actual data; therefore, if we copy the pointer in the process of copying a variable, both pointers hold the same address. This means that changes to one of the variables affects the other one, which is not how concrete data types behave.

Susan: I think I actually understand this now. At least, I'm not as confused as I was before.

Steve: Good; it's working.

Assignment of Responsibility

Although it's actually possible to get the effect of two independent strings without the extra work of allocating memory and copying data every time an assignment is done, the mechanisms needed to do that are beyond the scope of this book. By far the easiest way to have the effect of two independent strings is to actually make another copy of a string's data whenever we copy the string, and that's how we'll do it here. The results will be as indicated in Figure 7.12.

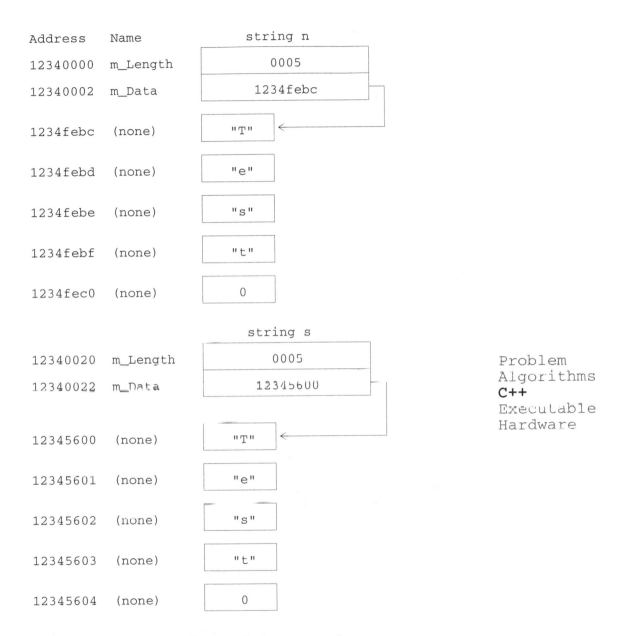

Figure 7.12: strings n and s in memory after custom =

With this arrangement, a change to one of the string variables will leave the other one unaffected, as the user would expect. To make this happen, we have to implement our own operator =, which will copy the data rather than just the pointer to the data. That's the operator declared in Figure 7.1 by the following line:

```
void operator = (const string& Str);
```

What exactly does this mean? Well, as with all function declarations, the first token[13] indicates the return type of the function. In this case, however, that token is void; that is, there is no return value from this function. Actually, that shouldn't seem too odd; after all, there's no obvious reason why an assignment needs to supply a return value. If we say a = b;, after a has been set to the same value as b, we're done; that operation is performed by the = operator, so no return value is needed after the assignment is completed.

C (and C++) programmers may be taken aback by this statement. As we've already seen, operator = for native types *does* return a value, which is equal to the value that was assigned to the left hand argument of =. That way, you can write an if statement such as if (a = b), when you really meant if (a == b); of course, this will cause a bug in your program, since these two statements don't have the same meaning. The first one sets a to b and returns the value of a; if a isn't 0, then the if condition is considered true. The latter statement, of course, compares a and b for equality and makes the if condition true if they are equal. To help prevent the error of substituting = for == in this situation, many compilers have a warning that indicates your use of, say, if (a = b); unfortunately, this is a legal construction with native types, and so cannot generate a compiler error. As it happens, using = in this way is an illegal operation with class objects, so even if you want to use this error-prone construction, you can't. Since I never use that construction with native variables, I don't mind not having it for class objects.

The other potential use of the return value from operator = is to allow statements such as a = b = c; where the current value of c is assigned to b and the return value from that assignment is assigned to a. I don't use that construction either, since I find it more confusing than useful. Therefore, I see no reason to provide a return value from operator =.

Next, we have the class name, string, followed by the membership operator ::. As we've already seen, these two characters merely tell the compiler that this function is a member function of class string. Now we're up to the mysterious looking construct operator =. This

Problem
Algorithms
C++
Executable
Hardware

---

13. A **token** is the smallest part of a program that the compiler treats as a separate unit; it's analogous to a word in English, with a statement being more like a sentence. For example, string is a token, as are :: and (. On the other hand, x = 5; is a statement.

portion of the function declaration tells the compiler the name of the function we're defining; namely, operator =. The operator keyword lets the compiler know that the "name" of this function is actually an operator name, rather than a "normal" function name. We have to say operator = rather than merely =, for two reasons. First, because normal function names can't have a = character in them, but are limited to upper and lower case letters, numbers, and the underscore (_). Second, because when we're redefining *any* operator, even one (like new) whose name is made of characters allowed in identifiers, we have to tell the compiler that we're doing that on purpose. Otherwise, we'll get an error telling us that we're trying to define a function or variable with the same name as a keyword.[14]

We're ready to look at the argument to this function, specified by the text inside the parentheses, const string& Str. We've already seen in Chapter 6 that & in this context means that the argument to which it refers is a *reference argument* rather than a *value argument*.[15] In other words, the variable Str is actually just another name for the argument provided by the caller of this function, rather than being a separate local variable with the same value as the caller's argument. However, there is a new keyword in this expression: const, which is short for "constant". In this context, it means that we promise that this function will not modify the argument to which const refers, namely string& Str. This is essential in the current situation, but it will take some discussion to explain why.

Problem
Algorithms
C++
Executable
Hardware

References Required

As you may recall from Chapter 5, when you call a function using a *value argument*, the argument that you give in the calling function isn't the one that the called function receives. Instead, a copy is made of the calling function's argument, and the called function works on the copy. While this is fine most of the time, in this case it won't

---

14. As this explanation may suggest, we can't make up our own operators with strange names by prefixing those names with operator; we're limited to those operators that already exist in the C++ language.

15. In this section, you're going to see a lot of hedging of the form "in this context, *x* means *y*". The reason is that C and C++ both reuse keywords and symbols in many different situations, often with different meanings in each situation. In my opinion, this is a flaw in the design of these languages, as it makes learning them more difficult. The reason for this reuse is that every time you add a keyword, it's possible that formerly working code will break as a result. Personally, I think this is an overrated problem compared to the problems caused by overuse of the same keywords; however, I don't have a lot of old C or C++ code to maintain, so maybe I'm biased.

work properly, for reasons that will be apparent shortly; instead, we have to use a reference argument. As we saw in the discussion of reference arguments in Chapter 6, such an argument is *not* a copy of the caller's argument, but another name for the actual argument provided by the caller. This has a number of consequences. First, it's more efficient than a "normal" argument, because the usual processing time needed to make a copy for the called function isn't required. Second, any changes made to the reference argument change the caller's argument as well. The use of this mechanism should be limited to those cases where it is really necessary, since it can confuse the readers of the calling function. There's no way to tell just by looking at the calling function that some of its variables can be changed by calling another function.

In this case, however, we have no intention of changing the input argument. All we want to do is to copy its length and data into the output string, the one for which operator = was called. Therefore, we tell the compiler, by using the const modifier, that we aren't going to change the input argument. This removes the drawback of non-const reference arguments: that they can change variables in the calling function with no indication of that possibility in the calling function. Therefore, using const reference arguments is quite a useful and safe way to reduce the number of time-consuming copying operations needed to make function calls.

The use of a const reference argument in this case is more than just efficient, however; as we'll see in the discussion in Chapter 8 under the heading "Temporary Help Wanted", such an argument allows us to assign a C string (i.e., bytes pointed to by a char*) to one of our string variables without having to write a special operator = for that purpose.

You might be surprised to hear that Susan didn't have too much trouble accepting all this stuff about const reference arguments. Obviously her resistance to new ideas was weakening by this point.

Problem
Algorithms
C++
Executable
Hardware

> **Susan**: OK, so the reference operator just renames the argument and doesn't make a copy of it; that is why it is important to promise not to change it?
>
> **Steve**: Right. A non-const reference argument can be changed in the function, because unlike a "regular" (i.e., value) argument, which is really a copy of the calling function's variable, a reference argument is just another name for the caller's variable. Therefore, if we change the reference argument, we're really changing the caller's variable, which is generally not a good idea.

Susan: OK. But in this case since we are going to want to change the meaning of = in all strings it is OK?

Steve: Not quite. Every time we define an operator we're changing the meaning of that operator for all objects of that class. The question is whether we're intending to change the value of the caller's variable that is referred to by the reference argument. If we are, then we can't use const to qualify the reference; if not, we can use const. Does that answer your question?

Susan: Well, yes and no. I think I have it now: When you write that code it is for that class only and won't affect other classes that you may have written, because it is contained within that particular class code. Right?

Steve: Correct.

Susan: So we don't want to change the input argument because what we are doing is basically defining a new = for this class, right?

Steve: Right. The input argument is where we get the data to copy to the string we're assigning to. We don't want to change the input argument, just the string we're assigning to.

Back to the discussion of the function declaration, we now have enough information to decode the function declaration

```
Problem
Algorithms
C++
Executable
Hardware
```

```
void string::operator = (const string& Str)
```

as illustrated in Figure 7.13.

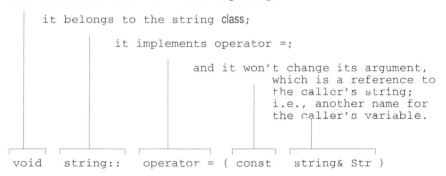

Figure 7.13: The declaration of operator = for the string class

Putting it all together, we're defining a void function (i.e., one that returns no value) belonging to class string. This function implements operator = and takes an argument named Str that's a constant reference to a string. That is, the argument Str is another name for the string passed to us by the caller, not a copy of the caller's string. Furthermore, we're vowing not to use this argument to change the caller's variable.

Hello, operator?

Now that we've dissected the header into its atomic components, the actual implementation of the function should be trivial by comparison. But first there's a loose end to be tied up. That is, why was this function named string::operator = called in the first place? The line that caused the call was very simple: s = n;. There's no explicit mention of string or operator.

This is another of the ways in which C++ supports classes. Because you can use the = operator to assign one variable of a native type to another variable of the same type, C++ provides the same syntax for user defined variable types. Similar reasoning applies to operators like >, <, and so on, for classes where these operators make sense.

Problem
Algorithms
C++
Executable
Hardware

When the compiler sees the statement s = n;, it proceeds as follows:

1. The variable s is an object of class string.
2. The statement appears to be an assignment statement (i.e., an invocation of the C++ operator named operator =) setting s equal to the value of another string value named n.
3. Is there a definition of a member function of class string that implements operator = and takes one argument of class string?
4. Yes, there is. Therefore, translate the statement s = n; into a call to operator = for class string.
5. Compile that statement as though it were the one in the program.

Susan was appreciative of the reminder that we started out discussing the statement s = n;.

Susan: Oh, my gosh, I totally forgot about s = n; thanks for the reminder. We did digress a bit, didn't we? Are you saying you have to go through the same thing to define other operators in classes?

Steve: Yes.

Susan: So are you saying that when you write the simple statement
s = n; that the = calls the function that we just went through?

Steve: Right.

Following this procedure, the correspondence between the tokens in the original program and the call to the member function should be fairly obvious, as we see them in Figure 7.14.

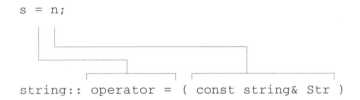

Figure 7.14: Calling the operator = implementation

But we've left out something. What does the string s correspond to in the function call to operator =?

What Is the Meaning of this?

The string s corresponds to a hidden argument called this, which is automatically included in every call to a member function in C++.[16] Its type is always a constant pointer to an object of the class that a member function belongs to. In this case its type is const string*; that is, a constant pointer to a string; the const means that we can't change the value of this by assigning a new value to it. The value of this is the address of the class object for which the member function call was made. In this case, the statement s = n; was translated into s.operator = (n); by the compiler; therefore, when the statement s = n; is being executed, the value of this is the address of the string s.

To see why we need to be concerned about this, let's start analyzing the implementation of operator =. Figure 7.15 shows the code for that function.

Problem
Algorithms
C++
Executable
Hardware

---

16. For the C++ purist, I should mention that this applies to all the member functions in this book. There's another kind of member function that doesn't get a this pointer passed to it, but we won't get to discuss that other type.

```
void string::operator = (const string& Str)
{
    if (&Str != this)
        {
        delete [] m_Data;
        m_Length = Str.m_Length;
        m_Data = new char [m_Length];
        memcpy(m_Data,Str.m_Data,m_Length);
        }
    return;
};
```

Figure 7.15: The assignment operator (operator =) for the string class (from code\string1.cc)

Equality Now!

Problem
Algorithms
C++
Executable
Hardware

In the case of the string class, as in most cases, the only reason why we have to worry about this is to be able to determine whether two objects that are referred to by different names are actually the same object. You can see this use of this in the first line of the code in string::operator = (const string& Str), which is

if (&Str != this)

Most of this statement should be familiar by now. Like other if statements, it tests a condition for truth or falsity. The != is the comparison operator that tests for "not equal", and of course we've just seen that this is the address of the variable for which the operator = function was called; in the expression s = n, this would be the address of the variable s. However, that still leaves the expression &Str.

Unfortunately, & is one of the tokens that is used in several different ways depending on context; when it precedes the name of a variable without itself being preceded by a data type like string, it means "the address of the following variable". In this case, &Str means "the address of Str". The variable Str is the argument passed to us by the caller; remember, as a reference argument, Str is another name for the caller's variable, rather than a copy of it. Therefore, &Str is the address of the caller's variable (n, in our example).

Clearly, then, the expression if (&Str != this) is comparing the address of the caller's string (i.e., &Str) to this. As we just saw, this represents the address of the object that we're operating on; in the case of operator =, it's the address of (i.e., a pointer to) the string that is going to be changed by operator =.[17] Therefore, this if statement is checking whether the string that was passed to us by the caller is a different string from the one to which the assignment is supposed to be made. For example, if the source line that caused operator = to be called was a = a; then the if statement would be false and therefore the block controlled by the if wouldn't be executed. Of course, there's no reason to do anything if we've been asked to set the value of a to the value of a! However, there are good reasons besides efficiency to check for the attempt to assign a string to itself; those reasons are the subject of one of the exercises in this chapter. For now, let's continue with the contents of the block controlled by the if, assuming that the two strings are actually distinct.

The first statement in the controlled block of the if statement is delete [] m_Data;. This corresponds to the new statement that we used to allocate memory for a string in the constructor string::string(char* p) (Figure 7.6).[18] That is, the delete operator returns the memory to the available pool called the *heap*. There are actually two versions of the delete operator: One version frees memory for a single data item, and the other frees memory for a group of items that are stored consecutively in memory. Here, we're using the version of the delete operator that frees a group of items rather than a single item, which we indicate by means of the [] after the keyword delete; the version of delete that frees only one item doesn't have the [].[19] So after this statement is executed, the memory that was allocated in the constructor to hold the characters in our string has been handed back to the memory allocation routines for possible reuse at a later time.

Susan had a few minor questions about this topic, but nothing too alarming.

> **Susan**: So delete just takes out the memory new allocated for m_Data?

> **Steve**: Right.

Problem
Algorithms
C++
Executable
Hardware

---

17. By the way, this is another keyword; you can't have a variable or function named this.

18. Or any other constructor that allocates memory in which to store characters. I'm just referring to the char* constructor because we've already analyzed that one.

19. By the way, this is one of the previously mentioned times when we have to explicitly deal with the difference between a pointer used as "the address of an item" and one used as "the address of some number of items"; the [] after delete tells the compiler that the latter is the current situation. The C++ standard specifies that any memory that was allocated via a new expression containing [] must be deleted via delete [].

Susan: What do you mean by "frees a group of items"?

Steve: It returns the memory to the heap, so it can be used for some other purpose.

Susan: Is that all the addresses in memory that contain the length of the string?

Steve: Not the length of the string, but the data for the string, such as "Test".

Please delete Me, Let Me Go

A point that we should not overlook is the possibility of calling delete for a pointer that has never been assigned a value. Calling delete on a pointer that doesn't point to a valid block of memory allocated by new will cause the system to malfunction in some bizarre way, usually at a time considerably after the improper call to delete.[20] This occurs because the dynamic memory allocation system will try to reclaim the "allocated" memory pointed to by the invalid pointer by adding it back to the heap. Eventually, some other function will come along, ask for some memory, and be handed a pointer to this "available" block that is actually nothing of the sort. The result of trying to use this area of memory depends on which of three cases the erroneous address falls into: The first is that the memory at that address is nonexistent, the second is that the memory is already in use for some other purpose, and the third is that the invalid address points to data that is already in the heap. In the first case, the function that tries to store its data in this nonexistent area of memory will cause a system crash or error message, depending on the system's ability and willingness to check for such errors; the "General Protection Fault" message so familiar to Windows users is caused by this sort of error. In the second case, the function that is the "legal" owner of the memory will find its stored values changed mysteriously and will misbehave as a result. In the third case, the heap management routines would probably get confused and start handing out wrong addresses. Errors of this kind are common in programs that use pointers heavily and are extremely difficult to find.

Susan was interested in this topic of errors in memory allocation, so we discussed it.

Problem
Algorithms
C++
Executable
Hardware

---

20. There's an exception to this rule: Calling delete for a pointer with the value 0 will not cause any untoward effects, as such a pointer is recognized as "pointing to nowhere".

Susan: Can you give me an example of what an "invalid pointer" would be? Would it be an address in memory that is in use for something else rather than something that can be returned to the heap?

Steve: That's one kind of invalid pointer. The other type would be an address that doesn't exist at all; that is, one that is past the end of the possible legal addresses.

Susan: Oh, wait, so it would be returned to the heap but later if it is allocated to something else, it will cause just a tiny little problem because it is actually in use somewhere else?

Steve: You bet.

Susan: Is this a crash?

Steve: This is a major cause of crashes.

Susan: Oh yeah, this is cool, this is exciting. So this is what really happens when a crash occurs?

Steve: Do you know what a GPF (General Protection Fault) is? It's the operating system detecting the attempt by a program to access memory that doesn't belong to it.

Susan: I like this. So when there is no memory address allocated you get a error message?

Steve: Yes, or if it belongs to someone else. Of course, you'll be lucky to get anything other than a hard crash if it's a DOS program; at least in Windows you'll probably get a GPF instead.

```
Problem
Algorithms
C++
Executable
Hardware
```

Another way to go wrong with dynamic memory allocation is the opposite one. Instead of trying to delete something that was never dynamically allocated, you can forget to delete something that has been dynamically allocated. This is called a **memory leak**; it's very insidious, because the program appears to work correctly when tested casually. The usual way to find these errors is to notice that the program runs apparently correctly for a (possibly long) time and then fails due to running out of available memory. I should mention here how we can tell that we've run out of memory: The new operator returns a pointer with a 0 value. By convention, a pointer with the value 0 means "a pointer that doesn't point to anything". Hence, 0 is a reasonable value to return when there is no memory left. Our sample programs don't check the return value from new, so they will go along merrily as though they have actually allocated memory successfully. The result will be a spectacular failure when we actually try to use the "allocated" memory at location 0. Of course, a real program should check for this problem and tell the user that no more memory is left (if no better solution is available); however, even programs that have been in use for some time fail to check this situation sometimes.[21]

Given all of the ways to misuse dynamic memory allocation, we'll use it only when its benefits clearly outweigh the risks. To be exact, we'll restrict its use to controlled circumstances inside class implementations, to reduce the probability of such errors.

Susan had some questions about the idea of new returning a 0 if no memory is left.

> **Susan**: Where is it written that new returns a value of 0?
>
> **Steve**: That's what new does when it doesn't have anything to give you. By convention, 0 isn't a valid pointer value; therefore, getting a 0 from new means you're hosed.
>
> **Susan**: How does a real program check for this?

Problem
Algorithms
C++
Executable
Hardware

> **Steve**: By saying something like this:
>
> ```
> p = new char[1000];
> if (p == 0)
>     {
>     cout << "You're hosed!" << endl;
>     exit(1);
>     }
> ```
>
> For your information, exit means "bail out of the program right now, without returning to the calling function, if any". The argument to exit is reported back to DOS as the return value from the program; 0 means OK, anything else means some sort of error.

The error prone nature of dynamic memory allocation is ironic, since it would be entirely possible for the library implementers (that is, the people who write the functions that are used by new and delete) to prevent or at least detect the problem of deleting something you haven't allocated or failing to delete something that you have allocated. After all, those routines handle all of the memory

---

21. The forthcoming standard for the C++ language will change the behavior of new when no more memory is left. Instead of returning 0, new will notify the application programmer via a mechanism called an *exception*. Unfortunately, this mechanism is outside the scope of this book.

allocation and deallocation for a C++ program, so there's no reason that they couldn't keep track of what has been allocated and not released.[22] In fact, replacement libraries and other tools enable the programmer to find these problems more easily; such tools are so valuable that all professional programmers should use them to check for memory problems before they cause difficulties for their customers.[23]

Susan was intrigued by the possible results of forgetting to deallocate resources such as memory. Here's what resulted from her interest:

> **Susan**: So when programs leak system resources, is that the result of just forgetting to delete something that is dynamically allocated?
>
> **Steve**: Yes.
>
> **Susan**: Then that would be basically a programming error or at least sloppiness on the part of the programmer?
>
> **Steve**: Yes.

The Next Assignment

Having discussed some of the possible problems with dynamic allocation, let's continue with the code for operator = (Figure 7.15).

The next statement is m_Length = Str.m_Length;. Here's the first use we've made of the . operator, which allows us to access a member variable of an object other than the one for which the member function was called. Up until now, we've been satisfied to refer to a member variable such as m_Length just by that simple name, as we would with a local or global variable. The name m_Length is called an **unqualified name** because it doesn't specify which object we're referring to. The expression m_Length by itself refers to the occurrence of the member variable m_Length in the object for which

Problem
Algorithms
C++
Executable
Hardware

---

22. It's also possible to write programs so that this type of error is much less likely, basically, this approach requires keeping all dynamic memory allocation inside class implementations, rather than exposing it to the application programmer. We're following this approach with our string class, but it's not quite as easy to do so in the general case for reasons which are unfortunately beyond the scope of this book.

23. If these tools are so important, you may wonder why the standard implementations of new and delete don't check for common errors, such as freeing memory that was never deleted? The only answer to this question I've found is that "checking these operations would slow down the program". While performance is important, the first law of optimization states that "The speed of a nonworking program is irrelevant". In other words, who cares how fast it is if it doesn't work?

the current function was called; i.e., the string whose address is this (the string n in our example line s = n;). If you think about it, this is a good default, because member functions refer to member variables of their "own" object more than any other kinds of variables. Therefore, to reduce the amount of typing the programmer has to do, whenever we refer to a member variable without specifying the object to which it belongs the compiler will assume that we mean the variable that belongs to the object for which the member variable was called (i.e, the one whose address is the current value of this). However, when we want to refer to a member variable of an object other than the one pointed to by this, we have to indicate which object we're referring to, which we do by using the . operator. This operator means that we want to access the member variable (or function) whose name is on the right of the . for the object whose name is on the left of the .. Hence, the expression Str.m_Length specifies that we're talking about the occurrence of m_Length that's in the variable Str, and the whole statement m_Length = Str.m_Length; means that we want to set the length of "our" string (i.e., the one pointed to by this) to the length of the argument string Str.

Susan had some questions about this issue of accessing variables of another string and how that relates to operator =.

Problem
Algorithms
C++
Executable
Hardware

Susan: I still don't get the . thingy.

Steve: All . does is separate the object (on the left) from the member variable or function (on the right). So s.operator=(n); might be roughly translated as "apply the operator = to the object s, with the argument n".

Susan: So wait: the . does more than separate; it allows access to other string member variables?

Steve: It separates an object's name from the particular variable or function that we're accessing for that object. In other words, Str.m_Length means "the instance of m_Length that is part of the object Str."

Susan: So in the statement m_Length = Str.m_Length; what we are doing is creating a new m_Length equal to the length of Str's m_Length for the = operator?

Steve: What we're doing is setting the value of the length (m_Length) for the string being assigned to (the left-hand string) to the same value as the length of the string being copied from (the right-hand string).

Susan: But it is going to be specific for this string?

Steve: If I understand your question, the value of m_Length will be set for the particular string that we're assigning a new value to.

Susan: When we say Str, does that mean that we are not using the variable pointed to by this? I am now officially lost.

Steve: Yes, that's what it means. In a member function, if we don't specify the variable we are talking about, it's the one pointed to by this; of course, if we do specify which variable we mean, then we get the one we specify.

Next, we use the statement m_Data = new char [m_Length]; to acquire the address of some memory that we will use to store our new copy of the data from Str; along with the address, new gives us the right to use that memory until we free it with delete.

Finally, we use memcpy to copy the data from by Str (i.e., the group of characters starting at the address stored in Str.m_Data) to our newly allocated memory, which of course is pointed to by m_Data (i.e., the occurrence of m_Data in the string being assigned to). Now our target string is a fully independent entity with the same value as the string that was passed in. Equality is ours.

Although the individual statements weren't too much of a problem, Susan didn't get the big picture. Here's how I explained it to her:

Problem
Algorithms
C++
Executable
Hardware

Susan: I don't get this whole code thing for Figure 7.15, now that I think about it. Why does this stuff make a new operator =? This is weird.

Steve: Well, what does operator = do? It makes the object on the left side have the same value as the object on the right side. In the case of a string, this means that the left-hand string should have the same length as the one on the right, and all the chars used to store the data for the right-hand string need to be copied to the address pointed to by m_Data for the left-hand string. That's what our custom = does.

Susan: Let's see. First we have to get some new memory for the new m_Data; then we have to make a copy. . . So then the entire purpose of writing a new operator = is to make sure that variables of that class can be made into separate entities when using the = sign rather than sharing the same memory address for their data?

Steve: Right.

Susan: I forget now why we did that.

Steve: We did it so that we could change the value of one of the variables without affecting the other one.

Before we move on to the next member function, I should mention that Susan and I had quite a lengthy correspondence about the notion of this. Here are the highlights of that discussion.

Susan: I don't understand this.

Steve: this refers to the object that a member function is being called for. For example, in the statement xyz.Read();, when the function named Read is called, the value of this will be the address of the object xyz.

Susan: OK, then, is this the result of calling a function? Or the address of the result?

Steve: Not quite either of those; this is the address of the object for which a class function is called.

Susan: Now that I have really paid attention to this and tried to commit it to memory it makes more sense. I think that what is so mysterious is that it is a hidden argument. When I think of an argument I think of something in (), as an input argument.

Problem
Algorithms
C++
Executable
Hardware

Steve: It actually is being passed as though it were specified in every call to a member function. The reason it is hidden is not to make it mysterious, but to reduce the amount of work the programmer has to do. Since almost every member function needs to access something via this, supplying it automatically is a serious convenience.

Susan: Now as far as my understanding of the meaning of this, it is the address of the object whose value is the result of calling a member function.

Steve: Almost exactly right; this is the address of the object for which a member function is called. Is this merely a semantic difference?

Susan: Not quite. Is there not a value to the object? Other than that we are speaking the same language. We usually do.

Steve: Yes, the object has a value. However, this is merely the address of the object, not its value.

Susan: How about writing this as if it were not hidden and was in the argument list; then show me how it would look. See what I mean? Show me what you think it would look like if you were to write it out and not hide it.

Steve: OK, that sounds good. Actually, I was thinking of doing that anyway.

Figure 7.16 shows what the code for operator = might look like if the this pointer weren't supplied automatically, both in the function declaration and as a qualifier for the member variable names.[24]

```
void string::operator = (const string* this, const string& Str)
{
   if (&Str != this)
      {
      delete [] this->m_Data;
      this->m_Length = Str.m_Length;
      this->m_Data = new char [this->m_Length];
      memcpy(this->m_Data,Str.m_Data,this->m_Length);
      }
   return;
};
```

Figure 7.16: A hypothetical assignment operator (operator =) for the string class with explicit this

Note that every reference to a member variable of the current object would have to specify this. That would actually be more significant in writing the code than that we would have to supply this in the call. Of course, how we would actually supply this when calling the operator = function is also a good question. Clearly the necessity of passing this explicitly would make for a messier syntax than just s = n;.

Problem
Algorithms
C++
Executable
Hardware

The Terminator

Now that we have seen how operator = works in detail, let's look at the next member function in the initial version of our string class, the *destructor*.[25] A destructor is the opposite of a constructor; that is, it is responsible for deallocating any memory allocated by the constructor

---

24. I've introduced another new notation here: the operator –>. This does the same thing for pointer variables that . does for objects. That is, if the token on the right of –> is a member variable, that token refers to the specific member variable belonging to the object pointed to by the pointer on the left of –>; if the token on the right of –> is a member function, then it is called for the object pointed to by the pointer on the left of –>. For example, this–>m_Data means "the m_Data that belongs to the object pointed to by this.

25. Susan has suggested that the constructor, the destructor, and the assignment operator would make good action figures: perhaps Saturday morning cartoons would be a good outlet for getting children interested in programming?

and performing whatever other functions have to be done before a variable dies. It's quite rare to call the destructor for a variable explicitly; as a rule, the destructor is called automatically when the variable goes out of scope. As we've seen, the most common way for this to happen is that a function returns to its calling function; at that time, destructors are called for all local variables that have destructors, whereas local variables that don't have destructors, such as those of native types, just disappear silently.[26]

Susan had some questions about how variables are allocated and deallocated. Here's the discussion that ensued.

> **Susan**: I remember we talked about the stack pointer and how it refers to addresses in memory but I don't remember deallocating anything. What is that?

> **Steve**: Deallocating variables on the stack merely means that the same memory locations can be reused for different local variables. Remember the function mess?

> **Susan**: Oh, that is right, the data stays in the memory locations until the location is used by something else. It really isn't meaningful after it has been used unless it is initialized, is that right?

> **Steve**: Yes, that's right.

> **Susan**: When I first read about the destructor my reaction was, "well, what is the difference between this and delete?" But basically it just is a function that makes delete go into auto-pilot?

> **Steve**: Basically correct.

> **Susan**: How does it know you are done with the variable, so that it can put the memory back?

> **Steve**: By definition, when the destructor is called, the variable is history. This happens automatically when it goes out of scope. For an auto variable, whether of native type or class type, this occurs at the end of the function where the variable was defined.

> **Susan**: I don't understand this. I reread your explanation of "going out of scope" and it is unclear to me what is happening and what the alternatives are. How does a scope "disappear"?

Problem
Algorithms
C++
Executable
Hardware

---

26. If we use new to allocate memory for a variable that has a destructor, then the destructor is called when that variable is freed by delete. However, we won't be using new to create class objects in this book.

Steve: The scope doesn't disappear, but the execution of the program leaves it. For example, when a function terminates, the local variables (which have local scope), go out of scope and disappear. That is, they no longer have memory locations assigned to them, until and unless the function starts execution again.

Susan: What if you need the variable again?

Steve: Then don't let it go out of scope.

Because destructors are almost always called automatically when a variable goes out of scope, rather than by any explicit statement written by the programmer, the only information guaranteed to be available to a destructor is the address of the variable to be destroyed. For this reason, the C++ language specifies that a destructor cannot have arguments. This in turn means that there can be only one destructor for any class, since there can be at most one function in a given class with a given name and the same type(s) of argument(s) (or, as in this case, no arguments).

As with the constructor(s), the destructor has a special name to identify it to the compiler. In this case, it's the name of the class with the token ~ (the tilde) prefixed to it, so the destructor for class string is named ~string.[27] The declaration of this function is the next line in Figure 7.1, ~string();. Its implementation looks like Figure 7.17.

Problem
Algorithms
C++
Executable
Hardware

```
string::~string()
{
    delete [] m_Data;
};
```

Figure 7.17: The destructor for the string class (from code/string1.cc)

This function doesn't use any new constructs; we've already seen that the delete [] operator frees the memory allocated to the pointer variable it operates on.[28] In this case, that variable is m_Data, which holds the address of the first one of the group of characters that make up the actual data contained by the string.

---

27. In case you're wondering, this somewhat obscure notation was chosen because the tilde is used to indicate logical negation; that is, if some expression x has the logical value true, then ~x will have the logical value false, and vice-versa.

28. By the way, in case you were wondering what happened to the old values of the m_Data and m_Length member variables, we don't have to worry about those because the string being destroyed won't ever be used again.

Now that we've covered nearly all of the member functions in the initial version of the string class, it's time for some review.

Review

We've almost finished building a concrete data type called the string class, which provides a means of storing and processing a group of characters similar to the facilities provided by a *C string*, but without some of the drawbacks of the latter data type. The fact that string is a concrete data type means that a string that is defined as a local variable in a function should be created when the function starts up and automatically deleted when the function ends. Also, we need to be able to copy a string to another string and have the two copies behave like independent variables, not linked together in the manner of Siamese twins.

Susan didn't have much trouble picking up on one consequence of making a string a concrete data type.

Problem
Algorithms
C++
Executable
Hardware

Susan: Oh, I guess that the statement that "a string that is defined as a local variable in a function should be created when the function starts up and automatically deleted when the function ends" explains why you put the memory back when you are done with the variable.

Steve: Right.

The creation of an object is performed by a special member function called a *constructor*. Any class can have several constructors, one for each possible way that a newly created object can be initialized. So far, we've examined the interface and implementation of the *default constructor*, which takes no arguments, and a constructor that takes a char* argument. The former is needed to create a string that doesn't have an initial value, while the latter allows us to create a string that has the same contents as a C string. The default constructor is one of the required member functions in a concrete data type.

Continuing with the requirements for a concrete data type, we've implemented our own version of operator =, which can set one string to the same value as another string while leaving them independent of one another.

We've also created one other required member function for a concrete data type, the *destructor*, which is used to clean up after a string when it expires. This member function is called automatically for an auto variable at the end of the function where that variable is defined.

We're still short a *copy constructor*, which can create a string that has the same value as another pre-existing string. This may sound just like operator =, but it's not exactly the same. operator = is used to set a string that already exists to the same value as another extant string, whereas the *copy constructor* creates a brand-new string with the same value as one that already exists. We'll see how this works in the next chapter; in the meantime, let's take a look at some exercises intended to test your understanding of this material.

Exercises

1. What would happen if we compiled the program in Figure 7.18? Why?

```
class string
{
public:
    string();
    string(const string& Str);
    string(char* p);
    void operator = (const string& Str);
    ~string();
private:
    short m_Length;
    char* m_Data;
};

int main()
{
    string s;
    string n("Test");
    string x;
    short Length;

    Length = n.m_Length;

    s = n;
    n = "My name is: ";

    x = n;
    return 0;
}
```

Problem
Algorithms
C++
Executable
Hardware

Figure 7.18: Exercise 1 (code\strex1.cc)

2.   What would happen if we compiled the program in Figure 7.19? Why?

```
class string
{
public:
    string(const string& Str);
    string(char* p);
    void operator=(const string& Str);
    ~string();
private:
    string();
    short m_Length;
    char* m_Data;
};

int main()
{
    string s("Test");
    string n;

    n = s;

    return 0;
}
```

Problem
Algorithms
C++
Executable
Hardware

Figure 7.19: Exercise 2 (code\strex2.cc)

3.   What would happen if we compiled the program in Figure 7.20? Why?

```
class string
{
public:
    string();
    string(const string& Str);
    string(char* p);
    void operator=(const string& Str);
private:
    ~string();
    short m_Length;
    char* m_Data;
};

int main()
{
    string s("Test");

    return 0;
}
```

Figure 7.20: Exercise 3 (code\strex3.cc)

4. What would happen if a user of our string class wrote an expression that tried to set a string variable to itself (e.g., a = a;) and we hadn't bothered to check for that situation in our operator =?

5. What would happen if we compiled the program in Figure 7.21? Why?

```
class string
{
public:
    string(const string& Str);
    string(char* p);
    void operator = (const string& Str);
    ~string();
private:
    string();
    short m_Length;
    char* m_Data;
};

int main()
{
    string n("Test");
    string x = n;

    n = "My name is: ";

    return 0;
}
```

Problem
Algorithms
C++
Executable
Hardware

Figure 7.21: Exercise 5 (code\strex5.cc)

Conclusion

We've covered a lot of material about how a real, generally useful class such as string works in this chapter. In the next chapter, we'll continue with the saga of the string class, finishing up the additional functionality needed to turn it into a full-fledged concrete data type. We'll put this new functionality to the test in a modified version of the sorting algorithm from the early chapters that sorts strings rather than numeric values.

Answers to Exercises

1. The output of the compiler should look something like this:

    strex1.cc: In function 'int main()':
    strex1.cc:21: member 'm_Length' is a private member of class 'string'

    This one is simple; since m_Length is a private member variable of string, a nonmember function such as main can't access it.

2. The output of the compiler should look something like this:

    strex2.cc: In function 'int main()':
    strex2.cc:9: constructor 'string::string()' is private
    strex2.cc:17: within this context
    strex2.cc:17: in base initialization for class 'string'

    This is also pretty simple. Since the default constructor string::string() is in the private area, it's impossible for a nonmember function such as main to use it. Notice that there was no error message about string::string(char* p); that constructor is in the public area, so main is permitted to create a string from a C string. It's just the default constructor that's inaccessible.

3. The output of the compiler should look something like this:

    strex3.cc:12: warning: 'class string' only defines a private destructor and has no friends[29]
    strex3.cc: In function 'int main()':
    strex3.cc:16: destructor for type 'string' is private in this scope

    This answer is considerably less obvious than the previous ones. To be sure, the destructor is private and can't be called from main, but that doesn't explain why main is trying to call the destructor in the first place. The reason is that every auto variable of a type that has a destructor must have its destructor called at the end of that function. That's part of

Problem
Algorithms
C++
Executable
Hardware

---

29. In case you're wondering what a friend is, it's a class or a function that has special access to the internal workings of another class. We'll get into that mechanism in Chapter 8.

the mechanism that makes our objects act like "normal" variables, which also lose their values at the end of the function where they are declared.[30] In the case of a user defined variable, though, more cleanup may be required; this is certainly true for strings, which have to deallocate the memory that they allocated to store their character data.

Therefore, you cannot create an object of a class whose destructor is private as an auto variable, as the automatic call of the destructor at the end of the scope would be illegal.

Susan didn't get this one exactly right, but she was obviously in the ballpark.

> **Susan**: I have a note here that this program would not work because the ~string () thingy should be public and that, if this were to run, it would cause a memory leak. Am I on the right track?

> **Steve**: Yes, you're close. Actually, what would happen is that the compiler would refuse to compile this program because it wouldn't be able to call ~string at the end of the function, since ~string is private. If the compiler were willing to compile this program without calling the destructor, there would indeed be a memory leak.

4. Let's take a look at the sequence of events that would have transpired if the user had typed a = a; and we hadn't taken the precaution of checking for that situation in the operator = code.[31]

The first statement to be executed would be delete [] m_Data;. This gives the memory that had been allocated to store characters in string a back to the operating system.

The second statement to be executed would be m_Length = Str.m_Length;. Since m_Length and Str.m_Length are actually the same memory location in this case, this statement wouldn't do anything.

The third statement to be executed would be m_Data = new char [m_Length];. This would allocate memory for the target string, and assign it to the member variable m_Data.

Problem
Algorithms
C++
Executable
Hardware

---

30. To be more precise, the destructor is called at the end of the *scope* in which the variable was defined. It's possible for a variable to have scope smaller than an entire function; in that case, the variable is destroyed when its scope expires.

31. See Figure 7.15 for the code.

The fourth statement to be executed would be memcpy(m_Data,Str.m_Data,m_Length);. This would copy m_Length bytes of data to the address stored in m_Data, which points to the newly allocated piece of memory, from the address stored in Str.m_Data, which points to. . . the same address. Remember, if this and &Str are the same, as they are in this case, then m_Data and Str.m_Data are two names for the same memory location. Therefore, this operation will have no effect. Furthermore, the preceding step has assigned the address of the newly allocated memory to m_Data, overwriting the previous contents of m_Data, that is, the address of the original contents of the string a. Therefore, the original value of a, which was pointed to by m_Data when we started, is no longer accessible. Even if we had a copy of that address, we couldn't use it because the memory to which it refers to has already been returned to the operating system and no longer belongs to us.

The net result of all of this is that the m_Data member variable of string a would point to uninitialized data.

For a further explanation of this, you might want to take a look at the discussion I had with Susan. The topic is the if statement if (&Str != this), which checks whether the source string is the same as the destination string:

Problem
Algorithms
C++
Executable
Hardware

> **Susan**: I don't get the purpose of this if statement. Do we want the two strings to be the same or to be different?
>
> **Steve**: We want them to be the same *after* we do the copy; if they're the same *before* the copy, we don't need (or want) to do anything. This may not be completely obvious, so here's a more detailed explanation:
>
> If the two strings are different when the if statement is executed, then we can safely execute the code controlled by the if statement, because executing delete on the old contents of the string on the left-hand side of the = sign won't affect the string on the right-hand side.
>
> If the two strings are actually the same string, then the delete call will deallocate the memory that was used to hold the string's data; therefore, the memcpy will be copying from a pointer that is no longer valid. Even if this code would work, there's no reason to execute it if the two strings are already the same at the beginning of the code for the assignment statement.

Susan: OK, so if the two strings are the same then the if statement won't go into effect, but if they are different, then it will; it is important that they are different otherwise you would be deleting the original address of the caller?

Steve: Right, with one very small modification: It's the data at the original address of the string that would get freed prematurely.

5. This one was a little tricky. I'll bet you thought that making the default constructor private would keep this from compiling, but it turns out that we're not using the default constructor. That should be obvious in the line string n("Test");, which clearly uses string::string(char* p), but what does the compiler do with the line string x = n;? You might think that it calls the default constructor to make x and then uses operator = to copy the value of n into it. If that were true, the private status of the default constructor would prevent the program from compiling. However, what actually happens is that the copy constructor string::string(const string&) is used to make a brand new string called x with the same value as n. So, in this case, the private access specifier on the default constructor doesn't get in the way.

However, this leaves one question unanswered: Since there's an = sign in the statement string x = n;, why is a constructor called instead of operator =? Because we can't assign a value to a variable that doesn't exist before the beginning of the statement. Thus, when we define a variable and provide an initial value for it, as this statement does, we're actually calling a constructor to create the variable with that initial value, rather than constructing the variable first with no value and then calling operator =.

Problem
Algorithms
C++
Executable
Hardware

Chapter 8

Down the Garden Path

Objectives of This Chapter

By the end of this chapter, you should

1. Understand how to implement all the concrete data type functions for a class that uses pointers.
2. Have a string class that is useful in some real programming situations.
3. Understand how to write appropriate input and output functions (operator >> and operator <<) to handle the objects of our string class.
4. Learn how to use some additional C library functions such as memcmp and memset.
5. Learn about the (dreaded) C data type, the *array*, and some of the reasons why it is hazardous to use.
6. Learn about the friend declaration, which allows access to private members by selected nonmember functions.

For Reference Only

Now we're finally ready to examine exactly why the code for our operator = needs a *reference argument* rather than a *value argument*.

I've drawn two diagrams that illustrate the difference between a value argument and a reference argument. First, Figure 8.1 illustrates what happens when we call a function with a value argument of type string using the compiler-generated copy constructor.[1]

---

1. In case you were wondering where you'd seen this diagram before, it's the same as the one illustrating the problem with the compiler-generated operator =, Figure 7.11.

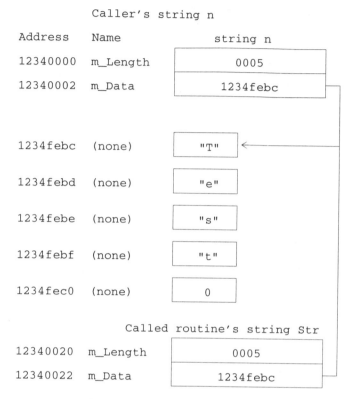

Problem
Algorithms
C++
Executable
Hardware

Figure 8.1: Call by value ("normal argument") using the compiler-generated copy constructor

In other words, with a value argument, the called routine makes a copy of the argument on its stack. This won't work properly with a string argument, and will result in destroying the value of the caller's variable. Why is this?

Unfair Copy

The problem occurs when the destructor is called at the end of a function's execution, to dispose of the copy that was made of the input argument during the function call. Since the copy points to the same data as the caller's original variable, the destruction of the copy causes the memory allocated to the caller's variable to be freed.

This is due to the way in which a variable is copied in C++ by the compiler-generated *copy constructor*. This mechanism for variable copying uses the same approach as the compiler-generated operator =; it makes a copy of all of the parts of the variable (a so-called **memberwise copy**). In the case of our string variable, this results in copying only the length m_Length and the pointer m_Data, and not the data that m_Data points to. That is, both the original and the copy refer to the same data, as indicated by Figure 8.1. If we were to implement our operator = with a string argument rather than a string&, then the following sequence of events would take place during the execution of the statement s = n;:

1. A default copy like the one illustrated by Figure 8.1 would be made of the input argument n, so that the variable Str in the operator = code would point to the same data as the caller's variable n.
2. The Str variable would be used in the operator = code.
3. The Str variable would be destroyed at the end of the operator = function. During this process, the destructor would free the memory that Str.m_Data points to by calling delete [].

Since Str.m_Data holds the same address as the caller's variable n.m_Data, the latter now points to memory that has been freed and may be overwritten or assigned to some other use at any time. This is a bug in the program, caused by the destructor for string being called for a temporary copy of a string that shares data with a caller's variable.

When we use a reference argument, however, the variable in the called function is nothing more (and nothing less) than another name for the caller's variable. No copy is made on entry to the operator = code; therefore, the destructor is not called on exit. This allows the caller's variable n to remain unmolested after operator = finishes executing.

That may sound good, but Susan wanted some more explanation.

> **Susan**: I don't get why a value argument makes a copy and a reference argument doesn't. Help.

> **Steve**: The reason is that a value argument is actually a new auto variable, just like a regular auto variable, except that it is initialized to the value of the caller's actual argument. Therefore, it has to be destroyed when the called function ends. On the other hand, a reference argument just renames the caller's variable; since the compiler hasn't created a new auto variable when the called routine starts, it doesn't need to call the destructor to destroy that variable at the end of the routine.

Problem
Algorithms
C++
Executable
Hardware

Figure 8.2 helped her out a bit by illustrating the same call as the one in Figure 8.1, but using a reference argument instead of a value argument.

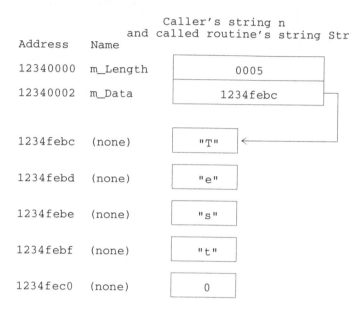

Figure 8.2: Call by reference

Problem
Algorithms
C++
Executable
Hardware

Finally, we're finished examining the intricacies that result from the apparently simple statement s = n; in our test program (Figure 8.3).

```cpp
#include "string1.h"

int main()
{
    string s;
    string n("Test");
    string x;

    s = n;
    n = "My name is: ";

    x = n;
    return 0;
}
```

Figure 8.3: Our first test program for the string class (code\strtst1.cc)

Now let's take a look at the next statement in that test program, n = "My name is: ";. The type of the expression "My name is: " is char*; that is, the compiler stores the character data somewhere and provides a pointer to it. In other words, this line is attempting to assign a char* to a string, something that the compiler again has no built-in code for. Unlike the previous case, however, the code we've already written is sufficient to handle this situation. That's because if we supply a value of type char* where a string is needed, the constructor string::string(char*) is automatically invoked, much as the default constructor is invoked when we create a string with no arguments. Such automatic conversion is another of the features of C++ that makes our user defined types more like native types.[2]

The sequence of events during compilation of the line n = "My name is: "; is something like this:

1. The compiler sees a string on the left of an =, which it interprets as a call to some version of string::operator =.
2. It looks at the expression on the right of the = and sees that it is not a string, but a char*.
3. Have we defined a function with the signature string::operator = (char*)? If so, use it.
4. In this case, we have not defined such an operator. Therefore, the compiler checks to see whether we have defined a constructor with the signature string::string(char*) for the string class.
5. Yes, there is such a constructor. Therefore, the compiler interprets the statement as n.operator = (string("My name is: "));. If there were no such constructor, then the line would be flagged as an error.

Problem
Algorithms
C++
Executable
Hardware

So the actual interpretation of n = "My name is: "; is n.operator = (string("My name is: "));. What exactly does this do?

Figure 8.4 is a picture intended to illuminate the compiler's "thoughts" in this situation; that is, when we assign a C string with the value My name is: " to a string called n via the constructor string::string(char*).[3]

---

2. There are situations, however, where this usually helpful feature is undesirable; for this reason, the new draft standard for C++ provides a way of preventing the compiler from supplying such conversions automatically.

3. Rather than showing each byte address of the characters in the strings and C strings as I've done in previous diagrams, I'm just showing the address of the first character in each group, so that the figure will fit on one page.

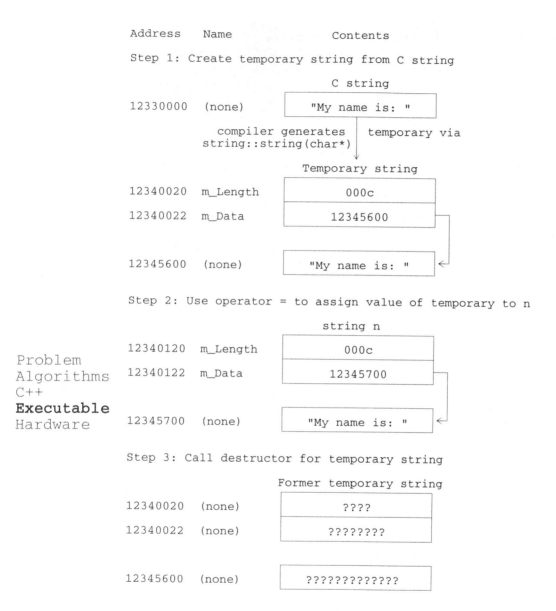

Figure 8.4: Assigning a C string to a string via string::string(char*)

Temporary Help Wanted

Let's go over Figure 8.4, step by step. The first thing that the compiler does is to call the constructor string::string(char*) to create a

temporary (jargon for **temporary variable**) of type string, having the value "My name is: ". This temporary is then used as the argument to the function string::operator = (const string& Str) (see Figure 7.15). Since the argument is a reference, no copy is made of the temporary; the variable Str in the operator = code actually refers to the (unnamed) temporary variable. When the operator = code is finished executing, the string n has been set to the same value as the temporary (i.e., "My name is: "). Upon return from the operator = code, the temporary is automatically destroyed by a destructor call inserted by the compiler.

This sequence of events also holds the key to understanding why the argument of string::operator = should be a const string& (that is, a constant reference to a string) rather than just a string& (that is, a reference to a string). You see, if we declared the function string::operator = to have a string& argument rather than a const string& argument, then it would be possible for that function to change the value of the argument. However, any attempt to change the caller's argument wouldn't work properly if, as in the current example, the argument turned out to be a temporary string constructed from the original argument (the char* value "My name is: "); clearly, changing the temporary string would have no effect on the original argument. Therefore, if the argument to string::operator = were a string&, the line n = "My name is: "; would produce a compiler warning to the effect that we might be trying to alter an argument that was a temporary value. The reason that we don't get this warning is that the compiler knows that we aren't going to try to modify the value of an argument that has the specification const string&; therefore, constructing a temporary value and passing it to string::operator = is guaranteed to have the behavior that we want.[4]

Problem
Algorithms
C++
Executable
Hardware

This example is anything but intuitively obvious and, as you might imagine, led to an extended discussion with Susan.

> **Susan:** So no copy of the argument is made, but the temporary is a copy of the variable to that argument?
>
> **Steve:** The temporary is an unnamed string created from the C string that was passed to operator = by the statement n = "My name is: ";.
>
> **Susan:** Okay. But tell me this: Is the use of a temporary the result of specifying a reference argument? If so, then why don't you discuss this when you first discuss reference arguments?

---

4. By the way, the compiler doesn't just take our word that our operator = function isn't going to modify an argument with the const specifier; if we wrote an operator = that tried to modify such an argument, it wouldn't compile.

Steve: It's not exactly because we're using a reference argument. When a function is called with the "wrong" type of argument but a constructor is available to make the "right" type of argument from the "wrong" one that was supplied, then the compiler will supply the conversion automatically. In the case of calling operator = with a char* rather than a string, there is a constructor that can make a string from a char*; so, the compiler will use that constructor to make a temporary string out of the supplied char* and use that temporary string as the actual argument to the function operator =. However, if the argument type were specified as a string& rather than a const string&, then the compiler would warn us that we might be trying to change the temporary string that it had constructed; since we have a const string& argument, the compiler knows that we won't try to change that temporary string, so it doesn't need to warn us about this possibility.

Susan: Well, I never looked at it that way, I just felt that if there is a constructor for the argument then it is an OK argument.

Steve: As long as the actual argument matches the type that the constructor expects, there is no problem.

Susan: So, if the argument type were a string& and we changed the temporary argument, what would happen? I don't see the problem with changing something that was temporary; I see that it would be a problem for the original argument but not the temporary.

Problem
Algorithms
C++
Executable
Hardware

Steve: The reason why generating a temporary is acceptable in this situation is that the argument is a const reference. If we didn't add the const in front of the argument specifier, then the compiler would warn us about our possibly trying to modify the temporary. Since we have a const reference, the compiler knows that we won't try to modify the argument, and thus it's safe for the compiler to generate the temporary value.

Susan: OK, then the temporary is created any time you call a reference argument? I thought that the whole point of a temporary was so you could modify it and not the original argument and the purpose of the const was to ensure that would be the case.

Steve: The point is precisely that nothing would happen to the original argument if we changed the copy. Since one of the reasons that reference arguments are available is to allow changing of the caller's argument, the compiler warns us if we appear to be interested in doing that (a non-const reference argument) in a situation where such a change would have no effect because the actual argument is a temporary.

Susan: So, if we have a non-const string& argument specification with an actual argument of type char* then a temporary is made that can be changed (without affecting the original argument). If the argument is specified as a const string& and the actual argument is of type char* then a temporary is made that cannot be changed.

Steve: You've correctly covered the cases where a temporary is necessary, but haven't mentioned the other cases. Here is the whole truth and nothing but the truth:

1.   If we specify the argument type as string& *and* a temporary has to be created because the actual argument is a char* rather than a string, then the compiler will warn us that any change we make to that temporary will no effect on the original argument.
2.   If we specify the argument type as const string& *and* a temporary has to be created because the actual argument is a char*, then the compiler won't warn us about our (hypothetical) change not doing anything, because it knows that we aren't going to make such a change.
3.   However, if the actual argument is a string, so that no temporary needs to be made in either of these cases (string& or const string&), then the argument that we see in the function is actually the real argument, not a temporary. Therefore, the compiler won't warn us about trying to change a (nonexistent) temporary.

Susan: OK, this clears up another confusion I believe, because I was getting confused with the notion of creating a temporary that is basically a copy but I remember that you said that a reference argument doesn't make a copy; it just renames the original argument. So that would be the case in 3 here, but the temporary is called into action only when you have a situation such as in 1 or 2, where a reference to a string is specified as the argument type in the function declaration, while the actual argument is a char*.

Steve: Right.

Copy Cat

Assuming you've followed this so far, you might have noticed one loose end. What if we want to pass a string as a value argument to a function? As we have seen, with the current setup bad things will happen, since the compiler-generated copy constructor doesn't copy strings correctly. Well, you'll be relieved to learn that this, too, can be fixed. The answer is to implement our own version of the *copy*

```
Problem
Algorithms
C++
Executable
Hardware
```

constructor, created precisely to solve the problem of copying variables of a given class, in this case string. Let's take another look at the header file, now in Figure 8.5.

```
class string
{
public:
    string();
    string(const string& Str);
    void operator = (const string& Str);
    ~string();

    string(char* p);

private:
    short m_Length;
    char* m_Data;
};
```

Figure 8.5: The string class interface (code\string1.h)

The line we're interested in here is string(const string& Str);. This is a constructor, since its name is the class name string. It takes one argument, which is a const string&, that is, a reference to a constant string. This means that we're not going to change the argument's value "through" the reference, as would be possible if it were a non-const reference. Figure 8.6 has the code that implements this new constructor.

Problem
Algorithms
C++
Executable
Hardware

```
string::string(const string& Str)
{
    m_Length = Str.m_Length;
    m_Data = new char [m_Length];
    memcpy(m_Data,Str.m_Data,m_Length);
};
```

Figure 8.6: The copy constructor for the string class

You may notice the resemblance to the code for operator =. This makes sense, since both of these functions are in the copying business. However, there are also some differences, which also makes sense; otherwise, we wouldn't need two separate functions.

The first difference is that we don't have to check whether the argument refers to the same string as this. That's because a constructor always creates a new, never before seen, object of whatever class it's a constructor for. There's no equivalent of the statement a = a; that can cause trouble for operator = without special handling.

The second difference is that we don't have to delete any previously held storage that might have been assigned to m_Data. Of course, this is also because we're building a new string, not reusing one that already exists. Therefore, we know that m_Data has never had any storage assigned to it previously.

Now that we have a correct copy constructor, we can use a string as a value argument to a function, and the copy that's made by the compiler when execution of the function starts will be an independent string, not connected to the caller's variable. When this copy is destroyed at the end of the function, it will go away quietly and the caller's original variable won't be disturbed.

This is all very well in theory, but it's time to see some practice. Let's write a function that we can call with a string to do some useful work, like displaying the characters in the string on the screen.

Screen Test

As I hope you remember from the previous chapters, we can send output to the screen via cout, a predefined output destination. For example, if we wished to write the character 'a' to the screen, we would use the statement cout << 'a';. Although we have previously used cout and << to display string variables, our current version of the string class doesn't support them. If we want this ability, we'll have to provide it ourselves. Since variables that can't be displayed are limited in usefulness, we're going to start to do just that right now. Figure 8.7 is the updated header file.

Problem
Algorithms
C++
Executable
Hardware

```
class string
{
public:
    string();
    string(const string& Str);
    void operator = (const string& Str);
    ~string();

    string(char* p);
    void Display();

private:
    short m_Length;
    char* m_Data;
};
```

Figure 8.7: The string class interface, with Display function (code\string3.h)

As you can see, the new function is declared as void Display();. This means that it returns no value, its name is Display, and it takes no arguments. This last characteristic may seem odd at first, because surely Display needs to know which string we want to display. However, as we've already seen, each object has its own copy of all of the variables defined in the class interface. In this case, the data that are to be displayed are the characters pointed to by m_Data.

As is often the case, Susan thought she didn't understand this idea, but actually did.

> **Susan**: This Display stuff. . . I don't get it. Are you having to write also the information that the classes need to display information on the screen?

> **Steve**: Yes.

Figure 8.8 is an example of how Display can be used.

```
#include <iostream.h>
#include "string3.h"
```

Problem
Algorithms
C++
Executable
Hardware

```
int main()
{
        string s;
        string n("Test");
        string x;

        s = n;
        n = "My name is: ";

        n.Display();

        s = "";

        return 0;
}
```

Figure 8.8: The string class test program, using the Display function
(code\strtst3.cc)

See the line that says, n.Display();? That is how our new Display function is called. Remember, it's a member function, so it is always called with respect to a particular string variable; in this case, that variable is n. Now, let's look at the implementation of this new member function, in Figure 8.9.

```
void string::Display()
{
    short i;

    for (i = 0; i < m_Length-1; i ++)
        cout << m_Data[i];
};
```

Figure 8.9: The string class implementation of the Display function

This should be looking almost sensible by now; here's the play by play. We start out with the function declaration, which says we're defining a void function (i.e., one that returns no value) that is a member function of the class string. This function is named Display, and it takes no arguments. Then we define a short called i. The main part of the function is a for loop, which is executed with the index starting at 0 and continuing while it (the index, that is) is less than the number of displayable characters that we use to store the value of our string; of course, we don't need to display the null byte at the end of the string. So far, so good. Now comes the tricky part. The next statement, which is the controlled block of the for loop, says to send something to cout; that is, display it on the screen. This makes sense, because after all that's the purpose of this function. But what is it that is being sent to cout?

Problem
Algorithms
C++
Executable
Hardware

A Character Study

It's just a char but that may not be obvious from the way it's written. This expression m_Data[i] looks just like a vector element, doesn't it? In fact, m_Data[i] is an element but not of a vector. Instead, it's an element of an *array*, the C equivalent of a C++ vector.

What's an array? Well, it's a bunch of data items (elements) of the same type; in this case, it's an array of chars. The array name, m_Data in this case, corresponds to the address of the first of these elements; the other elements follow the first one immediately in memory. If this sounds familiar, it should; it's very much like Susan's old nemesis, a pointer. However, like a vector, we can also refer to the individual elements by their indexes; so, m_Data[i] refers to the ith element of the array, which in the case of a char array is, oddly enough, a char.

So now it should be clear that each time through the loop, we're sending out the ith element of the array of chars where we stored our string data.

Susan and I had quite a discussion about this topic, and here it is.

Susan: And if this is an array or a vector (I can't tell which), how does the class know about it if you haven't written a constructor for it?

Steve: Arrays are a native feature of C++, left over from C. Thus, we don't have to (and can't) create a constructor and the like for them.

Susan: The best I can figure out from this discussion is that an array is like a vector but instead of numbers it indexes char data and uses a pointer to do it?

Steve: Very close. It's just like a vector except that it's missing some rather important features of a vector. The most important one from our perspective is that an array doesn't have any error-checking; if you give it a silly index, you'll get something back, but exactly what is hard to determine.

Susan: If it is just like a vector and it is not as useful as a real vector, then why use it? What can it do that a vector can't?

Steve: A vector isn't a native data type, whereas an array is. Therefore, you can use arrays to make vectors, which is in fact how I did it. We also wouldn't want to use vectors to hold our string data because they're much more "expensive" (i.e., large and slow) to use. I'm trying to illustrate how we could make a string class that would resemble one that would actually be usable in a real program, and although simplicity is important, I didn't want to go off the deep end in hiding arrays from the reader.

Susan: So when you say that "we're sending out the ith element of the array of chars where we stored our value." does that mean that the "ith" element would be the pointer to some memory address where char data is stored?

Steve: No, the ith element of the array is just like the ith element of a vector. If we had a vector of four chars called x, we'd declare it as follows:

```
vector<char> x(4);
```

Problem
Algorithms
C++
Executable
Hardware

Then we could refer to the individual chars in that vector as x[0], x[1], x[2], or x[3]. It's much the same for an array. If we had an array of four chars called y, we'd declare it as follows:

char y[4];

Then we could refer to the individual chars in that array as y[0], y[1], y[2], or y[3].

That's all very well, but where did that array come from? We defined m_Data as a char*, which is a pointer to (i.e., the address of) a char. As is common in C and C++, this particular char* is the first of a bunch of chars one after the other in memory. In case this isn't immediately obvious, don't worry; it wasn't obvious to Susan, either.

Susan: And when you say that "that is, a pointer (i.e., the address of) a char, which may be the first of a bunch of chars one after another in memory", does that mean the char* points to the first address and then the second and then the third individually, and an array will point at all of them at the same time?

Steve: No, the char* points to the first char, but we can figure out the addresses of the other chars because they follow the first char sequentially in memory. The same is true of the array; the array name refers to the address of the first char, and the other chars in the array can be addressed with the index added to the array name. In other words, y[2] in the example means "the char that is 2 bytes past the beginning of the array called y".

Problem
Algorithms
C++
Executable
Hardware

Array of Hope?

Brace yourself for this one. In C++, a pointer and the address of an array are for almost all purposes the same thing. You can treat an array address as a pointer and a pointer as an array address, pretty much as you please. This is a holdover from C, necessary for compatibility with C programs.

People who like C will tell you how "flexible" the equivalence of pointers and arrays in C is. That's true, but it's also extremely dangerous, because arrays have no error checking whatsoever. You can use whatever index you feel like, and whatever happens to be at the address that that index would have corresponded to will be your target of opportunity. The program in Figure 8.10 is an example of what can go wrong when using arrays.

```
#include <iostream.h>

int main()
{
    char High[10];
    char Middle[10];
    char Low[10];
    char* Alias;
    short i;

    for (i = 0; i < 10; i ++)
        {
        Middle[i] = 'A' + i;
        High[i] = '0';
        Low[i] ='1';
        }

    Alias = Middle;

    for (i = 10; i < 20; i ++)
        {
        Alias[i] = 'a' + i;
        }

    cout << "Low: ";
    for (i = 0; i < 10; i ++)
        cout << Low[i];

    cout << endl;

    cout << "Middle: ";
    for (i = 0; i < 10; i ++)
        cout << Middle[i];

    cout << endl;

    cout << "Alias: ";
    for (i = 0; i < 10; i ++)
        cout << Alias[i];

    cout << endl;

    cout << "High: ";
    for (i = 0; i < 10; i ++)
        cout << High[i];

    cout << endl;
};
```

Problem
Algorithms
C++
Executable
Hardware

Figure 8.10: Dangerous characters (code\dangchar.cc)

Let's look at what this program does when it's executed. First, we define three variables High, Middle, and Low, each as an array of 10 chars. Then we define a variable Alias as a char*; as you may recall, this is how we specify a pointer to a char. Such a pointer is essentially equivalent to a plain old memory address.

In the next part of the program, we use a for loop to set each element of the arrays High, Middle, and Low to a value. So far, so good, except that the statement Middle[i] = 'A' + i; may look a bit odd. How can we add a char value like 'A' and a short value such as i?

A Slippery Character

Let us return to those thrilling days of yesterycar, or at least Chapter 3. Since then, we've been using chars to hold ASCII values, which is their most common use. However, every char variable actually has a "double life"; it can also be thought of as a "really short" numeric variable, which can take on any of 256 values. Thus, we can add and subtract chars and shorts, as long as we're careful not to try to use a char to hold a number greater than 255 (or greater than 127, for a signed char). That won't work very well, since there's not enough room to keep such a value. In this case, there's no such problem with the magnitude of the result, since we're starting out with the value *A* and adding a number between 0 and 9 to it; the highest possible result is *J*, which is still well below the maximum value that can be stored in a char.

Problem
Algorithms
C++
Executable
Hardware

With that detail taken care of, let's proceed with the analysis of this program. The next statement after the end of the first for loop is the seemingly simple line alias = middle; This is obviously an assignment statement, but what is being assigned?

The value that Alias receives is the address of the first element of the array Middle. That is, after the assignment statement is executed, Alias is effectively another name for Middle. Therefore, the next loop, which assigns values to elements 10 through 19 of the "array" Alias, actually operates on the array Middle, setting those elements to the values *k* through *t*.

The rest of the program is pretty simple. It just displays the characters from each of the Low, Middle, Alias, and High arrays. Of course, Alias isn't really an array, but it acts just like one; to be precise, it acts just like Middle, since it points to the first character in Middle. Therefore, the Alias and Middle loops will display the same characters. Then the final loop displays the values in the High array.

Overwrought

That's pretty simple, isn't it? Not quite as simple as it looks. If you've been following along closely, you're probably thinking I've gone off the deep end. First, I said that the array Middle had 10 elements (which are numbered 0 through 9, as always in C++); now I'm assigning values to elements numbered 10 through 19. Am I nuts?

No, but the program is. When you run it, you'll discover that it produces output similar to Figure 8.11.

```
Low: 1111111111
Middle: ABCDEFGHIJ
Alias: ABCDEFGHIJ
High: mnopqrst00
```

Figure 8.11: Reaping the whirlwind

Problem
Algorithms
C++
Executable
Hardware

Most of these results are pretty reasonable: Low is just as it was when we initialized it, and Middle and Alias have the expected portion of the alphabet. But look at High. Shouldn't it be all 0s?

Yes, it should. However, we have broken the rules by writing "past the end" of an array, and the result is that we have overwritten some other data in our program, which in this case turned out to be the original values of High. You may wonder why we didn't get an error message, as we did when we tried to write to a nonexistent vector element in an earlier chapter. The reason is that, in C, an array is no more (and no less) than the address of some data. In other words, it's just like a pointer, except that the address it refers to can't be changed at run time. Because of this near-identity between pointers and arrays, the compiler does not and cannot keep track of how many elements are in an array. To the compiler, keeping track of such information makes no sense, any more than it can tell how many elements there are "in a pointer".

This is why pointers and (equivalently) arrays are the single most error-prone construct in C (and C++, when they're used recklessly). It's also why we're not going to use either of these constructs except when there's no other reasonable way to accomplish our goals; even then, we'll confine them to tightly controlled circumstances in the implementation of a user defined data type. For example, we don't have to worry about going "off the end" of the array in our Display function, because we know exactly how many characters we've stored (m_Length), and we've written the function to send exactly that many characters to the screen via cout. In fact, all of the member functions of our string class are carefully designed to allocate, use, and dispose of the memory pointed to by m_Data so that the user of this class doesn't have to worry about pointers or arrays, or the problems they can cause. After all, one of the main benefits of using C++ is that the users of a class don't have to concern themselves with the way it works, just with what it does.

You can run this program under gdb by switching to the normal subdirectory, then typing trace dangchar and hitting ENTER. The program will start up and show you the first line of executable code. Type z and hit ENTER to execute each line. The values of the relevant variables will be displayed immediately before the execution of each line in main. When you get to the end of the program (or when you're tired of tracing), type q (for *quit*) and hit ENTER to exit from the debugger.

Susan and I had quite a discussion about this program:

> **Susan**: It is still not clear to me why you assigned values to elements numbered 10–19. Was that for demonstration purposes to force "writing past the end"?
>
> **Steve**: Yes.
>
> **Susan**: So by doing this to Middle then it alters the place the pointer is going to point for High?
>
> **Steve**: No, it actually uses some of the same addresses that High uses, with the result being. . . well, do you remember the function mess?
>
> **Susan**: Oh, don't remind me. So then when High runs there isn't any memory to put its results in? Why does Middle overwrite High instead of High overwrite Middle? But it was Alias that took up high's memory?
>
> **Steve**: Actually High is filled up with the correct values, but then they're overwritten by the loop that stores via Alias, which is just another name for Middle. I'll explain that in detail.
>
> **Susan**: Is that why High took on the lower case letters? Because Middle took the first loop and then Alias is the same as middle, so that is why it also has the upper case letters but then when High looped it picked up the pointer where Alias left off and that is why it is in lower case? But how did it manage two zeros at the end? I better stop talking, this is getting too weird. You are going to think I am nuts.

Problem
Algorithms
C++
Executable
Hardware

Steve: No. You're not nuts, but the program is. We're breaking the rules by writing "past the end" of the array Middle, using the pointer Alias to do so. We could have gotten the same result by storing data into elements 10 through 20 of Middle, but I wanted to show the equivalence of pointers and arrays.

Susan: Oops, I got ahead of myself, and yes, I was just going to ask if Middle alone would have been sufficient to do the job.

Steve: Yes, it would have been. However, it would not have made the point that arrays and pointers are almost identical in C++.

Susan: I am confused as to why the lower case letters are in High and why k and l are missing and two zeros made their way in. You never told me why those zeros were there.

Steve: Because the end of one array isn't necessarily immediately followed by the beginning of the next array; this depends on the sizes of the arrays and on how the compiler allocates local variables on the stack. What we're doing here is breaking the rules of the language, so it shouldn't be a surprise that the result isn't very sensible.

```
Problem
Algorithms
C++
Executable
Hardware
```

Susan: OK, so if you are breaking the rules you can't predict an outcome? Here I was trying to figure out what was going on by looking at the results even knowing it was erroneous. Ugh.

Steve: Indeed.

private **Property: Keep Out!**

Now that we have disposed of the correspondence between arrays and pointers, it's time to return to our discussion of the private access specifier that we've used to control access to the member variables of the class. First of all, let me refresh your memory as to what this access specifier means: only member functions of the string class can refer to variables or functions marked private. As a rule, all the member variables of a class should be private, for reasons that we'll get into later. By contrast, most member functions are public, because such functions provide the interface that is used by programmers who need the facilities of the class being defined. While private member functions are sometimes useful for handling implementation details that aren't of interest or use to the "outside world" beyond the class boundaries, they aren't needed in most classes, including the classes defined in this book.

Now that I've clarified the role of these access specifiers, let's take a look at the program in Figure 8.12, which won't compile because it tries to refer to m_Length, a private member variable of string.

```
#include <iostream.h>
#include "string3.h"

int main()
{
    string n("Test");

    n.m_Length = 12;

    n.Display();

    return 0;
}
```

Figure 8.12: Attempted privacy violation (code\strtst3a.cc)

Here's the result of trying to compile this program:

```
strtst3a.cc: In function 'int main()':
strtst3a.cc:8: member 'm_Length' is a private member of class 'string'
```

Problem
Algorithms
C++
Executable
Hardware

Why would we want to prevent access to a member variable? Because public member variables have problems similar to those of global variables. To begin with, we want to guarantee consistent, safe behavior of our strings, which is impossible if a nonmember function outside our control can change one of our variables. In this example, assigning a new value to the m_Length member variable would trick our Display member function into trying to display 12 characters, when our string contains only four characters of displayable data. Similar bad results would occur if a nonmember function were to change the value of m_Data; we wouldn't have any idea of what it was pointing to or whether we should call delete in the destructor to allow the memory formerly used for our string data to be reused.

Of course, Susan had some questions about this notion of access restriction.

> **Susan**: Now let me see if I get the problem here with this Figure 8.12. When you originally wrote m_Length, it was placed in a private area, so it couldn't be accessed through this program?

Steve: Right.

Susan: I am confused on your use of the term *nonmember function*. Does that mean a nonmember of a particular class or something that is native? For this reason I am not understanding the first paragraph.

Steve: A nonmember function is any function that is not a member of the class in question.

Susan: A simple concept, but one that is easy to forget for some reason.

Steve: Probably because it's stated negatively.

While this may be a convincing argument against letting nonmember functions change our member variables, what about letting them at least retrieve the values of member variables? Surely that must be harmless.

Maintenance Required

Problem
Algorithms
C++
Executable
Hardware

Unfortunately this would be hazardous too. The problem here is akin to the other difficulty with global variables: Removing or changing the type of a global variable can cause repercussions everywhere in the program. If we decide to implement our string class by a different mechanism than a char* and a short, or even change the names of the member variables from m_Data and m_Length, any programs that rely on those types or names would have to be changed. If our string class were to become popular, this might amount to dozens or even hundreds of programs that would need changes if we were to make the slightest change in our member variables. Therefore, allowing nonmember functions even to retrieve the values of member variables is dangerous to the maintainability of programs using a class.

However, it is sometimes useful for a program that is using an object to find out something about the object's internal state. For example, a user of a string variable might very well want to know how long the string is; that is, how many characters it is storing at the moment.[5] Susan wanted to know how this requirement could be

---

5. Why would the user of this class want to know how long a particular string is? One possible use for this information would be in formatting a report, when you would want to pad each string with blanks to the same length so that the columns would line up. Each string might require a different amount of padding, depending on the number of visible characters in the string; however, we don't want the length the user sees to include the null byte, which doesn't

accommodated.

> **Susan**: So how would you "fix" this so that it would run? If you don't want to change m_Length to something public, then would you have to rewrite another string class for this program?

> **Steve**: No, you would generally fix this by writing a member function that returns the length of the string; the GetLength function to be implemented in Figure 8.14 is an example of that.

> **Susan**: Oh, so then m_Length stays private but GetLength is public. Is that how it would work?

> **Steve**: Exactly.

As I've just mentioned to Susan, it is indeed possible to provide such a service without compromising the safety or maintainability of our class by writing a function that tells the user how long the string is. Figure 8.13 has the new interface definition that includes the GetLength function.

```
class string
{
public:
    string();
    string(const string& Str);
    void operator = (const string& Str);
    ~string();

    string(char* p);
    void Display();
    short GetLength();

private:
    short m_Length;
    char* m_Data;
};
```

Problem
Algorithms
C++
Executable
Hardware

Figure 8.13: Yet another version of the string class interface (code\string4.h)

As you can see, all we have to do here is to add the new function, GetLength. The implementation in Figure 8.14 is extremely simple: it merely returns the number of char in the string, deducting 1 for the null byte at the end.

---

take up any space on the page. As you will see, satisfying this requirement complicates the function needed to return the "correct" length.

```
short string::GetLength()
{
   return m_Length-1;
};
```

Figure 8.14: The string class implementation of the GetLength function (from code\string4.cc)

This solves the problem of letting the user of a string variable find out how long the string is without allowing functions outside the class to become dependent on our implementation. With this mechanism in place, we can make whatever changes we like in how we store the length of our string;[6] as long as we don't change the name or return type of GetLength, no function outside the string class would be affected.[7] The example program in Figure 8.15 illustrates how to use this new function.

```
#include <iostream.h>
#include "string4.h"

int main()
{
        short len;
        string n("Test");

        len = n.GetLength();

        n.Display();

        cout << endl;

        cout << "The string has " << len << " characters." << endl;

        return 0;
}
```

Problem
Algorithms
C++
Executable
Hardware

Figure 8.15: Using the GetLength function in the string class (code\strtst4.cc)

---

6. For example, we could eliminate our m_Length member variable and just rely on the null byte at the end of the data rather than keeping the length separately. In that case, we could still supply a GetLength function which would call strlen to figure out the length); thus, the user's source code wouldn't have to be changed just because we changed the way we keep track of the length. However, because this change would affect the size of a string object, the user would have to recompile and relink his program if we were to make this change.

7. The alert reader will notice that we actually don't have free rein to change the implementation of the string class, because if we were to allow strings longer than 32767 bytes, we would have to change the return type of GetLength to something more capacious than an short. However, this still gives us a lot more leeway to make changes in the implementation than we would have if we allowed direct access to our member variables.

First Review

After finishing most of the requirements to make the string class a concrete data type in the previous chapter, we went back to look at why the operator = needs a *reference argument* rather than a *value argument*. The problem is that using a value argument results in making a copy of the argument on the stack. Compiler-generated copy constructors use *memberwise copy*; that is, simply copying all of the member variables in the object. While a memberwise copy is fine for simple objects whose data are wholly contained within themselves, it isn't sufficient for objects that contain pointers to data stored in other places, because copying a pointer from one object to another results in the two objects sharing the same actual data. Since our string class does contain such a pointer, the result of this simple(minded) copy is that the newly created string points to the same data as the caller's string. Therefore, when the newly created local string expires at the end of the operator = function, the destructor for that string frees the memory that the caller's string was using to store its data.

This problem is very similar to the reason why we had to write our own operator = in the first place; the compiler-generated operator = just copies the member variables from the source to the destination object, which causes similar havoc when one of the two "twinned" strings is changed. In the case of our operator =, we can solve the twinning problem by using a reference argument rather than a value argument. Since a reference argument is actually another name for the caller's variable rather than a copy of the value in that variable, no destructor is called for a reference argument when the function exits; therefore, the caller's variable is left unmolested.

Next, we examined how it was possible to assign a C string to one of our string variables. This didn't require us to write any more code because we already had a constructor that could create a string from a C string, and an operator = that could assign one string to another one. The compiler helps us out here by employing a rule that can be translated roughly as follows: If we need an object of type A (string, in this case) and we have an object of type B (char*, in this case), and there is a constructor that constructs an A and requires exactly one argument, which is of type B, then invoke that constructor automatically. The example code is as follows:

```
n = "My name is: ";
```

Problem
Algorithms
C++
Executable
Hardware

where n is a string, and "My name is" is a C string, whose type is char*. We have an operator = with the declaration:

   void string::operator = (const string& Str);

which takes a string reference argument, and we have a constructor of the form:

   string::string(char* p);

which takes a char* argument and creates a new string. So we have a char*, "My name is: ", and we need a string. Since we have a constructor string::string(char*), the compiler will use that constructor to make a temporary string with the same value as the char*, and then use the assignment operator string::operator = (const string& Str) to assign the value of that temporary string to the string n. The fact that the temporary is created also provides the clue as to why the argument to string::operator = (const string& Str) should be a const reference, rather than just a (non-const) reference, to a string. The temporary value of type string having the value "My name is: " that is created during the execution of the statement n = "My name is: "; disappears after operator = is executed, taking with it any changes that operator = might have wanted to apply to the original value. With a constant reference, the compiler knows that operator = doesn't wish to change that argument, and therefore doesn't give us a warning that we might be changing a temporary value.

At this point, we've taken care of operator =. However, to create a concrete data type, we still have to allow our string variables to be passed as value arguments. Unfortunately, the compiler-generated copy constructor suffers from the same drawback as the compiler-generated operator =; namely, it copies the pointer to the actual data of the string, rather than the data itself. Logically, therefore, the solution to this problem is quite similar to the solution for operator =: We write our own copy constructor that allocates space for the character data to be stored in the newly created string and then copies the data from the old string to the new string.

However, we still can't use a value argument to our copy constructor, because a value argument needs a copy constructor to make the copy. This obviously won't work, and will be caught by the compiler. Therefore, as in the case of operator =, we have to use a reference argument; since this is actually just another name for the caller's variable rather than a copy of it, no destructor for the reference argument is called at exit from our copy constructor. Since

Problem
Algorithms
C++
Executable
Hardware

we are not going to change the caller's argument, we specify a constant reference argument of type string, or a const string& in C++ terms.

At that point in the chapter, we had met the requirements for a concrete data type, but such a type is of limited usefulness as long as we can't get the values displayed on the screen. Therefore, the next order of business was to add a Display member function that takes care of this task. This function isn't particularly complicated, but it does require us to deal with the notion of a C legacy type, the *array*. Since the compiler treats an array in almost the same way as a pointer, we can use array notation to extract each character that needs to be sent out to the screen. Continuing with our example of the Display function's use, the next topic is a discussion of how chars can be treated as numeric variables.

Then we saw a demonstration of how easy it is to misuse an array so that you destroy data that belong to some other variable. This is an important warning of the dangers of uncontrolled use of pointers and arrays; these are the most error-prone constructs in both C and C++, when not kept under tight rein.

We continued by revisiting the topic of access control and why it is advantageous to keep member variables in the private section of the class definition. The reasons are similar to those of using global variables; it's too hard to keep track of where the value of a public member variable is being referenced and therefore to update all the affected areas of the code when changing the class definition. However, it is sometimes useful to allow external functions access to some information about a class object. We saw how to do this by adding a GetLength member function to our string class.

Problem
Algorithms
C++
Executable
Hardware

Stringing Along

At this point, we have a fairly minimal string class. We can create a string, assign it a literal value in the form of a C string, and copy the value of one string to another; we can even pass a string as a value argument. Now we'll use the techniques that we've already covered (along with others that we find necessary in the process) to improve the facilities that the string class provides.

To make this goal more concrete, let's suppose that we want to modify the sorting program of Chapter 4 to sort strings, rather than shorts. To use the sorting algorithm from that program, we'll need to be able to compare two strings to see which would come after the other in the dictionary, as we can compare two shorts to see which is greater. We also want to be able to use cout and << to display strings on the screen, and cin and >> to read them from the keyboard, just as we can with native types.

Before we go into the changes needed in the string class to allow us to write a string sorting program, Figure 8.16 shows our goal: The selection sort algorithm adapted to sort a vector of strings.

```
#include <iostream.h>
#include "string6.h"
#include "vector.h"

int main()
{
    vector<string> Name(5);
    vector<string> SortedName(5);
    string FirstName;
    short FirstIndex;
    short i;
    short k;
    string HighestName = "zzzzzzzz";

    cout << "I'm going to ask you to type in five last names." << endl;

    for (i = 0; i < 5; i ++)
      {
      cout << "Please type in name #" << i+1 << ": ";
      cin >> Name[i];
      }

    for (i = 0; i < 5; i ++)
        {
        FirstName = HighestName;
        FirstIndex = 0;
        for (k = 0; k < 5; k ++)
            {
            if (Name[k] < FirstName)
                {
                FirstName = Name[k];
                FirstIndex = k;
                }
            }
        SortedName[i] = FirstName;
        Name[FirstIndex] = HighestName;
        }

    cout << "Here are the names, in alphabetical order: " << endl;
    for (i = 0; i < 5; i ++)
        cout << SortedName[i] << endl;

    return(0);
};
```

Problem
Algorithms
C++
Executable
Hardware

Figure 8.16: Sorting a vector of strings (code\strsort1.cc)

You can run this program either normally or under gdb. In either case, start by switching to the normal subdirectory. Then, to run it normally, type strsort1 and hit ENTER.

To run it under gdb, type trace strsort1 and hit ENTER. The program will start up and show you the first line of executable code. Type z and hit ENTER to execute each line. The values of the relevant variables will be displayed immediately before the execution of each line in main. When you get to the end of the program (or when you're tired of tracing), type q (for *quit*) and hit ENTER to exit from the debugger.

Susan had a couple of comments and questions about this program:

> **Susan**: OK, I have this figured out now. I mentioned to you a long time ago that I was confused with the code here when you ask for last names but you are using a variable FirstName. This is a little confusing to a novice because it seems that you don't know what you are asking for. Now I get it: you are asking for the first one of the *last* names. This takes awhile to figure out, you know. You may need a footnote to explain this, as we novices can get sidetracked with this type of thing for quite awhile. This might save another novice some time.

> **Steve**: Actually, FirstName is the "lowest" name that we've found so far in the current pass, sort of like HighestWeight in the original program. I think we're saying the same thing here.

> **Susan**: Why aren't you using caps when you initiate your variable of HighestName; I don't understand why you use "zzzzzzzzzz" instead of "ZZZZZZZZZZ" ? Are you going to fix this later so that caps will work the same way as lower case letters?

> **Steve**: If I were to make that change, the program wouldn't work correctly if someone typed their name in lower case letters, because lower case letters are higher in ASCII value than upper case letters. That is, "abc" is higher than "ZZZ". Thus, if someone typed in their name in lower case, the program would fail to find their name as the lowest name. Actually, the way the string sorting function works, "ABC" is completely different from "abc"; they won't be next to one another in the sorted list. We could fix this by using a different method of comparing the strings that would effectively convert everything to upper case before sorting it, if that were necessary.

As you can see, this program looks very similar to the code that sorts short values, which is reasonable; after all, that's what we

Problem
Algorithms
C++
Executable
Hardware

wanted to achieve. Let's take a look at the differences between this program and the original one in Figure 4.5.

1. One difference is that we're sorting the names in ascending alphabetical order, rather than descending order of weight as with the original program. This means that we have to start out by finding the name that would come first in the dictionary (the "lowest" name). By contrast, in the original program we were looking for the highest weight, not the lowest one; therefore, we have to do the sort "backward" from the previous example.

2. The next difference is that the vectors Name and SortedName are collections of strings, rather than the corresponding vectors of shorts in the first program: Weight and SortedWeight.

3. We've added a new variable called HighestName, which plays the role of the value 0 that was used to initialize HighestWeight in the original program; that is, it is used to initialize the variable FirstName to a value that will certainly be replaced by the first name we find, just as 0 was used to initialize the variable HighestWeight to a value that had to be lower than the first weight we would find. The reason why we need a "really high" name rather than a "really low" one is because we're sorting the "lowest" name to the front, rather than sorting the "highest" weight to the front as we did originally.

Problem
Algorithms
C++
Executable
Hardware

You may have noticed that these changes to the program aren't very significant. That's a correct conclusion; we'll spend much more time on the changes we have to make to our string class before this program will run, or even compile. The advantage of making up our own data types (like strings) is that we can make them behave in any way we like. Of course, the corresponding disadvantage is that we have to provide the code to implement that behavior and give the compiler enough information to use that code as necessary to perform the operations we want to use. In this case, we'll need to tell the compiler how to compare strings, read them in via >> and write them out via <<. Let's start with the header file that provides the new interface specification of the string class, including all of the new member functions needed to implement the comparison and I/O operators. We find this in Figure 8.17.[8]

---

8. I've also thrown in the declaration of operator ==, which we'll implement later in the chapter.

```
class string
{
friend ostream& operator << (ostream& S, const string& Str);
friend istream& operator >> (istream& S, string& Str);

public:
    string();
    string(const string& Str);
    void operator = (const string& Str);
    ~string();

    string(char* p);
    short GetLength();
    bool operator < (const string& Str);
    bool operator == (const string& Str);

private:
    short m_Length;
    char* m_Data;
};
```

Figure 8.17: The updated string class interface, including comparison and
I/O operators (code\string5.h)

Let's start by implementing operator < (the "less than" operator) so
that we can use the selection sort to arrange strings by their dictionary
order. The signature of this operator is similar to that of operator =,
except that rather than defining what it means to say x = y; for two
strings x and y, we are defining what it means to say x < y. Of course,
we want our operator < to act analogously to the < operator for short
values; that is, our operator will compare two strings and return true if
the first string would come before the second string in the dictionary
and false otherwise. That's all we need for the selection sort.

Problem
Algorithms
C++
Executable
Hardware

Less than Obvious

All right, then, how do we actually implement this undoubtedly
useful facility? Let's start by examining the function declaration bool
string::operator < (const string& Str); a little more closely. This means
that we're declaring a function that returns a bool and is a member
function of class string; its name is operator <, and it takes a constant
reference to a string as its argument. As we've seen before, operators
don't look the same when we use them as when we define them. In
the sorting program in Figure 8.16, the line if (Name[k] < FirstName)
actually means if (Name[k].operator < (FirstName)). In other words, if

the return value from the call to operator < is false, then the if expression will also be considered false and the controlled block after the if won't be executed. On the other hand, if the return value from the call to operator < is true, then the if expression will also be considered true and the controlled block of the if will be executed. To make this work correctly, our version of operator < will return the value true if the first string is less than the second string and the value false otherwise.

Now that we've seen how the compiler will use our new function, let's see how it does its work. The basic approach we will use to compare two strings is as follows:

1. Determine the length of the shorter of the two strings.
2. Compare a character from the first string with the corresponding character from the second string.
3. If the character from the first string is less than the character from the second string, then we know that the first string precedes the second in the dictionary, so we're done and the result is true.
4. If the character from the first string is greater than the character from the second string, then we know that the first string follows the second in the dictionary, so we're done and the result is false.
5. If the two characters are the same, and we haven't come to the end of the shorter string, then move to the next character in each string, and go back to step 2.
6. When we run out of characters to compare, if the strings are the same length, then the answer is that they are identical, so we're done and the result is false.
7. On the other hand, if the strings are different in length, and if we run out of characters in the shorter string before finding a difference between the two strings, then the longer string follows the shorter one in the dictionary. In this case, the result is true if the second string is longer and false if the first string is longer.

```
Problem
Algorithms
C++
Executable
Hardware
```

One question that might occur to you on looking over the preceding explanation is why we care whether two strings differ in length. Wouldn't it be simpler just to compare up to the length of the longer string?

Down for the Count

As it happens, the comparison would work properly so long as both of the strings we're comparing have a null byte at their ends *and* neither of them has a null byte anywhere else. To see why this restriction is necessary, let's look at what the memory layout might look like for two string variables x and y, with the contents "post" and "poster" respectively. In Figure 8.18, the letters in the box labeled "string contents" represent themselves, while the 0s represent the null byte, not the digit 0.

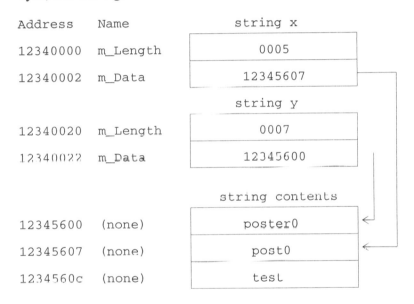

Problem
Algorithms
C++
Executable
Hardware

Figure 8.18: strings x and y in memory

If we were to compare the strings up to the longer of the two lengths with this memory layout, the sequence of events would go like this:

1. Get character *p* from location 12345600.
2. Get character *p* from location 12345607.
3. They are the same, so continue.
4. Get character *o* from location 12345601.
5. Get character *o* from location 12345608.
6. They are the same, so continue.
7. Get character *s* from location 12345602.

8.   Get character *s* from location 12345609.
9.   They are the same, so continue.
10.   Get character *t* from location 12345603.
11.   Get character *t* from location 1234560a.
12.   They are the same, so continue.
13.   Get character *e* from location 12345604.
14.   Get a null byte from location 1234560b.
15.   The character *e* from the first string is higher than the null byte from the second string, so we conclude (correctly) that the first string comes after the second one.

The reason why this works is that the null byte, having an ASCII code of 0, in fact is less than any byte that might be in the corresponding position of the other string.

However, one reason we're storing the actual length of the string rather than relying on the null byte to mark the end of a string, as is done with C strings, is that keeping the length separately makes it possible to have a string that has any characters whatever in it, even nulls. In the event that we had a string with a null in the middle of it, the preceding mechanism wouldn't work reliably. To see why, let's change the memory layout slightly to stick a null byte in the middle of string y. Figure 8.19 shows the modified layout.

Problem
Algorithms
C++
Executable
Hardware

Address	Name	string x
12340000	m_Length	0005
12340002	m_Data	12345607

		string y
12340020	m_Length	0007
12340022	m_Data	12345600

		string contents
12345600	(none)	post0r0
12345607	(none)	post0
1234560c	(none)	test

Figure 8.19: strings x and y in memory, with an embedded null byte

If we were to compare the strings up to the longer of the two lengths with this memory layout, the sequence of events would go like this:

1. Get character *p* from location 12345600.
2. Get character *p* from location 12345607.
3. They are the same, so continue.
4. Get character *o* from location 12345601.
5. Get character *o* from location 12345608.
6. They are the same, so continue.
7. Get character *s* from location 12345602.
8. Get character *s* from location 12345609.
9. They are the same, so continue.
10. Get character *t* from location 12345603.
11. Get character *t* from location 1234560a.
12. They are the same, so continue.
13. Get a null byte from location 12345604.
14. Get a null byte from location 1234560b.
15. They are the same, so continue.
16. Get character *r* from location 12345605.
17. Get character *t* from location 1234560c.
18. The character *r* from the first string is less than the character *t* from the second string, so we conclude that the first string comes before the second one.

Problem
Algorithms
C++
Executable
Hardware

Unfortunately, this conclusion is completely fallacious; what we have actually done is run off the end of the second string and started retrieving data from the next location in memory. Since we want to be able to handle the situation where one of the strings has one or more embedded nulls, we have to stop the comparison as soon as we get to the end of the shorter string; whatever happens to be past the end of that string's data, it's not anything relevant to our comparison of the two strings.

Let's listen in on the conversation Susan and I had about this function.

Susan: Why is the return value from operator < a bool?

Steve: Because it has to return a value indicating whether the first string is less than the second string. An if statement using this operator < will work properly if the result of this function is false for "not less than" and true for "less than". Thus, a bool is appropriate for this use.

Susan: Again I am not seeing where we're using string::operator < (const string& Str); in the sorting program.

Steve: That's because all you have to say is a < b, just as with operator =; the compiler knows that a < b, where a and b are strings, means string::operator < (const string&).

Susan: Why are you bringing up this stuff about what the operator looks like and the way it is defined? Do you mean that is what is really happening behind the curtain even though it looks like built in code?

Steve: Yes.

Susan: How do those null bytes get into memory? Who puts them there?

Steve: The compiler supplies a null byte automatically at the end of every literal string, such as "abc".

Susan: I don't get where you say you are not using a null byte when storing the length. . . it looks to me that you are. This is confusing. Ugh.

Problem
Algorithms
C++
Executable
Hardware

Steve: I understand why that's confusing, I think. I am including the null byte at the end of a string when we create it from a literal C string, so that we can mix our strings with C strings more readily; however, because we store the length separately, it's possible to construct a string that has null bytes in the middle of it as well as at the end. This is not possible with a C string, because that has no explicit length stored with it; instead, the routines that operate on C strings assume that when they get to a null byte, the C string is finished.

Susan: Why do you jump from a null byte to a *t*? Didn't it run out of letters? Is this what you mean by retrieving data from the next location in memory? Why was a *t* there?

Steve: Yes, this is an example of retrieving random information from the next location in memory. We got a *t* because that just happened to be there. The problem is that since we're using an explicit length rather than a null byte to indicate the end of our strings, we can't count on a null byte stopping the comparison correctly. Thus, we have to worry about handling the case where there is a null byte in the middle of a string.

Now that we've examined why the algorithm for operator < works the way it does, Figure 8.20 shows one way to implement it.

```
bool string::operator < (const string& Str)
{
      short i;
      bool Result;
      bool ResultFound;
      short CompareLength;

    if (Str.m_Length < m_Length)
         CompareLength = Str.m_Length;
    else
         CompareLength = m_Length;

    ResultFound = false;
    for (i = 0; (i < CompareLength) && (ResultFound == false); i ++)
            {
            if (m_Data[i] < Str.m_Data[i])
                   {
                   Result = true;
                   ResultFound = true;
                   }
            else
                   {
                   if (m_Data[i] > Str.m_Data[i])
                          {
                          Result = false;
                          ResultFound = true;
                          }
                   }
            }

        if (ResultFound == false)
           {
           if (m_Length < Str.m_Length)
                  Result = true;
           else
                  Result = false;
           }

      return Result;
};
```

```
Problem
Algorithms
C++
Executable
Hardware
```

Figure 8.20: The implementation of operator < for strings (from code\string5a.cc)

The variables we'll use in this function are:

1. i, which is used as a loop counter in the for loop that steps through all of the characters to be compared.
2. Result, which is used to hold the true or false value that we'll return to the caller.
3. ResultFound, which we'll use to keep track of whether we've found the result yet.
4. CompareLength, which we'll use to determine the number of characters to compare in the two strings.

It will probably be easier to understand the code if we follow an example, and I've written a program called strtst5x.cc for this purpose. Figure 8.21 has the code for that program.

```
#include <iostream.h>
#include "string5.h"

int main()
{
    string x;
    string y;

    x = "ape";
    y = "axes";

    if (x < y)
       cout << x << " comes before " << y << endl;
    else
       cout << x << " doesn't come before " << y << endl;

    return 0;
}
```

Problem
Algorithms
C++
Executable
Hardware

Figure 8.21: Using operator < for strings (code\strtst5x.cc)

You can see that in this program the two strings being compared are "ape" and "axes", which are assigned to strings x and y respectively. As we've already discussed, the compiler translates a comparison between two strings into a call to the function string::operator <(const string Str&); in this case, the line that does that comparison is if (x < y).

Now back to our implementation of operator < in Figure 8.20. After variable definition, the next four lines of the code determine how many characters from each string we actually have to compare; the value of CompareLength is set to the lesser of the lengths of our string and the string referred to by Str. In this case, that value is 4, the length of our string (including the terminating null byte).

Now we're ready to do the comparison. This takes the form of a for loop that steps through all of the characters to be compared in each string. The header of the for loop is for (i = 0; (i < CompareLength) && (ResultFound == false); i ++). The first and last part of the expression controlling the for loop should be familiar by now; we're setting i, the index variable, to 0, and incrementing i each time through the loop. But what about the continuation expression (i < CompareLength) && (ResultFound == false)?

For Better or Worse?

What we're doing here is specifying a two-part condition for continuing the loop. The first part, (i < CompareLength), is the usual condition that allows the program to execute the loop as long as the index variable is within the correct range. The second part, (ResultFound == false) should also be fairly clear; we want to test whether we've already found the result we're looking for, and continue only as long as that isn't the case (i.e., ResultFound is still false). The () around each of these expressions are used to tell the compiler that we want to evaluate each of these expressions first, before the && is applied to their results. That leaves the && symbol as the only mystery.

It's really not too mysterious. The && operator is the symbol for the "logical AND" operation, which means that we want to combine the truth or falsity of two expressions each of which has a logical value of true or false. The result of using && to combine the results of these two expressions will also be a logical value. Here is the way the value of that expression is determined:

1. If both of the expressions connected by the && are true, then the value of the expression containing the && is also true;
2. Otherwise, the value of the expression containing the && will be false.

If you think about it for a minute, this should be comprehensible. We want to continue the loop as long as both of the conditions are true; that is,

1. i is less than CompareLength; *and*

Problem
Algorithms
C++
Executable
Hardware

2.   ResultFound is false (i.e, we haven't found what we're looking for yet).

That's why the && operator is called *logical AND*; it checks whether condition 1 *and* condition 2 are both true. If either one is false, we want to stop the loop, and this continuation expression will do just that.

Now let's trace the path of execution through the for loop in Figure 8.20. On the first time through the loop, the index i is 0 and ResultFound is false. Therefore, the continuation expression allows us to execute the statements in the loop, where we test whether the current character in the current string, m_Data[i], is less than the corresponding character from the string Str, Str.m_Data[i].

By the way, in case the expression in the if statement doesn't make sense immediately, perhaps I should remind you that the array notation m_Data[i] means the ith character of the data pointed to by m_Data; an index value of 0 means the first element, as is always the case when using a C array. We've already covered this starting on page 387; you should go back and reread that section if you're not comfortable with the equivalence between pointers and arrays.

Problem
Algorithms
C++
Executable
Hardware

The code in Figure 8.22 compares the characters from the two strings.

```
if (m_Data[i] < Str.m_Data[i])
    {
    Result = true;
    ResultFound = true;
    }
```

Figure 8.22: Is our character less than the other one? (from code\string5a.cc)

In the event that the current character in our string is indeed less than the corresponding character in Str, we have our answer: Our string is less than the other string. If that were the case, we would set Result to true and ResultFound to true, and we would be finished with this execution of the for loop.

As it happens, in our current example both m_Data[0] and Str.m_Data[0] are equal to *a*, so they're equal to each other as well. What happens when the character from our string is the same as the one from the string Str?

In that case, the first if, whose condition is stated as if (m_Data[i] < Str.m_Data[i]), is false. So we continue with the else clause of that if statement, which looks like Figure 8.23.

```
else
    {
    if (m_Data[i] > Str.m_Data[i])
        {
        Result = false;
        ResultFound = true;
        }
    }
```

Figure 8.23: The else clause in the comparison loop (from code\string5a.cc)

This clause contains another if statement that compares the character from our string to the one from Str. Since the two characters are the same, this if also comes out false, so the controlled block of the if isn't executed. After this if statement, we've reached the end of the controlled block of the for statement. The next iteration of the for loop starts by incrementing i to 1. Then the continuation expression is evaluated again; i is still less than CompareLength, and ResultFound is still false, so we execute the controlled block of the loop again with i equal to 1.

On this pass through the for loop, m_Data[1], the character from our string, is p, and Str.m_Data[1], the character from the other string, is x. Therefore, the condition in the first if statement (that the character from our string is less than the character from the other string) is true, so we execute the controlled block of the if statement; this sets Result to true, and ResultFound also to true, as you can see in Figure 8.22.

We're now at the end of the for loop, so we return to the for statement to continue execution. First, i is incremented again, to 2. Then the continuation expression (i < CompareLength) && (ResultFound == false) is evaluated. The first part of the condition, i < CompareLength is true, since i is 2 and CompareLength is 4. However, the second part of the condition, ResultFound == false, is false, because we've just set ResultFound to true. Since the result of the && operator is true only when both subconditions are true, the for loop terminates, passing control to the next statement after the controlled block of the loop (Figure 8.24).

```
if (ResultFound == false)
    {
    if (m_Length < Str.m_Length)
        Result = true;
    else
        Result = false;
    }
```

Figure 8.24: Handling the return value (from code\string5a.cc)

In the current scenario, ResultFound is true because we have found a character from m_Data that differs from the corresponding character from Str.m_Data; therefore, the condition in the first if is false, and we proceed to the next statement. That statement is return Result;. This shouldn't come as too much of a surprise; we know the answer to the comparison, namely, that our string is less than the other string, so we're ready to tell the caller the information that he requested by calling our routine.

A Greater Cause

The path of execution is almost exactly the same if, the first time we find a mismatch between the two strings, the character from our string is greater than the character from the other string. The only difference is that the if statement that handles this scenario sets Result to false rather than true (Figure 8.23), because our string is not less than the other string; of course, it still sets ResultFound to true, since we know the result that will be returned.

Problem
Algorithms
C++
Executable
Hardware

There's only one other possibility: That the two strings are the same up to the length of the shorter one (e.g., "post" and "poster"). In that case, the for loop will expire of natural causes when i gets to be greater than or equal to CompareLength. Then the final if statement shown in Figure 8.24 will evaluate to true, because ResultFound is still false. In this case, if the length of our string is less than the length of the other string, we will set Result to true, because a shorter string will precede a longer one in the dictionary if the two strings are the same up to the length of the shorter one.

Otherwise, we'll set Result to false, because our string is at least as long as the other one; since they're equal up to the length of the shorter one, our string can't precede the other string. In this case, either they're identical, or our string is longer than the other one and therefore should follow it. Either of these two conditions means that the result of operator < is false, so that's what we tell the caller via our return value.

Simple Pleasures

This implementation of operator < for strings definitely works. However, there's a much simpler way to do it. Figure 8.25 shows the code.

```
bool string::operator < (const string& Str)
{
    short Result;
    short CompareLength;

    if (Str.m_Length < m_Length)
        CompareLength = Str.m_Length;
    else
        CompareLength = m_Length;

    Result = memcmp(m_Data,Str.m_Data,CompareLength);
    if (Result < 0)
        return true;
    else if (Result > 0)
        return false;
    else if (m_Length < Str.m_Length)
        return true;
    else
        return false;
};
```

Figure 8.25: Implementing operator < for strings (from code\string5.cc)

This starts out in the same way as our previous version, by figuring out how much of the two strings we actually need to compare character by character. Right after that calculation, though, the code is very different; where's that big for loop?

Problem
Algorithms
C++
Executable
Hardware

It's contained in the standard library function memcmp, a carryover from C, which does exactly what that for loop did for us. Although C doesn't have the kind of strings that we're implementing here, it does have primitive facilities for dealing with arrays of characters, including comparing one array with another, character by character. One type of character array supported by C is the C string, which we've already encountered. However, C strings have a serious drawback for our purposes here, their use of a null byte to mark the end of a group of characters. This isn't suitable for our strings, whose length is explicitly stored; as noted previously, our strings could theoretically have null bytes in them. There are several C functions that compare C strings, but they rely on the null byte for their proper operation, so we can't use them.

However, these limitations of C strings are so evident that the library writers have supplied another set of functions that act almost identically to the ones used for C strings, except that they don't rely on null bytes to determine how much data to process. Instead, whenever you use one of these functions, you have to tell it how many characters to manipulate. In this case, we're calling memcmp, which compares two C arrays of characters up to a specified length. The first argument is the first array to be compared (corresponding to our string), the second argument is the second array to be compared (corresponding to the string Str), and the third argument is the length for which the two arrays are to be compared. The return value from memcmp is calculated by the following rules:

1. It's less than 0 if the first array would precede the second in the dictionary;
2. It's 0 if they are the same up to the length specified;
3. It's greater than 0 if the first array would follow the second in the dictionary.

This is very convenient for us, because if the return value from memcmp is less than 0, we know that our result will be true, while if the return value from memcmp is greater than 0, then our result will be false. The only complication, which isn't very complicated, is that if the return value from memcmp is 0, meaning that the two arrays are the same up to the length of the shorter character array, we have to see which is longer. If the first one is shorter, then it precedes the second one; therefore, our result is true. Otherwise, it's false.

Susan had some questions about this version of operator <, including why we had to go through the previous exercise, if we could just use memcmp.

Problem
Algorithms
C++
Executable
Hardware

> **Susan**: What is this? I suppose there was a purpose to all the confusing prior discussion if you have an easier way of defining operator <? UGH! This new stuff just pops up out of the blue! What is going on? Please explain the reason for the earlier torture.
>
> **Steve**: I thought it would be better to go through the character-by-character version of operator < before taking the shortcut. For one thing, that should make it easier to follow the explanation of the "string overrun" problem, as each character comparison shows up in the code.
>
> **Susan**: So, memcmp is another library function, and does it stand for memory compare? Also, are the return values are built into memcmp? This is very confusing, because you have return values in the code.
>
> **Steve**: Yes, memcmp stands for "memory compare". As for return values: yes, it has them, but they aren't exactly the ones that we want. We have to return the value true for "less than" and false for "not less than", which aren't the values that memcmp returns. Also, memcmp doesn't do the whole job when the strings aren't the same length; in that case, we have to handle the trailing part of the longer string manually.

One small point that shouldn't be overlooked is that in this version of the operator < code, we have more than one return statement; in fact, we have four! That's perfectly legal and should be clear to a reader of this function. It's usually not a good idea to scatter return statements around in a large function, because it's easy to overlook them when trying to follow the flow of control through the function. In this case, though, that's not likely to be a problem; any reasonably fluent reader of C++ code will find this organization easy to understand.

Equalization of Opportunity

Although our current task requires only operator <, another comparison operator, operator ==, will make an interesting contrast in implementation; in addition, a concrete data type that allows comparisons should really implement more than just operator <. Since we've just finished one comparison operator, we might as well knock this one off now (Figure 8.26).

```
bool string::operator == (const string& Str)
{
    short Result;
    if (m_Length != Str.m_Length)
        return false;

    Result = memcmp(m_Data,Str.m_Data,m_Length);
    if (Result == 0)
        return true;
    else
        return false;
};
```

Problem
Algorithms
C++
Executable
Hardware

Figure 8.26: Implementing operator == for strings (from code\string5.cc)

This function is considerably simpler than the previous one. Why is this, since they have almost the same purpose? It's because in this case we don't care which of the two strings is greater than the other, just whether they're the same or different. Therefore, we don't have to worry about comparing the two char arrays if they're of different lengths. Two arrays of different lengths can't be the same, so we can just return false. Once we have determined that the two arrays are the same length, we do the comparison via memcmp. This gives us the answer directly, because if Result is 0, then the two strings are equal; otherwise, they're different.

Even though this function is simpler than operator <, it's not simple enough to avoid Susan's probing eye:

Susan: Does == only check to see if the lengths of the arrays are the same? Can it not ever be used for a value?

Steve: It compares the values in the arrays, but only if they are the same length. Since all it cares about is whether they are equal, and arrays of different length can't be equal, it doesn't have to compare the character data unless the arrays are of the same length.

Displaying Expertise

Before moving on to see how we will display a string on the screen via operator <<, I should bring up a couple of points here, because otherwise they might pass you by. First, we didn't have to change our interface header file string5.h (Figure 8.17) just because we changed the implementation of operator <. Since the *signature* of this function didn't change, neither the header file nor the user program had to change. Second, we didn't even implement operator == in the string5a.cc version of the string library and yet our test program still compiled without difficulty. How can this be?

Problem
Algorithms
C++
Executable
Hardware

In C++, you can declare all of the functions you want to, whether they are member functions or global functions, without actually defining them. As long as no one tries to actually use the functions, everything will work fine. In fact, the compiler doesn't even care whether any functions you *do* refer to are available; that's up to the linker to worry about. This is very handy when you know that you're going to add functions in a later revision of a class, as was the case here. Of course, you should warn your class users if you have listed functions in the interface header file that aren't available. It's true that they'll find out about the missing functions the first time they try to link a program that uses one of these functions, because the linker will report that it can't find the function; however, if they've spent a lot of time writing a program using one of these functions, they're likely to get mad at you for misleading them. So let them know what's actually implemented and what's "for later".

Now let's continue with our extensions to the string class, by looking at how we send a string out to the screen.

Down by the Old cout Stream

We've been using cout and its operator << for quite awhile now, but have just taken them for granted. Now we have to look under the hood a bit.

The first question is what type of object cout is. The answer is that it's an ostream (short for "output stream"), which is an object that you can use to send characters to some output device. I'm not sure of the origin of this term, but you can imagine that you push the characters out into a "stream" that leads to the output device.

As you may recall from our uses of cout, you can chain a bunch of << expressions together in one statement, as in Figure 8.27.

```
#include <iostream.h>

int main()
{
    short x;
    char y;

    x = 1;
    y = 'A';

    cout << "On test #" << x << ", your mark is: " << y << endl;

    return 0;
}
```

Problem
Algorithms
C++
Executable
Hardware

Figure 8.27: Chaining several operator << expressions together
(code\cout1.cc)

If you compile and execute that program, it will produce the following output:

On test #1, your mark is: A

Notice that it displays the short as a number and the char as a letter, just as we want it to do. This desirable event occurs because there's a separate version of << for each type of data that can be displayed; in other words, operator << uses function overloading, just like the constructors for the StockItem class and the string class. We'll also use function overloading to add support for our string class to the I/O facilities supplied by the iostreams library.

Gently Down the Stream

Before we examine how to accomplish this goal, though, we'll have to go into some detail about how the pre-existing output functions behave. Let's start with a simple case using a version of operator << supplied by the iostream.h header file. The simplest possible use of ostream's operator <<, of course, uses only one occurrence of the operator. Here's an example where the value is a char:

cout << 'a';

As you may remember, using an operator such as << on an object is always equivalent to a "normal" function call. This particular example is equivalent to the following:

cout.operator << ('a');

which calls ostream::operator << (char) (i.e.,the version of the operator << member function of the iostream class that takes a char as its input) for the predefined destination cout, which writes the char on the screen.

Problem
Algorithms
C++
Executable
Hardware

That takes care of the single occurrence of operator <<. However, as we've already seen, it's possible to string together any number of occurrences of operator <<, with the output of each successive occurrence following the output created by the one to its left. We want our string output function to behave just like the ones predefined in iostream.h, so let's look next at an example that illustrates multiple uses of operator <<, taking a char and a C string:

cout << 'a' << " string";

This is equivalent to

(cout.operator << ('a')).operator << (" string");

What does this mean? Well, since an expression in parentheses is evaluated before one outside the parentheses, the first thing that happens is that ostream::operator << (char) is called for the predefined destination cout, which writes the *a* to the screen. Now here's the tricky part: the return value from every version of ostream::operator << is a reference to the ostream that it operates on (cout, in this case). Therefore, after the *a* has been written on the screen, the former expression reduces to this:

cout.operator << (" string");

That is, the next output operation behaves exactly like the first one. In this case, ostream::operator << (char*) is the function called, because char* is the type of the argument to be written out. It too returns a reference to the ostream for which it was called, so that any further << calls can add their data to that same ostream. It should be fairly obvious how the same process can be extended to handle any number of items to be displayed.

Friends of Global Progress

That illustrates how the designers of ostream could create member functions that would behave in this convenient way. However, we can't use the same mechanism that they did; we can't modify the definition of the ostream class in the library, because we didn't write it in the first place and don't have access to its source code.[9] Does that mean that we can't give our strings convenient input and output facilities?

In fact, we can. To do this, we create a *global* function called operator << that accepts an ostream& (that is, a reference to an ostream), adds the contents of our string to the ostream, and then returns a reference to the same ostream. This will support multiple occurrences of operator << to be chained together in one statement, just as with the operator << member functions from the iostreams library. We can see the implementation of this function in Figure 8.28.

```
ostream& operator << (ostream& S, const string& Str)
{
        short i;
        for (i=0; i < Str.m_Length-1; i ++)
                S << Str.m_Data[i];

        return S;
};
```

Figure 8.28: An operator << function to output a string (from code\string5.cc)

Problem
Algorithms
C++
Executable
Hardware

---

9. Even if we did have the source code to the ostream class, we wouldn't want to modify it, for a number of reasons. One excellent reason is that every time a new version of the library came out, we'd have to make our changes again. Also, there are other ways to reuse the code from the library for our own purposes; unfortunately, these mechanisms are beyond the scope of this book.

As usual, we should first examine the function declaration; in this case, a couple of points are worth noting. We've already seen that the first argument is an ostream&, to which we will add the characters from the string that's the second argument. Also notice that the second argument is a const string&, that is, a reference to a constant string. This is the best way to declare this argument because we aren't going to change the argument, and there's no reason to make a copy of it.

But possibly the most important point about the function declaration is that this operator << is *not* a member function of the string class, which explains why it isn't called string::operator <<. It's a global function that can be called anywhere in a program that needs to use it, so long as that program has included the header file that defines it. Its operation is pretty simple: It simply calls ostream::operator << (char), which writes out each character from the C array called m_Data that we use to store the data for our string. Since there is no ostream function to write out a specified number of characters from a char array, we have to call ostream::operator << (char) for each character in the C array.[10] After all the characters have been written to the ostream, we return it so that the next operator << call in the line can continue producing output.

However, there's a loose end here. How can a global function, which by definition isn't a member function of class string, get at the internal workings of a string? We declared that m_Length and m_Data were private, so that they wouldn't be accessible to just any old function that wandered along to look at them. Is nothing sacred?

Problem
Algorithms
C++
Executable
Hardware

Members and Friends Only

In fact, private data aren't accessible to just any function. However, operator << (ostream&, const string&) isn't just any function. Take a look at string5.h in Figure 8.17 to see why. The line we're interested in here is this one:

friend ostream& operator << (ostream& S, const string& Str);

The key word here is friend. We're telling the compiler that a function with the signature ostream& operator << (ostream&, const string&) is

---

10. In case it's not obvious that we're calling ostream::operator <<(char) here, it's because S is an ostream&, which is just another name for the ostream that is the first argument to this function.

permitted to access the information normally reserved for member functions of the string class; that is, anything marked private. It's possible to make an entire class a friend to another class; here, we're specifying one function that is a friend to this class.[11]

You probably won't be surprised to learn that Susan had some questions about this operator. Let's see how the discussion went:

Susan: Let's start with friend. . . what is that?

Steve: A friend is a function or class that is allowed to access internals of this class, as though the friend were a member function. In other words, the private access specifier doesn't have any effect on friends.

Susan: What is an ostream?

Steve: An ostream is a stream that is used for output; streams can be either input (istream) or output (ostream).

Susan: This stream character seems to have a lot of relatives.

Steve: You're right; there are lots of classes in the stream family, including istream, ostream, ifstream, and ofstream.

Problem
Algorithms
C++
Executable
Hardware

That explains why this global function can access our private data. But why did we have to create a global function in the first place, rather than just adding a member function to our string class?

Because a member function of a class has to be called for an object of that class, whose address then becomes the this pointer; in the case of the << operator, the class of the object is ostream, not string. Figure 8.29 is an example.

```
string x = "this is it";

cout << x;
```

Figure 8.29: Why we need a global function for operator <<

The line cout << x; is the same as cout.operator << (x);. Notice that the object to which the operator << call is applied is cout, not x. Since cout is an ostream, not a string, we can't use a member function of string to do our output, but a global function is perfectly suitable.

---

11. The signature of the function is important here, as elsewhere in C++; this friend declaration would not permit a function with the same name and a different signature, for example ostream& operator << (ostream&, int) to access private members of string.

Before we move on to our next topic, one little point in the implementation of operator << for strings could use some more explanation: Why is the loop continuation expression i < Str.m_Length–1;? The reason is that the stored length of the string (m_Length) includes the null byte at the end of the string; thus, if we write out all the bytes indicated by the length, we'll include the null byte as well. This would work all right if we were writing the data out to the screen, because we can't read the data back from the screen. However, it would cause trouble if we wrote the data to a file and then tried to reread the data later, as we did in the StockItem class (see the discussion starting on page 272). Therefore, we have to be careful to avoid writing the null byte.

Reader and Advisor

Now that we have an output function that will write our string variables out to an ostream like cout, it would be very handy to have an input function that could read a string in from an istream like cin. You might expect that this would be pretty simple now that we've worked through the previous exercise, and you'd be mostly right. As usual, though, there are a few twists in the path.

Problem
Algorithms
C++
Executable
Hardware

Let's start by looking at the code in Figure 8.30.

```
istream& operator >> (istream& S, string& Str)
{
        const short BUFLEN = 256;

        char Buf[BUFLEN];
        memset(Buf,0,BUFLEN);

        if (S.peek() == '\n')
                S.ignore();
        S.getline(Buf,BUFLEN,'\n');
        Str = Buf;

        return S;
};
```

Figure 8.30: A operator >> function to input a string (from code\string5.cc)

The header is pretty similar to the one from the operator << function, which is reasonable, since they're complementary functions. In this case, we're defining a global function with the signature istream& operator >> (istream& S, string& Str). In other words, this function, called operator >>, has a first argument that is a reference to an istream, which is just like an ostream except that we read data from it rather than writing data to it. One significant difference between this function signature and the one for operator << is that the second argument is a reference, *not* a const reference, to the string into which we want to read the data from the istream. That's because the whole purpose of this function is to modify the string passed in as the second argument; to be exact, we're going to fill it in with the characters taken out of the istream.

Continuing with the analysis of the function declaration, the return value is another istream reference, which is passed to the next operator >> function to the right, if there is one; otherwise it will just be discarded.

After decoding the header, let's move to the first line in the function body, const short BUFLEN = 256;. While we've encountered const before, specifying that we aren't going to change an argument passed to us, that can't be the meaning here. What does const mean in this context?

It specifies that the item being defined, which in this case is short BUFLEN, isn't a variable, but a constant, or const value.[12] That is, its value can't be changed. Of course, a logical question is how we can use a const, if we can't set its value.

Problem
Algorithms
C++
Executable
Hardware

Initial Here

This is one of the places where it's important to differentiate between *initialization* and *assignment*. We can't assign a value to a const, but we can initialize it; in fact, because an uninitialized const is useless, the attempt to define a const without specifying its initial value is a compile-time error. In this case, we're initializing it to the value 256; if we just wrote const short BUFLEN;, we'd get an error something like the one in Figure 8.31 when we tried to compile it.

```
gcc -c -I. -g string5x.cc
string5x.cc: In function 'class istream & operator >>(class istream &, class string &)':
string5x.cc:84: uninitialized const 'short int BUFLEN'
```

Figure 8.31: Error from an uninitialized const (code\string5x.out)

---

12. In case you were wondering how I came up with the name BUFLEN, it's short for "buffer length". Also, I should mention the reason that it is all caps rather than mixed case or all lower case: there is an old C convention (carried over into C++) that named constants should be named in all caps to enable the reader to distinguish them from variables at a glance.

Susan wanted some further explanation.

Susan: I still don't get why const is used here.

Steve: This is a different use of const than we've seen before; in this case, it's an instruction to the compiler meaning "the following 'variable' isn't really variable, but constant. Don't allow it to be modified." This allows us to use it where we would otherwise have to use a literal constant, like 256 itself. The reason that using a const is better than using a literal constant is that it makes it easier to change all the occurrences of that value. In the present case, for example, we use BUFLEN three times after its definition; if we used the literal constant 256 in all of those places, we'd have to change all of them if we decided to make the buffer larger or smaller. As it is, however, we only have to change the definition of BUFLEN, and all of the places where it's used will use the new value automatically.

Susan: Okay, I think I have it now.

Problem
Algorithms
C++
Executable
Hardware

Now that we've disposed of that detail, let's continue with our examination of the implementation of operator >>. The next nonblank line is char Buf[BUFLEN];. This is a little different from any variable definition we've seen before; however, you might be able to guess something about it from its appearance. It seems to be defining a variable called Buf[13] whose type is related in some way to char. But what about the [BUFLEN] part?

This is a definition of a variable of that dreaded type, the *array*; specifically, we're defining an array called Buf, which contains BUFLEN chars. As you may recall, this is somewhat like the vector type that we've used before, except that it has absolutely no error checking; if we try to access a char that is past the end of the array, something will happen, but not anything good.[14] In this case, as in our previous use of pointers, we'll use this dangerous construct only in a very small part of our code, under controlled circumstances; the user of our string class won't be exposed to the array. We'll see how it's used in this function.

First, though, I should point out that there's a rule in C++ that says that the number of elements of an array has to be known at compile time. That is, the program in Figure 8.32 isn't legal C++.

---

13. This is another common C practice; using "buf" as shorthand for "buffer", or "place to store stuff while we're working on it".

14. This is covered in the discussion starting on page 385.

```
#include <iostream.h>
#include "string.h"
#include "string5.h"

istream& operator >> (istream& S, string& Str)
{
    short BUFLEN = 256;

    char Buf[BUFLEN];
    char ch;

    memset(Buf,0,BUFLEN);
    cin.get(Buf,BUFLEN,'\n');
    cin.get(ch);
    Str = Buf;

    return S;

};
```

Figure 8.32: Use of a non-const array size (code\string5y.cc)

I'll admit that I don't understand exactly why using a non-const array size is illegal; a C++ compiler has enough information to create and access an array whose length is known at run time.[15] In fact, the DJGPP compiler supplied with this book by default does accept this construct: You have to set a special *warning option* (*pedantic-errors*) to treat this as an error. I've added this option to the batch file mknorm.bat, which you can use to compile your programs. Figure 8.33 shows the output that you would get if you used that batch file to compile the program in Figure 8.32.

```
Problem
Algorithms
C++
Executable
Hardware
```

```
gcc -o string5y.o -c -I. -g string5y.cc -pedantic-errors
string5y.cc: In function 'class istream & operator >>(class istream &, class
string &)':
string5y.cc:9: ANSI C++ forbids variable-size array 'Buf'
```

Figure 8.33: Trying to compile a program with a non-const array size
(code\string5y.out)

Although the ability to declare an array whose size isn't known until run time is sometimes very convenient and is provided by the DJGPP

---

15. According to Eric Raymond, a well-known historian of programming and the author of *The New Hacker's Dictionary*, there is no good reason for this limitation; it's a historical artifact.

compiler, you should avoid it. No other compiler I'm familiar with will accept this construct; it also won't be part of the C++ standard, so when such compilers are available, they won't accept it either.

Therefore, we'll use the const value BUFLEN to specify the number of chars in the array Buf, by the statement char Buf[BUFLEN];.

Pointers and Setters

Now we're up to the executable part of the function, where the first line is memset(Buf,0,BUFLEN);. This is a call to a function called memset, which is in the standard C library. You may be able to guess from its name that it is related to the function memcmp that we used to compare two arrays of chars. If so, your guess would be correct; memset is C-talk for "set all the bytes in an area of memory to the same value". The first argument is the address of the area of memory to be set to the value, the second argument is the char value to be used, and the third argument is the number of characters to be set to that value, starting at the address given in the first argument. In other words, we're setting all of the characters in the array called Buf to 0. This is important because we're going to treat that array as a C string later. As you may recall, a C string is terminated by a null byte, so we want to make sure that no junk is lying around in the array Buf, which would be misinterpreted as part of the data we're reading in from the istream.

Next, we have an if statement:

```
if (S.peek() == '\n')
    S.ignore();
```

What exactly does this do? It solves a problem with reading C string data from a file; namely, where do we stop reading? With a numeric variable, that's easy; the answer is "whenever we see a character that doesn't look like part of a number". However, with a data type that can take just about any characters as part of its value, this is more difficult. The solution adopted in C++ was to stop reading when we get to a newline ('\n') character; that is, an end-of-line character. This is no problem when reading from the keyboard, as long as each data item is on its own line, but what about reading from a file?

When we read a C string from a file, the newline at the end of the line is discarded, so the next C string to be read in starts at the beginning of the next line of the file, as we wish. This approach to handling newline characters works well as long as all of the variables

(margin note)
Problem
Algorithms
C++
Executable
Hardware

being read in are strings. However, in the case of the StockItem class, we needed to be able to mix shorts and strings in the file. In that case, reading a value for a short stops at the newline, because that character isn't a valid part of a numeric value. This is OK as long as the next variable to be read is also a short, because spaces and newlines at the beginning of a line are ignored when we're reading a numeric value. However, when the next variable to be read is a string, the leftover newline from the previous read is interpreted as the beginning of the data for the string, which messes up everything. Therefore, we have to check whether the next available char in the input stream is a newline, in which case we have to skip it. On the other hand, if the next character to be read in is something other than a newline, we want to keep it as the first character of our string. That's what the if statement does: the S.peek() function returns the next character in the input stream without removing it from the stream; then, if it turns out to be a newline, we tell the input stream to ignore it, so it won't mess up our reading of the actual data in the next line.

You won't be surprised to hear that Susan had a couple of questions about this function.

Problem
Algorithms
C++
Executable
Hardware

> **Susan**: Where do peek and ignore come from?
>
> **Steve**: They're defined in the iostreams header file iostream.h.
>
> **Susan**: How did you know that they were available?
>
> **Steve**: By reading a book called *C++ IOstreams Handbook* by Steve Teale.

Now that we've dealt with that detail, we're ready to read the data for our string. That's the job of the next line in the function: S.getline(Buf,BUFLEN,'\n');. Since S is an istream, this is a member function of istream. To be precise, it's the member function that reads a number of characters into a char array. The arguments are as follows:

1. The array into which to read characters
2. The number of characters that the array can contain
3. The "terminating character", where getline should stop reading characters

This function will read characters into the array (in this case Buf) until one of two events occurs:

1.   The size of the array is reached
2.   The "terminating character" is the next character to be read

Note that the terminating character is not read into the array.

Before continuing with the rest of the code for operator >>, let's take a closer look at the following two lines, so we can see why it's a bad idea to use the C string and memory manipulation library any more than we have to. The lines in question are

```
memset(Buf,0,BUFLEN);
S.getline(Buf,BUFLEN,'\n');
```

The problem is that we have to specify the length of the array Buf explicitly (as BUFLEN, in this case). In this small function, we can keep track of that length without much effort, but in a large program with many references to Buf, it would be all too easy to make a mistake in specifying its length. As we've already seen, the result of specifying a length that is greater than the actual length of the array would be a serious error in the functioning of the program; namely, some memory belonging to some other variable would be overwritten. Whenever we use the mem functions in the C library, we're liable to run into such problems, which is a good reason to avoid them except in strictly controlled situations, such as the present one, where the definition of the array is in the same small function as the uses of the array. By no coincidence, this is the same problem caused by the indiscriminate use of pointers; the difficulty with the C memory manipulation functions is that they use pointers (or arrays, which are essentially interchangeable with pointers), with all of the hazards that such use entails.

Now that I've nagged you sufficiently about the dangers of C arrays, let's look at the rest of the operator >> code. The next statement is Str = Buf;, which sets the argument Str to the contents of the array Buf. Buf is the address of the first char in an array of chars, so its type is char*; Str, on the other hand, is a string. Therefore, this apparently innocent assignment statement actually calls string::string(char*) to make a temporary string, and then calls string::operator=(const string&) to copy that temporary string to Str.[16]

Finally, we have the statement return S;. This simply returns the same istream that we got as an argument, so that the next input operator in the same statement can continue reading from the istream where we left off.

Problem
Algorithms
C++
Executable
Hardware

---

16. The details of this sequence can be found starting on page 376.

Now our strings can be read in from an input stream (such as cin) and written out to an output stream (such as cout), so our program that sorts strings can do some useful work.[17] To see how it works, change to the normal directory, type strsort1 and follow the directions.

Now that we've finished our improvements to the string class, it's time to look back at what we've covered since our first review in this chapter.

Second Review

After finishing up the requirements to make the string class a concrete data type, we continued to add more facilities to the string class; to be precise, we wanted to make it possible to modify the sorting program of Chapter 4 to handle strings rather than shorts. To do this, we had to be able to compare two strings to determine which of the two would come first in the dictionary and to read strings from an input stream (like cin) and write them to an output stream (like cout). Although the Display function provided a primitive mechanism for writing a string to cout, it's much nicer to be able to use the standard >> and << operators that can handle all of the native types, so we resolved to make those available for strings as well.

We started out by implementing the < operator so that we could compare two strings x and y to see which would come before the other in the dictionary, simply by writing if (x < y). The implementation of this function turned out to be a bit complicated because of the possibility of "running off the end" of one of the strings, when the strings are of different lengths.

Once we worked out the appropriate handling for this situation, we examined two implementations of the algorithm for operator <. The first compared characters from the two strings one at a time, while the second used memcmp, a C function that compares two sets of bytes and returns a different value depending on whether the first one is

Problem
Algorithms
C++
Executable
Hardware

---

17. The implementation of operator << will also work for any other output destination, such as a file; however, our current implementation of operator >> isn't really suitable for reading a string in from an arbitrary input source. The reason is that we're counting on the input data being able to fit into the Buf array, which is 256 bytes in length. This is fine for input from the keyboard, at least under DOS, because the maximum line length in that situation is 128 characters. It will also work for our inventory file, because the lines in that file are shorter than 256 bytes. However, there's no way to limit the length of lines in any old data file we might want to read from, so this won't do as a general solution.

Of course, increasing the size of the Buf array wouldn't solve the problem; no matter how large we make it, we couldn't be sure that a line from a file wouldn't be too long. The solution would be to handle long lines in sections; unfortunately, we don't have all of the infrastructure needed to implement that version of operator>>.

"less than", "equal to", or "greater than" the second one, using dictionary ordering to make this determination.

Then we developed an implementation of operator == for strings, which turned out to be considerably simpler than the second version of operator <, even though both functions used memcmp to do most of the work; the reason is that we have to compare the contents of the strings only if they are of the same length, because strings of different lengths are not equal.

Then we started looking beneath the covers of the output functions <<, starting with the predefined versions of << that handle char and C string arguments. The simplest case of using this operator, of course, is to display one expression on the screen via cout. Next, we examined the mechanism by which several uses of this operator can be chained together to allow the displaying of a number of expressions with one statement.

The next question was: How could we provide these handy facilities for the users of our string class? Would we have to modify the ostream classes to add support for strings? Luckily, the designers of the stream classes were foresightful enough to enable us to add support for our own data types without having to modify their code. The key is to create a *global* function that can add the contents of our string to an existing ostream variable and pass that ostream variable on to the next possible user, just as in the chaining mentioned previously for native types.

The implementation of this function wasn't terribly complicated; it merely wrote each char of the string's data to the output stream. The unusual part of this function was that it wasn't a member function of string, but a global function, as is needed to maintain the same syntax as the output of native types. We used the friend specifier to allow this version of operator << access to private members of string such as m_Length and m_Data.

After we finished the examination of our version of operator << for sending strings to an ostream, we went through the parallel exercise of creating a version of operator >> to read strings from an istream. This turned out to be a bit more complicated, since we had to make room for the incoming data, which limited the maximum length of string that we could read in. In the process of defining this maximum length, we also encountered a new construct, the const value. This is a data item that is declared just like a variable, except that its value is initialized once and cannot be changed, which makes it ideal for specifying a constant size for an array, a constant loop value, or other value that doesn't change from one execution of the program to the next.

Problem
Algorithms
C++
Executable
Hardware

Next, we used this const value to declare an *array* of chars to hold the input data to be stored in the string, and filled the array with null bytes, by calling the C function memset. We followed this by using some member functions of the istream class to eliminate any newline ('\n') character that might have been left over from a previous input operation.

Finally, we were ready to read the data into the array of chars, in preparation for assigning it to our string. After doing that assignment, we returned the original istream to the caller, to allow chaining of operations as is standard with operator << and operator >>.

That completes the review of this chapter. Now let's do some exercises to help it all sink in.

Exercises

1. What would happen if we compiled the program in Figure 8.34? Why?

```
class string
{
public:
    string();
    string(const string& Str);
    void operator = (const string& Str);
    ~string();
private:
    string(char* p);
    short m_Length;
    char* m_Data;
};

int main()
{
    string s;
    string n;
    string x;

    s = n;
    n = "My name is: ";

    x = n;
    return 0;
}
```

Problem
Algorithms
C++
Executable
Hardware

Figure 8.34: Exercise 1 (code\strex6.cc)

2.   We have already implemented operator < and operator ==. However, a concrete data type that allows for ordered comparisons such as < should really implement all six of the comparison operators. The other four of these operators are >, >=, <=, and != ("greater than", "greater than or equal to", "less than or equal to", and "not equal to", respectively). Add the declarations of each of these operators to the string interface definition.

3.   Implement the four comparison operators that you declared in the previous exercise.

4.   Write a test program to verify that all of the comparison operators work. This program should test that each of the operators returns the value true when its condition is true; equally important, it should test that each of the operators returns the value false when the condition is *not* true.

Conclusion

Problem
Algorithms
C++
Executable
Hardware

In this chapter, we have significantly improved the string class, learning some generally useful techniques and lessons in the process. Now it's time to wrap up this book, so once you finish doing the exercises, turn to Appendix A, where we'll tie up some loose ends, including some indications of your likely future path in learning more about C++.[18]

Answers to Exercises

1.   The output of the compiler should look something like this:[19]

```
strex6.cc: In function 'int main()':
strex6.cc:9: constructor 'string::string(char *)' is private
strex6.cc:21: within this context
strex6.cc:6: in passing argument 1 of 'string::operator =(const string &)'
```

---

18. You have been doing the exercises, haven't you? If not, you should definitely go back and do them. If you can get all of the answers right, including the reasons *why* the answers are the way they are, then you have a pretty firm grasp of the fundamentals of C++.

19. By the way, in case you're wondering what char * means, it's the same as char*. As I've mentioned previously, I prefer the latter as being easier to understand, but they mean the same to the compiler.

This one is a bit tricky. The actual problem is that making the constructor string::string(char*) private prevents the automatic conversion from char* to string required for the string::operator = (const string&) assignment operator to work. As long as there is an accessible string::string(char*) constructor, the compiler will use that constructor to build a temporary string from a char* argument on the right side of an =. This temporary string will then be used by string::operator = (const string&) as the source of data to modify the string on the left of the =. However, this is not possible if the constructor that makes a string from a char* isn't accessible where it is needed.

2.   The new class interface is shown in Figure 8.35.

```
class string
{
friend ostream& operator << (ostream& S, const string& Str);
friend istream& operator >> (istream& S, string& Str);
public:
    string();
    string(const string& Str);
    void operator = (const string& Str);
    ~string();
    string(char* p);
    short GetLength();
    bool operator < (const string& Str);
    bool operator == (const string& Str);
    bool operator > (const string& Str);
    bool operator >= (const string& Str);
    bool operator <= (const string& Str);
    bool operator != (const string& Str);
private:
    short m_Length;
    char* m_Data;
};
```

Problem
Algorithms
C++
Executable
Hardware

Figure 8.35: The string class interface file (code\string6.h)

3.   The implementations of the comparison operators are shown in Figure 8.36 through Figure 8.39.

```
bool string::operator > (const string& Str)
{
        short Result;

        if (Str.m_Length < CompareLength)
                CompareLength = Str.m_Length;
        else
                CompareLength = m_Length;

        Result = memcmp(m_Data,Str.m_Data,CompareLength);
        if (Result > 0)
                return true;
        else if (Result < 0)
                return false;
        else if (m_Length > Str.m_Length)
                return true;
        else
                Return false;
};
```

Figure 8.36: The string class implementation of operator > (from code\string6.cc)

Problem
Algorithms
C++
Executable
Hardware

```
bool string::operator >= (const string& Str)
{
        short Result;

        if (Str.m_Length < CompareLength)
                CompareLength = Str.m_Length;
        else
                CompareLength = m_Length;

        Result = memcmp(m_Data,Str.m_Data,CompareLength);
        if (Result > 0)
                return true;
        else if (Result < 0)
                return false;
        else if (m_Length >= Str.m_Length)
                return true;
        else
                return false;
};
```

Figure 8.37: The string class implementation of operator >= (from code\string6.cc)

```
bool string::operator <= (const string& Str)
{
        short Result;

        if (Str.m_Length < CompareLength)
                CompareLength = Str.m_Length;
        else
                CompareLength = m_Length;

        Result = memcmp(m_Data,Str.m_Data,CompareLength);
        if (Result < 0)
                return true;
        else if (Result > 0)
                return false;
        else if (m_Length <= Str.m_Length)
                return true;
        else
                return false;
};
```

Figure 8.38: The string class implementation of operator <= (from
code\string6.cc)

Problem
Algorithms
C++
Executable
Hardware

```
bool string::operator != (const string& Str)
{
        short Result;

        if (m_Length != Str.m_Length)
                return true;

        Result = memcmp(m_Data,Str.m_Data,m_Length);
        if (Result == 0)
                return false;
        else
                return true;
};
```

Figure 8.39: The string class implementation of operator != (from
code\string6.cc)

4.   The test program appears in Figure 8.40.

```
#include <iostream.h>
#include "string6.h"

int main()
{
    string x = "x";
    string xx = "xx";
    string y = "y";
    string yy = "yy";

// testing <
    if (x < x)
        cout << "ERROR: x < x" << endl;
    else
        cout << "OKAY: x NOT < x" << endl;
    if (x < xx)
        cout << "OKAY: x < xx" << endl;
    else
        cout << "ERROR: x NOT < xx" << endl;
    if (x < y)
        cout << "OKAY: x < y" << endl;
    else
        cout << "ERROR: x NOT < y" << endl;

// testing <=
    if (x <= x)
        cout << "OKAY: x <= x" << endl;
    else
        cout << "ERROR: x NOT <= x" << endl;
    if (x <= xx)
        cout << "OKAY: x <= xx" << endl;
    else
        cout << "ERROR: x NOT <= xx" << endl;
    if (x <= y)
        cout << "OKAY: x <= y" << endl;
    else
        cout << "ERROR: x NOT <= y" << endl;

// testing >
    if (y > y)
        cout << "ERROR: y > y" << endl;
    else
        cout << "OKAY: y NOT > y" << endl;
    if (yy > y)
        cout << "OKAY: yy > y" << endl;
    else
        cout << "ERROR: yy NOT > y" << endl;
    if (y > x)
        cout << "OKAY: y > x" << endl;
```

Problem
Algorithms
C++
Executable
Hardware

Figure 8.40: Testing the string class comparison operators (code\strcmp.cc)

```
        else
            cout << "ERROR: y NOT > x" << endl;

// testing >=
        if (y >= y)
            cout << "OKAY: y >= y" << endl;
        else
            cout << "ERROR: y NOT >= y" << endl;
        if (yy >= y)
            cout << "OKAY: yy >= y" << endl;
        else
            cout << "ERROR: yy NOT >= y" << endl;
        if (y >= x)
            cout << "OKAY: y >= x" << endl;
        else
            cout << "ERROR: y NOT >= x" << endl;

// testing ==
        if (x == x)
            cout << "OKAY: x == x" << endl;
        else
            cout << "ERROR: x NOT == x" << endl;
        if (x == xx)
            cout << "ERROR: x == xx" << endl;
        else
            cout << "OKAY: x NOT == xx" << endl;
        if (x == y)
            cout << "ERROR: x == y" << endl;
        else
            cout << "OKAY: x NOT == y" << endl;

// testing !=
        if (x != x)
            cout << "ERROR: x != x" << endl;
        else
            cout << "OKAY: x NOT != x" << endl;
        if (x != xx)
            cout << "OKAY: x != xx" << endl;
        else
            cout << "ERROR: x NOT != xx" << endl;
        if (x != y)
            cout << "OKAY: x != y" << endl;
        else
            cout << "ERROR: x NOT != y" << endl;

        return 0;
}
```

Problem
Algorithms
C++
Executable
Hardware

Figure 8.40 continued

Appendix A

Tying up Loose Ends

Where Am I, Anyway?

Now that you've reached the end of this book, there are some questions that have probably occurred to you. For example,

1. Am I a programmer now?

2. What am I qualified to do?

3. Where do I go from here?

4. Is that all there is to C++?

The answers to the first three of these questions, as usual with such open-ended topics, is "It all depends". Of course, I can give you some general answers; let's start with questions 1 and 2.

Yes, in the broadest sense, you are a programmer. You've read a fair amount of code and written some programs yourself. But, of course, this doesn't mean that you're a professional programmer. As I said way back at the beginning, no book can turn a novice into a professional programmer. Being a professional in any field takes a lot of hard work, and although you've undoubtedly worked hard in understanding this book, you've just begun the exploration of programming.

Questions 3 and 4 are also closely related. You now have enough background that you should be able to get some benefit from a well-written book about C++ that assumes you are already acquainted with programming; that would be a good way to continue.

As for whether we've covered everything about C++, the answer is unequivocal: absolutely not. I would estimate that we have examined perhaps 5% of the very large, complicated, and powerful C++ language; however, that 5% is the foundation for the rest of your learning in this subject. Most books try to cover every aspect of the language and, as a result, cannot provide the deep coverage of fundamentals; I've worked very hard to ensure that you have the correct tools to continue your learning.

Tying up Loose Ends

I've skipped over some topics because they weren't essential to the discussion. However, since they are likely to be covered in any other book that you might read on programming in C++, I'll discuss them here briefly. This will ensure that they won't be completely foreign to you when you encounter them in your future reading.

Operator Precedence

```
Problem
Algorithms
C++
Executable
Hardware
```

You may recall from high school arithmetic that an expression like 5 + 3 * 9, is calculated as though it were written 5 + (3 * 9), not (5 + 3) * 9; that is, you have to do the * before the +, so that the correct result is 32, not 72, as it would be under the latter interpretation. The reason for performing the operations in the former order is that multiplication has a higher *precedence* than addition. Well, every operator in C++ also has a precedence that determines the order of application of each operator in an expression with more than one operator. This seems like a good idea at first glance, since after all, arithmetic does follow precedence rules like the one we just saw. Unfortunately, C++ is just a little more complicated than arithmetic, and so its precedence rules are not as simple and easy to remember as those of arithmetic. In fact, there are 17 different levels of precedence, which no one can remember. Therefore, everyone[1] ends up using parentheses to specify what order was meant when the expression was written; of course, if we're going to have to use parentheses, then why do we need the precedence rules in the first place?[2]

---

1. At least, everyone who is sensible.

2. In the event that you're worried about using redundant parentheses, you might want to check with the Department of Redundancy Department.

Other Native Data Types

We've confined our use of native data types to short, unsigned short, char, int (for the return type of main only), and bool. As I mentioned in Chapter 6, there are other native types; you'll be seeing them in other programs and in other textbooks, so I should tell you about them now. By the way, I haven't avoided them because they're particularly difficult to use; the reason is simply that they weren't necessary to the task at hand, which was teaching you how to program, using C++. Now that we have accomplished that task, you might as well add them to your arsenal of tools. These other native types are

1.   float

2.   double

3.   long (signed or unsigned)

The float and double types are used to store values that can contain fractional parts, (so-called *floating-point* numbers), rather than being restricted to whole numbers as in the case of short and the other integral types. Of course, this raises two questions: First, why don't we use these types all the time, if they're more flexible? Second, why are there two of these types rather than only one? These questions are related, because the main difference between float and double is that a float is 4 bytes long and a double is 8 bytes long; therefore, a double can store larger values and maintain higher accuracy. However, it also uses up twice the amount of memory of a float, which may not be important when we're dealing with a few values but is quite important if we have a vector or array of thousands or tens of thousands of elements.

So that explains why we'd use a float rather than a double, but not why we would use a long rather than a float; after all, they both take up four bytes. The reason that we would use a long is that it can store larger whole values than a float while retaining exact accuracy in results. Also, on a machine that doesn't have a built-in numeric processor, longs can be processed much more rapidly than than floats.

Problem
Algorithms
C++
Executable
Hardware

protected **Species**

The protected keyword is another access specifier, like public and private. The reason that we haven't covered it in this book is that it is not used except in situations where we create a class that is "descended" from another class. The topic of creating a class that descends from another class is sufficiently complex as to be the subject of several chapters in the sequel to this book, *Who's Still Somewhat Apprehensive of C++?*, and is therefore not covered in this book due to space limitations.[3]

```
Problem
Algorithms
C++
Executable
Hardware
```

3. As you might have guessed, that title is a joke, but I'm definitely planning to write a sequel to this book in the relatively near future. Look for it sometime in 1997.

Glossary

Special Characters

& has a number of distinct meanings. When it precedes the name of a *variable* without following a *type* name, it means "the address of the following variable". For example, &Str means "the address of the variable Str". When & follows a type name and precedes a variable name, it means that the variable which is being declared is a *reference*; that is, another name for a pre-existing variable. In this book, references are used only in argument lists, where they indicate that the variable being defined is a new name for the caller's variable rather than a new local variable.

< is the "less than" operator, which returns the value true if the expression on its left has a lower value than the expression on its right; otherwise, it returns the value false; also see operator < in the index.

= is the *assignment* operator, which assigns the value on its right to the *variable* on its left; also see operator = in the index.

> is the "greater than" operator, which returns the value true if the expression on its left has a greater value than the expression on its right; otherwise, it returns the value false; also see operator > in the index.

[is the left square bracket; see *square brackets* for usage.

] is the right square bracket; see *square brackets* for usage.

{ is the left curly brace; see *curly braces* for usage.

} is the right curly brace; see *curly braces* for usage.

!= is the "not equals" operator, which returns the value true if the expression on its left has a value different from the expression on its right; otherwise, it returns the value false; also see operator != in the index.

&& is the "logical AND" operator. It produces the result true if both of the expressions on its right and left are true; if either of those expressions is false, it produces the result false.

++ is the *increment* operator, which adds 1 to the variable to which it is affixed.

+= is the *add to variable* operator, which adds the value on its right to the variable on its left.

-= is the *subtract from variable* operator, which subtracts the value on its right from the variable on its left.

// is the comment operator; see *comment* for usage.

<< is the "stream output" operator, used to write data to an ostream; also see operator << in the index.

<= is the "less than or equal to" operator, which returns the value true if the expression on its left has the same value or a lower value than the expression on its right; otherwise, it returns the value false; also see operator <= in the index.

== is the "equals" operator, which returns the value true if the expression on its left has the same value as the expression on its right; otherwise, it returns the value false; also see operator == in the index.

>= is the "greater than or equal to" operator, which returns the value true if the expression on its left has the same value or a greater value than the expression on its right; otherwise, it returns the value false; also see operator >= in the index.

>> is the "stream input" operator, used to read data from an istream; also see operator >> in the index.

[] is used after the delete operator to tell the compiler that the *pointer* for which delete was called refers to a group of elements rather than just one data item. This is one of the few times when we have to make that distinction explicitly, rather than leaving it to context.

|| is the "logical OR" operator. It produces the result true if at least one of the two expressions on its right and left is true; if both of those expressions are false, it produces the result false.

A #include **statement** has the same effect as copying all of the code from a specified file into a source code file at the point where the include statement is written. For example, if we wanted to use definitions contained in a file called iostream.h in the source code file test.cc, we could insert the include statement #include <iostream.h> in test.cc rather than physically copying the lines from the file iostream.h into test.cc.

A

An **access specifier** controls the access of nonmember functions to the member functions and variables of a class. The two access specifiers used in this book are public, which allows general access to member functions and variables and private, which forbids access by nonmember functions. Also see friend.

Access time is a measure of how long it takes to retrieve data from a storage device, such as a hard disk or *RAM*.

Address; see *memory address*.

An **algorithm** is a sct of precisely defined steps guaranteed to arrive at an answer to a problem or set of problems. As this implies, a set of steps that might never end is not an algorithm.

An **argument** is a value that is supplied by one function (the *calling function*) that wishes to make use of the services of another function (the *called function*). There are two main types of *argument*s: *value argument*s, which are *copies* of the values from the *calling function*, and *reference argument*s, which are not copies but actually refer to *variable*s in the calling function.

An **argument list** is a set of *argument* definitions specified in a *function declaration*. The argument list describes the types and names of all the *variables* that the *function* receives when it is called by a *calling function*.

An **array** is a group of *elements* of the same type; for example, we can create an array of chars. The array name corresponds to the address of the first of these elements; the other elements follow the first one immediately in memory. As with a vector, we can refer to the individual elements by their indexes; so, if we have an array of chars called m_Data, m_Data[i] refers to the ith char in the array. Also see *pointer*.

The **ASCII code** is a standardized representation of characters by binary values. For example, the letter *A* is represented as a char with the *hexadecimal* value 41, and the digit *0* is represented as a char with the *hexadecimal* value 30. All other printable characters also have representations in the *ASCII* code.

An **assembler** is a program that translates *assembly language* instructions into *machine instructions*.

An **assembly language** instruction is the human-readable representation of a *machine instruction*.

Assignment is the operation of setting a *variable* to a value. The operator that indicates assignment is the equal sign, =.

An **assignment operator** is a function that sets a pre-existing variable to a value of the same type. There are three varieties of assignment operators:

1. For a variable of a native type, the compiler supplies a native assignment operator.
2. For a variable of a class type, the compiler will generate its own version of an assignment operator (a *compiler-generated* assignment operator), if the class writer does not write one.
3. The class writer can write a *member function* to do the assignment; see operator = in the index.

An **assignment statement** such as x = 5;, is *not* an algebraic equality, no matter how much it may resemble one. It is a command telling the computer to assign a value to a variable. In the example, the variable is x and the value is 5.

The auto **storage class** is the default storage class for *variables* declared within C++ *functions*. When we define a variable of the auto storage class, its *memory address* is assigned *auto*matically upon entry to the function where it is defined; the memory address is valid for the duration of that function.

B

A **binary** number system uses only two digits, 0 and 1.

A **bit** is the fundamental unit of storage in a modern computer; the word *bit* is derived from the phrase *bi*nary digi*t*. Each bit, as this suggests, can have one of two states: 0 and 1.

A **block** is a group of *statement*s that are considered one logical statement. A block is delimited by the "curly braces", { and }; the first of these symbols starts a block, and the second one ends the block. A block can be used anywhere that a statement can be used, and is treated in exactly the same way as if it were one statement. For example, if a block is the *controlled block* of a if statement, then all of the statements in the block are executed if the condition in the if is true, and none is executed if the condition in the if is false.

A bool (short for *boolean*) is a type of variable whose range of values is limited to true or false. This is the most appropriate return type for a function that uses its return value to report whether some condition exists, such as operator <; in that particular case, the return value true indicates that the first argument is less than the second, while false indicates that the first argument is not less than the second.

Brace; see *curly brace*s.

A break **statement** is a loop control device that interrupts processing of a *loop* whenever it is executed within the *controlled block* of a *loop control statement*. When a break statement is executed, the flow of control passes to the next statement after the end of the *controlled block*.

A **byte** is the unit in which data capacities are stated, whether in *RAM* or on a disk. In modern computers, a byte consists of eight *bit*s.

C

A **C string** is a literal value representing a variable number of characters. An example is "This is a test.". C strings are surrounded by double quotes ("). Please note that this is *not* the same as a C++ string.

A **cache** is a small amount of fast memory where frequently used data are stored temporarily.

Call; see *function call* or call *instruction*.

A call **instruction** is an *assembly language* instruction that is used to implement a *function call*. It saves the *program counter* on the *stack*, and then transfers execution from the *calling function* to the *called function*.

A **called function** is a *function* that starts execution as the result of a *function call*. Normally, it will return to the *calling function* via a return *statement* when finished.

A **calling function** is a *function* that suspends execution as a result of a *function call*; the *called function* begins execution at the point of the function call.

A char is an *integer variable* type that can represent either one character of text or a small whole number. Both signed and unsigned chars are available for use as "really short" integer variables; a signed char can represent a number from −128 to +127, whereas an unsigned char can represent a number from 0 to 255.

In case you were wondering how to pronounce this term, the most common pronunciation has an *a* like the *a* in "married", while the *ch* sounds like *k*. Other pronunciations include the standard English pronunciation of "char", as in overcooking meat, and even "car" as in "automobile".

A char* (pronounced "char star") is a *pointer* to (i.e., the *memory address* of) a char or the first of a group of chars.

cin (pronounced "see-in") is a predefined istream; it gets its characters from the keyboard.

A class is a user defined type; for example, string is a class.

A class **implementation** tells the compiler how to implement the facilities defined in the class interface. A class implementation is usually found in a *source code file*, which by convention has the extension .cc.

A class **interface** tells the compiler what facilities the class provides. This interface is usually found in a header file, that is, one with the extension .h.

The class **membership** operator, ::, indicates which class a function belongs to. Thus, the full name of the default constructor for the string class is string::string().

class **scope** describes the visibility of *member variable*s: that is, those that are defined within a class. These *variable*s can be accessed by any *member function* of that class; their accessibility to other *function*s is controlled by the *access specifier* in effect when they were defined in the class *interface*.

A **comment** is a note to yourself or another programmer; it is ignored by the compiler. The symbol // marks the beginning of a comment; the comment continues until the end of the line containing the //. For those of you with BASIC experience, this is just like REM (the "remark" keyword); anything after it on a line is ignored.

Compilation is the process of translating *source code* into an *object program*, which is composed of *machine instructions* along with the data needed by those instructions. Virtually all of the *software* on your computer was created by this process.

A **compiler** is a program that performs the process of compilation.

A **compiler-generated** function is supplied by the compiler because the existence of that function is fundamental to the notion of a concrete data type. The compiler will generate its own version any of the following functions that are not written by the class writer: the *assignment operator*, the *copy constructor*, the *default constructor*, and the *destructor*.

Compile time means "while the compiler is compiling the source code of a program".

A **concrete data type** is a class whose objects behave like variables of native data types. That is, the class gives the compiler enough information that *object*s of that class can be created, copied, assigned, and automatically destroyed just as native variables are.

The keyword const has two distinct meanings as employed in this book. The first is used as a modifier to an *argument* of a function; in this context, it means that we are promising not to modify the value of that argument in the function. An example of this use might be the function declaration void operator = (const string& Str);.
    The second use of const in this book is to define a data item similar to a *variable*, except that its value cannot be changed once it has been initialized. For this reason, it is mandatory to supply an initial value when creating a const. An example of this use is const short x = 5;.

A **constructor** is a *member function* that creates new *object*s of a (particular) class type. All constructors have the same name as the class for which they are constructors; therefore, the constructors for the string class also have the name string.

A **continuation expression** is the part of a for *statement* computed before every execution of the *controlled statement*. The statement controlled by the for will be executed if the result of the computation is true, but not if it is false; see the entry for the for statement for an example.

A **controlled block** is a *block* under the control of a *loop control statement* or an if or else statement. The controlled block of a loop control statement can be executed a variable number of times, whereas the controlled block of an if or else statement is executed either once or not at all.

Controlled statement; see *controlled block*.

A **copy constructor** makes a new *object* with the same contents as an existing object of the same type.

cout (pronounced "see out") is a predefined ostream; characters sent to it are displayed on the screen.

CPU is an abbreviation for Central Processing Unit. This is the "active" part of your computer, which executes all the *machine instructions* that make the computer do useful work.

The **curly brace**s { and } are used to surround a *block*. The *compiler* treats the *statement*s in the block as one statement.

D

Data are the pieces of information that are operated on by programs. The singular of "data" is "datum"; however, the word "data" is commonly used as both singular and plural.

A **debugger** is a program that controls the execution of another program, so that you can see what the latter program is doing. The CD-ROM in the back of this book contains the gdb debugger, which works with the djgpp compiler on the CD-ROM.

A **dedicated register** is a *register* such as the *stack pointer* whose usage is predefined, rather than being determined by the programmer as with *general register*s such as eax.

A **default constructor** is a *member function* that is used to create an *object* when no initial value is specified for that object. For example, string::string() is the default constructor for the **string class**.

The **delete** operator is used to free memory that was previously used for *variable*s of the *dynamic storage class*. This allows the memory no longer needed for those variables to be reused for other variables.

A **destructor** is a *member function* that cleans up when an *object* expires; for an object of the auto *storage class*, the destructor is called automatically at the end of the *function* where that object is defined.

A **double** is a type of *floating-point variable* that can represent a range of positive and negative numbers of magnitude from approximately 4.940656e–324 to approximately 1.79769e+308 (and 0), with approximately 16 digits of precision.

The **dynamic storage class** is used for *variable*s whose size is not known until *run time*. Variables of this storage class are assigned *memory address*es at the programmer's explicit request.

Dynamic type checking refers to the practice of checking the correct usage of *variable*s of different types during execution of a program rather than during *compilation*; see the *type system* entry for further discussion.

E

An **element** is one of the *variable*s that makes up a vector or an array.

The keyword else causes its *controlled block* to be executed if the condition in its matching *if* statement turns out to be false at run time.

An **empty stack** is a *stack* that currently contains no values.

Executable; see *executable program*.

An **executable program** is a program in a form suitable for running on a computer; it is composed of *machine instructions* along with data needed by those instructions.

F

The keyword false is a predefined value, representing the result of a conditional expression whose condition is not satisfied. For example, in the conditional expression x < y, if x is not less than y, the result of the expression will be false. Also see bool.

A **fencepost error** is a logical error that causes a loop to be executed one more or one less time than the correct count. A common cause of this error is confusing the number of *elements* in a vector or *array* with the *index* of the last *element*. The derivation of this term is by analogy with the problem of calculating the number of fence sections and fence posts that you need for a given fence. For example, if you have to put up a fence 100 feet long, and each section of the fence is 10 feet long, how many sections of fence do you need? Obviously, the answer is 10. Now, how many fenceposts do you need? 11. The confusion caused by counting fenceposts when you should be counting segments of the fence (and vice-versa) is the cause of a fencepost error.

To return to a programming example; if you have a vector with 11 elements, the index of the last element is 10, not 11. Thus, confusing the number of elements with the highest index has much the same effect as the fencepost problem.

This sort of problem is also known, less colorfully, as an *off-by-one* error.

A float is a type of *floating-point variable* that can represent a range of positive and negative numbers of magnitude from approximately 1.401298e–45 to approximately 3.40282e+38 (and 0), with approximately 6 digits of precision.

A **floating-point variable** is a C++ approximation of a mathematical "real number". Unlike mathematical real numbers, C++ floating-point variables have a limited range and precision, depending on their types; see the individual types float and double for details.

A for statement is a *loop control statement* that causes its *controlled block* to be executed while a specified logical expression (the *continuation expression*) is true. It also provides for a *starting expression* to be executed before the first execution of the controlled statement, and a *modification expression* to be executed after every execution of the controlled statement. For example, in the for statement for (i = 0; i < 10; i ++), the initialization expression is i = 0, the continuation expression is i < 10, and the modification expression is i ++.

The keyword friend allows access by a specified class or *function* to private members of a particular class.

A **function** is a section of code having a name, optional *arguments*, and a *return type*. The name makes it possible for one function to start execution of another one via a *function call*; the arguments are used to provide input for the function, and the return type allows the function to provide output to its *calling function* when the return *statement* causes the calling function to resume execution; see figure 5.2 for a diagram illustrating a function call and return.

A **function call** (or *call* for short) causes execution to be transferred temporarily from the current *function* (the *calling function*) to the one named in the function call (the *called function*). Normally, when a called function is finished with its task, it will return to the calling function, which will pick up execution at the statement after the function call.

A **function declaration** tells the compiler some vital statistics of the function: its name, its *arguments*, and its *return type*. Before we can use a *function*, the compiler must have already seen its function declaration. The most common way to arrange for this is to use a #include *statement* to insert the function declaration from the header file where it exists into our source code module.

Function header; see *function declaration*.

Function overloading is the C++ facility that allows us to create more than one *function* with the same name. So long as all such functions have different *signature*s, we can write as many of them as we wish, and the compiler will be able to figure out which one we mean.

G

A **general register** is a *register* whose usage is determined by the programmer, rather than being predefined as with *dedicated register*s such as the *stack pointer*. On an Intel CPU such as the 486 or Pentium, the 16-bit general registers are ax, bx, cx, dx, si, di, and bp; the 32-bit general registers are eax, ebx, ecx, edx, esi, edi, and ebp.

Global scope describes the visibility of *variable*s that are defined outside any *function*; such variables can be accessed by code in any function. It also describes the visibility of *function*s that are defined outside any class.

H

Hardware refers to the physical components of a computer, the ones you can touch. Examples include the keyboard, the monitor, the printer.

A **header file** is a file that contains class *interface* definitions and/or global *function declaration*s. By convention, header files have the extension .h.

The **heap** is the area of memory where *variable*s of the *dynamic storage class* store their data.

Hex is an abbreviation for *hexadecimal*.

A **hexadecimal** number system 16 digits, 0–9 and a–f.

I

An **identifier** is a user defined name; both *function* names and *variable* names are identifiers. Identifiers must not conflict with *keyword*s such as if and for; for example, you cannot create a function or a variable with the name for.

An if **statement** is a *statement* that causes its *controlled block* to be executed if the *logical expression* specified in the if statement is true.

An ifstream (pronounced "i f stream") is a stream used for input from a file.

Implementation; see class *implementation*.

Include; see #include *statement*.

To **increment a *variable*** means to add 1 to its value. This can be done in C++ by using the increment operator, ++.

An **index** is an expression used to select one of a number of *element*s of a vector or an *array*. It is enclosed in *square bracket*s ([ ]). For example, in the expression a[i+1], the index is the expression i+1.

An **index variable** is a *variable* used to hold an .

Initialization is the process of setting the initial value of a *variable*. It is very similar to *assignment* but is not identical: Initialization is done only once for each variable, when that variable is created, whereas assignment can be done as many times as desired. In particular, you cannot assign a value to a const, but you can, and indeed must, initialize it when it is created.

Input is the process of reading data into the computer from the outside world. A very commonly used source of input for simple programs is the keyboard.

Instruction; see *machine instruction*.

An int (short for *integer*) is a type of *integer variable* that is essentially equivalent to either a short or a long, depending on the compiler you are using.[1] A 16-bit compiler such as Borland C++ 3.1 has 16-bit ints, which are the same size as shorts. A 32-bit compiler such as DJGPP (the compiler on the CD-ROM that comes with this book) has 32-bit ints, which are the same size as longs.

An **integer variable** is a C++ representation of a whole number. Unlike mathematical integers, C++ integers have a limited range, depending on their types; see the individual types char, short, int, and long for details. The type bool is sometimes also considered an integer variable type.

Interface; see class *interface*.

I/O is an abbreviation for "input/output". This refers to the process of getting information into and out of the computer; see *input* and *output* for more details.

iostream.h is the name of the *header file* that tells the *compiler* how to compile code that uses predefined stream *variable*s like cout and operators like <<.

An **istream** is a stream used for input. For example, cin is a predefined istream that reads characters from the keyboard.

K

A **keyword** is a word defined in the C++ language, such as if and for. It is illegal to define an *identifier* such as a *variable* or *function* name that conflicts with a keyword; for example, you cannot create a function or a variable with the name for.

---

1. Pedants will point out that it is not absolutely guaranteed that an int is the same size as either a short or a long; it's theoretically possible that all three of these variable types are different in size. However, at this writing, all commonly available C++ compilers for microcomputers in fact equate an int with either a short or a long. and it does not appear likely that this situation will change in the near future.

L

A **library** (or library module) contains the *object code* generated from several *source code module*s, in a form that the *linker* can search when it needs to find general-purpose functions.

The **linker** is a program that combines information from all of the *object file*s for our program, along with some previously prepared files called *libraries*, to produce an *executable program*.

Linking is the process of creating an *executable program* from *object file*s and *libraries*.

A **literal** value doesn't have a name, but represents itself in a literal manner. Some examples are 'x' (a char literal having the ASCII value that represents the letter *x*), and 5 (a numeric literal with the value 5).

Local scope describes the visibility of *variable*s that are defined within a *function*; such variables can be accessed only by code in that function.[2]

A **logical expression** is an expression that takes on the value true or false, rather than a numeric value. Some examples of such expressions are: x > y, which will be true if x has a greater value than y and false otherwise; and a == b, which will be true if a has the same value as b, and false otherwise; see bool.

A **long** is a type of *integer variable* that can represent a whole number in either the range -2147483648 to 2147483647 (if signed) or the range 0 to 4294967295 (if unsigned).

A **loop** is a means of executing a *controlled block* a variable number of times, depending on some condition. The statement that controls the controlled block is called a *loop control statement*. This book covers the while and for loop control statements; see those headings for details.

---

2. In fact, a variable can be declared in any *block*, not just in a *function*; in that case, its scope is from the point where it is declared until the end of the block where it is defined. However, in this book all local variables have function scope, so this distinction is not critical here and omitting it simplifies the discussion.

A **loop control statement** is a *statement* that controls the *controlled block* in a *loop*.

M

Machine address; see *memory address*.

Machine code is the combination of *machine instructions* with the data used by those instructions. A synonym is *object code*.

A **machine instruction** is one of the fundamental operations that a *CPU* can perform. Some examples of these operations are addition, subtraction, or other arithmetic operations; other possibilities include operations that control what instruction will be executed next. All C++ programs must be converted into machine instructions before they can be executed by the *CPU*.

A **machine language** program is a program composed of *machine instructions*.

A **member function** is a *function* defined in a class interface. It is viewed as "belonging" to the class, which is the reason for the adjective *member*.

A **member variable** is a *variable* defined in a class interface. It is viewed as "belonging" to the class, which is the reason for the adjective *member*.

Memberwise copy means to copy every *member variable* from the source *object* to the destination object. If we don't define our own copy constructor or assignment operator for a particular class, the *compiler-generated* versions will use memberwise copy.

A **memory address** is a unique number identifying a particular *byte* of *RAM*.

A **memory hierarchy** is the particular arrangement of the different kinds of storage devices in a given computer. The purpose of using various kinds of storage devices having different performance characteristics is to provide the best overall performance at the lowest cost. See Figure 2.2 for a sample memory hierarchy.

A **memory leak** is a programming error in which the programmer forgot to delete something that had been dynamically allocated. Such an error is very insidious, because the program appears to work correctly when tested casually. The usual way to find these errors is to notice that the program runs apparently correctly for a (possibly long) time and then fails due to running out of available memory.

A **modification expression** is the part of a for *statement* executed after every execution of the *controlled block*. It is often used to *increment* an *index variable* to refer to the next *element* of an *array* or a vector; see the entry for the for statement for an example.

N

A **nanosecond** is one-billionth of a second.

A **native** data type is one that is defined in the C++ language, as opposed to a user defined data type (class).

The new operator is used to allocate memory for *variable*s of the *dynamic storage class*; these are variables whose storage requirements aren't known until the program is executing.

Nondisplay character; see *nonprinting* character.

A **nonmember function** is one that is not a member of a particular class being discussed, although it may be a *member function* of another class.

A **nonnumeric variable** is a *variable* that is not used in calculations like adding, multiplying, or subtracting. Such variables might represent names, addresses, telephone numbers, Social Security numbers, bank account numbers, or drivers license numbers. Note that just because something is called a *number* or even is composed entirely of the digits 0–9, does not make it a *numeric variable* by our standards; the question is how the item is used. No one adds, multiplies, or subtracts drivers license numbers, for example; they serve solely as identifiers, and could just as easily have letters in them, as indeed some of them do.

A **nonprinting character** is used to control the format of our displayed or printed information, rather than to represent a particular letter, digit, or other special character. The *space* ( ) is one of the more important nonprinting characters.

A **null byte** is a byte with the value 0, commonly used to indicate the end of a *C string*. Note that this is not the same as the character '0', which is a normal printable character having the *ASCII* code 48.

A **null object** is an object of some (specified) class whose purpose is to indicate that a "real" object of that class does not exist, analogously to a *null pointer*. One common use for a null object is as a *return value* from a *member function* that is supposed to return an object with some specified properties but cannot find such an object. For example, a null StockItem object might be used to indicate that an item with a specified UPC cannot be found in the inventory of a store.

A **null pointer** is a *pointer* with the value 0. This value is particularly suited to indicate that a pointer isn't pointing to anything at the moment, due to some special treatment of zero-valued pointers built into the C++ language.

A **numeric variable** is a *variable* representing a quantity that can be expressed as a number, whether a whole number (an *integer variable*), or a number with a fractional part (a *floating-point variable*), and which can be used in calculations such as addition, subtraction, multiplication, or division. The integer variable types in C++ are char, short, int, and long. Each of these types can be further subdivided into signed and unsigned versions; the former of these can represent both negative and positive values (and 0), whereas the latter can represent only positive values (and 0), but provides a greater range of positive values than the corresponding signed version does.

The floating-point variable types are float and double, which differ in their range and precision. Unlike the integer variable types, the floating-point types are not divided into signed or unsigned versions; all floating-point variables can represent either positive or negative numbers as well as 0; see the individual headings float and double for details on range and precision.

O

An **object** is a *variable* of a class type, as distinct from a variable of a *native* type. The behavior of an object is defined by the code that implements the class to which the object belongs. For example, a variable of type string is an object whose behavior is controlled by the definition of the string class.

Object code; see *machine code*. This term is unrelated to C++ *object*s.

An **object code module** is the result of compiling a *source code module* into *object code*. A number of object code modules are combined to form an *executable program*. This term is unrelated to C++ *object*s.

Object file; see *object code module*. This term is unrelated to C++ *object*s.

Object-oriented programming is an approach to solving programming problems by creating *object*s to represent the entities being handled by the program, rather than relying solely on *native* data types. This approach has the advantage that you can match the language to the needs of the problem you're trying to solve. For example, if you were writing a nurse's station program in C++, you would want to have objects that represented nurses, doctors, patients, various sorts of equipment, and so on. Each of these objects would display the behavior appropriate to the thing or person it was representing.

Off-by-one error; see *fencepost error*.

An ofstream (pronounced "o f stream") is a stream used for output to a file.

An **op code** is the part of a *machine instruction* that tells the *CPU* what kind of instruction this is and sometimes also specifies a *register* to be operated on.

An **operating system** is a program that deals with the actual hardware of your computer; it supplies the lowest level of the software infrastructure needed to run a program. By far the most common operating system for Intel CPUs, at present, is MS-DOS, followed by OS/2 and Windows NT.

The keyword operator is used to indicate that the following symbol is the name of a C++ operator that we are redefining, either globally or for a particular class. For example, to redefine =, we have to specify operator = as the name of the function we are writing, rather than just =, so that the *compiler* does not object to seeing an operator when it expects an *identifier*.

An **ostream** is a stream used for output. For example, cout is a predefined ostream that displays characters on the screen.

Output is the process of sending data from the computer to the outside world. The most commonly used source of output for most programs is the screen.

P

A **pointer** is essentially the same as a *memory address*. The main difference between these two concepts is that a memory address is "untyped" (i.e., it can refer to any sort of *variable*), but a pointer always has an associated data type. For example, char* (pronounced "char star"), means "pointer to a char.

To say "a variable points to a memory location" is almost exactly the same as saying "a variable's value is the address of a memory location". In the specific case of a variable of type char*, to say "the char* x points to a C string" is equivalent to saying "x contains the address of the first byte of the C string".

Technically, a pointer does have some properties that differ from those of a memory address. However, in our use of pointers, the differences between a pointer and a memory address will never matter.

Also see *array*.

Pop means "remove the top value from a *stack*".

The keyword private is an *access specifier* that denies *nonmember functions* access to *member functions* and *member variables* of its class.

A **program** is a set of instructions specifying the solution to a set of problems, along with the data used by those instructions.

The **program counter** is a *dedicated register* that holds the address of the next instruction to be executed. During a *function call*, a call *instruction pushes* the contents of the program counter on the *stack* so that the *called function* can return to the *calling function* when it is finished executing.

Programming is the art and science of solving problems by the following procedure:

1. Find or invent a general solution to a set of problems,

2. Express this solution as an *algorithm* or set of algorithms,

3. Translate the algorithm(s) into terms so simple that a stupid machine like a computer can follow them to calculate the specific answer for any specific problem in the set.

Warning: This definition may be somewhat misleading since it implies that the progression of a program is straightforward and linear, with no revision. This is known as the "waterfall model" of programming, since water going over a waterfall follows a preordained course in one direction. However, real-life programming doesn't usually work this way; rather, most programs are written in an incremental process as assumptions are changed and errors are found and corrected.

The keyword public is an *access specifier* that allows *nonmember functions* access to *member functions* and *member variables* of its class.

Push means "add another value to a *stack*".

R

RAM is an acronym for Random Access Memory. This is the working storage of a computer, where data and programs are stored while we're using them.

A **reference argument** is another name for a variable from the *calling function*, rather than an independent variable in the *called function*. Changing a reference argument therefore *does* affect the corresponding *variable* in the calling function.

A **register** is a storage area that is on the same chip as the *CPU* itself. Programs use registers to hold data items that are actively in use; data in registers can be accessed within the time allocated to instruction execution, rather than the much longer times needed to access data in *RAM*.

A **retrieval function** is a *function* that retrieves data, which may have been previously stored by a *storage function* or may be generated when needed by some other method such as calculation according to a formula.

A **return address** is the *memory address* of the next *machine instruction* in a *calling function*. It is used during execution of a return *statement* in a *called function* to transfer execution back to the correct place in the calling function.

A return **statement** is used by a *called function* to transfer execution back to the *calling function*. The return statement can also specify a value of the correct *return type* for the called function; this value is made available to the calling function to be used for further calculation. An example of a return statement is return 0;, which returns the value 0 to the calling function.

A **return type** tells the *compiler* what sort of data a *called function* returns to the *calling function* when the called function finishes executing. The *return value* from main is a special case; it can be used to determine what action a batch file should take next.

ROM is an abbreviation for Read Only Memory. This is the permanent internal storage of a computer, where the programs needed to start up the computer are stored. As this suggests, ROM does not lose its contents when the power is turned off, as contrasted with *RAM*.

Run time means "while a (previously compiled) program is being executed".

S

A **scalar** *variable* has a single value (at any one time); this is contrasted with a vector or an *array*, which contains a number of values, each of which is referred to by its *index*.

The **scope** of a *variable* is the part of the program in which the variable can be accessed. The scopes with which we are concerned are *local*, *global*, and *class*; see the entry for each specific scope for more details.

A **selection sort** is a sorting algorithm that selects the highest (or lowest) *element* from a set of elements (the "input list"), moving that selected element to another set of elements (the "output list"). The next highest (or lowest) element is then treated in the same manner; this operation is repeated until as many elements as desired have been moved to the output list.

A short is a type of *integer variable* that can represent a whole number in either the range −32768 to 32767 (if signed) or the range 0 to 65535 (if unsigned).

A **side effect** is any result of calling a *function* that persists beyond the execution of that function. For example, writing data to a file is a side effect.

The **signature** of a *function* consists of its name and the types of its *arguments*. In the case of a *member function*, the class to which the function belongs is also part of its signature. Every function is uniquely identified by its signature, which is what makes it possible to have more than one function with the same name; this is called *function overloading*.

A signed char is a type of *integer variable*; see char for details.

A signed int is a type of *integer variable*; see int for details.

A signed long is a type of *integer variable*; see long for details.

A signed short is a type of *integer variable*; see short for details.

A signed **variable** can represent either negative or positive values; see the individual variable type char, short, int, or long for details.

Software refers to the other, nonphysical components of a computer, the ones you cannot touch. If you can install it on your hard disk, it's software. Examples include a spreadsheet, a word processor, a database program.

Source code is a program in a form suitable for reading and writing by a human being.

Source code file; see *source code module*.

A **source code module** is a file containing part or all of the source code for a program.

The **space** character ( ) is one of the *nonprinting characters* (or *nondisplay characters*) that controls the format of displayed or printed information.

The **square bracket**s, [and], are used to enclose an *array* or vector *index*, which selects an individual *element* of the *array* or vector. Also see [].

A **stack** is a data structure with characteristics similar to a spring-loaded plate holder such as you might see in a cafeteria. The last plate deposited on the stack of plates will be the first one to be removed when a customer needs a fresh plate; similarly, the last value deposited (*push*ed) onto a stack is the first value retrieved (*pop*ped).

The **stack pointer** is a *dedicated register*. The stack pointer is used to keep track of the most recently *push*ed value on the *stack*.

A **starting expression** is the part of a for *statement* executed once before the *controlled block* of the for statement is first executed. It is often used to initialize an *index variable* to 0, so that the index variable can be used to refer to the first element of an *array* or vector; see the entry for the for statement for an example.

A **statement** is a complete operation understood by the C++ compiler. Each statement is ended with a semicolon (;).

The static **storage class** is the simplest of the three *storage class*es in C++; *variables* of this storage class are assigned *memory address*es in the *executable program* when the program is *link*ed.

Static type checking refers to the practice of checking the correct usage of variables of different types during compilation of a program rather than during execution. C++ uses static type checking; see the *type system* entry for further discussion.

Stepwise refinement is the process of developing an *algorithm* by starting out with a "coarse" solution and "refining" it until the steps are within the capability of the C++ language.

Storage: syn. *memory*.

A **storage class** is the characteristic of a *variable* that determines how and when a *memory address* is assigned to that variable. C++ has three different storage classes: static, auto and *dynamic*; see the descriptions of each of these storage classes for more details. Please note that the term *storage class* has nothing to do with the C++ term class.

A **storage function** is a *function* that stores data for later retrieval by a *retrieval function*.

A stream is a place to put (in the case of an ostream) or get (in the case of an istream) characters. Some predefined streams are cin and cout.

The string class defines a type of *object* that contains a group of chars; the chars in a string can be treated as one unit for purposes of *assignment*, *I/O*, and *comparison*.

T

Temporary; see *temporary variable*.

A **temporary variable** is automatically created by the *compiler* for use during a particular operation, such as a *function call* with an *argument* that has to be converted to a different type.

The keyword this represents a hidden argument automatically supplied by the compiler in every *member function* call. Its value during the execution of any member function is the address of the class object for which the member function call was made.

A **token** is a part of a program that the *compiler* treats as a separate unit. It's analogous to a word in English; a *statement* is more like a sentence. For example, string is a token, as are :: and (. On the other hand, x = 5; is a statement.

The keyword true is a predefined value representing the result of a conditional expression whose condition is satisfied. For example, in the conditional expression x < y, if x is less than y, the result of the expression will be true.

The **type** of a class variable is the class to which it belongs. The type of a native variable is one of the predefined variable types in C++; see *integer variable*, *floating-point variable*, and bool for details on the native types.

The **type system** refers to the set of rules that the compiler uses to decide what uses are legal for a variable of a given *type*. In C++, these determinations are made by the compiler (*static type checking*). This makes it easier to prevent type errors than it is in languages where type checking is done during execution of the program (*dynamic type checking*).

U

An **uninitialized variable** is one that has never been set to a known value. Attempting to use such a *variable* is a logical error that will cause a program to act very oddly.

An **unqualified name** is a reference to a *member variable* that doesn't specify which *object* the member variable belongs to. When we use an unqualified name in a *member function*, the compiler assumes that the object we are referring to is the object for which that member function has been called.

An unsigned char is a type of *integer variable*; see char for details.

An unsigned int is a type of *integer variable*; see int for details.

An unsigned long is a type of *integer variable*; see long for details.

An unsigned short is a type of *integer variable*; see short for details.

An **unsigned variable** is an *integer variable* that represents only positive values (and 0); see the individual variable type (char, short, int, or long) for details.

A **user defined** data type is one that is, well, defined by the user. In this case, however, *user* means "programmer". The primary mechanism used to define a user defined type is the class.

V

A **value argument** is a *variable* of *local scope* created when a *function* begins execution. Its initial value is set to the value of the corresponding *argument* in the *calling function*. Changing a value argument does not affect any variable in the calling function.

A **variable** is a programming construct that uses a certain part of *RAM* to represent a specific item of data that we wish to keep track of in a program. Some examples are the weight of a pumpkin or the number of cartons of milk in the inventory of a store.

A vector is a group of *variable*s that can be addressed by their position in the group; each of these variables is called an *element*. A vector has a name, just like a regular variable, but the elements do not. Instead, each element has a number, corresponding to its position in the vector.

A void return type specifier in a *function* declaration indicates that the function in question does not return any value when it finishes executing.

W

A while **statement** is a *loop control statement* that causes its *controlled block* to be executed while a specified logical expression is true.

Z

Zero-based indexing refers to the practice of numbering the *element*s of an *array* or vector starting at 0 rather than 1. Although it might seem arbitrary to start counting at 0 rather than at 1, there are historical reasons for this decision, stemming from the *assembly language* ancestry of the C language.

About the Author

Steve Heller had always been fascinated by writing. In his childhood days in the 1950s and 1960s, he often stayed up far past his bedtime reading science fiction; even in adulthood, if you came across him in his off-hours, he was more likely to be found reading a book than doing virtually anything else.

After college, Steve got into programming more or less by accident; he was working at an actuarial consulting firm, and was selected to take charge of programming on their timesharing terminal, because he was making much less than most of the other employees. Finding the programming itself to be more interesting than the actuarial calculations, he decided to become a professional programmer.

Until 1984, Steve remained on the consuming side of the writing craft. Then one day he was reading a magazine article on some programming-related topic and said to himself, "I could do better than that". With encouragement from his wife of the time, he decided to try his hand at technical writing. Steve's first article submission, to the late lamented *Computer Language Magazine*, was published, as were a dozen more over the next ten years.

But although writing magazine articles is an interesting pastime, writing a book is something entirely different. Steve got his chance at this new level of commitment when Harry Helms, then an editor for Academic Press, read one of his articles in *Dr. Dobb's Journal* and wrote him a letter asking whether he would be interested in writing a book for AP. He answered, "Sure, why not?", not having the faintest idea of how much work he was letting himself in for.

The resulting book, *Large Problems, Small Machines* received favorable reviews for its careful explanation of a number of facets of program optimization, and sold a total of about 20,000 copies within a year after publication of the second edition, entitled *Efficient C/C++ Programming*.

By that time, Steve was hard at work on his next book, *Who's Afraid of C++*, which is designed to make object-oriented programming intelligible to anyone from the sheerest novice to the programmer with years of experience in languages other than C++. To make sure that his exposition was clear enough for the novice, he posted a message on Compuserve requesting the help of someone new to programming. The responses included one from a woman named Susan Spino, who ended up contributing a great deal to the book; in fact, about 100 pages of the book consist of email between Steve and Susan. Her contribution was wonderful, but not completely unexpected.

What **was** unexpected was that Steve and Susan would fall in love during the course of this project, but that's what happened. Since she lived in Texas and he lived in New York, this posed some logistic difficulties. The success of his previous book now became extremely important, as it was the key to Steve's becoming a full-time writer. Writers have been "telecommuting" since before the invention of telephone, so his conversion from "programmer who writes" to "writer" made it possible for him to relocate to her area, which he promptly did.

Steve and Susan hope to be married before the end of 1996.

Index

& 274, 352
< (*See Also:* operator <) , 87, 118
= (*See Also:* operator =) , 58, 97, 100
> (*See Also:* operator >) , 92, 118
[122
] 122
{ 90
} 90
!= (*See Also:* operator !=) , 118
&& 411
++ 128
+= 163
 = 283
// 57
<< (*See Also:* operator <<) , 84, 91
<= (*See Also:* operator <=) , 118
== (*See Also:* operator ==) , 118
>= (*See Also:* operator >=) , 118
>> (*See Also:* operator >>) , 85, 91
[] 353
|| 303
#include 91

A

access specifier 280, 286-288

address (*See:* memory address)
algorithm 3, 91, 140-147, 161-176, 399, 400, 408
argument 204-210, 212-214, 358-392, 401-413
argument list 174, 176
array 373, 385, 413-420, 412, 426, 443-461
ASCII code 80, 110, 406
assembler 37, 56
assembly language 37, 84-103
assignment 58, 425
assignment operator (*See:* operator =)
assignment statement (*See.* assignment, operator =)
auto storage class 221-262, 324, 362, 365, 368

B

batch file 96
binary 10, 40-41, 52-78
bit 12
block 90, 167
bool 282
boot program 96
bootstrapping 96
brace (*See:* {, })
break 277
byte 12, 60

C

C string 107-112, 256, 323, 324, 345-368, 368, 378, 406-409, 399, 415, 456-458
cache 47-51
call instruction 198, 201, 229
called function 195-262
calling function 195-262
char 103-110
char* 405-409, 415-417, 394
character sets 76
cin 85, 91, 452-459
class implementation 236, 241, 283-333, 349-392, 382, 413-415, 423-424, 432-446, 449-458, 434, 435
class interface 236, 268-333, 347-392, 410-431, 418, 434, 435
class membership (*See Also:* member function) , 255
class scope 286-288
comment 57
compilation 4, 92-103
compile time 72, 92-100
compiler 4, 56
compiler-generated function 275-277, 319, 369-372, 402-403, 409-411
concrete data type 245, 273-283, 292, 347-392
constructor 245, 253
continuation expression 127
controlled block 104, 127
controlled statement (*See:* controlled block)
copy constructor 245, 246, 319, 320, 375, 381, 402-411
cout 85, 91, 383, 447-452
CPU 11, 17

curly brace (*See:* {, })

D

data 11
data type
    user defined (*See:* class)
debugger (*See:* gdb)
dedicated register 23, 61
default constructor 245, 246, 253, 261, 319, 320, 349-358
delete (*See:* operator delete)
destructor 245, 246, 319, 320, 361
disk 11
double 235, 443
Dvorak keyboard 126
dynamic storage 353-392
dynamic type checking 82

E

element 149-182, 271, 307-308, 413-420, 426
empty stack 197, 199
executable (*See:* executable program)
executable program 4, 58
exit code 96

F

fail() 277
false 283
fencepost error 307-309
file input 299-309, 291, 293
file output 313
fixed-length data 79
float 235, 443
floating-point variable (*See Also:* double, float) , 24, 55, 126
for loop 127
for statement 127
friend 422

function 167, 195-262
function call 167, 195-262
function declaration 174, 179, 255, 263, 275, 313, 381, 385, 403, 422, 425
function overloading 262, 419

G

gdb 98
general register 23, 61
global function 449-452
global scope 230-251, 256-262, 285-287
global variable (*See:* global scope)

H

hardware 4, 37-79, 54, 191, 201
header file 77, 95, 121, 160, 188, 236, 253, 269, 272, 313, 330, 331, 382, 402, 418, 420, 422, 429
heap 338, 353
hex (*See:* hexadecimal)
hexadecimal 10, 59-65, 92, 102

I

I/O (*See Also:* <<, >>, operator >>, operator <<, cin, cout) , 84
identifier 53, 175
if statement 86
ifstream 300-311
implementation (*See:* class implementation)
include (*See:* #include)
incrementing 128
index 150-182
index variable (*See:* index)
initialization 113, 137, 171-176, 150, 156, 158, 180, 210-211, 220-247, 223, 255-261, 236, 245, 253, 254, 256, 259, 260, 262, 274, 307, 328, 332, 362, 370, 371, 376, 425, 432
input 85, 132, 135, 143, 179-182, 156, 188-190, 191, 275, 318, 452-459
instruction (*See:* machine instruction)
int 78, 96
integer variable (*See:* char, short, int, long)
iostreams 95, 191, 266, 419, 421, 429
istream 452-459
iteration 130

K

keyword 53, 176

L

library (*See:* library module)
library module 165, 188
library modules 191
linker 188
linking 188
literal 58
local 246
local scope 230-251
local variable (*See:* local scope)
logical expression 283
long 235, 443
loop (*See:* for loop, while loop)
loop control statement (*See:* for loop, while loop)

M

machine address (*See:* memory address)

machine code (*See:* machine instruction)
machine instruction 45-52, 65-76, 84-103, 95, 128, 163
Mega 12
member function 236, 255, 272-295, 300-304
member variable 237, 271-272, 295-296
memberwise copy 375
memory (*See:* memory address)
memory address 15, 43-44, 60, 85-103
memory hierarchy 19
memory leak 355
memset 428
modification expression 127

N

native 317
native variable 263-280, 260
nesting 195
new (*See:* operator new)
nondisplay character 82
nonnumeric variable 56
nonprinting character 82
null byte 80, 333
null object 294
numeric variable (*See:* integer variable, floating-point variable)
numeric variables 24

O

object 236, 265-296
object code 4
object code module 165, 188
octal 32
off by one error (*See:* fencepost error)
ofstream 313

operating system 190
operator < 431-445
operator = 245, 246, 247, 249, 307, 319, 320, 369-389, 367, 369, 371, 375
operator > 435
operator != 435
operator << 77, 373, 447-452, 446-459
operator <= 435
operator == 417
operator >= 435
operator >> 373, 452-459, 447-459
operator delete 353-367, 381-385, 381-392, 375, 383, 393
operator new 353-367, 381-385, 381-392
ostream 419, 447-452
output 85, 87, 94, 99, 136-138, 130, 188-190, 191, 304, 447-452

P

pointer 350-392
pop 196
preprocessor directive 91
private 253, 286-288, 295, 283, 284, 368, 369, 371, 373, 420-423, 450-451, 434, 435
processor (*See:* CPU)
program counter 198, 201
public 279-280, 286-288, 267, 283, 368, 369, 393, 395
push 196

R

RAM 11, 14
reference (*See:* reference argument)

reference argument 302-303, 347, 348, 373
register 22
retrieval function 168
return address 225-229, 250
return statement 168, 198-203
return type 174, 266
ROM 15, 96
run time 100-103

S

scalar (*See:* scalar variable)
scalar variable 122
scope (*See:* class scope, global scope, local scope)
selection sort 133
short 24, 27, 57-59, 35, 37, 51, 58, 89-92
side effect 171
signature 263, 331, 418, 423
signed char (*See:* char)
signed int (*See:* int)
signed long (*See:* long)
signed short (*See:* short)
signed variable (*See Also:* char, short, int, long) , 29, 65
software 4
source code 4, 58
source code file (*See:* source code module)
source code module 165
space 79
square bracket 122
stack 224-230, 250-251, 257-261
stack pointer 225-230
standard library 326, 333
starting expression 127
statement 57, 58
static storage class 220-256, 234, 324
static type checking 82, 174

stepwise refinement 6
storage (*See:* memory address)
storage class 219-262
storage function 168
stream 187-190, 300-306, 447-459
string 345-461
subscript 122

T

temporary 403-409, 430, 435
temporary variable (*See:* temporary)
this 379-381, 358, 388-389, 370, 382, 423
token 346
true 283
type 263-269
type system 82

U

uninitialized variable (*See Also:* initialization) , 143, 173, 228
unqualified name 357
unsigned char (*See:* char)
unsigned int (*See:* int)
unsigned long (*See:* long)
unsigned short (*See:* short)
unsigned variable (*See Also:* char, short, int, long) , 29
user defined data type (*See:* class)

V

value argument 205-208, 223, 274, 347, 373, 401-404, 410-411
variable 51-52, 57-59
variable-length data 79
vector 112, 149-182, 270, 279, 290, 293, 386, 400

W

while loop 88, 127
while statement (*See:* while
   loop)

Z

zero-based indexing 124

4. To check whether the compiler has been set up correctly, run the go32-v2.exe program by typing the following command at a DOS prompt:

go32-v2

The last two lines of its output should report how much DPMI memory and swap space DJGPP can use on your system, like this:

DPMI memory available: 8020 Kb
DPMI swap space available: 240 Kb

If you don't get output that looks like this, with the exception of different numbers, check that you've followed the instructions exactly.

Windows 95 Compiler Installation Instructions

If you are going to run the compiler in a DOS box under Windows 95, you should follow the above instructions, with the following change:

1c/2a. Add the lines to the file that is executed when you start up a DOS box, NOT autoexec.bat.

Copying and Compiling the Sample Programs

After you have set up the compiler as shown above, you can copy the sample programs to your hard disk. They are in the directory d:\whos\code (assuming that your CD-ROM is drive D:).

1. To copy the sample files to your hard disk, change to the root directory on the CD-ROM and run the batch file "copysamp", supplying a parameter to indicate where you want the sample files to go. For example, if you want the sample files to be placed under the directory "c:\whos", type:

d:
cd\
copysamp c:\whos

2. Now you can compile any of the sample programs by changing to the directory "c:\whos\code" and running the batch file "mknorm.bat", giving the name of the sample program as a parameter. For example, to compile "itemtst1", type:

"mknorm itemtst1".

The compiled version will be placed in the "\whos\normal" directory. You can also use this same method to compile programs you write that use the string and vector classes, as well as any classes you create yourself.

Further Assistance

If you have any problems setting up the compiler or compiling the sample code, or have any other questions, you might want to check my Web page for updates to the instructions or sample code. That address is:

http://ourworld.compuserve.com/homepages/steve_heller

About the CD-ROM

DOS Compiler Setup Instructions

Here are the instructions on setting up the DJGPP compiler from the CD-ROM in the back of this book if you are going to run under DOS. If you don't have a printed copy of these instructions, you should print them out first.

1. If you wish to copy the compiler from the CD-ROM to your hard disk:
   (Warning: the compiler requires approximately 20 MB of disk space!)
   a. Make a directory on your hard disk, say c: \djgpp
   b. Use XCOPY to copy all the files in the CD-ROM directory \djgpp and below to your hard disk. If you want to install to c:\djgpp and your CD-ROM drive is drive D:, then you can type:

      xcopy d:\djgpp c:\djgpp /s

   c. Add the following lines to the end of your "autoexec.bat" file: (To save typing, you might want to cut and paste them from this file, which is d:\readme.txt)

      subst z: c:\
      subst y: c:\
      set DJGPP=z:\DJGPP\DJGPP.ENV
      set PATH=z:\DJGPP\BIN;%PATH%
      setdjgpp c:\djgpp c:/djgpp

   d. Make sure that your "config.sys" file contains the following lines:

      DEVICE=C:\DOS\HIMEM.SYS
      DOS=HIGH
      FILES=30
      lastdrive=z

2. If you prefer to run the compiler from the CD-ROM, assuming your CD-ROM is drive D:
   a. Add the following lines to the end on your autoexec.bat file:

      subst z: d:\
      subst y: c:\
      set DJGPP=z:\DJGPP\DJGPP.ENV
      set PATH=z:\DJGPP\BIN;%PATH%
      setdjgpp d:\djgpp d:/djgpp

   b. Make sure that your "config.sys" file contains the following lines:

      DEVICE=C:\DOS\HIMEM.SYS
      DOS=HIGH
      FILES=30
      lastdrive=z

3. After either of these alternatives, make sure to reboot so that the changes to your autoexec.bat and config.sys files can take effect.